Unsettling
Mobility

THE ARCHAEOLOGY OF INDIGENOUS-COLONIAL INTERACTIONS
IN THE AMERICAS

Series Editors
*Liam Frink, Aubrey Cannon, Barbara Voss, Steven A. Wernke,
and Patricia A. McAnany*

Unsettling Mobility

Mediating Mi'kmaw Sovereignty in Post-contact Nova Scotia

Michelle A. Lelièvre

THE UNIVERSITY OF
ARIZONA PRESS
TUCSON

The University of Arizona Press
www.uapress.arizona.edu

Printed in the United States of America
22   21   20   19   18   17   6   5   4   3   2   1

ISBN-13: 978-0-8165-3485-2 (cloth)

Cover design by Leigh McDonald
Cover photo: *Group on a boat going to Merigomish Island, 1930.* Courtesy of National Museum of the American Indian, Smithsonian Institution (N19809). Photo by NMAI Photo Services.

Original series design: David Alcorn, Alcorn Publication Design

Publication of this book is made possible in part by the proceeds of a permanent endowment created with the assistance of a Challenge Grant from the National Endowment for the Humanities, a federal agency.

Library of Congress Cataloging-in-Publication Data
Names: Lelièvre, Michelle A., author.
  Title: Unsettling mobility : mediating Mi'kmaw sovereignty in post-contact Nova Scotia / Michelle A. Lelièvre.
  Description: Tucson : The University of Arizona Press, 2017. | Series: The archaeology of indigenous-colonial interactions in the Americas | Includes bibliographical references and index.
  Identifiers: LCCN 2016041552 | ISBN 9780816534852 (cloth : alk. paper)
  Subjects: LCSH: Micmac Indians—Nova Scotia. | Sovereignty.
  Classification: LCC E99.M6 L45 2017 | DDC 971.5004/97343—dc23 LC record available at https://lccn.loc.gov/2016041552

⊖ This paper meets the requirements of ANSI/NISO Z39.48-1992 (Permanence of Paper).

For my parents, Ronald and Elizabeth,
and
the people of the Pictou Landing First Nation
Wela'lioq

Contents

Illustrations

Still image of the procession of St. Anne on
Maligomish, circa 1965

Figures

Tables

Procession of St. Anne on Maligomish, circa 1965. Still image captured from DVD transfer of Super 8 film. Original film shot by Noel Martin, Pictou Landing First Nation. Reproduced with permission of Noel Martin.

Acknowledgments

THE SUCCESSFUL COMPLETION OF THIS PROJECT is due to a great number of people—some of whom contributed their time and expertise and others who encouraged and guided me throughout the fieldwork and writing process. It is my pleasure to thank many of these people publicly. For those whom I have forgotten to mention, please know that I remain grateful for your support.

Perhaps most importantly, I would like to acknowledge the members of the Pictou Landing First Nation who welcomed me into their community and—after a period of negotiation—agreed to allow me to conduct the research for this book with them. The people I met during my first visits to Pictou Landing were patient with me as I fumbled to get to know the community and its members. I am deeply grateful for their friendship and the knowledge they have shared over the years. I would like to offer a special thanks to my field assistants, Edie Nicholas, Mary Irene Nicholas, and Laura Prosper. Thanks also to Darlene Bachiri, Mary Gladys Bernard, Diane Denny, Dominic Denny, Martha Denny, Mary Ellen Denny, Michelle Francis Denny, Debbie Dykstra, Janet Francis, Javenny Francis, Ralph and Lorraine Francis, Sarah (Sadie) Francis, Caroline Martin, Noel and Madeline Martin, Mary Lou and Anthony Nicholas, Louise and Martin (Junior) Sapier, Catherine (Katalin) Thomas, and many, many others. Mi'kmaq from other communities beyond Pictou Landing were also instrumental in the success of the project. For example, Florence Walsh very generously allowed me to use her cabin on Maligomish while my field assistants and I were completing our test excavations. Bernie Francis was very patient with my many questions about Mi'kmaw grammar.

The bulk of the research conducted for this book was conducted as a doctoral dissertation project. The early stages of my dissertation research were funded, in part, with two Nova Scotia Museum Research Grants in Industrial History. In addition to the much-needed funding, the staff at the Nova Scotia Museum was unceasingly generous with their time and resources. Debra McNabb, the Manager of the Nova Scotia Museum of Industry (MOI), was steadfast in her support of my research. Mary Guildford, the MOI's then–Curator of Collections, facilitated my access to the museum's library, collections, and technical resources. Stephen Powell, the Assistant Curator in Archaeology at the Nova Scotia Museum, devoted dozens of hours over the years to answering my questions about archaeology in Nova Scotia. Roger Lewis, the Curator of Ethnology, was instrumental in helping me earn the trust of Mi'kmaq at the Pictou Landing First Nation. Scott Robson, then–Curator of History, helped me to navigate the historical sources at the museum and the provincial archives. Ruth Holmes Whitehead, the former Curator of Ethnology, guided me to the resources she had curated during her tenure at the museum. Chris Lavergne, the Collections Conservator, guided me through the Nova Scotia Museum Research Grant application process. Finally, David Christianson, then–Manager of Collections, served as one of my dissertation committee members. I am grateful that David lent his expertise on the Mi'kmaq and archaeology in Nova Scotia to push me to represent the sources accurately. More recently, Lisa Bower, the Assistant Curator of History, has made scanned copies of the Harry Piers accession ledgers available to me for review.

The later stages of my fieldwork were supported with grants from the University of Chicago, Division of the Social Sciences' Janco Travel Fund and travel grants from the Marion R. & Adolph J. Lichtstern Fund at the Department of Anthropology at the University of Chicago. I also received grants from the Jacobs Research Fund at the Whatcom Museum in Bellingham, Washington, and a Sigma Xi Grant. The Culture and Heritage Working Committee of the Mi'kmaq + Nova Scotia + Canada Tripartite Forum provided funding to the Pictou Landing First Nation, which allowed the band to hire my field assistants. Thank you to Bill Greenlaw, David Christianson, Calum Ewing, and Tim Bernard for helping to secure this funding.

Several Mi'kmaw organizations in Nova Scotia offered a variety of support for the field and archival research. My thanks to Don Julien, Tim Bernard, Theresa LeBlanc, Craig Marshall, and Leah Rosenmeier at the Confederacy of Mainland Mi'kmaq, and Jim Michael and Jennifer Copage at the Treaty and Aboriginal Rights Research Centre. The Assembly of Nova Scotia Mi'kmaq Chiefs, the Kwilmu'kw Maw-klusuaqn Negotiation Office (Mi'kmaq Rights Initiative), the Confederacy of Mainland Mi'kmaq, and the Chief and Council of the Pictou Landing First Nation all wrote letters of support for the project, which helped me to secure clearance from Mi'kmaw Ethics Watch (MEW). Thank you to the staff at Unama'ki College, Cape Breton University, for facilitating my proposals to MEW.

The archaeological stage of my fieldwork would not have been completed without the assistance of several colleagues in Nova Scotia. The Departments of Anthropology and Earth Sciences at St. Francis Xavier University in Antigonish and the Department of Anthropology at Saint Mary's University in Halifax all generously lent me field equipment. Scott Buchanan, Leah Rosenmeier, and Lauren Zych assisted me in the field. Michael Haller and students from his archaeological methods and zooarchaeology classes at St. Francis Xavier also helped with the excavations and later processed the faunal remains collected from Maligomish. I was able to gain invaluable field experience while working with Michael Deal and Rob ("Stumpy") Ferguson on their respective field projects in Nova Scotia. I also consulted several archaeologists working in the Northeast as I prepared to excavate the shell midden on Maligomish. I extend my thanks to David Black, David Sanger, and Arthur Spiess for their time and advice.

Much of the research was conducted in archives and artifact repositories in Nova Scotia and beyond. Sister Josephine MacLellan assisted me as I applied for permission to consult the Diocese of Antigonish Archives. The staff at the Hector Heritage Centre in Pictou guided me through the local newspapers and indices. The staff at the Northumberland Fisheries Museum in Pictou generously shared the results of a research project the museum had conducted with fishers from the Pictou Landing First Nation. Stella Maris Catholic Church in Pictou allowed me to consult and copy the parish's registers. The reference archivists at Nova Scotia Archives guided me to the relevant record groups. They also granted me permission to view original documents when microfilm copies were illegible. Matthew Betts and Stacey Girling-Christie at the Canadian Museum of History (CMH) lent their time and expertise in the archaeological artifacts from Merigomish Harbour collected by Harlan Smith and John Wintemberg in the early twentieth century. The staff at the CMH Archives retrieved the original field notes of some of the archaeologists who had worked in the Merigomish area, including Smith, Wintemberg, and David Keenleyside. At Library and Archives Canada, Jessica Squires and Patricia Kennedy offered tremendous help as I fumbled through the resources on indigenous peoples. Janet Stoddard, the Collections Manager for Archaeology at the Parks Canada in Dartmouth, Nova Scotia, granted me access to the documentation for Birgitta Wallace's excavations on Rustico Island. Sandy Balcom, Anne Marie Jonah, and Heather Gillis assisted me at the Fortress of Louisbourg archives. I would like to extend a general thank you to the reference archivists, librarians, and staff at the following institutions: the University of New Brunswick Archives and New Brunswick Archaeological Services, both in Fredericton; the Maine Folklife Center at the University of Maine in Orono; the Acadia University Archives in Wolfville; and the Newberry Library in Chicago.

I would not have been able to process the soil samples from the excavations without the guidance, patience, and skills of several researchers at laboratories around Atlantic Canada. Thanks to Peta Mudie, Owen Brown, and Kate Jarrett at the Bedford Institute of Oceanography. Thanks also to Yana Fedortchouk in the Earth Sciences Department at Dalhousie University. Michael Deal granted me access to the Paleoethnobotanical Laboratory in the

Department of Archaeology at the Memorial University of Newfoundland (MUN). Also at MUN, Helen Gillespie conducted the acetolysis treatment of the pollen samples. David Garbary very generously lent me use of a microscope in his laboratory in the Department of Biology at St. Francis Xavier University.

Thank you to Clare Fawcett, Susan Vincent, Leslie Jane McMillan, and Mikael Haller in the Department of Anthropology at St. Francis Xavier University for welcoming me as a visiting professor while I was conducting my fieldwork in Nova Scotia. As a faculty member I was able to access the consortium of university libraries in Nova Scotia and its interlibrary loan system, an invaluable resource when I was so far away from my home institution.

There are many people at the University of Chicago without whose encouragement, support, and expertise I would not have been able to complete the dissertation research that has become this book. Thank you to my dissertation committee members for your comments, encouragement, and countless letters of support throughout my entire graduate career at the University of Chicago. Kathleen Morrison and Adam T. Smith cochaired my committee. Raymond Fogelson and Shannon Dawdy joined David Christianson in rounding out the committee members. Nicholas Kouchoukos lent much inspiration to my project during its early stages.

While at the University of Chicago, I was very fortunate to be a member of two writing groups. I am deeply grateful for my colleagues' close reading and constructive criticism of the various documents I circulated over the years. Special thanks to Andrew Bauer, Royal Ghazal, Rebecca Graff, Alan Greene, Laura-Zoë Humphreys, Sarah Luna, and Maureen Marshall. My many conversations with Maureen Marshall on mobility and politics have critically shaped the ideas presented in this book. I am grateful for her close reading of my work and for her pushing me to clarify my ideas. Several other colleagues and friends from the University of Chicago have continued to provide much welcome support. They include Betsey Brada, Elizabeth Fagan, Phoebe France, Kathryn Franklin, Debora Heard, Brian Horne, Kelda Jamison, Madeleine McLeester, Melissa Rosenzweig, and Lauren Zych. A very special shout-out to Maureen Marshall and Elizabeth Fagan, whose near-daily check-in emails as I revised the book kept me focused, inspired, and still unconvinced of the existence of red pandas.

During my time at the University of Chicago I was very fortunate to have the support of several extraordinary staff members, including the inimitable Anne Ch'ien, who manages the Department of Anthropology's student affairs. The staff members of the interlibrary loan office were able to fulfill 99 percent of even my most obscure requests. David Forero, Bart Longacre, and Joshua Letzter lent me much-needed computer and technical support.

Unsettling Mobility has been revised and rethought with much support and encouragement from my friends and colleagues at the College of William and Mary and in my adopted homes of Williamsburg and Richmond, Virginia. Thank you to Kathleen Bragdon, Martin Gallivan, Jonathan Glasser, Grey Gundaker, Jennifer Kahn, Danielle Moretti-Langholtz, Ali Colleen Neff, Kara Thompson, and Brad Weiss. Kerry Murphy and Bill Vega helped me get various drafts of this manuscript out to editors and publishers. Funds provided by the Dean of Arts and Sciences at the College of William and Mary allowed me to work with Laura Helper-Ferris in the early stages of developing the dissertation into a book manuscript and to conduct follow-up archival research in Nova Scotia. I extend warm thanks to Peter Henry for reminding me not to take myself (or him) too seriously.

At the University of Arizona Press I would like to thank Allyson Carter and the editors of the Archaeology of Indigenous-Colonial Interactions in the Americas series, especially Liam Fink and Aubrey Cannon. Aubrey was a supporter of this work long before I imagined it being published as a book. Thank you also to Celia Braves for creating the index. Special thanks to Elizabeth LeLievre for proofreading the page proofs.

Finally, I would like to thank my family and friends in Nova Scotia who have been unfailingly supportive through the many long years of this project. My parents, Ronald and Elizabeth LeLievre, remain my most steadfast supporters. Their encouragement, shelter, financial support, and love continue to inspire me. My siblings, Mark and Megan, have always reminded me to explore life beyond work. My aunt, Patricia O'Sullivan, made a generous and welcome financial contribution toward the project. Meaghan Beaton, Dennis Lever, Bernadette and Neil MacPhee, Rosanne MacPhee, and Norma Jean MacPhee have all given me places to sleep, food to eat, and sympathetic ears. I would also like to thank some very influential people in my life who supported me from the beginning, but are no longer here to read this book: Annie Jane and Severin LeLievre, Harry and Pearl O'Sullivan, and Jolane MacPhee—you have my deepest gratitude.

A Note About Language and Names

IN MAY 2016, I met with many of the members of the Pictou Landing First Nation who are featured in this book to discuss their comments on its accuracy and tone. It was a wide-ranging conversation in which I did my best to explain academic publishing, tenure, and the anthropological conventions of using pseudonyms in publications. For their part, the community members asked questions that have since helped me to clarify and—in some cases—reinterpret the arguments presented here.

We returned to two topics several times throughout the conversation: language and names. One elder, Sarah (Sadie) Francis, expressed a polite but forceful concern over the use of one word that is repeated throughout the book: *civilization*. I often use this word in reference to the attempts of the Nova Scotia colonial and later the Canadian federal governments to "civilize" indigenous populations whom they believed to be "uncivilized savages." Sadie requested that I remove this word from the manuscript. In response to this request, I tried to explain the context of the word and why I believed it was important to explain that context to the book's audience. I tried to remain the detached, objective researcher, while Sadie seems to have been expressing a frustration and quiet anger over a repeated reminder of how Euro-Canadians have viewed her and her ancestors. Indeed, the title of Mi'kmaw historian Daniel Paul's book, *We Were Not the Savages* (2000) might capture Sadie's motivation in requesting that the word be struck from the manuscript. "Civilization" remains, but it is written in scare quotes because the belief that the Mi'kmaq needed to be "civilized" was held by a limited (but powerful) number of newcomers.

A second topic of conversation during the May 2016 meeting was names—the names I gave to my Mi'kmaw interlocutors from the Pictou Landing First Nation, and the names that scholars have used to identify the Mi'kmaq. Originally, I had given most of my interlocutors pseudonyms. During the May 2016 meeting several people asked the purpose of doing so, and I offered an abbreviated history of the conventions of informed consent and protection of anonymity in anthropological research. In the end, some of the gathered community members requested that I use their real names. Others were satisfied with keeping their pseudonyms. Individuals who have been given pseudonyms are indicated in the manuscript with an asterisk (*) at the end of their names.

Mi'kmaq is a word that newcomers to eastern Canada gave to some of this region's indigenous peoples. The Mi'kmaq refer to themselves as *l'nu* (person) or *l'nu'k* (people). Although commonly used in the archival sources of the nine-teenth century, today most Mi'kmaq and other indigenous peoples through-out Canada consider the term *Indian* to be derogatory, especially when used by nonindigenous peoples. The term appears in this book in quotations from archival sources and when referring to the official titles of the colonial (and later federal) bureaucrats—for example, "Indian Agents," the "Commissioner for Indian Affairs," and so on. Other quotations use similarly derogatory terms—for example, *savage* and the French *sauvage*.

When referring to Mi'kmaq and other nations in North America collec-tively, I use the term *indigenous*. I use the terms *First Nations* and *aboriginal* when referring specifically to Canada's indigenous populations, although see Gerald Taiaiake Alfred (2009) for a discussion among Canadian indigenous leaders, many of whom take issue with these terms because they have been imposed upon their peoples by colonizing powers. Finally, I use the term *Native American* when referring collectively to the United States' indigenous populations. However, whenever possible, I use the name of the particular indigenous nation under discussion.

Throughout the book I use the Smith-Francis orthography (Pacifique 1990) to write Mi'kmaw words. This is the orthography used most com-monly by Mi'kmaq in Nova Scotia, and it is the official orthography of the *Sante' Mawi'omi* or Grand Council (see Battiste 1997). In this orthography *Mi'kmaq* is a plural noun that refers to the Mi'kmaq as a people. *Mi'kmaw* is a singular noun and an adjective that modifies both singular and plural nouns. Many anthropologists recognize the Mi'kmaq as "the Micmacs," and this spell-ing appears in some quotations cited in the book. I occasionally quote authors who use different orthographies, and I note these differences throughout the text.

The two places I discuss most frequently in this book are Pictou Landing and Maligomish, both of which are part of the Pictou Landing First Nation. In the settler geography of Nova Scotia, Pictou Landing and Maligomish are located in Pictou County, which is in the northeastern region of mainland Nova Scotia. Pictou County was established in 1835 when it was separated from the County of Halifax. Some archival sources reference the original names of counties within the province; for example, what is currently known as Antigonish and Guysborough Counties was originally Sydney County until the early nineteenth century. Most of the places described in this book are located within the three counties of Pictou, Colchester, and Antigonish. Taken together, I refer to this region as northeastern Nova Scotia (see fig. 1 in chapter 1).

As a final prefatory note, I will say that the work presented here is not a Mi'kmaw story, any more than it is a settler story, or a story about the Catholic Church. It is one interpretation—among many possible interpretations—of what has happened in this part of the world since Europeans began to settle it. In this book I attempt to address questions of interest to anthropologists, such as the sociality of mobility and the conditions of possibility for settler colonialism. But I can't help but wonder if my interpretation of Mi'kmaw sovereignty might be one of the "academic" attempts to understand indigenous politics that the Mi'kmaw scholar Stephen J. Augustine (2008) has said often make him laugh. Augustine and other Mi'kmaw scholars, writers, and leaders have described the Mi'kmaw worldview through stories of the Mi'kmaq's creation and long-term development, reflections on the Mi'kmaw language and visual culture, and discussions of concepts such as *Netukulimk* or the ability to provide for yourself and your family (see Battiste 1997; Clarke and Patterson 1987; D. Marshall et al. 1989; J. B. Marshall 2006; cf. Barsh 2002). These scholars may not need (or want) another academic interpretation of their history, culture, and politics written by an *aklasie'wi'skw* (literally, an English-speaking woman). In that spirit, I offer the chapters that follow not as a replacement for Mi'kmaw voices but as a site for distilling one story from the over two-hundred-year-old conversation among representatives of the Mi'kmaq, the Crown, and the Catholic Church in Nova Scotia.

Unsettling Mobility

Introduction

THE END(S) OF SETTLEMENT

"Neither Settled nor Migratory"

BY THE TIME HE ARRIVED ON MALIGOMISH, James Dawson was already too late.[1] For several weeks in the spring of 1842 he had been planning the roughly seventeen-kilometer journey from his home in the town of Pictou located on Nova Scotia's northeastern shore to Maligomish, better known to the mostly British settlers of the region as "Indian Island" (see fig. 1). Dawson, father of the noted geologist John William Dawson, had been recruited by Joseph Howe, the newly appointed commissioner for Indian affairs, to help the provincial government enforce the recently passed Act to Provide for the Instruction and Permanent Settlement of the Indians. The primary goal of this legislation was to make the province's indigenous Mi'kmaq[2] self-sufficient subjects of the British Crown. In his capacity as commissioner, Howe had visited many Mi'kmaw communities to see firsthand the conditions in which they housed and supported themselves and to encourage them to conform to the recently introduced legislation. Being unable to travel to the northeastern county of Pictou, Howe requested Dawson's assistance to ascertain the willingness of the local Mi'kmaq to abide with the provisions of this act.

There is an apparent restlessness in the early letters Dawson wrote to Howe after being recruited for this duty. Describing his eventual visit to Maligomish in June 1842, Dawson noted that he had planned to travel to the island with William O'Reilly, the local priest who ministered to the devoutly Catholic Mi'kmaq. But settling on a date for the journey had taken some time. When the agreed-upon day had finally arrived, Dawson was disappointed to learn that Father O'Reilly had been called away to travel an even greater distance across the Northumberland Strait to Prince Edward Island, where he was needed to

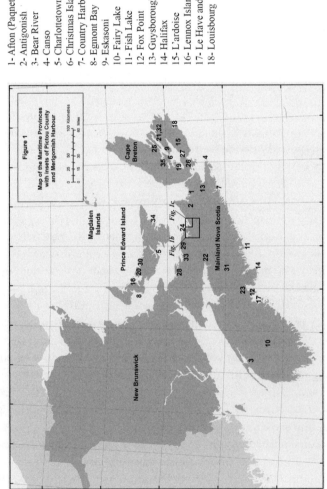

Figure 1

Map of the Maritime Provinces
with insets of Pictou County
and Merigomish Harbour

1- Afton (Paqnetek)
2- Antigonish
3- Bear River
4- Canso
5- Charlottetown
6- Christmas Island
7- Country Harbour
8- Egmont Bay
9- Eskasoni
10- Fairy Lake
11- Fish Lake
12- Fox Point
13- Guysborough
14- Halifax
15- L'ardoise
16- Lennox Island
17- Le Have and Lunenburg
18- Louisbourg

19- Malagawatch
20- Malpeque
21- Membertou
22- Millbrook
23- Panhook
24- Pictou Harbour Area
25- Port Dauphin/St. Ann's
26- Port Toulouse/St. Peter's
27- Potlotek
28- Pugwash
29- River John
30- Rustico
31- Shubenacadie
32- Sydney
33- Tatamagouche
34- Three Rivers
35- Waycobah

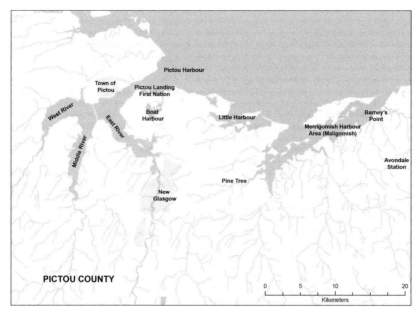

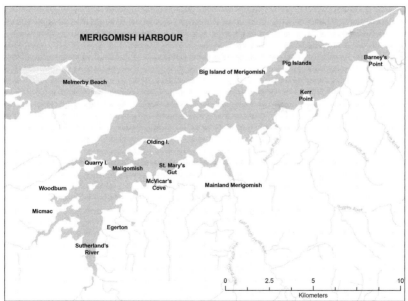

FIGURE 1. Map of the maritime provinces of Canada (*facing page*) with insets of Pictou County (*top*) and Merigomish Harbour (*bottom*). Figures created by Nick Belluzo.

consult with the bishop. Setting out from Pictou on his own, Dawson met with a settler named MacDonald who lived close to Maligomish, and the two of them visited the island to consult with the Mi'kmaq living there. Dawson wrote that he again was "doomed to disappointment" having discovered that the very people with whom he wanted to consult—the adult males of the island—had just left that morning "for different destinations to pursue the herring and cod fisheries" (LAC 1842c). Dawson had to settle for speaking with John Sapier, whom he described as an "intelligent old fellow," and the Mi'kmaw women who had stayed behind on Maligomish (LAC 1842c).

The letter that Dawson wrote to Howe describing his visit provides a window into the daily lives of a mid-nineteenth-century community of Mi'kmaq on this tiny island, which Dawson described as "a beautifully romantic and exceedingly fertile spot" (LAC 1842c). Dawson had caught John Sapier in the midst of planting potatoes, which appear to have been a staple crop. Dawson observed "15 to 30 bushels" in each of the root cellars the Mi'kmaq kept on the island (LAC 1842c). He also commented on a magnanimous gesture that John Sapier had made by giving five bushels of potatoes from his own stock to a widow to plant for herself and her children.

Dawson also noted the "neat little chapple [sic]" on Maligomish—an island that had been a Catholic mission site at least since the mid-eighteenth century. The chapel became an important site in the conversation between Dawson, Sapier, and the Mi'kmaw women about the government's Act to Provide for the Instruction and Permanent Settlement of the Indians. Dawson reported that, while those assembled agreed with the spirit of the law, they could not support its letter. They feared that sending their children to a "White man's school" would weaken their social and familial bonds (LAC 1842c). Recognizing this fear as justified, Dawson suggested a compromise that would allow the children to be instructed in the chapel for several hours a day during the summer months. For this arrangement to work, Dawson suggested that some Mi'kmaw women would have to become more permanently settled on the island to be guardians to the children, while a non-Mi'kmaw teacher would have to become more mobile by traveling to and from Maligomish each day.

In his letter to Howe, Dawson did not betray the irony of having traveled to Maligomish to discuss the "permanent settlement" of a traditionally mobile people only to find that a significant number of those people had moved precisely to be able to support themselves and their communities independently of the Crown. Not wanting to overstep the bounds of his role as a deputized Indian commissioner, Dawson was cautiously optimistic in his recommendations to Howe that instruction of the children and the teaching of basic agricultural practices to adults be undertaken on Maligomish. In late

November 1842 Dawson reported that he had not succeeded "in getting any of their young people instruction," but he hoped that in the following year he "might get some benefit extended toward them in this way" (LAC 1842e).

Such has been the history of white settler interventions on the Mi'kmaw island of Maligomish. Because Maligomish has been a gathering place for the indigenous peoples of northeastern Nova Scotia at least since 1500 BP, it has also been a site where representatives of the British Crown and the Catholic Church have attempted—in overt and subtle ways—to assimilate Mi'kmaq into a broader society that they imagined to be predominately white, Protestant, middle class, and permanently settled. Indeed, for all of Dawson's optimism and willingness to compromise, his ultimate goal—and that of the British Crown whom he represented—was the "civilization" of the Mi'kmaq, a goal that Dawson had stated in a previous letter to Howe was his "favourite subject" (LAC 1842a). *Civilizing* meant transforming the Mi'kmaq into ideal, liberal, political subjects—loyal to the Crown but independent of it. To construct such subjects, the Mi'kmaq would have to be instilled with values, skills, and resources that would assure independence. The first step in this process was to make the mobile Mi'kmaq sedentary (cf. Raibmon 2007, 177).[3]

Chapters 1 through 4 will discuss some of the efforts undertaken by both the Catholic Church and the British Crown to sedentize the Mi'kmaq in nineteenth- and twentieth-century Nova Scotia. But the takeaway is easily anticipated: the Mi'kmaq did not become sedentary. They continued to move in the nineteenth century—and continue to move today—for food procurement, religious devotion, the renewal of political ties, and for many other reasons. Movement is inherent to the Mi'kmaw worldview, which the linguist Bernie Francis has described as being in constant motion. Mi'kmaw language and stories reflect a cosmology that is processual, relational, and animate. For example, whereas in most Indo-European languages colors are classified primarily as adjectives or nouns, they are verbs in Mi'kmaw. Thus, the word for "red"—*mekwe'k*—translates as "being in the process of becoming red" (Sable and Francis 2012, 28; see also Battiste 1997, 13). The characters in Mi'kmaw stories move over land and through water not only in the "Earth World" of the here and now; they also move between this world and the other five that make up the Mi'kmaw universe (see Hornborg 2006; Whitehead 1988). In her interpretations of Mi'kmaw legends and myths, Ruth Whitehead has argued that Mi'kmaq experience the land and its features not as inanimate objects but as animate persons who are able to change their shape at will. Many of the human and nonhuman characters that inhabit these worlds can change their form, including the Mi'kmaw culture hero Kluskap (see Rand 1894; Speck 1922, 145–49; Wallis and Wallis 1955; Whitehead 1988, 1989). These stories also indicate the types of places where, and seasons during which, Mi'kmaq stopped along their journeys through the Earth World and beyond. For example, in Rand's rendition of "A Child Nourished by a Bear," time passes from autumn to spring, and the characters travel from a Mi'kmaw settlement to berry patches, a bear den, and smelting grounds (Rand 1894, 259–62).

Early anthropological scholarship drawing on ethnohistorical sources describes a pre-contact settlement pattern characterized by a biseasonal mode of subsistence (see Bock 1966; Hoffman 1955; Miller 1982; Nietfeld 1981; Prins 1996a; Wallis and Wallis 1955).[4] Large communities of extended families—each of which consisted of approximately ten to twelve people—fished and gathered along the ocean coast and estuaries in the spring and summer. In the winter, these families scattered and traveled upriver to inland hunting grounds. "They were a typical migratory people who lived in the woods during the winter months hunting moose, caribou, and porcupine, then moved down to the seashore in spring to gather shell-fish, to fish at the mouths of the rivers, and to hunt the seal near the coast" (Jenness 1958, 267–68, quoted in Bock 1966, 3). Nietfeld (1981, 396) quotes Lescarbot (1611) and Denys (1672) in her description of a summer village as "a large enclosure upon a rising ground enclosed with trees, great and small, fastened to one another, and within the enclosure many lodges large and small." She argues that warm-weather villages could accommodate between one hundred and three hundred people in the sixteenth century (Nietfeld 1981, 398). These numbers would have varied throughout the post-contact period as disease and war caused significant declines in the Mi'kmaw population during the early seventeenth century (Nietfeld 1981, 398; see also Miller 1982).

Reexaminations of the ethnohistorical documents and archaeological investigations have revealed a more complex system than simply coastal fishing in the summer and inland hunting in the winter (Nash and Miller 1987; Sanger 1996; Stewart 1989). In some regions Mi'kmaq moved back and forth as different resources became available. "From the spring to the early autumn, they lived in large summer villages on the coast or near river mouths gathering shellfish, eggs, nuts and berries and catching sturgeon, herring, salmon, trout and smelt. In the late autumn and winter, the Mi'kmaq were occupied with a combination of inland hunting of big game and beaver and coastal dwelling to harvest tom cod and seal" (Prins 1996a, 28). Based on his archaeological surveys along the Gulf of Maine, Sanger has gone so far as to suggest that there may have been two entirely separate populations—one that maintained a four-season coastal dwelling, and the other based in the interior (Sanger 1996, 521). Stewart's (1989) review of faunal collections from several sites throughout the Maritime Provinces suggests that the seasonality of sites is highly variable between regions, with some being occupied year-round and others occupied only during certain seasons.

The Mi'kmaq traveled to and from these sites through a network of rivers, lakes, and portages. Early European writers commented on "the exact knowledge of all rivers and landmarks which enable the Micmac, given only slight indication of a wigwam's location, to find it successfully at a distance of a hundred leagues and through dense forests" (LeClerq 1691, quoted in Wallis and Wallis 1955, 54). Mi'kmaw shelters and material culture accommodated this mobile existence. Wigwams, containers, baskets, and mats were made from water-resistant and lightweight materials such as birch bark and cattails (*Typha latifolia*; see Gordon 1993, 1995, 1997).

That movement has been essential to how Mi'kmaq have constructed their worldviews, language, religion, and modes of subsistence is not a new insight. Nor is the consideration of indigenous movement as a response to, resistance against, or codependency with British settler colonialism a unique contribution.[5] Instead, *Unsettling Mobility* attempts to offer an anthropological analysis of the ways in which movement has mediated the social, political, and economic relationships between individuals and institutions that fall within the broader categories of "Mi'kmaq," "British Crown," and "Catholic Church" from the late eighteenth century to the present in a region whose indigenous peoples have never ceded territory to the Crown. Much work in anthropology, indigenous studies, and history has been done to demonstrate how such categories have been constructed through interactions between individuals, communities, institutions, and, indeed, through the production of knowledge in disciplines such as anthropology (see, for example, Brooks 2008; Byrd 2012; Cipolla 2013; Harris 2002; Raibmon 2005, 2007; Roy 2010; Wicken 2012; Wolfe 1991, 1999). The current volume contributes to these discussions. However, while recognizing that these categories are socially and historically constructed—and that there are many fissures along which they fracture—the book uses the terms *Mi'kmaq*, *Crown*, and *Church* heuristically to allow for a different perspective on what is, by now, a familiar story of colonization in northeastern North America. This perspective places mobility at the center of interactions between the Mi'kmaq, the Crown, and the Church to explore how individuals and institutions representing each category not only negotiated their encounters with each other but were also changed by them.[6] It is in these encounters that the categories of Mi'kmaq, Church, and Crown were constructed. Indeed, one of the objectives of the book is to elucidate a contradiction at the core of the settler project: that the attempts of the Church and

Crown to assimilate people such as the Mi'kmaq have more often than not served to further mark those people as indigenous and, therefore, "Other" than the settler majority.

I use the term *mediating* purposefully to describe the work that mobility is doing in the colonial (and postcolonial) context of Nova Scotia.[7] I understand mobility to have affected the transitions that have occurred during the ongoing processes of contact between indigenous peoples and "newcomers" in settler colonies. Mediating can connote reconciliation or union, but it can also link these relationships indirectly in ways that create tensions, misunderstandings, resistances, or even indifference. In these ways, mediating is comparable to Richard White's (1991) conceptual framework for understanding colonial relationships in the eighteenth-century *pays d'en haut*[8] known as the "middle ground." White describes the middle ground as both a space and a process. As a process, it creates mutual misunderstandings between the protagonists of a colonial encounter, and these misunderstandings create new meanings (R. White 2006, 9). As a historical space, the middle ground requires specific conditions that allow the processes of mutual misunderstanding to become the basis of relationships between distinct peoples. These conditions include "a rough balance of power, mutual need or a desire for what the other possesses, and an inability by either side to commandeer enough force to compel the other to change" (R. White 2006, 10). The period between the late eighteenth century and the early twenty-first century, which this book covers, saw very different conditions with the balance of power shifting decisively to the British Crown and its settlers. And yet, if we understand power as something that is "exercised rather than possessed" (Foucault 1977, 26), then using a mediator such as mobility can be productive for tracing how various kinds of power are negotiated, diffused, and exercised in a colonial context.

Analyzing the mediating power of mobility in colonial and postcolonial Nova Scotia allows the book to achieve its two primary objectives: First, its conceptual objective is to reimagine *settlement*—both as an analytical category and also as a political category that forms the legal foundation of settler colonies such as Nova Scotia. The second objective is to examine the bias toward sedentism that underlies both the anthropological study of indigenous peoples and also the political and legal management of them. This bias has affected how Mi'kmaq have been defined—and have defined themselves—as political subjects. Following Ortner (2005) and Adam Smith (2003), Maureen Marshall and I define political subjects as "historically and culturally-situated individuals and collectives who assert authority while also submitting some degree of will to one or more political institutions" (see Lelièvre and

Marshall 2015, 436; see also Ortner 2005, 34; Smith 2003, 155). Political institutions are collective bodies such as the British Crown and Catholic Church that "exert some authority over subject populations" (Lelièvre and Marshall 2015, 436). Much of the work that these two institutions have done in colonial contexts has been focused on making indigenous subjects legible (*sensu* J. Scott 1998)—in other words, to render them quantifiable and measureable to allow for their management, conversion, and eventual assimilation into the settler population.[9] Technologies that render populations legible—such as censuses, tax collection, and property management—require political subjects to be in one place most of the time. In this way, a fully realized political subject of a settler colony is a sedentary one (cf. Raibmon 2007: 177).

The analysis that *Unsettling Mobility* offers includes identifying the bias toward sedentism evident in archival documents describing the Mi'kmaq, in the system of British common law that arbitrates the rights and title of indigenous peoples such as the Mi'kmaq, and in the social-scientific study of Mi'kmaq and other traditionally mobile peoples. It examines what the historian Paige Raibmon (2007) has described as the "sedentarist ideology" that underlay nineteenth-century anxieties about indigenous movements and has mediated the relationships between Mi'kmaq, settlers, the Crown, and the Church from the eighteenth century to the present. This ideology prevented nineteenth-century observers from seeing that Mi'kmaw movements were with purpose; that they supported Mi'kmaw society in its economic, political, and spiritual practices; and that their movements at times supported settler economies and politics. The sedentarist ideology further prevented settlers, missionaries, and colonial administrators from seeing that movement was inherent to their own social practices (cf. Ferris 2009; Raibmon 2005, 2007; Roy 2010).[10]

The European missionaries and explorers who first wrote about societies like the Mi'kmaq—and those settlers who later tried to wean them from their hunting and gathering subsistence practices—made moral assumptions about the Mi'kmaq's seeming unwillingness to conform to a sedentary life-style; they were seen as aimless, improvident, and even lazy.[11] As Cole Harris concluded in his discussion of indigenous land dispossession in colonial and postcolonial British Columbia, these characterizations of indigenous peoples were assumed, not debated, among the settler population (Harris 2004, 170). Such moral characterizations had material effects for the indigenous people who were denied title to land or squeezed out of their territories, in part, because of the assumption that their land use did not comprise an act of ownership (see Arneil 1996; Barker 2005; Cronon 1983). Moreover, these effects continue to be felt today as indigenous peoples across North America struggle to maintain access to their ancestral lands and waters.

Running parallel to the nineteenth-century settler colonial efforts to "civilize" the Mi'kmaq was the development of the nascent discipline of ethnology.[12] Along with a rich archive of ethnographic, ethnohistorical, and archaeological studies of mobile peoples comes an epistemological legacy that emphasizes classification and typology. In the hierarchical typologies of the nineteenth and early twentieth centuries, mobile societies were almost invariably relegated to the lowest rung on the social evolutionary ladder that proceeded from "simple" to "complex" (see Engels [1884] 1978; Hobhouse et al. 1915; Morgan 1877; Wilson 1862). In these models, the ability to control the production of food was the sign of true "civilization." Mobility was considered a trait of "simple" societies because the peoples who represented these groups tended not to produce surplus agriculture, relying instead on the seasonal availability of animals and plants, which they procured by moving to these resources and harvesting them through hunting, fishing, and gathering. Mobile peoples lived in small groups without stratified political or social organizations that could mobilize the labor power necessary to build permanent architecture—all characteristics of more "complex" societies (see chapter 1; see also Lelièvre and Marshall 2015).

Anthropologists have traditionally classified the indigenous Mi'kmaq of eastern Canada among the so-called "simple" societies (see Binford 1980, 1990; Hobhouse et al. 1915; Hoffman 1955; Kroeber 1939; Speck 1915, 1922). Early settler images of the Mi'kmaq, such as the 1791 untitled watercolor by H. N. Binney shown in figure 2, highlight their hunting and gathering mode of subsistence. Here a group of Mi'kmaq is depicted encamped at a lakeshore. Three adults and one child are returning from fishing and fowling, pulling their birch-bark canoe from the water. Their lightweight and portable birch-bark wigwams stand in the middle ground, while, in the foreground, Mi'kmaw women fashion wood-splint baskets and birch-bark containers. *Hunter-gatherer* is a label that describes a subsistence practice; but bound up in this term are deep-seated assumptions that subsistence is the prime mover of sociopolitical change.[13]

This book lays bare these assumptions and overcomes the sedentarist bias by treating mobility as an object of ethnographic study. By doing so, the present work might best be described as a historical ethnography of mobility.[14] While it integrates the results of an archaeological surface survey of Maligomish and test excavations conducted in the island's shell midden, the book is not an archaeological monograph.[15] My initial objectives for the archaeological work on Maligomish were to excavate the shell midden stratigraphically and to collect samples of shellfish, whose incremental growth patterns I could observe to infer if the island had been occupied seasonally or year-round, and

FIGURE 2. H. N. Binney. 1791. Painting of Mi'kmaq, possibly at Tufts Cove (Nova Scotia). Courtesy of the Nova Scotia Museum Mi'kmaq Portraits Collection. Reproduced with permission of the Nova Scotia Museum.

whether these occupational patterns changed over time. However, as I describe in chapter 2, the extent of the test excavations and the materials recovered from the shell midden proved to be inadequate for answering questions about seasonal occupation changes over time. Instead, I integrate the modest results from the survey and test excavations with archival, oral-historical, and ethnographic data to examine mobility as a mediator between the Mi'kmaq, the British Crown, and the Catholic Church.[16]

The Road to Pugwash

This interdisciplinary and integrative approach to examining mobility in the settler colony of Nova Scotia developed directly from my experiences working with members of the Pictou Landing First Nation. Pictou Landing is a small Mi'kmaw community on the northeastern shore of mainland Nova Scotia. It is located at the mouth of the East River of Pictou in what is now Pictou County (see fig. 1). The Mi'kmaw words for describing this place and its relationship to the broader landscape of Mi'kma'ki are variable and reflect the history of attempts to capture in the written word what—for thousands of years—had been shared only orally.[17] The Capuchin missionary Pacifique drew on the Baptist missionary Silas Rand and the local historian George Patterson to write his *Le Pays des Micmacs* (1934), which records hundreds of Mi'kmaw toponyms. Pacifique lists *Pogsagtegenegatig* for Pictou Landing, *Oisasôg* for Boat Harbour, and *Maligômitjg* for Maligomish or Indian Island (see Pacifique 1934, 240, 241).[18] The colonial government of Nova Scotia and later the Canadian federal government gradually reserved these and other lands for the Mi'kmaq of this area to form the Pictou Landing First Nation. They are located in *Piwktuk* ("the explosive place"), which is one of the seven traditional regions of Mi'kma'ki.[19]

The Pictou Landing First Nation has 625 registered members.[20] One of those members was an elder named Katalin (Catherine) Thomas. I had known Katalin only a few months when we decided on a bright Friday in September 2007 to drive the two hours from her home at the Pictou Landing First Nation to the village of Pugwash in northeastern Nova Scotia (see fig. 1). We drove along Nova Scotia's Trunk Highway 6. Better known as the "Sunrise Trail," Highway 6 hugs the northeastern shore of mainland Nova Scotia, providing spectacular views of the Northumberland Strait. Katalin and I were not out for a leisurely drive, however. We were each searching for Louis Thom. Katalin was looking for people who may have known Louis—who was her husband's grandfather—before his passing in the mid-1950s. I was looking for people who might recall the location of the house where Katalin had heard he lived and died.

I met Katalin in June 2007 during a community meeting where I had proposed to conduct ethnographic and archaeological research on Mi'kmaw movements within and beyond the Pictou Landing First Nation. Throughout that summer, I had several one-on-one conversations with Katalin. She was elderly and in failing health, which meant that she spent most of her days in her small house on the reserve. During most of our visits, Katalin shared stories about herself and her relations. She was descended from two Mi'kmaw men whose names are well known to ethnohistorical and archaeological researchers in Nova Scotia—Charlie Wilmot and his father, Peter.[21] Born in Pictou Landing during the 1930s, Katalin lived with her parents until her mother died when Katalin was about seven years old. She was then sent to the state-sanctioned and Catholic-operated Indian Residential School for Mi'kmaw children about one hundred kilometers southwest of Pictou Landing in Shubenacadie (see fig. 1). Katalin attended the school until she was fourteen, returning to Pictou Landing to stay with relatives during the school holidays.

During our very first conversation, Katalin mentioned Louis Thom, who was a World War I veteran. She believed that Louis had been granted land at the Pictou Landing First Nation through Canada's Soldiers Settlement Act.[22] Yet, despite having a home on the reserve, Louis lived alone in a cabin near the Pugwash Junction rail station. Katalin understood that Louis Thom had owned the land on which he built the cabin. She remembered him traveling by train between the town of Pictou and Pugwash Junction, but her memory was that Louis Thom spent most of his time in the latter location. Over the summer of 2007, Katalin shared more details about her life, her family, and her involvement in Mi'kmaw politics. Some of our talks were simply about the weather or the television program she was watching. But Louis Thom—and his life in Pugwash Junction—remained a continued topic of conversation.

Through these conversations either Katalin, or I, or both of us decided that we should travel to Pugwash to try to find people who might remember Louis. Katalin had the inspired idea of asking at branches of the Royal Canadian Legion in the small villages between Pictou Landing and Pugwash. Although the gentlemen we met at our first stop—Branch 64 in Tatamagouche—did not recall Louis, they gave us the names of people to ask for at the Branch 60 Legion in Pugwash. When we asked about him at Branch 60, the bartender was uncertain at first, but eventually remembered that a Legion member named Stewart MacDonald* had supposedly found Louis in his cabin after he had passed away.[23] Stewart was a non-Mi'kmaw man who lived just outside Pugwash. The bartender gave us Stewart's phone number, I called him, and after a brief conversation, Stewart invited us to his house. When we arrived, Katalin filled in the details that we had sketched over the phone and asked Stewart what he could tell us about Louis Thom. He said that Louis had built a small cabin near Pugwash Junction, not far from the rail tracks and close to Stewart's childhood home. He told us that Louis made baskets that he would trade with the MacDonald family for eggs and milk. He also recalled that Louis traveled by train from Pictou to Pugwash Junction and from the Junction into the village of Pugwash to visit places such as the Legion hall. Stewart remembered at least one woman and three girls from Pictou Landing who visited Louis in the summer months. He said that they all made baskets from the ash that they collected from the forest around Louis's cabin.

When I asked Stewart about whether Louis Thom had owned the land on which he built his cabin, he said no. He remembered the land being owned by a family called Sampson* and that they had given Louis permission to build. Stewart offered to take us to the site of the cabin, which was only a few kilometers from his house. But the day was growing late, and we had a long drive back to Pictou Landing. I expressed an interest in returning in the near future so we could see the site and perhaps record its location.

It was more than a year before I returned to Pugwash in December 2008. When I arrived at Stewart's home, he called his brother Robert* to ask him to join our excursion to Pugwash Junction. We piled into Robert's SUV and drove the six kilometers to the site of the former train station. We parked about a kilometer down the lane in what appeared to be the middle of no-where. The snow and fallen trees made for precarious walking, but the Mac-Donald brothers eventually found the spot. The thin cover of snow provided an excellent contrast to allow us to distinguish the foundations very clearly. They were situated at the base of a small knoll that overlooked a sharp bend in Dochtery's Creek, which was running quite high on that December day. The area was surrounded mostly by softwood trees; one wayward spruce was growing in the middle of what remained of Louis Thom's cabin. The broth-ers said that the area had been less dense with trees in Louis Thom's time and that there had been a path cleared from what was the rail line to the cabin. I attempted to record the coordinates of the cabin's location, but the cold and tree cover rendered my handheld GPS unit useless. I photographed the foun-dations and the surrounding area. The brothers helped me to measure the foundations, which were a mere four-by-three meters. They recalled that the cabin had contained a bed with a straw mattress, a table, and a wood-burning stove, parts of which were visible outside the foundation. At only twelve square meters, the cabin would have had room for little else.

As we explored the area around the foundations, I revisited the conversa-tion that Katalin, Stewart, and I had shared the year before. Contrary to the impression that Katalin and I were given the previous autumn, Stewart did not find Louis Thom's body. Stewart explained that it was the section men from the Canadian National Railway who found Louis. Both brothers said that in the morning Louis would catch a ride with this crew to meet friends at the Legion and would ride back with them in the afternoon. They recalled that Louis had also occasionally hitched rides with the local mail carriers. Stewart and Robert also corrected my impression that the women who came to visit Louis Thom had stayed for the entire summer. In their memories, the women had stayed only a few weeks in May and June.

In the months that followed my second visit to Pugwash, I prepared a report to submit to the Nova Scotia government, which administers per-mits to conduct archaeological fieldwork in the province. The permit re-quired me to document any newly recorded archaeological site by describing its location, features, and cultural and chronological affiliations. After I submitted my permit report, the departmental staff assigned Louis Thom's cabin a site number (BkCv-08) and added it to the provincial database of archaeological sites. With this information entered into the official record, Louis Thom's cabin became a legible feature of Nova Scotia's archaeological landscape.[24]

Toward a Revitalized Anthropology of Mobility

One response to legal and political systems that define political subjectivity by the degree of a subject's sedentism could be to suggest that the Mi'kmaq were perhaps less mobile than the descriptions by early explorers and ethnographers suggest. This book takes a different approach, arguing instead for a reconceptualization of settlement itself to include movement and impermanent occupation that worked to emplace individuals and communities.[25] The movements that Louis Thom and Katalin Thomas experienced over their lifetimes—some voluntary, others forced; some to places near, others far; some shared with social and kin relations, others undertaken alone; and many beyond the boundaries of the Pictou Landing First Nation—illustrate the importance of including movement and impermanence in our understanding of how people settle. Louis Thom was born and raised in one community, chose to spend most of his time in another, and traveled between and around each at various spatial and temporal scales.[26] Katalin traced a very different path as she traveled—involuntarily—between Pictou Landing and the residential school at Shubenacadie. Her later trips to places farther afield allowed her to earn some wages working as a laborer on blueberry and potato farms.[27] These trips also provided a venue to renew social ties with Mi'kmaq from Pictou Landing and other communities. By examining such movements and others, this book demonstrates that Mi'kmaq have embedded themselves in Nova Scotia's (post)colonial landscape by moving across it. Doing so has frequently taken Mi'kmaq off their reserved lands to areas that have been alienated by European settlers. Drawing on archaeological, archival, ethnographic, and oral-historical data, this book demonstrates that both Mi'kmaq and Europeans were settling colonial and postcolonial Nova Scotia not by being fixed in one place but by moving across its lands and waters.

This approach to reconceptualizing settlement also requires what my colleague Maureen Marshall and I have described as a revitalized anthropological concept of mobility (see Lelièvre and Marshall 2015). In the case of colonial and postcolonial Nova Scotia, archaeological, archival, ethnographic, and oral-historical evidence exists not only for the actual physical movements of

Mi'kmaq (such as Louis Thom and Katalin Thomas) and non-Mi'kmaq (such as James Dawson and Father O'Reilly) but also for what people were saying about these movements, which were often moralizing statements about the apparent backwardness of being mobile and the benefits of being sedentary. These lines of evidence demonstrate the need for anthropologists to understand mobility as not simply the act of moving from one place to another but also the conceptions people have of those movements, the sensual perceptions of the experience of moving, and the work that moving does to emplace people on lands and waters that have been constructed by diverse subjects in colonies, even as they are being claimed by them.

* * *

The conceptual framework that Marshall and I have developed calls for more rigorous archaeological and ethnographic analyses of movement and the relationship between movement and politics. We sought a framework that would overcome what we consider to be the three most significant challenges facing an anthropology of mobility: first, the need to address the movements of subjects in both the present and the past; second, the difficulty of analyzing both the local, quotidian movements of individuals, families, and communities and also regional and global movements of workers, internally displaced persons, refugees, tourists, athletes, and others; and, third, the entrenched assumption that moving subjects are the marked or "Othered" category contrasted with a sedentary norm (see Lelièvre and Marshall 2015, 436). Katalin Thomas and Louis Thom's movements help illustrate these challenges because they occurred over multiple temporal and spatial scales. Katalin's movements in her late life were influenced, in part, by her experiences of moving as a child between her home in Pictou Landing and the residential school at Shubenacadie, and as a young married woman traveling between Pictou Landing and Maine. Louis Thom's experiences of moving included not only his daily journey from his cabin into the town of Pugwash but also his occasional travels between his cabin at Pugwash Junction and his house at Pictou Landing. The residential impermanence of some indigenous peoples in Canada has had direct bearing on their political status; they have been conceived as "Other" within a settler state whose common law traditions rely on sedentary attachment to a single location (cf. Raibmon 2005, 2007). Chapter 1 discusses in greater depth movement and politics as it relates to the interactions between the Mi'kmaq, the British Crown, and the Catholic Church in (post)colonial Nova Scotia. Here, I will review some of the basic terms that Marshall and I define and discuss in our conceptual framework for mobility (see Lelièvre and Marshall 2015).[28]

The foundation of our conceptual framework is an articulation of the difference between *movement* and *mobility*. In many of the previous ethnographic and archaeological discussions of mobility, there has been a tendency to confuse the ethnographically and archaeologically observable sociopolitical facts of movement with the analytical concept of mobility.[29] We understand movement to be an object of observation and mobility to be an object of study (*sensu* Trouillot 2001).[30] Thus, sociocultural anthropologists and archaeologists observe movement, or the ethnographic, historic, and archaeological proxies of movement, which we define as "a simultaneous change in space and time that subjects or objects experience actively and/or passively" (Lelièvre and Marshall 2015, 440). This definition can apply not only to human subjects but also to the movements of commodities, crafts, animals, and other objects. Marshall and I emphasize *change* in this definition, rather than the *displacement* of a subject or object from one position to another (Lelièvre and Marshall 2015, 440; see Merleau-Ponty 1962, 267; Massumi 2002, chap. 1). Displacement implies that the natural position of subjects/objects is stasis and that subjects/objects only passively experience removal from this stasis (Lelièvre and Marshall 2015, 440). These assumptions are what a sedentarist ideology masks.[31]

Revealing this ideology—and examining its role in the sociopolitics of British settler colonialism in North America—is possible when we consider movement not merely as a change in space and time experienced by an object or subject but more broadly as a commingling of *lived* practices, *conceived* imaginaries, and *sensual* perceptions (*sensu* Lefebvre [1974] 1991).[32] The lived, the conceived, and the perceived should not, however, be understood as discrete categories, for they all inform each other. Nor should this triad be mistaken for a "model"; Lefebvre ([1974] 1991, 40) argues for the logical necessity of the lived, conceived, and perceived being interconnected.[33]

The *lived practices* and experiences of movement are "repeated actions that shape and are shaped by the material and the social" (Lelièvre and Marshall 2015, 441). These actions might include the method by which people travel across land and water (e.g., by canoe, foot, automobile, train) and the material items that accompany them on their journeys (e.g., food, supplies, navigation equipment).[34] They also include the behaviors exhibited at places that afford rest and provide supplies while on long- and short-term journeys (e.g., the use of shellfish on Maligomish, or the construction of fish weirs). These actions manifest differently according to the historical, political, and social circumstances. For example, over the past four hundred years, the movements of Catholic clergy and congregants in Nova Scotia have shifted dramatically. In the seventeenth and eighteenth centuries, missionaries traveled to their congregations—Mi'kmaw and otherwise. By the nineteenth century, a formal diocesan structure meant that some priests were more permanently situated, while others maintained a peripatetic ministry. The twentieth century saw parish churches with dedicated priests established in larger Mi'kmaw communities. In smaller communities, such as Pictou Landing, the churches were missions in a larger parish; the parish priest would travel to the mission churches to offer Mass and administer sacraments.[35]

Practices of movement are facilitated and also limited by certain material conditions such as the presence or absence of mobile technologies and infrastructures, including roads, bridges, and railways (see Dalakoglou and Harvey 2015; Sheller and Urry 2006; Snead et al. 2009). For example, in his ethnoarchaeological research with Nunamiut hunters, Binford (1976) reported the changes in hunting practices that were prompted by the introduction of snowmobiles. Not only did the use of snowmobiles rather than dogsleds make it possible to travel farther without having to plan overnight stays, but it also permitted the pursuit of different animals, including wolves. But the snowmobiles also had problems that limited movement, including their frequent breakdowns in the field and the challenge of repairing the machines in cold weather (Binford 1976, 301). In nineteenth-century Nova Scotia, the representatives of the British Crown understood roads as literally and figuratively paving the way to "civilization" for the Mi'kmaq. The commissioner for Indian affairs wrote in 1843: "As the opening and improvement of cheap roads, in two or three places, is in some degree connected with the ultimate success of these experiments, it will be very desirable that a small sum should be placed at the disposal of your Excellency to connect the Reserves with adjoining settlements" (NSA 1843). But Sadie Francis shared a very different perspective on the presence of roads in her community during a 2004 roundtable discussion with Mi'kmaw elders of the Pictou Landing First Nation. The one road that ran through the reserve during her childhood was brought up in the context of discussing how children were selected to attend the residential school in Shubenacadie. To Sadie and her family, the road represented the outside world because the only people who drove on it were non-Mi'kmaq— usually the priest or the Indian agent, who was frequently the same person. She recalled being told by her parents and grandparents that if she saw a car on the reserve, she was to run home immediately to avoid being taken away (Francis, 2004).

Practices of movement also have social dimensions that shift through time and across space. For example, Mi'kmaw fishing practices became very differently gendered between the seventeenth and nineteenth centuries. Martijn

(1989) contrasts the differences between family units that traveled to the whaling sites around the Magdalene Islands in the seventeenth century and those who did so in the eighteenth century.[36] Using accounts from French military officers stationed at Louisbourg, Martijn demonstrates that in the earlier period an entire Mi'kmaw band, including women, children, and the elderly, might travel to the islands for the summer. In contrast, a report from the French administrator, Le Normant de Mézy in 1733, describes women and elders being left at the mission sites on the mainland while men pursued the whale fishery (Martijn 1989, 221). James Dawson observed a similar situation during his ill-timed visit to Maligomish in June 1842, when he found only one elderly man and the community's women with whom to converse.

As Martijn and others (see Pawling 2010; Rosenmeier 2010) have demonstrated, Mi'kmaq and other indigenous peoples in North America move at multiple spatial and temporal scales—from movements around a camp or across an island to journeys across vast distances for subsistence, to fetch a priest, to flee illness, and to seek aid from the colonial government. Chief Maltel (Matthew) Sapier documented one such journey in his 1836 petition: "Your Memorialists have been induced, to undertake a journey, at this Late Season of the year, from Merigomish, in the District of Pictou, where we have pitched our winter Wigwams, a distance of upwards of One hundred and Twenty Miles, to make known our wants to your Excellency" (NSA 1836).[37]

While some movements were regular and predictable, such as the annual pilgrimages to Maligomish and Chapel Island for the St. Anne's mission, others were less so, such as fetching a priest to have him perform the last rites. The seeming irregularity of Mi'kmaw journeys was one of the *conceptions* of movement—in other words, "the qualities, meanings, and values associated with movement" (Lelièvre and Marshall 2015, 442). These qualities include—among others—impermanence, itinerancy, transience, flexibility, and ephemerality. The positive and/or negative value of these "bundled" (*sensu* Keane 2003, 2005) qualities and their utility and relevance shift across contexts, making them historically and socially contingent (see Keane 2003, 414; Marshall and Lelièvre 2010, 9). This flexibility and contingency are important for how we understand relationships between political institutions and political subjects, for the qualities of movement can be equated with the qualities of moving subjects. For example, Raibmon (2005) cites a missionary in nineteenth-century British Columbia whose views of indigenous mobility were gendered—"the mobility of young men was improvident, while the mobility of women was immoral" (Raibmon 2005, 25). As the imagined value of the qualities of movement shifts, the relationships between institutions and subjects are affected. Some values are privileged, while others fade or are derided.

The conception of Mi'kmaw movements as aimless, improvident, and wandering was shared by many of the colonial agents, citizens, and missionaries who interacted with Mi'kmaq in nineteenth-century Nova Scotia. Other imaginaries are represented in the colonial discourse—for example, that Crown and Church agents were sedentary when, in fact, movement was inherent in many of their sociopolitical practices—especially with the Mi'kmaq. Ethnographic literature provides insight into non-Western imaginaries of movement. In her detailed ethnographic study among Gawan islanders, Munn (1986) demonstrates that for the Gawans motion can be imbued with positive qualities, as objects, rituals, and people who embody lightness and speed serve to extend intersubjective spacetime. Munn also interprets Gawans' relationship to movement as gendered such that activities associated with maleness (canoe building, sailing, net making) require movement from the village, while those associated with femaleness (child care, garden tending) are more sedentary (Munn 1986, 31–32).

Ethnographic observation can also provide evidence for the sensual *perceptions* of movement, which can be difficult to describe from written and archaeological sources because they represent the very immediate experiences of subjects as they move through both familiar and unfamiliar environments. However, Collignon (2006) laments the inadequate empirical data available for anthropological analyses of sensual perception. Referring to the senses of smell and sound that Inuit way-finders use in their navigation, she remarks that anthropologists who discuss senses other than sight "tend to do so more by their own 'intuition' than by observed facts" (Collignon 2006, 66). Analysis of its sociality is necessary because perception is "at once an immediate response of the body's senses and, at the same time, a relational accumulation of previous sensual experiences" that can "shape the practices of movement as well as affect the conceptions of movement" (Lelièvre and Marshall 2015, 441; see also Roth 2015). While engaging in participant observation on Maligomish, my attention was drawn to how its temporary residents perceived their movements through their camps and across the island. For example, Ralph Francis, who has diabetes and a heart condition, finds it difficult to negotiate the hills around his camp. The steep path from his camp leads to the churchyard where both religious and secular events are held throughout the St. Anne's mission. Some years Ralph climbs the hill; in others he does not. When he's not busy caring for his grandchildren, Ralph and his wife, Lorraine, generally relax in the shade at their picnic table or near the fire pit. When their grandchildren were younger, they were often heard before they were seen—yelling to their siblings, friends, parents, or grandparents as they approached the cluster of camps. The younger children often careened down the hill at breakneck speed and stumbled as they tried to stop themselves. The teenagers ambled down trying not to look too enthusiastic. As Ralph and Lorraine's adult children and extended family members walk up and down this hill, a common refrain is that it gets "steeper every year."

One's perception of walking across the island varies depending on the weather and time of day. The footpaths that connect various parts of the island can be pleasant, shade-covered avenues on a hot afternoon or treacherous tripping hazards after a heavy rainfall or in the dark. At night on Maligomish, the only illumination comes from kerosene or propane lamps, flashlights, children's glow sticks, solar-powered patio lanterns, and the occasional set of Christmas lights twinkling with electricity provided by a gas-powered generator. Archival records and ethnographic studies of Mi'kmaw religious practices also provide some insight into the sensual dimensions of movement. For example, Elsie Clews Parsons (1926) provides a detailed description from Potlotek (Chapel Island) of Mi'kmaw pilgrims crawling on their knees through the churchyard, up the stairs of the church, and down the main aisle in veneration of St. Anne (see chapter 4).

Taken together, the practices, conceptions, and perceptions of movement are the building blocks of the concept of *mobility*. Previous scholars have defined mobility, and some have distinguished movement from mobility. Wendrich and Bernard (2008) sought to free archaeologists from preconceived ideas based on universal definitions by identifying the temporal, spatial, and social dimensions of movement in particular social and historical settings. They define mobility as the combination of "moment" (time), "motion" (spatial pattern), and "motivation" (Wendrich and Barnard 2008, 8). But this definition does not consider perceptions or conceptions of movement. The philosopher Henri Bergson ([1889] 2001) accounts for the perceived and conceived in his definition of motion. Bergson argues against Eleatic philosophers such as Zeno, whose famous paradoxes posited that motion was impossible. Bergson suggests that Zeno's mistake is in equating the act of traversing across space (i.e., motion) with the space that is traversed ([1889] 2001, 112–13). Motion is the synthesis of the successive positions that a subject experiences while in the act of traversing a space. Bergson argues that this act of traversing has "no reality except in consciousness: it is a quality or an intensity" ([1889] 2001, 112). Cresswell (2006) distinguishes movement from mobility by defining them analogically in relation to location and place. He compares movement to space—in other words, abstract "contentless, apparently natural, and devoid of meaning, history, and ideology"—and mobility to place or something that is socially constructed (Cresswell

2006, 3). Thus, the Eleatic philosophers, Bergson ([1889] 2001), and Cresswell (2006) all rely on space as the ground against which to examine movement.

In the conceptual framework that Marshall and I offer, we aim to demonstrate how the practices, conceptions, and perceptions of movement are deeply interconnected with place without reducing movement to a displacement from one position to another (Lelièvre and Marshall 2015, 441–42). As discussed above, the mediating role of mobility in colonial and postcolonial Nova Scotia cannot be considered without also examining the places where Mi'kmaq, missionaries, and colonial agents stopped along their journeys and the practices performed at these places. Some, such as the shell midden on Maligomish, are places to which mobile populations have been returning for hundreds of years. Others, such as the reserves that were established for Mi'kmaq in the nineteenth century, represent attempts to constrain and sedentize an indigenous population. The literature on place and place-making provides a strong foundation for understanding the deep social connections that many traditionally mobile peoples share with particular landscapes (see Ashmore and Knapp 1999; Basso 1996; Bradley 2000; Bender 2002; Delucia 2015; Gallivan 2007; Hirsch and O'Hanlon 1995; Ingold 1993; Morphy 1993, 1995; Munn 1996; Rubertone 2009; Adam T. Smith 2003). For example, Basso (1996) demonstrates how an Apache community's collective knowledge, naming, and narrating of particular places builds a social landscape of great geographic and historical depth. From northern Maine and New Brunswick, Pawling (2010) examines petitions submitted by colonial settlers to illustrate the persistence of Wabanaki peoples' movements throughout the nineteenth century. He argues that these movements beyond the lands that had been reserved for them reinforced the Wabanaki idea of *homeland*, which he describes as something that was "not confined to a single place or surrounded by walls, but evoked a feeling of contentment and belonging to a network of people dispersed across the land" (see Pawling 2010, 503).

Emplacement, or "how people are drawn to, and into, places," at once refines and expands conceptions of place-making (Cobb 2005, 564. See also Rockefeller 2011). Marshall and I emphasize emplacement's subjective and political nature. Grounded in phenomenological approaches to conceptualizing place, we build on the work of Englund (2002) and Bachand (2006) to define emplacement as "embodied and historically contextual practices of situating, positioning and embedding subjects" (Lelièvre and Marshall 2015, 442). Subjects may emplace themselves, or they may be emplaced by others. Emplacement may occur in discrete locations, and/or they may occur over vast areas. Consequently, emplacement is not simply concerned with establishing and maintaining territory, for it may transcend borders (Lelièvre and Marshall 2015, 442). The relationship between movement and emplacement is perhaps best conceptualized as dialogical, as they have always already been copresent, mutually constitutive, and productive of new possibilities (*sensu* Bakhtin 1981; Kaplan and J. Kelly 1994, 1999).[38] Many Mi'kmaw toponyms capture the co-constitutive nature of movement and emplacement. For example, as reported by the missionary Pacifique, *Nemtogôoeg* is a strip of shoreline near the Caribou River meaning "running straight up," *Pagasepegiag* in Cape Breton is "something falls into the water," and *Mimsgolatjg* or "curving round and round" describes the Little Bass River in Colchester County (Pacifique 1934, 237, 250, 284).[39] The Mi'kmaw scholar Marie Battiste notes that "all spaces within Míkmáki [*sic*] have ancient names in the Míkmaq [*sic*] language that bear witness to their continuous use" (Battiste 1997, 17).[40] Much of the archaeological research conducted in Mi'kma'ki over the past thirty years has worked to respond to—and disprove—the negative and racist stereotypes of Mi'kmaq. Some research has addressed Mi'kmaw movements directly and demonstrated that, far from being aimless wanderers, the Mi'kmaq in the post-contact period engaged in movements that were part of an economic strategy, which involved subsistence not only from traditional food resources but also from wage labor and the sale of handmade crafts (see Abler 1990; Gonzalez 1981; Prins 1996b, 1997; N. R. Smith 1989). More recent scholarship has used oral histories and archaeological evidence of subsistence practices to identify places where Mi'kmaq have dwelled continuously or visited regularly over long periods of time (see Bernard et al. 2011; Blair 2004; Pentz 2008; Rosenmeier 2010; Rosenmeier et al. 2012). These are the places where Mi'kmaq returned seasonally or annually to hunt and fish, to gather resources, to practice their Catholic faith, and to renew political and family ties. This work has been important for demonstrating patterns of Mi'kmaw use of land and water (see Lewis 2007; cf. Brooks 2008).[41] And yet the focus on place has left the role of movement in Mi'kmaw society underexamined.[42] *Unsettling Mobility* builds on these studies to examine not only the places where Mi'kmaq dwelled but also how movements between these places (and the conceptions and perceptions of these movements) mediated sociopolitical relationships between Mi'kmaq, members of the Catholic Church, and representatives of the Crown. These include practices that served to emplace Mi'kmaq on their ancestral lands and waters by moving across them. They also include practices of the Church and Crown to emplace the Mi'kmaq by constraining and sometimes redirecting their movements. Emplacement is thus a particularly robust concept for examining the political consequences of positioning subjects in colonial settings.

Mobilizing Politics in Settler Colonies

By examining how mobility—defined as the practices, perceptions, and conceptions of movement entangled with emplacement—has mediated relationships between the Mi'kmaq, the Crown, and the Church, this book provides an avenue for exploring how Mi'kmaq have asserted their authority as political subjects in colonial and postcolonial Nova Scotia. Mi'kmaq such as Louis Thom, Katalin Thomas, the St. Anne's Day pilgrims, and the cod and herring fishers whom James Dawson missed on his visit to Maligomish have embedded themselves by moving across Nova Scotia's (post)colonial landscape. Doing so has frequently taken Mi'kmaq off the lands that have been reserved for their exclusive occupation to areas with which they have ancestral ties but from which they were long ago alienated by European settlers. The central argument of this book is that, by moving beyond the boundaries of their reserves—and by asserting their rights to access and use their traditional lands and waters—Mi'kmaq have been engaging in acts of sovereignty and, consequently, constituting themselves as political subjects.[43]

Three observations have drawn me to this conclusion. First, many practices of movement, such as hunting and traveling for political and social renewal, represent a persistence and transformation of those from the pre-contact period—what Neal Ferris (2009, 1) has described as "changed continuities."[44] Practices such as decorating handbags with dyed porcupine quills were not those in which Mi'kmaq engaged before the arrival of European settlers and the development of markets that demanded such products. However, neither were they entirely new practices. Indeed, while few Mi'kmaq from the Pictou Landing First Nation worked underground in the area's many coal mines, several did fashion wooden roof supports and ax handles that they then sold to the mining companies. The material and social dimensions of these practices—in other words, the raw materials used to produce the beams and handbags, the places the people traveled to harvest the materials, the tools they used, and the people with whom they traveled and worked—required Mi'kmaq to access places and use skills, such as navigation and wood working, that had persisted from the pre-contact period. Thus, many of the activities through which Mi'kmaq engaged the settler economy also allowed them to exercise their right to access the land and water.

Second, even some of the practices introduced through their contact with Europeans, such as subsistence digging for archaeological artifacts and performing pilgrimages to mission sites, have involved returning to places that Mi'kmaq used in the pre-contact period. For example, in the mid-twentieth century, while reporting on his excavations at Bear River in southwestern

Nova Scotia, the amateur archaeologist John Erskine noted a nineteenth-century Mi'kmaw occupation, as evidenced by the intrusion of nails and chinaware into the pre-contact site (Erskine 1958, 14).

Finally, Mi'kmaw movements in the post-contact period represent acts of sovereignty because many of the places to and by which Mi'kmaq have traveled are located on lands and waters that have long been alienated by Europeans. Non-Mi'kmaw residents of northeastern Nova Scotia, such as the MacDonald brothers, remember these temporary settlements. While recording the location of the abandoned rail station at Avondale during a 2004 archaeological survey, I spoke with Olive Wilson, a non-Mi'kmaw woman who was the daughter of the Canadian National Railway stationmaster and who had lived in Avondale Station since childhood (see Lelièvre 2005). She recalled that in the mid-1940s an extended family named Sylliboy had traveled 250 kilometers by train from Christmas Island near Eskasoni and sought permission from her uncle to camp on his property for the winter. Mrs. Wilson recalled that the family was trying to avoid complying with the Canadian government's policy to "centralize" Nova Scotia's Mi'kmaw population into two large settlements.[45] In the cases of Louis Thom and the Sylliboys, they did not own the land, but their impermanent settlement on it exercised their right to access it.

Beyond examining how Mi'kmaq emplaced themselves by moving across the post-contact Nova Scotia landscape, *Unsettling Mobility* also demonstrates how movement and emplacement operated in the European settlement of the province, and particularly in the settlers' management of the indigenous population. While exercising their rights to access the land worked to constitute the Mi'kmaq as political subjects, at the same time the Church and Crown worked to subjectify the Mi'kmaq through various projects of "civilization," which included first and foremost their sedentization. By encouraging them to settle with incentives of land, tools, and seed, the Church and Crown were attempting to remake the Mi'kmaq in the image of European colonial subjects.

This book holds these two perspectives on the constitution of Mi'kmaw political subjectivity in tension. It uses archaeological data, archival records, oral histories, and participant observation to expand our anthropological understanding of mobility. Building on the growing body of ethnographic, archaeological, and interdisciplinary research related to the movements of human subjects (see, for example, Andrushko et al. 2009; Beaudry and Parno 2013; Bettinger 2015; Binnie et al. 2007; Bonilla 2011; Braidotti 1994; Cunningham and Heyman 2004; Czeglédy 2004; de León 2012; Delugan 2010; Englund 2002; Fowles 2011; Henderson 2013; Kallius et al. 2016; Langan 2001; Magaña 2011; Ong 2005; Peña 2011; Roth 2015; Sellet et al. 2006; Sharma and Towns 2015; Sheller and Urry 2006; Smithers 2015; Truitt 2008; Wilcox 2009), this book demonstrates that—far from being indicative of "simple" societies, mobility has complex motivations, manifestations, and effects as it mediates, and is productive of, sociopolitical relationships.[46]

The Political Stakes of Mobility

In the summer of 2005, a decision from the Supreme Court of Canada (SCC) helped me to recognize the theme of mobility that had been recurring in my conversations with Mi'kmaq from the Pictou Landing First Nation. This decision also provided an initial understanding of the political and legal stakes of the relationship between mobility and settlement. That year the SCC heard an appeal case that upheld the convictions of Stephen Frederick Marshall and Joshua Bernard—two Mi'kmaq from Atlantic Canada who had been convicted by lower courts of having harvested timber illegally from provincial Crown land. Their lawyers had argued that the men had a right to this resource based both on promises made in a series of eighteenth-century treaties the Mi'kmaq had made with the British and also on their claim of aboriginal title, or exclusive occupation of the land in question before the assertion of British sovereignty over it. The court rejected this defense on both points; the Mi'kmaq did not demonstrate that their harvesting of timber represented "a logical evolution from the traditional trading activities at the time the treaties were made," and they did not demonstrate that they possessed aboriginal title to the land they had harvested (Supreme Court of Canada, 2005, summary).

Although the SCC decision was unanimous, the reasons behind it were not. Chief Justice MacLachlan, responding for the majority, emphasized the need for the evidence to demonstrate "exclusive occupation" of land before British sovereignty in order to claim aboriginal title. While the evidence presented in *R. v. Marshall/R. v. Bernard* did not demonstrate exclusive occupation, the majority respondents did, however, recognize the potential for traditionally mobile peoples such as the Mi'kmaq to provide such evidence in future cases. Chief Justice MacLachlan wrote, "In each case, the question is whether a degree of physical occupation or use equivalent to common law title has been made out" (Supreme Court of Canada 2005, para. 66). In his concurring decision, Justice LeBel expressed concern that the test for determining aboriginal title by *degree* of physical occupation may be impossible for nomadic and semi-nomadic peoples to meet (Supreme Court of Canada 2005, para. 126, emphasis added). He argued that the standards of a common law definition of title could not be the only criteria applied to the cases involving indigenous Canadians. Justice LeBel argued further that "the patterns and nature of aboriginal occupation of land should inform the standard necessary to prove aboriginal title," and these patterns included "nomadic and semi-nomadic modes of occupation" (Supreme Court of Canada 2005, para. 131). More than just considering indigenous perspectives on land access and use in rights cases, LeBel went so far as to argue that indigenous "conceptions of territoriality, land use and property should be used to *modify* and *adapt* the traditional common law concepts of property in order to develop an occupancy standard that incorporates both the aboriginal and common law approaches" (Supreme Court of Canada, para. 127, emphasis added).[47]

In making this argument to accommodate both common law and Mi'kmaw understandings of property and ownership, Justice LeBel appeared to be opening the door for a radical dialectics of property law that would break from the legal traditions of the "mother" country and introduce an approach uniquely designed to accommodate the contrasting worldviews at work in settler colonies. The research presented here was inspired by this idea; I sought to study Mi'kmaw mobility in order to shed light on the bias toward sedentism that suffuses not only the common law but also provincial and federal policies related to indigenous peoples. I also sought evidence to demonstrate that Mi'kmaw settlement practices may be impermanent, but they are nevertheless significant.[48] Whether the evidence of Mi'kmaw mobility presented here can be used in future Mi'kmaw land and rights claims is less critical than the contribution this study makes toward reconceptualizing mobility as a co-constitution of movement and emplacement. This idea has implications not only for the rights of traditionally mobile peoples such as the Mi'kmaq but also for how we understand the politics of settler colonialism.

* * *

On the surface, the role played by Mi'kmaq and other indigenous peoples as political subjects in the settler colony of Canada is straightforward. Before the introduction of the Indian Act in 1876, these peoples were considered autonomous nations. Indeed, that was the status conferred to the various communities of Mi'kmaq with whom the British Crown negotiated the Covenant Chain of treaties in the eighteenth century. After 1876, Mi'kmaq and other indigenous peoples were considered wards of the state with the federal government assuming responsibility for their welfare, education, and ultimate assimilation into settler society. The policies and legislation enacted since

1876—especially those designed to precipitate assimilation—have had dire consequences for the social, economic, and political lives of indigenous peoples in the present. Among these consequences are the oft-quoted statistics demonstrating that Canada's indigenous peoples experience unemployment, poverty, incarceration, inadequate housing, and unsafe drinking water at rates much higher than Euro-Canadians. And yet these problems only tell part of the story, because despite—or in spite of—them, indigenous peoples have not been so assimilated that they have abandoned practices that settler institutions most feared, including potlatches, ceremonial dancing, language, communal property, and movement. Even the prohibition on potlatches and dancing in the early twentieth century was insufficient to destroy these practices, which have been enjoying a revitalization in many Northwest Coast communities since the late twentieth century (see Glass 2006).

The failure of the sovereign to meet the terms of its social compact with its indigenous populations—as well as the responses of peoples such as the Mi'kmaq to this failure—has had consequences for how we understand "the political" and particularly "sovereignty," in settler colonies. Both the liberal model of "sovereign and subject" and the Foucauldian idea that diffuse and multiple sources of power work to create subjects not through relations of sovereignty but through relations of discipline (Foucault 1977, 208) can help us understand the ways in which the Catholic Church and the British Crown have attempted to construct the Mi'kmaq as subjects. In the liberal tradition, ultimate political authority rests with the sovereign. Those who recognize that authority are subject to it. Hence, as Adam T. Smith has argued, "the political," concerns "the creation and maintenance of sovereignty in practical negotiations between variously formalized authorities and a publically specified community of subjects" (2011, 416). We can recognize this model in the colonial and postcolonial history of Nova Scotia as the formalized authorities of the British Crown (e.g., lieutenant governors, legislative bodies, and judiciaries) have negotiated with those of the Mi'kmaq (e.g., the *Sante' Mawi'omi* or Grand Council) to enact and maintain treaties.

However, neither the liberal nor Foucauldian models of sovereignty have adequately conceptualized the political relationships between the multiple authorities, and multiple worldviews, operating in settler societies.[49] The Mi'kmaq's assertion of themselves as a sovereign nation exemplifies the contingent nature of sovereign authority in settler colonies. For while the British took the Mi'kmaq's entrance into treaties as a sign of their having surrendered some authority to that of the Crown—a submission of subject to sovereign— the Mi'kmaq understood the treaties to be an agreement between two nations (see D. Marshall et al. 1989; Wicken 2002, 2012). Even in the face of increasing encroachment, Mi'kmaq retained their faith in the legitimacy of the treaties and their rights to access the land and water.

Mi'kmaq refer to these treaties as the Covenant Chain.[50] Each of the eighteenth-century treaties is considered to be a link in a chain of agreements that Clarke and L. Patterson (1987) describe as being forged in mutual consent with the British Crown. The traditional governing body of the Mi'kmaw nation, the *Sante' Mawi'omi*, holds the responsibility for keeping both Mi'kmaq and the Crown accountable for the mutual promises made in the Covenant Chain of treaties. There is evidence in the archival record that Mi'kmaq treasured the treaty agreements. For example, in May 1812, Abbé Sigogne, who was a missionary to the Acadian and Mi'kmaw populations on Nova Scotia's south shore, responded to a request from Lieutenant Governor Sherbrooke for the Le Hève Mi'kmaq's copy of the "Treaty of Peace" (Belcher's Treaty/Proclamation of 1763). Sigogne prefaces his letter with the following comment: "Agreeable to you with I send a copy of the Treaty of Peace with the Indians. I cannot send the original which is dirty, somewhat damaged and worn out on the edges of the folds" (NSA 1812). This description of the wear that the document incurred suggests that the Le Hève Mi'kmaq had been preserving and repeatedly consulting their copy of the treaty for almost fifty years—something the Crown's archivists in Nova Scotia were apparently unable to do, as indicated by Sherbrooke's request for the document.

The Mi'kmaq's faith in these treaties stems from their self-ascribed status as a sovereign nation. The leaders of the *Sante' Mawi'omi* describe their nation's sovereignty in relation to the Covenant Chain of treaties (see D. Marshall et al. 1989).[51] Their arguments stem from the premise that the people of Mi'kma'ki represent an independent nation with the same status as Great Britain; as such, the treaties were negotiated by two equal nations. For example, the 1752 treaty, which the leaders referred to as the Elikawake ("in the King's house") Treaty, "affirmed Mikmaki [*sic*] and Britain as two states sharing one Crown—the crown pledging to preserve and defend Mi'kmaq [*sic*] rights against settlers as much as against foreign nations" (D. Marshall et al. 1989, 82). The authors maintain that the Crown was unwilling and/or unable to enforce the treaties and acted illegally when, in the nineteenth century, it sold land promised to Mi'kmaq. This action was illegal because the 1763 Royal Proclamation that "consolidated all previous policies . . . stated unequivocally that the tribes were not to be disturbed in their use and possession of their traditional lands, and that the only way in which such lands could be acquired was through treaty with the Crown" (D. Marshall et al.

1989, 82, 83). Thus, from the perspective of the *Sante' Mawi'omi*, when the colonial government in Nova Scotia introduced legislation in the mid-nineteenth century that allowed for the sale of Crown lands promised to the Mi'kmaq, the government was acting illegally.[52]

The above comments must be understood in the context of the political circumstances of late twentieth-century Nova Scotia and Canada, which was characterized by contentious relations between the federal and provincial governments and First Nations populations. But Mi'kmaw adherence to the treaty promises was not a product the Pan-Indian movement. The Mi'kmaq's understanding of the treaties' value has been passed down through the members of the *Sante' Mawi'omi*. For example, in 1852, almost a century after the last treaties were ratified, the Baptist minister Silas Rand related to Lieutenant Governor LeMerchant part of a conversation with Chief Francis Paul, in which at least one Mi'kmaw's understanding of his people's role within the British Empire was made clear: "It may also be proper to state that the Indians do not consider themselves subjects of Queen Victoria. I had written this expression at the close of the Petition. The venerable old chief—Francis Paul—shook his head that expression could not be admitted. 'We treated as an independant [*sic*] nation,' said he, 'and no steps had ever been taken to alter this relation.' I must say I admired the Independant [*sic*] spirit of the old man. I dashed my pen thro. the offensive expression" (NSA 1852).

Moreover, political authority in a colonial context is something of a moving target. The Mi'kmaq submitted some portion of will to a diverse range of formal and informal political authorities, including the French and British colonial regimes, the Catholic Church, trade companies, European immigrants, and authorities already extant in their own communities, such as the *Sante' Mawi'omi*. With so many authorities at work, the power of any one of them was diffuse, leaving much room for the Mi'kmaq to engage in practices that allowed them to use the lands and waters in ways that exercised their aboriginal and treaty rights.[53]

Indeed, the assertion of treaty rights was Donald Marshall Jr.'s defense when he was accused of fishing eels out of season in 1993. In the most famous of a series of court cases against Mi'kmaw hunters and fishers, Mr. Marshall was originally convicted. But that decision was eventually overturned by the Supreme Court of Canada, which heard Marshall's appeal in 1999 (see Coates 2000; Wicken 2002). In what became known as the "Marshall Decision," the SCC upheld these rights for all Mi'kmaq and Wolastoqiyik (Maliseet), granting them the right to fish and harvest other resources to earn a "moderate living." As the Marshall Decision and subsequent Supreme Court rulings on treaty rights have demonstrated, the Covenant Chain should not be interpreted as a static entity; the rights negotiated through these treaties have evolved. Over the past two centuries, these treaties have been linked through the practices in which Mi'kmaq engaged to assert their rights, many of which involved both movement and emplacement. Mi'kmaq moved to and from places that were significant for the resources they offered, the people they attracted, and the kin and spiritual associations they fostered. Seen as an exercise of treaty rights, these practices of movement and emplacement are political acts of sovereignty on the part of the Mi'kmaw nation. By extension, the individual Mi'kmaq who have engaged in these practices have been asserting themselves as political subjects.

This practice-based approach to the constitution of political subjectivity is inspired by the work of Simpson (2003, 2014) and Cattelino (2008, 2010a), who examine the material practices of sovereignty in indigenous communities. Cattelino grounds her definition of sovereignty in her ethnographic observations of daily life in a "casino-era" Seminole community. For her, sovereignty is "the Seminoles' shared assertions, everyday processes, intellectual projects, and lived experiences of political distinctiveness," all of which is materialized in forms as mundane as houses, kitchen appliances, universal health care, and seniors' meal service. In addition to emphasizing the lived experiences of sovereignty, Cattelino's ethnography challenges models that define sovereignty as autonomy. Cautioning against "overly juridical and unitary understandings," Cattelino argues that Seminole sovereignty is grounded in interdependent economic, political, and legal relationships (Cattelino 2008, 17, 128–29). These two ideas—that sovereignty can be materially constituted and that multiple sovereignties can be not only copresent but also co-constitutive—lay the groundwork for understanding the multiple authorities at work in Mi'kmaw communities.

Offering insight to how the Mi'kmaq constituted *themselves* as political subjects within colonial and postcolonial Nova Scotia helps to shift the tone of discourse on Mi'kmaw-settler relations away from that of victimization. Certainly the Mi'kmaq suffered—and many continue to suffer—greatly from the policies of the Crown and the Church. These institutions forged some policies in collusion; for example, the assimilation of indigenous children through a system of residential schools. But Nova Scotia's social and political history is more complex than a dichotomous model of perpetrator/victim or domination/resistance can describe. I approach this history from the perspective of intersubjectivity—in other words, "self-other relations constituted in terms of and by means of specific types of practices" (Munn 1986, 10). I engage the complexity of interactions in colonial and postcolonial Nova Scotia by assuming that they have obtained in the interactions between multiple individuals and institutions. These have included myriad permutations of interactions between Mi'kmaq, between Mi'kmaw organizations, between individual Mi'k-maq and Mi'kmaw institutions such as the *Sante' Mawi'omi*, between the *Sante' Mawi'omi* and the Catholic Church, between Mi'kmaq and settlers, and between Mi'kmaq and the numerous individuals who represented the institutions of the British Crown.

The complex nature of Mi'kmaw political subjectivity challenges liberal conceptions of the political based on a "sovereign-subject" framework. If a liberal politics is "an historical negotiation over the logics of authorization and subjection that stitch together the polity and differentiate the terrain of personal will from that of sovereign privilege" (Adam T. Smith 2011, 416), then this negotiation is complicated in settler colonies because of the copresence of competing definitions of the polity and convictions about who holds the privilege to determine life and death. Indeed, scholars, leaders, and activists have expressed skepticism that any concepts rooted in Western liberal political theory can be productive for even *describing* let alone *securing* indigenous rights in settler colonies because they are so alien to the worldviews of many indigenous peoples (see Alfred 1999, 2009; de la Cadena 2010; 2015; Ivison et al. 2000; Rifkin 2009). The basic ideas of Western political theory—sovereignty, citizenship, territory, and subjectivity—inadequately capture the complexity of societies that may operate through less structured, less patriarchal, and more collective practices and whose cosmologies recognize nonhuman animals and even the land itself as political actors.[54] Given the overlapping and competing authorities at work (in Nova Scotia, for example, between the Catholic Church, the *Sante' Mawi'omi*, and the British Crown), the sovereign-subject relationship seems inadequate for understanding politics in settler societies.

Recognizing the inadequacy of a liberal sovereign-subject model for politics in settler colonies is particularly important for the current work given the spatial metaphors that weave through much of the conceptual language that Western scholarship uses to describe political relationships; for example, the political versus public *sphere*, the political *landscape*, the political *field*, and the *placement* of subjects in relation to a sovereign.[55] Sovereignty itself is almost always associated with the authority to determine life and death within a specific territory. *Unsettling Mobility* builds on the work of anthropologists, historians, and geographers who have been articulating the precepts of that territoriality in specific historical and cultural contexts (see, for example, Brooks 2008; Simpson 2014; Adam T. Smith 2003; Sparke 2005). It also aims to expose the deep and extensive roots of many modern Western conceptions of the relationships between political subjects, including those in the Marxist and poststructuralist traditions. For example, in the revolutionary genealogy of political subjectivity, the spatial relationship between the urban and the rural (Marx and Fanon) and the north and the south (Gramsci) sets the stage for the development of a fully conscious proletariat. Arendt's conceptualization of citizenship is grounded in an understanding that political participation must occur in the public sphere. More recently, Agamben (1998, 19) has traced the "complex topological relations" of Western polities, arguing that it is the sovereign's ability to determine the threshold for what is included and what is excluded from the space of the polity that makes the validity of the juridico-political order possible. In attempting to "indigenize" Agamben, Rifkin (2009) has argued for a focus on *geo*- as much as *bio*politics. And in her analysis of Badiou's early conceptions of the political subject, Power (2006, 324) argues that what is at stake for the French philosopher is the topological framework that places the proletariat in opposition to the bourgeoisie. Although diverse in aim and scope, these conceptualizations of the political share a privileging of the *location* of subjects—either in the demarcated territories of geopolitics or in the abstract topologies of the philosophy of sovereignty—over their subjective experiences as moving bodies. Brian Massumi (2002) makes this point in his critique of cultural theory that emphasizes the formation of subjects by systemic structures into which a body is positioned. He argues that poststructuralist cultural and literary theory has privileged describing the position of a body on an *a priori* grid of interlocking binaries (male/female, gay/straight, black/white) over understanding how these binaries emerge. For Massumi, ontology is not about being but instead about becoming (Massumi 2002, 2–3).

Given the kinship that an ontology of becoming shares with the fluidity of the Mi'kmaw worldview, is a postpositional politics possible? Power's analysis of Badiou suggests a way of conceptualizing "the political" such that "sovereign," "subject," and "institution" do not exist *a priori* or necessarily relate to each other hierarchically. Rather, these positions are constituted relationally, and hierarchies may or may not emerge from these relationships. This conception of the political does not assume that all subjects and institutions have equal authority. The relations by which these positions are constituted are asymmetrical but not unidirectional (Lycett 2004, 358).[56] This book attempts to pose a postpositional politics by privileging mobility as a mediator between political subjects and institutions; in other words, political subjects and institutions are formed through their relationships with each other as mediated by mobility.

Integrating Pictou Landing

A recurrent theme in my conversations with elders from the Pictou Landing First Nation was the time in their younger lives that they spent living, working, and traveling in communities near and far from the reserve. To the extent that their stories were about people leaving a small place in search of better (or just different) opportunities, they may be unremarkable. Louis Thom's eighty-kilometer journey between his on- and off-reserve homes, Katalin Thomas's shuttling between the reserve and the Shubenacadie residential school as a child, and her short-term migrations to New Brunswick and Maine to harvest blueberries are experiences unique neither to Mi'kmaq of the Pictou Landing First Nation nor to indigenous peoples. Indeed, two decades ago the anthropologist Arjun Appadurai asserted that the "world we live in is one in which human motion is more often definitive of social life than it is exceptional" (Appadurai 1996, 43). Yet, the diversity of mobile experiences recounted by the people of this small community—and their persistent and strong connection to the island of Maligomish—proved to be a compelling setting for examining the very broad issues of political subjectivity in settler colonies and the relationship between mobility and settlement.

My very first introduction to the community was in December 2004 when I facilitated a roundtable discussion with elders as part of a research project sponsored by the Nova Scotia Museum of Industry. I met with several elders to discuss their employment experiences. We gathered in the meeting room of Our Lady of Perpetual Help, the community's Catholic church. I was assisted by Javenny Francis, a Mi'kmaw student who had been working for the Museum of Industry, and who had suggested the names of several elders as potential participants. Once the digital recorder and microphone were set up and everyone was assembled, I introduced myself, thanked everyone for coming, and directed the elders' attention to the written consent forms that I had distributed around the table. The Museum of Industry had requested that the participants sign written consent forms so that its staff and researchers could use the elders' comments in the future. I read my consent script, which informed the elders of their rights and described how their knowledge would be preserved and reproduced. I then asked the elders to sign the consent forms, which would authorize the Museum of Industry and me to use their knowledge in publications, presentations, and exhibits. While I was reading the consent script, one elder—Sadie Francis—interrupted me to ask what benefit the community would receive from the knowledge that she and her contemporaries were about to share. She was skeptical that the conversation would benefit anyone other than myself: "So it's not solely for your own personal use. You're not just—you're not using this just to get your PhD . . . you're not viewing us as a stepping stone. 'Cause it has been done before . . . it's still happening too. I guess that['s] . . . why I'm very cautious in stuff like that 'cause [we've] been stepped on, spit on, used, everything else along the way. . . . So, when a new face comes along you put your flags up, eh?" (Francis, 2004).

These comments reveal a sentiment shared by more than one individual in Pictou Landing and by many indigenous peoples who have been the objects of research. The Mi'kmaq of Pictou Landing have seen many strangers pass through their community, claiming that they want to make a difference, and implying that they have a better way of doing things. These strangers come, take what they want, and contribute very little back into the community. Interventions from outside the community are not limited to academic researchers. Many indigenous communities in Canada have a long history of being studied by various levels of government, by NGOs, and by commercial agencies. Many Pictou Landing community members told me that they felt the Mi'kmaq had been "studied to death." This feeling may be due to the countless environmental and health studies that have been conducted to measure the effects of water and air pollution from the pulp paper plant that is located across the East River of Pictou. The effluent treatment facility was constructed in the late 1960s on a tidal lagoon that is part of Pictou Landing's reserved lands.[57]

Although Sadie eventually agreed to participate in what turned out to be a lively discussion, her skepticism made me reluctant to pursue any follow-up research with the community. However, in the years that followed the 2004 roundtable, I gradually realized that I had misunderstood Sadie's initial response. I had mistaken her feelings for disinterestedness when they were, in fact, an expression of caution. My mistake was jumping into a community and asking for its collective knowledge when no one knew who I was, where I was from, or—as one community member later asked me—"what I'm all about."

When my fieldwork began in earnest in 2007, I sought opportunities to share what I was all about with members of the Pictou Landing First Nation. I spent much of my first year in the field volunteering at community events such as the annual powwow in June, the four-day St. Anne's mission in July, and the *salitey* or the combined feasts and fundraising benefits that follow Mi'kmaw funerals. I traded Mi'kmaw language instruction for my very rudimentary graphic design skills with Lorraine Francis, who was looking for help promoting her craft business. I also applied to Fisheries and Oceans Canada for a license that would allow me to fish lobster with Louise and Martin (Junior)

Sapier from Pictou Landing. I spent a couple of days on the boat, mostly trying to stay out of the way, but occasionally being allowed to bait traps.

The participant observation also extended beyond the Pictou Landing First Nation as I attended St. Anne's Day celebrations on Potlotek in Cape Breton Island, joined Treaty Day (October 1) events in the provincial capital of Halifax, and occasionally accompanied an elder on excursions to visit friends and relations in other Mi'kmaw communities. Engaging in these activities not only allowed community members to get to know me but also allowed me to observe kinship networks that often extended beyond Pictou Landing, informal and formal political and social organizations, and tensions between individuals and families. This breadth of knowledge may not have been possible had I worked in a larger community.

My work with the Pictou Landing First Nation began to build momentum after a community meeting in June 2007. I had organized this meeting to propose to the community a research project that would combine oral history and archaeology to examine changes in Mi'kmaw movement from the pre-contact to the post-contact periods. I had proposed to focus the project on Maligomish, a small island in Merigomish Harbour that is part of the Pictou Landing First Nation's reserved lands.[58] The objective of the 2007 community meeting was to outline the proposed research and get feedback on how to modify the research so that community members would be comfortable with it. Already from the 2004 roundtable and from subsequent conversations, I knew that any kind of research—but particularly archaeological fieldwork—would raise concerns for some community members. For example, Raymond Francis, a former chief and *Keptin* of the Pictou Landing First Nation, was one of the community members most wary of any archaeological work being conducted on Maligomish. He shared a very negative experience that he had had with an archaeologist (or someone claiming to be an archaeologist) who came to the island in the late 1960s or early 1970s. Mr. Francis recalled that this man had conducted archaeological work on Maligomish without asking for the community's permission. He further recalled that this man—who was accompanied by two younger people who referred to him as "Doctor"—did not even introduce himself. While Mr. Francis could not recall many details of this visit, he was able to convey to me a feeling of having his (and therefore the community's) authority undermined. Because of the anxieties associated with archaeological fieldwork, I wanted to be sure that I had the general approval of the community before proceeding with my project. The process of gaining approval was a gradual negotiation that unfolded on many fronts, involving a network of people and institutions that extended well beyond the Pictou Landing First Nation.

The individual who perhaps had the most influence on the project's approval was Roger Lewis, a Mi'kmaw archaeologist who has spent considerable time in Mi'kmaw communities explaining how archaeology supports land and treaty claims. Roger laid the groundwork for people like me—nonindigenous outsiders who are trying to overcome a century and a half of strained relations between archaeologists and Mi'kmaq in Nova Scotia. Roger attended the community meeting in June 2007 to follow up on a presentation that he had made in Pictou Landing two years previously. At this meeting, Roger was the headliner; I was making a guest appearance. After delivering his presentation, Roger introduced me and endorsed the work I was proposing to do. His endorsement made a significant difference in how the community viewed me and my proposed research. Many community members continued to have concerns, but they were more willing to engage in dialogues about the proposed fieldwork on Maligomish.

In subsequent conversations, several people articulated the reasons for their discomfort. One of the primary concerns was that the fieldwork would disturb the island itself. Many of the Mi'kmaq with whom I spoke described the island as sacred. Their observance of the island's sanctity manifested in practices such as a self-imposed prohibition on alcohol and drug consumption while on the island. Lorraine Francis, who made birch-bark wall hangings and baskets, said that she would not harvest bark from the trees on Maligomish, because they are sacred. The island's sanctity also derives from its role as a final resting place for many deceased Mi'kmaq. The cemetery associated with the St. Anne's mission church contains graves ranging in dates as early as 1858 to as recently as 2015. There are also several earth mounds distributed throughout the island, which many Mi'kmaq—and some non-Mi'kmaw archaeologists—believe to be burials.

In addition to the physical remains of their ancestors, many Mi'kmaq believe that Maligomish is home to ancestral spirits. The spirits on Maligomish include not only those of the deceased relatives who are buried on Maligomish but also the spirits that Ruth Holmes Whitehead describes as *Mn'tu'k* or persons, which she identifies as one of the many nonhuman animate beings that populate Mi'kmaw stories. These persons are "entities who do not necessarily need to take form, although they can and do, as it pleases them" (Whitehead 1988, 5). Almost every Mi'kmaw with whom I spoke shared a story of encountering these generally nocturnal spirits, which can appear as trickster figures. They call attention with sounds of distant voices and the scraping of boats and canoes being pulled up onto the rocky shore. But if anyone follows these sounds and goes to the shore, he or she will see no one. Thus, in addition to concerns that our archaeological fieldwork might disturb the ground in which their ancestors were buried, there was an implicit unease about the disrespect that disturbing the ground posed to nonhuman subjects such as animals, the soil, and landforms. Like those of other Algonquian societies, the Mi'kmaq's cosmology recognizes the animacy of nonhuman subjects.[59] The Mi'kmaw writer Murdena Marshall summarizes the collective responsibility that all animate beings have in the Mi'kmaw cosmology: "that all things in the world have their own spirit, and all things must work in harmony with each other" (Murdena Marshall, n.d., n.p.). Fellow Mi'kmaw scholar Marie Battiste concurs, noting that plants, rocks, and animals share the same life forces as humans (Battiste 1997, 15). In a world where the very earth itself is considered to be a sentient being, it is difficult to imagine an activity more disturbing to its harmony than an archaeological excavation. With a better understanding of these concerns, we eventually reached a compromise in which the archaeological fieldwork would be limited to a surface survey of the entire island and test excavations of the island's shell midden.

The archaeological fieldwork was conducted in three phases between November 2007 and November 2008. Equally important to the surface survey and test excavations was the experience of traveling to and living on Maligomish outside the bustle of the St. Anne's Day mission. Maligomish is accessible only by boat, and much of our time in the field was spent ensuring we had a suitable vessel to take us across the three hundred meters that separates Maligomish from the mainland. We were also occupied monitoring the weather, winds, and tides, which can make even this short journey precarious. During the autumn, our field crew shared the island with several hunters and fishers from Pictou Landing and other Mi'kmaw communities. Several families participated in the food fishery and had set salmon nets around the island to take advantage of the fall run. In the fall of 2008, we were using a band-owned boat, which we occasionally shared with families from Pictou Landing who were taking their children to check their nets for salmon.

These serendipitous encounters were perhaps the most crucial for understanding Maligomish as a Mi'kmaw place and the role that such places play in the constitution of Mi'kmaq as political subjects. For example, during the autumn salmon run, Merigomish Harbour is rife with tension as Mi'kmaw fishing practices are surveilled by federal officers from Fisheries and Oceans Canada. Our field crew experienced this surveillance firsthand one day as we came ashore after having collected samples of soft-shell clams. The officers were waiting for us, inquired about what we had been doing, and asked to inspect the bags of clams we had collected. After they left, I naively wondered at how these officers had just happened to be at the shore when we arrived. With a sardonic laugh, Edie Nicholas, one of the field crew members from the

Pictou Landing First Nation, assured me that the officers had been watching us the entire time we had been collecting. Yet despite—or in spite of—such surveillance, some Mi'kmaq from Pictou Landing knowingly violate the regulations associated with the food fishery by using improperly sized nets and not tagging their nets clearly. In the fall of 2008, three men from Pictou Landing were accused of using improper nets. One of these men had the boat he was using confiscated. While being surveilled by the state, Mi'kmaq who engage in the fall food fishery also compete with non-Mi'kmaw fishers who occasionally steal salmon or damage nets. Such incidents further mark the Mi'kmaq as indigenous subjects of a settler society. These moments of tension between practices of subjectification and practices of resistance and perseverance illuminate the construction of Mi'kmaw political subjectivity.

Mobility in the Field and in the Archive

Writing a historical ethnography of mobility has required an interdisciplinary approach both to the fieldwork and also to the subsequent data analysis and interpretation. My initial goal was to use multiple archaeological, historical, and ethnographic data sources to provide a richer, more complete narrative of the Mi'kmaw experience of colonial and postcolonial Nova Scotia. But as I reflected on the Pugwash road trips, it became clear that the nature of the various data sets would not allow for a cohesive narrative. Nor was constructing such a narrative desirable given the evidence that mobility mediated the social lives of several different subject groups. Instead, I aimed to integrate—rather than commensurate—the data sets by bringing the sometimes scant material remains into dialogue with both the contradictions and truncated memories contained within oral testimonies and also the biases inherent in archival records.[60] In the course of my research, the historical, archaeological, and ethnographic methods were always integrated even though they constantly shifted in prominence from one field site to the next. Indeed, without the living memories of Louis Thom, his cabin would never have been recorded as an archaeological site. The archive rarely records such sites and, if so, records them in such obscurity as to render the chances of finding any references almost negligible. Previous archaeological data would not have led me to this site because those related to the Mi'kmaq in Nova Scotia are generally from the pre-contact period.[61] The spatial arrangement of the cabin foundations and scattered remains would have provided a limited view on how Louis Thom arranged his furniture, who visited him, what he did to support himself, and how he traveled to the village of Pugwash and beyond. Thus, the methodology was not simply about using the methods of three disciplines to approach a question. The objective, rather, was to integrate these methods in such a way that they led to questions of sociopolitical significance for (post) colonial Mi'kmaq in Nova Scotia.

However, by integrating ethnographic, archaeological, and historical methods so closely—especially in a study that examines the past *and* the present—there is a risk of collapsing differences and creating ahistorical and unchanging subjects, similar to how early ethnographers and archaeologists discussed the pre-contact Mi'kmaq. In trying to integrate historical and archaeological data sets, Williamson identifies two potential issues: the ontological problem of "how to link the structure of the two data sets and the records produced from them" and the epistemological problem of "the manner in which the differing time periods, research areas, and theoretical and methodological approaches of the two disciplines might be incorporated" (Williamson 2004, 186). She suggests resolving these issues by treating prehistory and history as part of the same continuum (Williamson 2004, 191). I emulate this approach, first, by drawing on multiple data sets to examine mobility in different time periods in Nova Scotia and, second, by using Maligomish as an anchor from which to explore the mobility of Mi'kmaw and non-Mi'kmaw subjects. Yet the book is not a chronological history of Mi'kmaw-settler interactions or of Maligomish. Much like my conversations with Mi'kmaq from Pictou Landing and elsewhere, the discussions presented here move between the present and the deep and recent pasts.

The data sets I examine are the result of research conducted in the field and in the archive. The archaeological fieldwork conducted on Maligomish included a surface survey that inventoried the most ubiquitous feature on the island: the roughly forty-five cabins or "camps," as local Mi'kmaq call them. As discussed in chapter 3, these buildings embody impermanence, and yet their locations—and the kinship ties that they reflect and constitute—make the camps a significant marker of Mi'kmaw emplacement on Maligomish. The excavations that followed the surface survey were conducted in the shell midden on the south side of the island (site BjCo-02). As I describe in chapter 2, the materials recovered from the shell midden proved to be inadequate for answering the original research questions focused on changes in Mi'kmaw movement from the pre-contact to the post-contact periods. Yet the archival documentation existing for previous excavations of this midden (in other words, its archaeography) provided a new perspective from which to interpret the midden's significance to Mi'kmaq and their constitution as political subjects.[62] This study also relied on archival sources created by people who worked with Mi'kmaq or in Mi'kmaw places in northeastern Nova Scotia, including the personal papers, letters, research notes, and field notes of archaeologists, ethnographers, and priests.[63]

The archaeological and archival data often served as entry points for my ethnographic work with Mi'kmaq from Pictou Landing. From my conversations with community members, it became clear that there was a strong concern for the collective ownership and distribution of their knowledge. When I first proposed to interview Mi'kmaq at the Pictou Landing First Nation about their work experiences, then–band chief Ann Francis-Muise advised that a roundtable discussion would be more productive than one-on-one interviews. She thought that the participants would be more likely to share their experiences in a group setting. By 2007 and 2008, when I began conducting oral-historical research on mobility, I had thought that my time spent with the community and the observations that I had made through informal participant observation would have made my research partners more willing to share their experiences with me. I conducted a few formal interviews that were guided by—but not limited to—the prepared set of questions that had been approved by my university's Institutional Review Board and the Mi'kmaw equivalent, Mi'kmaw Ethics Watch. However, I recorded none of these interviews because most of my research collaborators in Pictou Landing were very uncomfortable having their voices recorded. Some people were merely shy, but one woman expressed a deeper concern that the information she would share might be incorrect. Despite my attempts to assure her that I was interested in her life history—and, therefore, there was no possibility of giving incorrect information (without her knowing it)—she steadfastly refused to be recorded.

The anxiety about giving false information reflects the attention to collectivity and consensus that is the foundation of Mi'kmaw social and political life. Decisions at the Pictou Landing First Nation, and in many other First Nations communities, are ideally reached through group discussion and consensus (see Bernard et al. 2015, 19). As such, many of the research participants were much more comfortable speaking as part of a group than individually with me. The one-on-one conversations that I had with members of the Pictou Landing First Nation were ongoing and open-ended like those I had with Katalin Thomas. These conversations took place over months and—in some cases—years. Another woman with whom I shared many conversations was Dorie Sapier, a British expat who met Fred Sapier in England and moved to Maligomish in the 1970s to be with him. Dorie and I discussed her life in England before coming to Canada and her life on Maligomish. She had a unique insight into the history of the island, from the stories Fred shared and the experience of living on Maligomish, which even today does not have the conveniences of running water, electricity, or phone landlines.

As my conversations with Pictou Landing residents became more frequent, I began a kind of metaphorical excavation of the palimpsest of oral traditions and oral data about Maligomish.[64] In comparing these stories, several concurrent influences on how Pictou Landing Mi'kmaq conceive of Maligomish as a Mi'kmaw place began to emerge. These include individuals' own memories of experiences on Maligomish and stories of the experiences of others—often those of kin relations from previous generations. The experiences that local Mi'kmaq have shared with visitors to the island also contribute to local conceptions of it. For example, several Mi'kmaq believe that all areas of Maligomish (not just the cemetery) may contain burials.[65] This belief was reinforced by Joel Denny, a Mi'kmaw man from the Eskasoni First Nation, who visited Maligomish in the early 1990s. He claimed to have the ability to identify the location of burials, and the age and gender of the interred individuals, by sensing the ambient energy around burial sites.[66] No archaeological investigations have been conducted to confirm Denny's identifications, but the possibility that they were correct has affected some local Mi'kmaq's conception of the sacredness of the island. And these conceptions, in turn, affected attitudes toward conducting archaeology and other research on Maligomish.

Conceptions of Maligomish have also been influenced by written and visual representations of the island. Excerpts of Nicholas Denys's 1672 *Description geographique et historique des costes de l'Amerique Septentrional*, for example, have woven themselves through several histories of the area, including George Patterson's *A History of the County of Pictou* (1877), A. A. Johnston's two-volume history of the Diocese of Antigonish (1960, 1971) and Christmas's *Wejkwapniaq* (or *Coming of the Dawn*), an account of Mi'kmaw history and culture for school children published in 1977 by the Micmac Association of Cultural Studies.[67]

A photograph of Maligomish's east end has also influenced local conceptions of the island (see fig. 3). In the summer of 1914, Harlan Smith conducted archaeological excavations on the islands around Merigomish Harbour and took several photographs of the area. One such image was taken from the shell midden at Olding Island, looking west toward the east end of Maligomish. Three houses are visible at the water's edge. A building locally remembered as the dance hall appears in the middle ground, with the church towering above. The glebe house (or priest's residence) is tucked behind hardwood trees to the left of the church. Smith's photograph has been reproduced many times. It is a favorite subject of Mi'kmaw artists who have personal experiences of Ma-

FIGURE 3. Top: Shell-heap on Donald MacDonald's farm, Olding Island, Pictou County, Nova Scotia, by Harlan I. Smith, 1914. Canadian Museum of History, 27728 (detail approved). The author has cropped the original image to highlight the eastern end of Maligomish. Reproduced with permission from the Canadian Museum of History. Bottom: Photocopy of a reproduced sketch of the east end of Maligomish, which appears on the cover of Mary Brooks's *Oral History of Indian Island*. Artist unknown. Date unknown.

ligomish. For example, Mary Brooks, who was raised in Pictou Landing, included a sketch that was possibly inspired by the Smith image on the cover of her unpublished history of Maligomish. There are several differences between the original and this reproduction. For example, the number of houses has doubled to six. These houses are made more prominent because much of the vegetation appears to have been cleared or changed. Perhaps most significantly, three wigwams appear along the shoreline, indexing that the place depicted is "Mi'kmaw," or, at the very least, "Indian."

These various conceptions of Maligomish remind us that the objective of integrating several data sets is neither to commensurate the various sources so that they can be arranged into a cohesive narrative, nor to determine which version or part of a story is the "right" one. In the case of the oral traditions of Maligomish, the point, rather, is to acknowledge that the expectation of "accuracy" and "cohesiveness" is one that is influenced by modernist values.[68] Additionally, an integrative methodology requires researchers to acknowledge that the conceptions described above have their own social and political efficacy. Thus, whether Joel Denny accurately identified burials on Maligomish is less important than the fact that some Pictou Landing Mi'kmaq believe that he did, precisely because these beliefs have consequences for how Maligomish is—and will be—conceived. In this book, I strive to understand the internal logics of these conceptions.

"A Most Romantic and Fertile Spot"

So, what happens if we read James Dawson's 1842 letter describing his visit to Maligomish, not as another example of a white, male settler ignorantly entering an indigenous space that he tries to change (or not *only* reading it that way), but as a vignette evoking the movement of Mi'kmaw and non-Mi'kmaw subjects, the conceptions of those movements, and the ways in which these movements to and from Maligomish over thousands of years have worked to construct it as a Mi'kmaw place?[69] Doing so shifts our perspective to see how non-Mi'kmaw settlers, priests, and Crown representatives were required to move to negotiate their way through their newly adopted homes (for which they moved across oceans to settle) and to manage the indigenous population. James Dawson moved from Pictou to Maligomish—a round-trip journey of twenty-four kilometers that required traveling over land and water and was likely completed in one day given the light that would have been available on the long June days in northeastern Nova Scotia. Father O'Reilly was unable to join Dawson on this journey because he traveled across the Northumberland Strait to Prince Edward Island on Church business. Dawson's description also suggests something of the social dynamics of Mi'kmaw subsistence in the mid-nineteenth century. The movements required to participate in the offshore fisheries appear to have been gendered—being restricted to adult males.

Dawson's letter also indexes the role Maligomish has played as a site of Church and Crown intervention on Mi'kmaw lifeways. In correspondence between settlers like Dawson, priests, and representatives of the Crown, Maligomish has frequently been cited as a gathering place for Mi'kmaq from within and beyond the northeastern region of Nova Scotia, making it ideal for deploying technologies of legibility because they could be delivered to a large and captive audience. But as Dawson discovered in June 1842, although some Mi'kmaq have made Maligomish their year-round home at different points in the island's occupational history, most have dwelled there impermanently. The nature of this impermanent occupation makes Maligomish a place that embodies mobility.

Although its occupational history has been almost exclusively impermanent, Mi'kmaq have returned to Maligomish—during all times of the year— for specific activities related to subsistence, worship, and the renewal of social and kin ties. Its occupation stretches back to at least circa AD 500 as evidenced by the shell midden located on the south side of the island (see Lelièvre 2017; Mudie and Lelièvre 2013). In the eighteenth century, Maligomish became the site of a Catholic mission. The revered missionary Abbé Maillard spent several months there after fleeing Isle Royale during the siege of Louisbourg in 1758 (see Burns 1936–37). In the late nineteenth and early twentieth centuries, Maligomish seems to have had an autonomous existence from Pictou Landing. In his response to a circular forwarded by the Indian Branch of the federal Department of the Interior in 1874, R. Stewart, the Indian agent for Nova Scotia's District 4, indicated that Pictou Landing and Maligomish were two separate communities. Yet, even if the state recognized Pictou Landing and Maligomish as separate communities, the families who dwelled at each location appear to have had close relationships. For example, in 1844 Angus McDobald [sic] wrote to the bishop of Halifax that the Pictou Mi'kmaq did not undertake any cultivation that year because they planned to share in the planting and harvest of Maligomish (NSA 1844). Two years later, several families from the Merigomish area relocated to Pictou Landing during an epidemic (NSA 1846).

Today, Maligomish is where many Pictou Landing Mi'kmaq travel to hunt, to attend the St. Anne's mission, or simply to relax. There are approximately forty-five cabins along the perimeter of the island, which Mi'kmaq use as summer homes and hunting camps. Some Mi'kmaq visit these camps regularly throughout the year (although winter visits have been rarer due to the lack of solid ice on which to cross). Others visit only in late July during the St. Anne's mission. Still others move to the island for the entire summer. Mi'kmaq from the communities of Waycobah on Cape Breton Island and Millbrook about eighty kilometers southwest of Pictou Landing also have cabins in Maligomish (see fig. 1). These visitors are often descendants of Mi'kmaq who were originally from Pictou Landing.

Using Maligomish as an anchor point, each chapter of this book integrates archaeological, ethnographic, and historical evidence to make a case for a

fundamental shift in how social scientists, legislators, and judiciaries understand human settlement. Chapter 1 elaborates the two theoretical objectives
of this book—namely, to revitalize mobility as an object of anthropological
study and to examine how a traditionally mobile people such as the Mi'kmaq
are constituted as political subjects (both by themselves and by others) in a
settler society founded on sedentarist ideologies. I use archival sources to describe the anxiety that settlers felt over the Mi'kmaq's mobile existence. These
sources also betray the mobile existence of the settlers, administrators, and
missionaries who came to Nova Scotia. Operating parallel to the settler project was the fledgling discipline of ethnology. I discuss the implications of the
social evolutionary paradigm on our anthropological understanding of mobility. I also consider the legacy of early ethnographic research on the Mi'kmaq.
Drawing on the work I have conducted with Maureen Marshall (see Lelièvre
and Marshall 2015), I discuss the implications that a reconsideration of settlement has for our understanding of the "political" in settler colonies.

Chapter 2 is the first of three chapters that each examine a different cultural form that embodies mobility—defined as the practices, perceptions, and
conceptions of movement, entangled with emplacement—at work on Maligomish. Chapter 2 uses the shell midden on Maligomish as a lens through
which to examine the political implications of mobility. Although an impermanent archaeological feature, the midden has served to emplace Mi'kmaq on
Maligomish since the pre-contact period in several different ways. Chapter 2
examines three moments in the archaeological history of the midden when
both the Western scientific and the local Mi'kmaw narratives of this feature
intersected. These moments allow us to observe the quotidian construction of
Mi'kmaw political subjectivity.

Chapter 3 examines the construction of dwellings on Maligomish, whose
impermanent and dynamic nature embody mobility. The chapter discusses
changes over time in patterns of dwelling construction on Maligomish to demonstrate how Mi'kmaq have emplaced themselves on the island. An examination of the typical life history of Maligomish dwellings demonstrates how they
embody the quality of impermanence. The chapter considers the contemporary
settlement practices on Maligomish in the context of the longer history of
Mi'kmaw dwellings in the post-contact period. It describes the five phases of a
camp's life history and argues that impermanent practices of settlement reflect—
and are productive of—social relationships (especially kinship) on Maligomish.

Chapter 4 examines Mi'kmaw practices of pilgrimage, which exemplify
mobility as the co-constitution of movement and emplacement. It also discusses the mobility inherent in the Catholic Church's continuing mission to
the Mi'kmaq. The chapter considers some of the unintended consequences of

the Mi'kmaq's conversion to Catholicism. For example, when the British Crown refused to send a new priest after the death of Abbé Maillard in 1762, the result was what one nineteenth-century missionary described as the development of "their Church" (Anonymous 1867)—a "Mi'kmaw Church" characterized by the performance of pilgrimages and strict adherence to a liturgy that had long since become passé. The chapter examines an incident during the procession of St. Anne in 2010 in which the authority of this "Mi'kmaw Church" was brought to bear against the authority of the resident Catholic priest, further constituting these Mi'kmaw pilgrims as political subjects.

The book's conclusion considers the contemporary political stakes of reconsidering settlement. Indigenous peoples across North America are increasingly using movement as a way to protest the unfulfilled promises of their social contracts with sovereign authorities. These mobile protests include a 1,600-kilometer journey that seven young Cree men undertook in the winter of 2013 *on foot* from northern Québec to the Canadian capital of Ottawa. *Unsettling Mobility* argues that such long-distance protests across the ancestral territories of the continent's indigenous nations demonstrate the historically contingent nature of the political and social boundaries created by the settler state. These protests also signal the fragility of these boundaries, which provides an opportunity to radically alter the sedentarist ideology underlying liberal models of civil society and reveals the movement and dynamism that animates politics in settler colonies.

I

The Sedentarist Ideology

"Vagrant and Intemperate Habits":
Mobility and Settler Anxiety

AT STAKE WAS NOTHING LESS THAN THE SALVATION of the Mi'kmaq's moral character.[1] That appears to have been the consensus among respondents to a circular that the Nova Scotia provincial secretary sent in 1835 asking for reports on the numbers and condition of the province's indigenous population. While the gentlemen from the mainland and Cape Breton Island offered differing opinions on the best course for educating Mi'kmaw children and compensating adults for the sale of craftwork, there was agreement on the underlying cause of what they commonly described as the "degraded" condition of the Mi'kmaq. "With the destruction of their hunting grounds," wrote Martin Wilkins of the northeastern town of Pictou, "came vagrant and intemperate habits" (LAC 1835). As European settlers encroached upon Mi'kmaw hunting and fishing grounds, the Mi'kmaq were made increasingly so as they sought new sources of subsistence.[2] Wilkins insisted that only when the Mi'kmaq were settled property owners would their condition improve. By clearing his own piece of land, a Mi'kmaw could "establish a good character to be an absolute owner" (LAC 1835). Wilkins's fellow informant, Cornelius White, reported from the south shore of the province that the "moral state" of the Mi'kmaq who had supposedly settled was better than those who had remained migratory (LAC 1835).

The circular was sent, in part, as a response to the dramatic population increase and demographic shift that the colony of Nova Scotia experienced from the late eighteenth to early nineteenth century. No longer valued only for its timber and fisheries, Nova Scotia (or Acadia, as it was then called) became a destination for immigrants—first fishers and traders from the New England states, then British Loyalists fleeing postrevolutionary America, then people from all over the British Isles (see A. H. Clark 1954, 295).[3] In the century between 1760 and 1860, the settler population of Nova Scotia increased exponentially from approximately 18,000 to 340,000, as recorded in the 1861 census.[4]

As increasing numbers of settlers came to the colony, the administrators based in the capital of Halifax faced many challenges managing its indigenous population. The treaties of peace and friendship that the Mi'kmaq signed with the British over the course of the eighteenth century preserved their right to access traditional hunting, fishing, and gathering lands and waters.[5] The vast swaths of land that afforded such activities were illustrated in a map of Cape Breton Island created around 1767 by J. F. W. DesBarres, then an engineer with the Royal Navy (see fig. 4).[6] The map shows most of the northern and western coasts and interior of the island as "Indian Hunting Country." Read critically, however, DesBarres's map may more accurately reflect British aspirations for the proportions of indigenous and settler territories rather than the on-the-ground reality. Indeed, as more settlers came to Nova Scotia, there was increasing competition for traditional Mi'kmaw lands. In contrast to the previous colonial settlement of Nova Scotia by the French Acadians, British settlement was considerably less complementary with the Mi'kmaq's mode of existence (see A. H. Clark 1968; Kennedy 2013; Wicken 1994). The British and Loyalist settlers favored the places where Mi'kmaq relied on the seasonal availability of game, fish, and plant resources—most commonly near estuaries and river mouths. The British cleared forests for grain cultivation and pasture, bounded their properties with fences, and dammed rivers for water-powered mills.[7] Consequently, the Mi'kmaq's access to their traditional hunting and fishing grounds became increasingly difficult. Species became depleted, and habitat was lost or destroyed. Nova Scotia's geography meant that there were fewer places to which Mi'kmaq could retreat, as George Henry Monk, superintendent for Indian affairs, cited in his letter to Lieutenant Governor Provost in 1808: "[T]he Province of Nova Scotia, being a Peninsula, has no back Country for the Aborigines to retract to, as the Population and Improvements by their Conquerors occupy the Rivers and Forests that were the sources of their means of Subsistance [sic]" (NSA 1808). Mi'kmaq supplemented their subsistence through the sale of food and handcrafted items to the settler population. But with fewer means to support themselves, Mi'kmaq relied increasingly on charity, whether by asking settlers for permission to camp on lands that were once theirs or by petitioning the government for food, muskets, shot, and winter coats.

By the early nineteenth century, Nova Scotia's colonial administrators were faced with increasing challenges as they tried to balance the interests of the

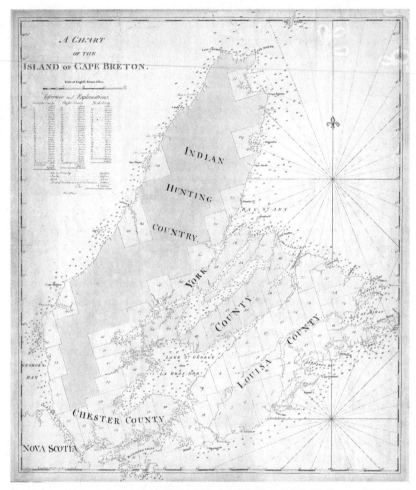

FIGURE 4. A chart of the Island of Cape Breton, 1767. J. F. W. DesBarres. Map 667. Beaton Institute, Cape Breton University. Reproduced with permission from the Beaton Institute, Cape Breton University, Sydney, Nova Scotia.

province's burgeoning settler population with those of the indigenous Mi'kmaq. Indeed, those who observed and interacted with the Mi'kmaq communicated a general anxiety about their peripatetic existence "on the chase." For example, the colony's administrators in the capital of Halifax were anxious about the possible (and eventual) war between the newly independent United States and what remained of British North America. George Henry Monk appears to have been particularly concerned about the role the indigenous population would play in the course of any war. In 1807, he sent a circular to the agents in districts around the province who were liaisons to the Mi'kmaq. Monk requested: "[Y]ou will, from time to time, inform me, at Halifax, of any movements of the Indians, with the Cause, and the Object of such movements" (NSA 1807). Monk's concerns about Mi'kmaw movements were also articulated in his 1808 letter to Lieutenant Governor Provost in which he related a report on the Mi'kmaq in Pictou: "That several Indians went last autumn from Pictou to Quebec as it was understood, to establish a Communication with the Indians of Canada" (NSA 1808).

The anxiety over Mi'kmaw movements was not limited to concerns for the safety of the colony from war and invasion. It also extended to the more mundane management of the indigenous population. The Executive Council and its appointed agents were frustrated by their inability to complete the most basic administrative tasks such as conducting a census. The constant movements of small groups of Mi'kmaq made taking an accurate census almost impossible, as Monk further explained in his 1808 letter to Provost: "They are so continually moving from place to place, that it has not been practicable to ascertain their numbers" (NSA 1808). In 1801, the District of Pictou's agent, Edward Mortimer, reported an additional challenge: "It is the universal custom of Indians to assume different names in the different settlements they frequent" (NSA 1801a).[8]

The frequent movements of the Mi'kmaq frustrated some of the settlers on whose lands they encountered Mi'kmaw families. The crafts that Mi'kmaq produced to sell to the non-Mi'kmaw population required access to particular tree species such as black ash (*Fraxinus nigra*) and white birch (*Betula papyrifera*). Petitions written by settlers reveal an anxiety about some of the Mi'kmaq's use of these trees and the cutting of firewood. William Powell, for example, petitioned the provincial government in 1860 for compensation in the amount of ninety pounds (NSA 1860). He claimed that he had allowed the local Mi'kmaq to winter on his property since 1842, "during which time they have used up his Hardwood and other valuable wood depeciating [*sic*] the value of His property very much" (NSA 1860). Similarly, in his 1862 petition, Donald McArthur claimed that Mi'kmaq had "ravaged our whole lot" due to their cutting "firewood and Materials for the manufacture of Baskets Buttertubs and other workmanship" (NSA 1862).

The colonial archive has preserved far fewer petitions for personal compensation, however, than petitions from settlers who believed that the Mi'kmaq's unsettled existence was the root cause of the Mi'kmaq's suffering from frequent want of sufficient food, adequate shelter, and protective clothing. Their greatest concern was that the Mi'kmaq's persistent movements—their seeming unwillingness to settle in one place and to cultivate the land—would mean the Mi'kmaq's suffering from potential starvation. Much of the anxiety betrayed in these documents was a realization on the part of some petitioners that the settlers themselves were the ultimate cause of Mi'kmaw suffering, as Lieutenant Governor Wentworth described in his letter to Michael Wallace in September 1802:

> By their own account, they are a sobor [sic] and industrious people, who plant and fish for subsistence. It seems however, that their good dispositions are discouraged by several white people who claim the land . . . these Indians and their ancestors have lived and occupied for many years. They also complain that white people set Nets intirely [sic] across the Brooks and small rivers, which intirely [sic] prevent any Fish running up the streams and of course deprive the upper residents of any share in this comfortable article of support, and that such practises [sic] will soon destroy the fisherys [sic]. (NSA 1802)

In these letters, reports, and petitions—from a wide range of settler subjects—the anxiety over Mi'kmaw mobility is represented in a particular vocabulary that is deployed repeatedly.[9] For example, Mi'kmaq are often described as wanderers, vagabonds, "children of the forest," erratics, transient, or *errans*. These terms suggest a moral judgment made against the Mi'kmaq—that they were aimless, shiftless, and lacked purpose in their movements across land and water. To the settler population—including Catholic missionaries and colonial administrators—moving in search of food was the hallmark of an anachronous society whose ancient customs were no longer compatible with modern life.[10] In an attempt to relieve the Mi'kmaq from what they perceived as a precarious existence—and also to relieve the province's coffers from expenditures on charity—the colonial agents turned their efforts toward "civilizing" the province's indigenous population.

The Protestant Ethic and the Spirit of Civilization

Following the death of Abbé Maillard in 1762, the Lords of Trade in London denied the governor of Nova Scotia's request for a priest for the Mi'kmaq, advising that the "Protestant missionaries may wean them from their prejudices" (Lenhart [1921] 1995, vi). But the Mi'kmaq's steadfast devotion to the Catholic faith they had adopted in 1610 outlasted even the most zealous Protestant missionary. In his forty-four years of service to—and study of— the Mi'kmaq, the Baptist minister Silas T. Rand was able to produce only one convert.[11] Yet an inability to foment a spiritual conversion did not prevent Nova Scotia's settlers and administrators from trying to create a temporal one by instilling in the Mi'kmaq a Protestant ethic.[12] The ethic was cultivated by encouraging in the Mi'kmaq values of self-reliance through various strategies. These strategies included issuing ultimatums, as suggested by the Committee of His Majesty's Council to two of its agents in northeastern Nova Scotia: "for, it will be in vain to look to Government for an annual support, it being the Determination of the Legislature, that they [the Mi'kmaq] shall cultivate the Ground, otherwise they will be abandoned to their Fate" (NSA 1800). Of course, Mi'kmaq were "cultivating the ground" well before the nineteenth century, but their planting sites were generally small plots for maize and beans that did not require year-round attention for their upkeep (see Deal et al. 1987). In his *History of the County of Pictou* (1877), the Reverend George Patterson describes how several Mi'kmaq were gradually driven away from their planting grounds around the county as settlers cleared and built on these plots. But when His Majesty's Committee declared that the Mi'kmaq would cultivate the ground or be abandoned to their fate, it meant that Mi'kmaq would have to plant a discrete plot and live on it permanently.[13]

There was a less fatalistic tone in the circular sent in early 1801 by a joint committee of the lower and upper chambers of Nova Scotia's General Assembly to correspondents in districts throughout the province. The objective of the circular was to ascertain, with as much accuracy as possible, the current Mi'kmaw population and what, if any, conditions existed for their permanent settlement. The committee was interested in identifying any leaders or chiefs among the various communities, the lands that might be suitable for settlement, and the availability of materials for making handcrafted items such as "Staves, Hoops, Shingles, Clapboards, Oar Rafters, Handpikes and Laths." The joint committee also wondered if it would be possible to obtain "Wool, Flax, and Wheels . . . for employing Indian Women, supposing them excited to industry" (NSA 1801b). But these initial queries and eventual programs to "excite" the Mi'kmaq were not an attempt to draw them into the wider colonial economy as a source of labor or as suppliers of raw materials. Their primary purpose was to reconnoitre the options available for creating an economically self-sufficient Mi'kmaw population. In this way, the economic role of Nova Scotia's indigenous peoples was markedly different from other settler colonies, such as South Africa and British Columbia, which relied on an indigenous labor force for mining operations and resource harvesting and processing.[14]

Another strategy that the Crown employed in the temporal conversion of the province's indigenous population was to help those Mi'kmaq who helped themselves. Several letters and reports detail the incentives and disincentives that were offered to Mi'kmaq to encourage them to remain stationary. For example, in his annual report of 1832, the commissioner for Indian affairs, Abraham Gesner, recommended "that as large a portion of the grant as possible be applied to aid them in their agricultural pursuits and that no blankets or clothing be supplied to any but the aged, sick or infirm" (NSA 1832). In 1843, James Dawson of Pictou appealed to the succeeding commissioner, Joseph Howe, for funding to help a Mi'kmaw named Stephen Toney to build a house on the island of Maligomish. Dawson was later authorized to "supply him [Toney] with a few pounds worth of materials" (LAC 1843). In his annual report of 1843, Howe described the settlement at Bear River, which he considered to be the only effectively managed Mi'kmaw community in Nova Scotia. One thousand acres of land had been reserved for the Mi'kmaq who dwelled near this community on the province's southeast coast. The reserve was divided into thirty-acre lots, which were assigned to the heads of families. But these lots came with conditions: "If they retained possession and improved, their title was respected—if they deserted the land for three years, it was given to others of more industrious habits" (NSA 1843). This strategy of helping Mi'kmaq who showed an inclination to settle and cultivate the land was part of a broader effort to lead by example. As early as 1808, the superintendent of Indian affairs, George Henry Monk, in outlining his plan to manage the Mi'kmaq, suggested, "That such assistance of Implements, and seed should be given to those who incline to clear, and cultivate Land, as would induce others to follow their example, and become reconciled to a stationary Residence, and Occupations affording a certain Subsistance [sic]" (NSA 1808). The strategy was still being employed by the middle of the century, as Joseph Howe described in his 1843 annual report: "It also struck me that . . . the sooner a good example was set, by placing in its midst one family enjoying a degree of comfort, which, by moderate exertion, all might emulate, the more probability was there of advancing civilization" (NSA 1843).[15]

Beyond these material strategies of incentivizing the Mi'kmaq toward sedentism, the archival documents associated with nineteenth-century Mi'kmaw-settler relations reveal a more general process of attempting to "colonize" Mi'kmaw consciousness by remaking Mi'kmaw conceptions of space, time, kinship relations, and property (sensu Comaroff and Comaroff 1986, 1992).[16] For example, as they moved across land and water, stopping in places to procure food and resources, to renew political and kin ties, and to practice their Catholic faith, Mi'kmaq used the land and waters in ways that transcended settler property boundaries. From the settler perspective, Mi'kmaq were everywhere and nowhere at once.

Yet, far from aimless "wandering," Mi'kmaw movements were by design, if not always by choice. For example, in December 1842, James Dawson described to Joseph Howe the difficulty that the Pictou-area Mi'kmaq had in finding firewood with the result that "the poor creatures had been driven from place to place with their camps, having been refused liberty to cut wood by the inhabitants about Fisher's Grant, Boat Harbour, etc." (LAC 1842f).

More than food procurement or even political strategizing, George Henry Monk considered the Mi'kmaq's religious practice to be their primary motivation for moving: "It is a Custom with the Indians periodically to visit their Priests:—and this Custom frequently calls them together from Considerable Distances, along the Coast, on the Rivers, and Lakes, and through the Forests, during which their Subsistence depends upon the Game they find in their Way. This Custom is a principal Cause of their continuing their Wandering Life" (NSA 1808). The Mi'kmaq had been visiting priests since their conversion to the Catholic faith in 1610, and the practice survived the transfer from French to British imperial rule. In June 1762, when the Le Hève (now La Have) Mi'kmaq from Nova Scotia's south shore traveled to the town of Lunenburg and stayed for over a month, they raised the suspicion of the British administrators in Halifax. When asked by the Governor's Council why his people had gathered in Lunenburg, Chief Paul Laurent responded that they had been expecting to see Abbé Maillard. Upon hearing that Maillard was ill in Halifax, they had waited in hope of his recovery (Burns 1936–37, 22). A century later, the anonymous author of an article titled "The Catholic Church in the Wilderness" (1867) made several references to the great distances Mi'kmaq would travel to receive blessings and sacraments from their priests and to make pilgrimages in honor of their patroness, St. Anne. What most seems to have concerned the colonial administrators is the apparent unpredictability of some Mi'kmaw movements. While the settlers and colonial authorities might have been able to observe some seasonal regularity in how Mi'kmaq timed their movements for food or even for the annual St. Anne's mission in late July, it was more difficult to predict when, for what purpose, or for what duration Mi'kmaq would move in order to meet a priest. As the anonymous author wrote in 1867, the Mi'kmaw is considered "by those who do not know the nature of the wanderer of the forests, as being lazy and improvident" (Anonymous 1867, 248).[17]

The accusation of improvidence underlies much of the correspondence between the administrators in Halifax and their agents throughout the province. The observers characterize the Mi'kmaq as too impetuous, too covetous of immediate gratification, and too undisciplined to devote themselves to the cultivation of the land. They are cast as so many grasshoppers, whiling away the summer when they should be toiling like ants. Thus, the "civilizing" project in Nova Scotia—and throughout the settler colonial world—aimed to transform the Mi'kmaq's worldview by instructing them in an ethics of self-reliance.[18] For example, when writing to their correspondents in northeastern Nova Scotia in December 1800, the Committee of His Majesty's Council instructed: "[Y]ou avail yourselves of all occasions, to impress upon the Minds of the Indians, the Necessity there is of their turning to Industry and providing themselves with some provisions in the Summer for their Winter Necessities" (NSA 1800). In his annual report for 1832, the commissioner for Indian affairs, Abraham Gesner, made the following note about the residents of the settlement at Bear River: "The abundance of Fish in the Annapolis Basin draws the Micmac off his little farm at that season when his labour is most required and his immediate and pressing wants compel him to seek his food in the fisheries" (NSA 1832). James Dawson described the following scene from Maligomish in a letter written to Joseph Howe in 1842: "We noticed one bad defect in the system of farming—after a crop they sow nothing on the spot, the consequence is that it becomes a bed of wild weeds and is consigned for a long series of years to sterility" (NSA 1842c). Howe himself lamented in 1843 that he "could have given away hundreds of bushels of Potatoes in the Spring, but they would have been eaten and not planted" (NSA 1843). He reported that he "in no instances assisted those who had not some cleared land in occupation, and who showed a disposition to help themselves" (NSA 1843).

Underlying this ethic is a sedentarist ideology that understands stasis to be the norm and movement to be a deviation from the norm (see Fowles 2011; Lelièvre and Marshall 2015; Malkki 1992; Marshall 2003; Marshall and Lelièvre 2010; Massumi 2002; Raibmon 2007; Sheller and Urry 2006). By *ideology*, I mean unconscious assumptions that take as natural and given what is, in fact, cultural and constructed (Leone 2005, 25; see also Althusser 1971; Bloch 1989; Comaroff and Comaroff 1991; Geertz 1973).[19] The sedentarist ideology laid the groundwork for the transformation of the settler anxiety about Mi'kmaw movements into moral judgments against the Mi'kmaq themselves. In nineteenth-century Nova Scotia—and in other settler colonies—the sedentary practices of land clearing, survey, demarcation, and cultivation were understood by the settler population not simply as the dominant practices of establishing a colony but as the normal ones. It was anathema to suggest anything beyond two options for the Mi'kmaq: proceed to "civilization" by means of becoming stationary, or perish. Joseph Howe concluded as much in his 1843 report. He described the Mi'kmaq as "a people . . . who

have, if not by treaty, at least by all the ties of humanity, a claim upon the
Government of the Country, which nothing but their entire extinction, or
their elevation to a more permanent and happy position in the scale of society,
can ever entirely discharge" (NSA 1843).

Yet the settlers, Crown agents, and missionaries who passed moral judgment on the Mi'kmaq's movements and encouraged the Mi'kmaq to "civilize" by remaining stationary seemed unaware of the importance of movement
to their own existence and, moreover, to the ways that movement mediated
their social and political relations with Mi'kmaw communities (cf. Raibmon
2007, 188–89). Casgrain (1895) cites the excellent example of the Abbey Mac-
Eachern, an early nineteenth-century missionary in the colony of Ile St. Jean
(now Prince Edward Island) who reported himself to be more mobile than
stationary in his proselytizing. The following excerpt was taken from an 1813
letter from Abbey MacEachern to the archbishop of the Diocese of Québec:

> On the 7th of January I went to visit a sick man from the Town [Char-
> lottetown] through the woods in one day. A few days after, I was called to
> Egmont Bay, returned then to Malpèque, and after having confessed such
> of our people as live round the Bay, I returned to M. Beaubien's Chateau
> at St. Augustine [Rustico] in the month of February. From that time
> until the middle of June, I seldom slept two nights in the same bed. . . . I
> went eight times to Three Rivers, and always in the winter and along the
> Bays. (Casgrain 1895, 223)

MacEachern's prodigious peripateticism was far from unique for Catholic
missionaries in the New World. There were too few priests to have one reside
in every community. Those who were available could rarely visit most rural
Catholic communities more than once a year. During these visits, the priests
would hear confessions and conduct all of the year's necessary blessings and
sacraments. This situation was as true for Mi'kmaw communities as it was
for the Acadians and also the Highland Scots who immigrated to Nova Scotia
in the late eighteenth and nineteenth centuries. More priests were eventually
brought to Nova Scotia, and men from the province entered the seminary. As
the number of priests increased, the frequency and distance of travel to obser-
vant communities became less of a burden. But priests retained some degree
of itinerancy, especially in their interactions with Mi'kmaw communities.

Just as priests had to move to their congregations, so too did the merchants who came to Nova Scotia to make their fortunes in trade and commerce. In a 1756 letter written at the French fortress town of Louisbourg, de
la Varenne described his view of the British attitudes toward the Mi'kmaq. In

making a case against any British claim to sovereignty over peninsular Acadia, de la Varenne considered the early British interest in Acadia to be primarily for trade. Consequently, the merchants had no time to settle and pursue agriculture, because they were "continually obliged to follow the savages in their vagabond journeys" (included in Maillard 1758, 104).[20]

Mobility continued to mediate relationships between Mi'kmaq and nonindigenous subjects well after the arrival of British settlers. For example, when Joseph Howe became the commissioner for Indian affairs in 1842, he spent considerable time touring the province to gather information about the state of the Mi'kmaq. The agents established in the various districts around the province were also moving to meet Mi'kmaq. James Dawson's visit to Maligomish in the spring of 1842 required him to travel approximately thirty kilometers from the town of Pictou. In the summer of 1846, Dr. William Anderson made frequent trips across the harbor from Pictou to Pictou Landing where twenty Mi'kmaw families were quarantined after an outbreak of an unidentified but deadly fever (NSA 1846).

In addition to being seemingly unaware of their agents' own mobility, the Church and Crown were at times ambivalent in their attitudes toward Mi'kmaw movements. In some cases, they relied on these movements in order to assist their management of the Mi'kmaq. For example, His Majesty's Council in Halifax wrote to its agents in the northeast of the province in December 1800 to forewarn them of a possible influx of Mi'kmaq to that area: "Not having had an opportunity of sending any supplys [sic] . . . it is highly probable that the Indians may be induced to collect in . . . your Neighbourhood the present Winter. This Disposition the Committee would rather wish to have encouraged than opposed; since it is much to be desired that the Indians should be kept as far from the Capital (Halifax) as possible" (NSA 1800). Here the colonial government sought not to keep the Mi'kmaq sedentary but to emplace them by disciplining their movements and segregating them from the most populous city in the province.[21]

The rhetoric of these dispatches reads as if the authors' objectives were to make order out of chaos. Although archaeological and ethnohistorical evidence indicates that the Mi'kmaq were stationary as much as they were mobile, this episodic and ephemeral sedentism was inadequate for the colonial (and postcolonial) "civilizing" project.[22] Encouraging the Mi'kmaq to abandon their "wanderings" meant keeping them fixed in one location at all times. While Martin Wilkins and the colonial government's other informants around Nova Scotia drew a direct connection between the ownership of property and the improvement of the general moral character of the collective Mi'kmaq, the material effects of this improvement could only be exacted upon Mi'kmaq as individuals. Thus, in attempting to make the Mi'kmaq stationary, the settlers, priests, and bureaucrats not only had to alienate the Mi'kmaq from their mobile practices by providing land for their permanent settlement; they also had to shift the Mi'kmaw worldview from one of flexibility, fluidity, and collective stewardship to one marked by boundedness in space, regularity in time, and individual ownership of land, water, and the resources they bear. This attempted transformation—and the Mi'kmaw response to it—has helped to shape the relationships between the Mi'kmaq, the Church, and the Crown by etching into the political and legal institutions of the settler society an understanding of mobile subjects as deviating from a sedentary norm.

"To Be an Absolute Owner"

Of course, the specific projects to induce the Mi'kmaq in Nova Scotia to "civilization" occurred within a broader context of British colonialism in the New World.[23] In her discussion of John Locke's influence on British colonial policy, Arneil (1996) argues that a change in the definition of private property was necessary in order to justify British settlers' taking land occupied by indigenous peoples. Before the seventeenth century, property was defined by occupation of land. Locke's *Two Treatises of Government* (1689–90) changed this definition to be rooted in labor: "*As much land* as a man tills, plants, improves, cultivates, and can use the product of, so much is his *property*. He by his labour does, as it were, inclose [*sic*] it from the common" (Locke [1690] 1980, 21; Arneil 1996, 18). By distinguishing the ownership of *land* from the ownership of the land's *resources*, Locke provided a moral and economic philosophy that would make the sedentary occupation and use of land the only legitimate form of property in the New World.

Whether the Mi'kmaq and other Eastern Algonquian peoples had their own conceptions of private property before their contact with Europeans was a topic of rigorous debate between twentieth-century North American anthropologists. In his 1915 study of northeastern Algonquian peoples, Frank Speck challenged the assumption of most contemporary anthropologists that primarily hunting societies "had little or no interest in the matter of claims and boundaries to the land which they inhabited" (Speck 1915, 289). Quite to the contrary, Speck observed a general tendency of the Algonquians to divide land into hunting territories "owned" by the family unit. In her review of the ethnohistorical sources, Nietfeld (1981, 410) describes this unit as "an extended family, consisting of a husband and wife, their young children, some of their married children with their spouses and children, and perhaps also a few other relatives (consanguine or affinal) or even nonrelatives who chose to reside with the family." Contrary to Speck, who believed the Mi'kmaw family was patrilocal, Nietfeld cites several early sources to suggest that the family was "bilocal in practice" (1981, 410).

Speck identified the family hunting territories as having boundaries and sometimes being named for the families who hunted them. The lands were generally inherited, but they could be traded outside of the family or given as a gift. Speck defined the family hunting unit as "a kinship group composed of folks united by blood or marriage, having the right to hunt, trap, and fish in a certain inherited district bounded by some rivers, lakes or other natural land-marks" (Speck 1915, 290).[24] The territories generally radiated around lakes and rivers (Speck 1922, 92; Snow 1968). Speck reported that the boundaries of these territories were so well defined that his informants were able to trace them onto maps that he re-created in his monographs (see Speck 1922, map 1).[25] He believed that Mi'kmaw hunting groups and their territories were deter-mined "on a purely economic basis, with no sociological phenomenon other than kinship involved" (Speck 1922, 88).

The crux of the so-called Algonquian Family Hunting Territory Debate concerned the origins of these territories. Speck argued that they existed be-fore European contact. But in her study of the Naskapi of northern Québec, Leacock (1954, 35) suggested that the apparent substitution of individualized subsistence patterns for cooperative ones was an effect of Naskapi engagement in the fur trade.[26] The protagonists of the debate also differed in their views of whether the lands qualified as being owned. For example, Leacock (1954) maintained that the relationship to the land itself resembled more usufruct than outright ownership. She argued that the Naskapi had private ownership of the resources on the land and that these rights developed in relation with the fur trade, laying the foundation for the inheritance of the land itself—a point that Lips had made in his 1947 ethnography on Naskapi law. Lips also noted that abstract terms such as *property*, *possession*, and *ownership* were not known to the Naskapi (Lips 1947, 427).[27]

For the colonial administrators in nineteenth-century Nova Scotia, the concern appears to have been less about whether Mi'kmaq had an abstract concept of property and more about encouraging the kind of property owner-ship that would induce them to settle and, therefore, "civilize." In their cor-respondence with the colonial government, the agents of the Crown conveyed their concern that the tradition of communal ownership would be an obstacle to inducing the Mi'kmaq to settle. In an 1844 letter to the bishop of Halifax, Angus McDobald [*sic*] described the planting activities of the Mi'kmaq on Maligomish. He praised the hard work of the Maligomish Mi'kmaq but reported that the Mi'kmaq in the town of Pictou made no such effort: "I also called on the Pictou Indians to see if they intended to sow or plant there, and they told me that they would not; as they all owned the Island [Maligomish] in common they would have an equal share in planting it" (NSA 1844). W. A. Hendry reported from Cape Breton Island in 1863: "Much patience will be necessary to accomplish anything like a satisfactory settlement of the Indians [*sic*] families upon their lands, without exciting jealousy and disturbance amongst them, because they like to 'have everything in common, even their wigwams—they wish to be as children of the same family'" (JLCNS 1863, appendix 16:4).[28] Encouraging individual rather than collective ownership was part of the broader work of assimilating the Mi'kmaq by transforming them from a nation into individual subjects of the Crown. Bernard Gilpin reported this objective in his 1877 address to the Nova Scotian Institute of Science, arguing that "the time has long passed to consider them as a nation. . . . The sooner all national feeling, language and traditions are gone the better. They must be approached as individual men and women" (Gilpin 1877, 275). The sedentarist ideology underlying these observations and recommendations was a product of the changing definition of property, which assumed that being an individual owner of a tract of land would inspire permanent occupation and the moral quality of self-reliance required to cultivate it successfully.

But while the Crown, Church, and settlers attempted to encourage in the Mi'kmaq the Protestant ideals associated with individual property ownership, they had no intention of actually granting the Mi'kmaq their own alienable land.[29] In the first half of the nineteenth century, as the system for managing the Mi'kmaq became increasingly bureaucratized, much effort was directed toward reserving land on which the Mi'kmaq could dwell permanently.[30] The land was never sold to the Mi'kmaq; the plots were owned by the Crown and licensed to them for their occupation and use.[31] The chiefs of the various communities throughout the province were to divide the reservations among the male heads of household, and each family was responsible for its respective tract's "improvement" (see Province of Nova Scotia 1842). The Mi'kmaq could not sell these tracts of land, because they belonged to the Crown. Thousands of acres were reserved across the province, and some Mi'kmaq took advantage of the legal means available to them by submitting petitions to the lieutenant governor in Halifax. For example, in 1829 James Lulan submitted his petition citing, "That for upwards of Fifty years The fathers of Your Petitioners, and your petitioners themselves have been in the possession of a piece of Land at the Mouth of the Harbour of Pictou and have made considerable clearing thereon" (NSA 1829a). In 1820, Peter Wilmot submitted the following petition:

The bearer Peter Wilmot finds it very difficult to maintain himself and family by hunting and fishing according to the Indian custom. He therefore is fully determined if Government will allow him to improve some of the ungranted lands near to the forks of the River John in the District of Pictou to follow . . . in the same manner as the English settlers by cutting down Timber clearing and Planting the Land, thereby to enable him to maintain his family by this industry in a comfortable manner pledging that his own industry here after shall entitle him to a grant of the Lands & Premises he may improve Provided it may be kept in reserve for him. (NSA 1829b)[32]

But the province's efforts to reserve land—and even their agreement to grant the requests of Mi'kmaq for these lands—did not ensure that Mi'kmaq would use them in ways that contributed to their becoming sedentary property owners. In his 1832 annual report, the commissioner of Indian affairs, Abraham Gesner, stated, "Since I entered upon my duties . . . it has been my aim to induce the Indians to enter upon and settle those exclusive tracts of land which have been reserved for their use: and in some instances I have been successful" (NSA 1832). Gesner was cautiously optimistic about the prospects of permanent occupation at Shubenacadie, Fish Lake, and Bear River. However, other fledgling settlements at Fairy Lake and Panhook "had not been followed up by the energy wished for" (NSA 1832). For Gesner, the mark of true settlement was cultivation of the land and/or the care of livestock that required year-round dwelling on the reserves. Indeed, he cared little for less permanent planting, reporting: "The smaller patches of cultivation made by the Indians . . . do not require particular notice" (NSA 1832).

The Mi'kmaq had little choice but to supplement their subsistence from cultivation and husbandry by continuing to move to seasonally available flora and fauna. The reserved lands were often located in the least desirable places. Joseph Howe himself acknowledged this significant flaw in the government's plan: "It is to be regretted that so little judgment has been exercised in the selection of them. . . . All the land reserved in this County [Halifax] is sterile and comparatively valueless" (NSA 1843). But leaving their plots in search of other means of subsistence, or for other reasons, left these reserved lands vulnerable to encroachment by non-Mi'kmaw settlers.[33] By 1837, the problem of encroachment had become so ubiquitous that the lieutenant governor issued a public notice naming specific settlers who had trespassed on reserves on Cape Breton Island and emphatically warning trespassers that if anyone settled, cut timber, or otherwise made "improvements" upon Indian lands, "such offender will be prosecuted by His Majesty's Attorney General, and punished with the utmost rigour of the Law" (NSA 1837).[34]

Yet the problem persisted. When the colonial government passed the Act to Provide for the Instruction and Permanent Settlement of the Indians in 1842, it made the primary responsibilities of the commissioner for Indian affairs the supervision and management of reserved lands and the prevention of encroachment on them (see Province of Nova Scotia 1842). In his first annual report as commissioner, Joseph Howe intimated that the failure of efforts to induce the Mi'kmaq to settle was due to their lack of education in the white man's ways. He cited the slow progress he was making on this score: "I at first found the whole tribe strongly prejudiced against learning to read or write any other language than their own. . . . By visiting the camps, conversing cheerfully . . . giving them familiar illustrations of the value of our rudimentary branches [of knowledge], to themselves, and showing how much they had lost from not knowing how to secure lands as the whites had done, or to protect those which they had, an impression was gradually made upon some" (NSA 1843). Throughout his report, Howe maintained that the material enticements to settle, such as supplies of tools and livestock and aid to construct houses and barns, mattered less than convincing the Mi'kmaq to conform to the settler way of obtaining and securing land. While the government could grant and survey lands, the Mi'kmaq would have to be responsible for securing them through "improvements"—ideally improvements such as planting and husbandry, whose success would require their stationary presence in one location.

But as the attempts to encourage the Mi'kmaq to settle continued to fail—and the encroachment of non-Mi'kmaq persisted—the colonial government placed greater emphasis on receiving compensation for reserved lands in the form of rent paid by the trespassers or the outright sale of lands that remained "unimproved" by the Mi'kmaq. In 1844, the legislature passed An Act to Regulate the Management and Disposal of the Indian Reserves in This Province. The act's preamble claimed that not only had the reservation of lands failed to sedentize the Mi'kmaq; it also prevented the full settlement of the colony by non-Mi'kmaq: "the extensive Tracts of valuable Land reserved for the Indians in various parts of this Province tend greatly to retard the Settlement of the Country" and "large portions of them are not, in their present neglected state, productive of any benefit to the people, for whose use they were reserved" (Province of Nova Scotia 1844). This act authorized the commissioner for Indian affairs to survey the reserves to determine what improvements had been made. If funds were collected through the sale or rent of lands that had been improved by non-Mi'kmaq, then the proceeds would be directed to a fund that could be used, "First, towards the relief of the indigent and infirm Indians of the several Tribes: Second, towards procuring seeds, implements of husbandry, and domestic animals" (Province of Nova Scotia 1844). As for the Mi'kmaq, the act would now require them to obtain Tickets of Location for five to fifty-acre plots of land that had been laid out into villages. The act provided Mi'kmaq the opportunity to earn an outright grant to the land, "after the Indians to whom such Location Tickets have [been] issued shall have resided upon and improved the same for a period of not less than ten years" (Province of Nova Scotia 1844). Further revisions to this act were made in 1851, 1859, and 1864. Thus, in the dwindling years of Nova Scotia's existence as a colony of the British Empire, the management of the indigenous population came full circle. Its failure to provide appropriate and adequate lands for the Mi'kmaq—and to defend these lands against the encroachment of non-Mi'kmaq—meant that it had to provide relief for a people it had further impoverished.

* * *

Seen from the perspective of the settler state, the fact that Mi'kmaq such as Peter Wilmot and James Lulan submitted petitions for land suggests that the efforts to create individual Mi'kmaw subjects may have been successful. Wilmot and Lulan were not petitioning on behalf of their communities; rather, they requested land for their own use and that of their families. Petitioning the Crown worked to reinforce the intimate relationship (if only symbolic) between the sovereign and his/her subjects. However, the ways in which Mi'kmaq used these reserved lands demonstrate that petitioning was only one of the many practices that mediated the construction of Mi'kmaq as political subjects in nineteenth-century Nova Scotia. While exercising their legal right as British subjects to petition the sovereign for discrete parcels of land, many Mi'kmaq were also asserting their aboriginal and treaty rights to access the resources that lay outside of these areas by continuing to move across lands and waters that had been bounded, planted, dammed, and built upon by European settlers. Even if the colonial government had provided the Mi'kmaq with arable land, the families who planted them would not have remained permanently settled as religious celebrations, political meetings, and family ties drew them from their individualized plots. Mi'kmaw movements in colonial and postcolonial Nova Scotia were not motivated only by the need to procure food or engage in wage labor; nor were they simply an act of resistance against a colonial power. Some movements, such as those associated with the Mi'kmaq's adopted Catholicism, were new practices developed through interactions with the colonizers. Others, such as working as hunting guides, were developed from pre-contact practices and were prompted in response to a demand from the colonial market. Even the "smaller patches of cultivation" dismissed by Abraham Gesner in 1832 represented a practice that was continued from at least the time of early contact with Europeans. Such practices—the old and the new—represented a perseverance of pre-contact Mi'kmaw activities (Ferris's "changed continuities" [2009, 1]) that were grounded in an intimate knowledge of the lands and waters through movement across them. In persisting to move, Mi'kmaq asserted their authority over the land and its resources.[35] Mi'kmaw political subjectivity was, therefore, a complex and dialogical entanglement of the individualizing and, ultimately, assimilatory structures of the settler state with the Mi'kmaq's collective assertion of authority to access their traditional lands and waters.[36]

"The Successive Arts of Subsistence": Anthropology's Sedentarist Legacy

While the efforts of the colonial government to induce the Mi'kmaq to settle and cultivate reserved lands were failing, early ethnologists used their observations of Mi'kmaq and other indigenous peoples as evidence for new models of social evolution.[37] Compared to the first descriptions of the New World's indigenous populations, the nineteenth-century Mi'kmaq and others may have appeared to the contemporary settler population as being caught in a timeless past—influenced not by organic changes from within but by external forces such as migration, diffusion, trade, and intermarriage with other societies. In the latter half of the nineteenth century, scholars such as Daniel Wilson (1862), Lewis Henry Morgan (1877), and Friedrich Engels ([1884] 1978) classified most North American indigenous societies as representing the earliest stages of human social development.

In *Ancient Society*, Morgan articulated a schema of social evolution that progressed from savagery to barbarism to civilization.[38] While Morgan's inventory of traits characterizing each phase of development included forms of government, family, religion, and property, he cast subsistence as the prime mover of social evolution:

> The important fact that mankind commenced at the bottom of the scale and worked up, is revealed in an expressive manner by their successive arts of subsistence. Upon their skill in this direction, the whole question of human supremacy on the earth depended. Mankind are the only beings

who may be said to have gained an absolute control over the production of food. . . . It is accordingly probable that the great epochs of human progress have been identified, more or less directly, with the enlargement of the sources of subsistence (Morgan 1877, 19).

Whether discussing language, political systems, marriage practices, or subsistence, Morgan's highest levels—those that represent "civilization"—were those of contemporary Europeans. Thus, field cultivation was the highest form of subsistence, and it was made possible by the ownership of property by individuals. These were the hallmarks of civilization and signaled the peak of humanity's progress thus far.[39] The Mi'kmaq, having not engaged in the full-time production of food, and having not conformed to the norms of individual property ownership, remained "uncivilized savages" in the eyes of colonial agents, settlers, and ethnologists.[40]

The teleological model of social evolution proposed by Morgan—and later taken up by Engels—has had deep and lasting effects on the development of anthropology and especially the subdiscipline of archaeology. Both have been influenced by the presumptive relationship between subsistence and social evolution, and both have grown up with the early ethnologists' legacy of social typologizing. Trigger (1980) has argued that the European stereotype of native North Americans as unprogressive has been the most important factor in the development of North American archaeology. He cites this stereotype as the root cause for a general lack of interest before 1914 in exploring cultural change of the continent's earliest peoples. McNiven and Russell (2005) surveyed more recent literature and concluded that archaeology and sociocultural anthropology continue to define hunter-gatherers through their cultural absence—particularly their absence of agriculture.[41] While some studies have questioned the reified nature of the hunter-gatherer category (see Bettinger 2015; Bird-David 2004; M. Hall 1988; Ingold et al. 1991a, 1991b; Kent and Vierich 1989; Morrison and Junker 2002; Rubertone 2000, 2001; Waguespack 2005; Wolf 1981; Woodburn 1980), many of the most popular introductory textbooks continue to place hunter-gatherers at the bottom of a sociopolitical hierarchy (see, for example, R. Kelly and D. Thomas 2013; Renfrew and Bahn 2012; Sharer and Ashmore 2003).[42]

In our call for a revitalized anthropological theory of mobility, Maureen Marshall and I (2015) trace anthropology's engagement with mobility and politics from Morgan (1877) and Hobhouse et al. (1915) to structural-functionalist (Evans-Pritchard 1940; Fortes and Evans-Pritchard 1940; Lowie 1920), diffusionist (Childe 1929; Petrie 1939; Rivers 1914), and cultural evolutionist thinkers (Adams 1966; Fried 1960; Sahlins and Service 1960; Steward 1955; L. White 1943). We discuss how mid-twentieth-century cultural evolutionary models of social change have influenced the "Othering" of many mobile subjects.[43] With an underlying focus on how economies are adapted to environments, cultural evolution defined broad categories of societies based on traits that existed along a continuum; for example, the degree to which a society was mobile or sedentary, the level of formal leadership, the complexity of architecture, and the size of the population (see Adams 1966; Childe 1950; Fried 1960; Marshall and Lelièvre 2010, 3; Radcliffe-Brown 1965; Renfrew and Bahn 1996, 167; Sahlins and Service 1960; Service 1975). Each of these traits was mutually determinative: Hunter-gatherers were defined by the observation that their environments provided scarce and limited resources—access to which required movement. This movement required a type of organization that would be flexible enough to accommodate changes in the availability of resources—that is, the "band." Likewise, a band level of organization was adapted to its environment and resources such that shifting to a mode of production that required sedentism would be difficult (see Steward 1955).

In cultural evolutionary models, the categories may have been refined (for example, the patrilineal band, the composite band), but the peoples whom these models categorized were understood more in terms of typological traits than the historical contexts of their sociopolitical complexity. For example, in the well-known Band → Tribe → Chiefdom → State model of Sahlins and Service (1960), the state was considered the apogee of sociopolitical organization and was dependent upon agriculture and a settled population (Lelièvre and Marshall 2015, 439). Mobility was treated primarily as a strategy for food procurement, relegating it to a trait of sociopolitical organization. Thus, practices of movement—and the people engaged in those practices— were reduced to the type "hunter-gatherer" (see Ames 1991; Binford 1990; Bettinger 1991; Casimir and Rao 1992; Gamble and Boismier 1991; Hurtado and Hill 1990; R. Kelly 1983, 1992, 1995; Marshall and Lelièvre 2010, 4; Steward 1955; Winterhalder and E. Smith 1981; Yesner 1980).[44]

The development of typological categories was part of the scientific turn in North American archaeology in the second half of the twentieth century. Steward (1955) recognized the futility of attempting to create universal developmental categories for band-level societies, opting instead to focus on the evolution of hunter-gatherers into other stages along the sociocultural hierarchy. He considered the primary objective of multilinear evolution to be ascertaining "the detailed processes by which hunters and gatherers were converted into farmers or herdsmen and these latter into more 'civilized' people" (Steward 1955, 25). Despite Steward's skepticism of their universal value, broad categories such as "hunter-gatherer," "forager," and "pastoralist" facilitated Binfordian aspirations for nomothetic generalizations from archaeological data by providing a common vocabulary—however problematic—for researchers working in different temporal and geographic settings. And yet the late twentieth-century introduction of the so-called complex hunter-gatherer—who exhibited traits from higher up on the cultural hierarchy—betrays the untenability of universal categories (see King 1978; Price and Brown 1985; cf. Asad 1979). Moreover, the focus on refining typologies meant that comparatively little attention was paid to either the historical contexts in which practices of movement were constituted or the motivations that induce subjects to move other than food procurement (Lelièvre and Marshall 2015, 439).[45] Thus, in many archaeological studies of North America, mobility remained an epiphenomenal trait of the categories "band" and "hunter-gatherer" and/or a reaction to an externally imposed crisis or influence (see Binford 1990; Bourque 1973; Bourque et al. 1978; Burke 2003; Davis 1986; Gamble and Boismier 1991; Martijn 1989; McWeeney 2002; Nash 1978; Nietfeld 1981; Rast et al. 2004; Renouf and Bell 2000; Sanger 1982, 1996; Sheldon 1988).

Turning to Mobility

By the late twentieth century most anthropologists had recognized the limitations of typological approaches that created strict dichotomies between mobile and sedentary populations. In his review of archaeological approaches to conceptualizing mobility and sedentism, Robert Kelly (1992, 60) argued that it was "no longer useful to speak of a continuum between mobile and sedentary systems, since mobility is not merely variable but multi-dimensional." For some anthropologists movement became a direct object for empirical observation, and greater attention was given to the historical contexts of mobile communities (Duff 2002; Fowles 2011; Lekson and Cameron 1995; Nelson and Strawhacker 2011; Wilcox 2009). Binford's ethnoarchaeological research among the Nunamiut in Alaska exemplifies the renewed commitment to empiricism (see Binford 1976; 1978). In April 1971, Binford observed forty-seven hunting trips made by Nunamiut males out of the village of Anaktuvuk. The study was primarily designed to understand the human behaviors that result in the formation of the archaeological record. However, the data he gathered to infer these processes are perhaps more interesting to our current discussion because they are the practices, conceptions, and perceptions of Nunamiut movement. Binford recorded many details for each trip including the time of departure, the composition of the party leaving the village, the expressed purpose of the trip, the anticipated destination, and the mode of transportation to be used. He also conducted an inventory of all gear—both before the trip commenced and after the hunters returned to the village. Upon the hunters' return, Binford recorded the route traveled, the locations of all stops, the activities performed at each stop, the duration of each stop, the total distance traveled, and the duration of the entire trip (Binford 1976, 300). These observations allowed Binford to conduct many different types of analyses, including drawing correlations between the material objects carried with the hunters and the distances traveled. Such information would form the foundation of his later models of logistical and residential mobility (see Binford 1980).

Despite the longevity of the residential versus logistical models, the more valuable contribution of Binford's research to the anthropology of mobility may be his detailed empirical observations. The conversations Binford had with his Nunamiut interlocutors about how they categorized the gear they brought with them on hunting trips demonstrates this point. His objective was to compare how archaeologists would categorize material culture with the hunters' own categories. Binford reported that "the hunters consistently recognized three categories: (1) 'tools and things,' (2) food, and (3) clothing" (Binford 1976, 323). Items that an anthropologist might recognize as "tools and things"—"big knife" and "extra line"—appeared in the hunters' "clothing" category. One hunter explained, "They are in that pile because I'm thinking about what may happend [sic] to me out there; suppose the dog team lead broke or I had to build a snow shelter" (Binford 1976, 324). When Binford noted that archaeologists would categorize "coffee can" and "cup" as "food" rather than "tools and things," another hunter responded: "Yes, but I carry them when I think about myself and how I will feel, not when I think about what I may have to do out there" (Binford 1976, 324). The conclusion Binford drew from the categorization exercise and the hunters' comments suggests that archaeologists need to focus more on the functions of artifacts rather than their formal properties when trying to interpret patterning in the archaeological record: "The Nunamiut, in this context, think of their gear in terms of the analogous functions of the items in regard to their dimensions of contingency planning, and not in terms of analogous formal properties of the items themselves" (Binford 1976, 324). More relevant to our discussion here is how this example illustrates the need for an anthropological approach to mobility that considers not only the practices of moving from one place to another—the forty-seven trips the Nunamiut hunters made, how they traveled, what they brought with them—but also the sensual perceptions of how the hunters felt while traveling these distances and camping overnight, and their conceptions of what these hunting journeys would entail. The hunter who explained that in planning his trip he is at once *thinking* about himself and—at the same time—imagining how he will *feel* when he is traveling away from his village captures the interconnection between the lived, the perceived, and the conceived.

A decade later, the ethnographer José Mailhot made an explicit appeal for more robust empirical research of traditionally mobile peoples. As one of the anthropologists who continued the debate regarding the origins and operations of the Algonquian family hunting territories, Mailhot (1986) approached her work with the Montagnais-Naskapi of Sheshatshit in Labrador with specific questions about the dynamism of territorial occupancy. She argued that previous studies had focused too much on the structure of Algonquian territories—and how that structure has endured or been modified over time—rather than the mobile nature of occupancy in those territories (Mailhot 1986, 105). She criticized previous research on Algonquian family hunting territories for either ignoring the existence of territories in areas with a "marked circulation of individuals" or treating mobility as a "minor phenomenon" in areas with documented systems of hunting territories (Mailhot 1986, 105). Mailhot was able to make this criticism because of the observations she made through her careful ethnographic research with members of the Sheshatshit community. Her linguistic analysis clarified that common property remained the more dominant institution than private ownership. Words that refer to possession— for example, "my lake"—were neologisms (Mailhot 1986, 94–95). Mailhot also demonstrated that the movements to various territories that she observed were structured by band exogamy and matrilocal residence (Mailhot 1986, 95; see also Mailhot 1993).

Although Binford and Mailhot's projects exemplify the empirical study of *movement* (the object of observation), many anthropological considerations of moving subjects over the past two decades have been focused on *mobility* (the object of study). In anthropology, the mobility "turn" (see Sheller and Urry 2006) seems to have emerged with the increasing interest in the processes of globalization during the late 1980s and early 1990s. The seemingly unhindered movement of people, goods, and ideas inspired researchers to examine the apparent dissolution of ethnic and political boundaries (see Appadurai 1996; Glick Schiller et al. 1995; Gupta 1992; Gupta and Ferguson 1997; Sassen 1998). In the wake of these economic and cultural "flows," several authors directly addressed the sedentarist bias inherent in the traditional approach to anthropological inquiry that relied on the boundedness of discrete cultural units (see Asad 1979; Clifford 1997; Malkki 1992; see also Rockefeller 2011). Indeed, Clifford (1997, 3) sought to upend anthropology's axiom that "roots precede routes" by suggesting that travel and displacement can be constitutive of the cultural meaning of human experiences, rather than simply transferring or extending them.

In introducing our framework for a revitalized anthropology of mobility, Marshall and I (2015) discuss promising work in sociocultural anthropology, archaeology, and history whose investigations of a variety of mobile subjects (from athletes, to refugees, to economic migrants, to ancient and modern pilgrims) can help meet the challenges of conceptualizing mobility in the past and the present, of observing movement simultaneously at multiple spatial scales, and of overcoming the tendency to "Other" what is mobile. Yet the sedentarist bias in anthropology persists, most notably in archaeological studies that continue to be influenced by the legacy of cultural evolutionism. Both Binford and Mailhot were able to participate, observe, and interview the mobile subjects they studied. Most archaeologists must rely on inferring movement only from the stationary features and artifacts they observe in the archaeological record. Without the advantage of ethnographic or historical data that can inform an understanding of the perceptions and conceptions of movement, archaeologists may be able to infer reliably only the practices of movement.[46] As Collignon has argued, making such inferences has too often relied on the personal experiences or intuitions of the researcher (Collignon 2006, 66).[47] These inferences have also relied on assumptions of so-called rational choice in the face of limited options presented to societies by their environments—a holdover of cultural evolutionism. Ideas that attempted to explain and predict movements and settlement—such as optimal foraging theory and central place theory—were built on assumptions of rational choice (see Evans and Gould 1982; E. Smith 1983; Winterhalder and E. Smith 1981). These theories continue to influence the tools that many archaeologists use to interpret their data, such as the spatial analysis applications (e.g., view-shed and line-of-site analyses) available in off-the-shelf geographic information systems software (see Adam T. Smith 2003, chap. 3; Kosiba and Bauer 2012).

Challenging the Sedentarist Ideology

The methodological and epistemological challenges facing the archaeological study of mobility have had legal and political implications for traditionally hunting, gathering, and fishing peoples such as the Mi'kmaq. Many such peoples have been denied access to land, resources, and full participation in settler polities because their impermanent and ephemeral activities have not been valued as legitimate practices for establishing ownership and authority (cf. Raibmon 2007). Beginning in the nineteenth century, court decisions against indigenous peoples in North America have been grounded in a sedentarist ideology that assumes indigenous engagements with the land and water have made no significant impact on them (see Arneil 1996; Barker 2005; Raibmon 2007). In the twentieth and early twenty-first centuries—as traditionally mobile indigenous peoples in Canada and other settler colonies have attempted to demonstrate their right to lands and waters—this impermanent existence has been considered insufficient or ineligible to qualify as evidence for continued occupancy (see Asch 1992; Culhane 1998; Daly 2005; M. Johnson 2008; Mills 2005; Monet and Skanu'u 1992; Povinelli 1995; Raibmon 2005). Disputes over indigenous access to land and resources in North America have been determined, in part, by the anthropological classification of indigenous social organization. For example, Pinkoski and Asch (2004) demonstrate Julian Steward's role in denying the land claims of Great Basin Indians with his assertion that their social organization was insufficiently complex for them to have developed concepts of property.[48] The sedentarist ideology means that the benchmarks for occupancy are those practices—such as monumental architecture, large-scale infrastructure, urban development, and agriculture—that permanently alter the land and water. Compared to societies that construct such features, how could a Mi'kmaw community claim rights to land upon which their ancestors have left little or no tangible trace?

One of the primary objectives of *Unsettling Mobility* is to demonstrate that impermanent and ephemeral activities can have a significant cultural impact, in part, because of their persistence.[49] The recent archaeological reconsiderations of site abandonment have contributed significantly toward recognizing the longevity of what Matson et al. (1988, 245) have described as "discontinuous occupations" (see also Cameron and Tomka 1993; Colwell-Chanthaphonh and Ferguson 2006; Kent 1993; Lekson and Cameron 1995; Nelson 1999; Nelson and Strawhacker 2011).[50] The island of Maligomish provides a compelling case study in this regard because the archaeological, historical, and ethnographic records document repeated use of the island from AD 1500 to the present.[51] Moreover, these data sets suggest that at various points in its history the island may have been used year-round, even though it may not have been settled permanently. For the pre-contact period, the remains recovered from the shell midden on the south side of the island include those of multiseasonal anadromous fish such as striped bass (*Morone saxatilis*) and smelt (*Osmerus mordax*) and megafauna such as moose (*Alces*

alces).[52] But such seasonal indicators may tell only part of the site's occupational history. For the post-contact period, ethnographic observations, oral histories, and archival sources provide evidence for how Mi'kmaq moved to and from Maligomish and how the island fit within the broader Mi'kma'ki landscape. Indeed, such evidence from the twentieth century indicates that Mi'kmaq continuously used Maligomish year-round. Censuses taken by the Canadian Department of Indian Affairs in 1904 and the Diocese of Antigonish in 1906 distinguish Maligomish as a separate reserve from the one located at Pictou Landing (also known as Fisher's Grant or Indian Cove), suggesting there was a steady population living on Maligomish. Harlan Smith's 1914 photograph of the eastern side of Maligomish clearly indicates buildings that were substantial enough to sustain year-round occupancy (see fig. 3). In 1926, the local Indian agent and priest for the Pictou-area Mi'kmaq, J. D. MacLeod, made reference to Maligomish in a letter to the Department of Indian Affairs, in which he stated that the Mi'kmaq "lived there the greater part of the year. But now Indian Island has been abandoned and now nobody lives or makes his home there" (LAC 1926).

But what constituted abandonment for MacLeod? The archival and oral-historical records indicate that Mi'kmaq did not leave Maligomish altogether after 1926. Several newspaper reports describe the St. Anne's Day celebrations that occurred on the island each July (see Diocese of Antigonish Archives 1932–38). Dorie Sapier lived year-round on the island with her husband, Fred, for almost thirty years between the mid-1970s and 2000. She recalled Fred's stories of growing up on Maligomish. She also described the cement foundations of Fred's grandfather's house. Foundations matching her description were visible near the northeast corner of the island during our surface survey in 2007 and 2008 (see chapter 3).[53] Finally, perhaps the most significant evidence of persistent cultural and spiritual activity on Maligomish is its most prominent building—the church that was constructed in 1897 and remains in use during the annual St. Anne's mission. These historical and ethnographic descriptions suggest that at least some Mi'kmaq have been using Maligomish for multiple purposes, at various times of the year, for at least the last two centuries. They also illustrate that places like Maligomish are significant despite their impermanent occupation.

Demonstrating this significance requires acknowledging the biases that have become entrenched in colonial and academic discourse about mobile peoples. From the observations by early explorers of a people who lived "on the chase," to the bureaucrats and settlers who reported their "wanderings" in search of fish and game, to the ethnographers who focused on subsistence as the primary organizing structure in their society, and to the archaeologists who retrieved the artifacts required for hunting, the Mi'kmaq have been cast as a hunting and gathering people. These classificatory schemes have had not only intellectual consequences for the anthropological study of mobility but also political consequences for how Mi'kmaq and other indigenous peoples constitute themselves (and are constituted by others) as political subjects. Intellectually, the relegation of movement to the status of "trait" in a sociopolitical hierarchy has left anthropology with an anaemic understanding of the work that mobility does in creating, challenging, and remaking social worlds. Politically, the failed attempts of the colonial government in Nova Scotia to remake Mi'kmaq into autonomous, sedentary farmers set a precedent for how the later Canadian government would conceive of Mi'kmaq and other indigenous peoples as subjects of the Crown. Apparently unable to provide for themselves, the indigenous populations of British North America—and later Canada—became wards of the state. Yet the objectives of both the British colonial and Canadian federal governments were to make the indigenous populations independent, autonomous subjects. Indeed, the ultimate objective was complete assimilation, as stated by Duncan Campbell Scott, the deputy superintendent general of Indian affairs, in his 1920 testimony to the Canadian Parliament on proposed amendments to the 1876 Indian Act: "Our objective is to continue until there is not a single Indian in Canada that has not been absorbed into the body politic and there is no Indian question and no Indian Department" (LAC 1920). If being "absorbed into the body politic" means becoming sedentary, foregoing collective property, and enjoying the same basic human rights of nonindigenous Canadians, then there is substantial evidence that Duncan Campbell Scott's objective has failed—not least of which is the chronic lack of adequate housing and safe drinking water on reserves. The following chapters examine some of this evidence, focusing on the movements of Mi'kmaq in northeastern Nova Scotia. The chapters also demonstrate that many of the efforts made by the Church and Crown to assimilate Mi'kmaq had the unintended consequences of further marking them as "Other."

2

Clam Beds and Arrowheads

AN INDIGENOUS ARCHAEOGRAPHY OF MALIGOMISH

Maligomish's Ghosts

MANY PICTOU LANDING MI'KMAQ REPORT encountering tricksters or spirits on Maligomish. As described in the introduction, some Mi'kmaq have heard voices and the scraping of canoes being dragged on shore, but when they searched for who was there, no one could be seen. Other all-too-human ghosts haunt Maligomish for some Mi'kmaq. Elder Sadie Francis has described memories of an incident on Maligomish from the early twentieth century involving her grandmother and a mission priest. Her grandmother had led a group of women in a dance around a sacred fire built on the southeastern shore of the island to mark the beginning of the St. Anne's mission. Sadie's grandmother later greeted the mission priest as he arrived on Maligomish, describing the ceremonies that had been performed. The ritual ended abruptly when the priest demanded that the dancing stop and the fire be extinguished. Sadie has described the pain she felt as she witnessed the priest chastise her grandmother for overstepping her bounds as a woman and a layperson.

During our archaeological fieldwork on Maligomish, my field assistants and I encountered ghosts of a very different kind. Our excavations were designed to observe and record the stratigraphy of the shell midden located on the south side of the island, just down the hill from the church. We had hoped to recover faunal and floral materials from the observed strata in order to determine whether during the pre-contact period Mi'kmaq had occupied Maligomish year-round or only seasonally, and if this settlement pattern had changed over time. Our excavations of the midden were challenged by the ghosts of archaeologists who had worked in the midden over the previous century. Traces of earlier test units scarred this portion of Maligomish. Harlan

Smith, who was then a preparator with the National Museum of Man in Ottawa, first excavated a portion of the midden in 1914. His excavations haunted
John Erskine, an avocational archaeologist who excavated another part of the
midden in 1961. Erskine reported that one of the supposed "sub-sites" within
the midden was "so thoroughly ruined by Smith's digging that we have no
evidence on which to orient it" (Erskine 1962, 22). More than fifty years later,
the ghost of John Erskine appeared as my field assistants and I were excavating one of two, one-meter by one-meter test units in a portion of the midden
that we hoped had been untouched by either Smith or Erskine. As we were
preparing to photograph the bottom of the third level in this unit, Mary Irene
Nicholas noticed something that had escaped my attention: a linear feature of
slightly darker soil on the east side of the unit that was likely one of Erskine's
backfilled trenches. Because this context was "disturbed," we ceased our excavations and directed our efforts to another test unit.

Our experience of being thwarted by the ghost of Erskine is one chapter in
a longer narrative of archaeological intervention on Maligomish. Mary Irene
Nicholas, Edie Nicholas, and I were part of a history that has involved the
movement of objects and people to and from Maligomish in pursuit of knowledge. That knowledge—constructed largely from the perspective of nonindigenous researchers working within a Eurocentric epistemology that places
high and universal value on the accumulation of new information—has offered insight into how Mi'kmaq in the pre-contact period lived and the role
that places such as Maligomish have played in the broader pre- and post-
contact landscapes. But the shell midden has another narrative that has little
to do with archaeology.

From the perspective of local Mi'kmaq—none of whom were trained as
archaeologists before Mary Irene and Edie—the midden by turns has provoked
curiosity and provided utilitarian value. As revealed through their oral histories and memories, Mi'kmaq have engaged the Maligomish midden in ways
that have had little to do with the scientific pursuit of archaeology. Some of
these experiences reflect a Mi'kmaw understanding of the value that non-
Mi'kmaq placed on the contents of the midden. Others demonstrate that the
midden was just part of the land that comprised Maligomish. For example,
when I asked two elders from the Pictou Landing First Nation, Matthew and
Sarah Knockwood,* about their knowledge of the midden, Sarah recalled
her father and his contemporaries digging in the midden in search of "arrow
heads." She remembered that one of their excavations unearthed a small leather
boot. Matthew described a time in the latter half of the twentieth century
when the community widened the path that runs through the midden. This
path is the main route that visitors to Maligomish walk after arriving at the

wharf on the south side of the island. It extends from the top of the wharf stairs to the churchyard. This path receives the heaviest foot traffic on Maligomish, especially during the annual St. Anne's mission. Matthew recalled that the widening project required digging into the bank on the north side of the path. He described seeing "clam beds" and "arrow heads" (Lelièvre field notebook, vol. 14:130). Other community members recalled collecting, not artifacts, but the midden itself; the rich, black soil was a favorite fertilizer for local gardeners. Still other Mi'kmaq understood the value that tourists and archaeologists placed on the artifacts contained within the midden. As will be discussed in greater depth later in this chapter, several Mi'kmaq collected and sold archaeological artifacts as part of their subsistence economy.

We risk erasing local Mi'kmaw experiences of the Maligomish midden if we reduce this feature to a mere "trash heap." Indeed, many archaeologists more accurately refer to these contexts as "shell-bearing sites" to reflect the multiple uses humans have made of shell accumulations, including as storage pits, roasting pits, and house floors (see Black 1988; Black and Whitehead 1988; Claassen 1991; Thomas and Thomson 1992; Waselkov 1987). In this chapter, I explore both archaeological and local Mi'kmaw narratives of this shell midden, known to archaeologists by its Borden number, BjCo-02.[1] I use these narratives as a lens through which to explore mobility and the constitution of political subjectivity from several different perspectives. One of these perspectives is epistemological—in other words, how archaeologists construct knowledge. I discuss the midden's archaeological narrative as a way to make explicit some of the assumptions that underlie the inferences of dynamic processes that archaeologists make from the static remains of human activities. This discussion contributes to the broader theoretical objective of the current work by further revealing the bias toward sedentism, which can exist even at the most basic levels of empirical observation in social sciences such as archaeology. Another perspective is empirical: I trace the movements of people, objects, and knowledge to and from the Maligomish midden and other archaeological sites in the ninety-four years between 1914 and 2008. A final perspective is paradigmatic: in North America and other settler colonies, the practice of archaeology—particularly archaeology conducted in the ancestral territories of indigenous peoples—has been slowly shifting from being conducted solely by nonindigenous archaeologists who set the research agenda to involving descendant communities in roles ranging from passive consultants to full collaborators. Several researchers have defined the elements of these subfields, which include collaborative, community, public, and indigenous archaeologies (see Agbe-Davies 2010; Atalay 2006, 2008, 2012; Bruchac et al. 2010; Colwell-Chanthaphonh 2009; Colwell-Chanthaphonh and Ferguson 2007,

2008; Colwell-Chanthaphonh et al. 2010; Conkey 2005; Little 2009; Lyons 2013; Y. Marshall 2002; McDavid 2002; McGhee 2008; Nicholas and Andrews 1997; Phillips and Allen 2005; Potter 1994; Swidler et al. 1997; Watkins 2000; Wylie 2015). Although they have been criticized for simply being reactive to indigenous communities that are increasingly being proactive in the protection of their cultural resources (see Dawdy 2009), these archaeologies of virtue share an objective to decolonize archaeological practice by decentering the production of knowledge away from the academy, promoting multivocality in defining research questions and interpreting the past, and thinking reflexively and critically about the role that archaeologists have played in the subjection of indigenous peoples. Building on the foundations that these scholars have laid, I explore whether this more collaborative approach to archaeological practice has the potential to change how archaeologists constitute "the field" (cf. Gupta and Ferguson 1997). If, as has long been accepted by sociocultural anthropologists, ethnographic fieldwork is constituted through "dialogic encounters" between the researcher and her interlocutors (see Bourdieu 1977; Gupta and Ferguson 1997, 2), then does a comparable relationship exist in the constitution of archaeological fieldwork—and, indeed, of the archaeological record itself? Can the archaeological "field" be constituted through a dialogic encounter, not only between contemporary archaeologists and the communities who claim to be the descendants of the people who created the archaeological record, but also between contemporary archaeologists and past subjects who accessed and used the sites, features, and artifacts that comprise the archaeological record (see Lelièvre 2016)?

At the heart of these questions is the argument that the shell midden on Maligomish (and *any* shell midden anywhere) is not de facto an archaeological feature but is, rather, an object that has been constructed by archaeologists and others in ways that impact the social world.[2] I trace these impacts by considering three moments in the history of the midden during which the two narratives—one archaeological and Eurocentric, the other social and Mi'kmaw—intersected. Each moment offers further illustration of mobility as the entanglement of the practices, perceptions, and conceptions of movement with emplacement by describing how people and objects circulated to and from the shell midden. Each also demonstrates the constitution of Mi'kmaw political subjectivity because the Maligomish midden and other archaeological sites have been among the many places where Mi'kmaq have asserted their right of access despite the encroachment of European settlers.

This approach to discussing the shell midden on Maligomish is due, in part, to encountering the ghost of Erskine in the middle of our excavations.

Unfortunately, the materials recovered from the midden were too few and too poorly preserved to answer definitively the original research questions regarding changes in Mi'kmaw settlement patterns from the pre- to post-contact periods (see Lelièvre 2009). The lack of reliable archaeological data may have been due to Erskine and Smith's respective excavations, despite the best efforts of my field assistants and I to avoid those sections of the midden. But as I reviewed the artifactual and archival information related to these previous excavations, several details emerged that suggested the evidence related to the recent history of the midden; in other words, the history recorded in the notes of archaeologists and the memories of local Mi'kmaq might be more compelling than the few broken points and scraps of ceramic sherds that we managed to salvage. This information included published articles and unpublished field reports and notebooks, newspaper announcements of local excavations, museum accession records, photographs, and artifacts. The details contained within these documents that most captured my attention were the fleeting references to individual Mi'kmaq. These references were often parenthetical, but some portrayed Mi'kmaq in roles not commonly seen for indigenous peoples in the history of archaeological research. They were not simply passive objects being acted upon by archaeologists, museum curators, and private collectors. For example, as will be discussed in greater depth below, during Harlan Smith's excavation of the Maligomish midden in 1914, the Mi'kmaw caretaker of the island accused the archaeologist of trespassing and asked him to leave. This is a detail, incidentally, that Smith himself neglected to mention in his field notes and published reports. It only came to light fifty years later when Erskine was told the story by one of the local field assistants who had witnessed Smith's dismissal (Erskine 1962, 1986). Thus, by comparing the documents and visual resources that comprise the archaeographic record of Maligomish, it is possible to observe a more agentive role for Mi'kmaq in the history of archaeological practice. These observations, coupled with Ann Stoler's innovation of seeing historical documents as "generative substances" (Stoler 2009, 1), suggested that I treat them not only as metadata of the excavations—in other words, as means to the end of knowing how the archaeologists excavated the midden and sampled its remains. Instead, these data became ends in themselves—pieces of evidence whose comparison and analyses could generate their own knowledge, specifically, on the constitution of Mi'kmaq as political subjects.[3]

In the previous chapters, I have argued that Mi'kmaw subjectivity has been constituted through both passive and agentive practices; in other words, Mi'kmaq have constructed their subjectivity through their own practices, and that subjectivity has been shaped by the practices of others.[4] As discussed in chapter 1, on the one hand, individuals and institutions representing the Catholic Church and the British Crown in nineteenth-century Nova Scotia attempted to transform Mi'kmaq into ideal modern subjects by instilling them with a Protestant ethic that would make them sedentary, provident, and self-sufficient. Elsewhere I have discussed how Nova Scotia and Canada's early archaeological explorations contributed to the constitution of Mi'kmaq as political subjects (Lelièvre 2012). In this chapter, I consider Mi'kmaw practices that worked to construct their own political subjectivity, thus resisting—or, in some cases, simply ignoring—colonial subjectification. For example, I examine the practice of collecting and selling archaeological artifacts. By traveling to Mi'kmaw places that—in some cases—existed for centuries before the arrivals of Europeans, these Mi'kmaw collectors embedded themselves in a Mi'kmaw landscape. Using archival data from archaeological investigations and details recorded in the accession ledgers of the Nova Scotia Museum, I trace the movements of Mi'kmaq who participated in the trade of archaeological artifacts. The spatial and temporal patterns in these collecting activities suggest that—like hunting, fishing, and gathering—the collection of archaeological artifacts worked to assert the Mi'kmaq's treaty right to access the land. Artifact collecting was one of the "changed continuities" (Ferris 2009) that helped to support the subsistence economies in which many Mi'kmaq engaged during the post-contact period. It required knowledge of the land, and it involved returning to places of Mi'kmaw experience long alienated by European settlers. As such, these Mi'kmaw practices of moving to and revisiting specific archaeological sites was, effectively, a political act of sovereignty.[5]

In the next section of this chapter I explore the epistemological limits and possibilities of archaeologists' attempts to infer human movement from the static remains that humans leave behind in what becomes the archaeological record. I then discuss three moments of intersection between the archaeological and the Mi'kmaw narratives of the Maligomish midden. The designation "1914" describes Harlan Smith's work on Maligomish. "1933" considers the subsistence collecting done by Charlie Wilmot, a Mi'kmaw man from the Millbrook First Nation who had deep connections in Pictou Landing. "2008" discusses how my approach to the archaeological survey and excavation I conducted on Maligomish was influenced, not only by the beliefs of many Pictou Landing Mi'kmaq regarding the sacredness of the island, but also by the personal experiences of my field assistants. In the conclusion to the chapter, I consider how these recent moments in the history of the Maligomish midden represent the persistence of Mi'kmaw presence on this small island in the Northumberland Strait.

Embodying Mobility: Overcoming
Archaeology's Sedentary Bias

Before discussing the three moments of intersection between the archaeological and local Mi'kmaw narratives of the shell midden on Maligomish, I explore the epistemological limits and possibilities of archaeologists' attempts to infer human movement from the static remains that humans leave behind. When I was writing grant applications to investigate changes in Mi'kmaw movement patterns from the pre- to post-contact period, one of the requirements with which I—and many anthropologically oriented archaeologists—struggled was articulating how I would identify, collect, and analyze the archaeological correlates of those changes. Because archaeologists cannot directly observe past human movement, they must indirectly infer movement from the artifacts and plant and animal remains that traditionally mobile peoples leave behind. Shell middens are ideal sites for attempting to infer past movement because of the wide variety of artifactual and ecofactual (plant and animal) remains that can be preserved within them. Found along coastal and riverine shores, they are formed by the discard of invertebrate shells over decades, centuries, and, in some regions, millennia (see Balbo et al. 2010; Claassen 1991, 1998; Kennett and Voorhies 1996; Spiess et al. 2006; Stein 1992; Sullivan 1984; Villagran et al. 2011). Over time, the piles of shell that humans have dumped become in-filled with soil, animal bones, artifacts, and other debris. The alkaline calcium carbonate from the shells gradually leaches into this matrix, neutralizing much of the acid that may be present in the soil. It is this neutral chemistry of most shell middens that makes them desirable sites for archaeologists. The chemically stable environment helps to preserve organic bone and plant remains, which are usually destroyed in acidic soils.

Preservation of these organic remains is important to archaeologists wanting to infer movement because many of the archaeological proxies of movement are the remnants of plants and animals that are available only during certain months of the year. Archaeologists can use the presence of these remains to infer a season in which an archaeological site was used (see Black 1993; Bonzani 1997; Bourque et al. 1978; Humphreys 1987; Monks 1981; Spiess 1976; Stewart 1989; Woodborne et al. 1995). Moreover, the accretional growth patterns of the shells themselves can be compared with contemporary analogues to determine the season in which they were harvested (see Andrus and Crowe 2000; Bemis and Geary 1996; Burchell et al. 2014a, 2014b; Custer and Doms 1990; Milner 2001; Quitmyer and Jones 1997; Quitmyer et al. 2005; Richardson 2001). The recovery and identification of seasonally variable animal and plant remains is one of the most common methods archaeologists use to infer the past movements of humans. Archaeologists may not be able to observe an extended family of Mi'kmaq moving from an inland camp site to the coast in February to fish for smelt, but they can infer from recovered smelt remains—using the analogue of contemporary observations of smelt migration—that Mi'kmaq were fishing in or near Merigomish Harbour in the late fall and winter. An archaeologist might combine this inference with those made from what is often termed "negative evidence"—in other words, the absence of evidence commonly associated with permanent settlement, such as the foundations of buildings and fortifications—to infer that Mi'kmaq had moved elsewhere during the spring and fall. Thus, the archaeological proxies of activities thought to be associated with human movement have very little to do with actual movement, defined as the simultaneous change in space in time by a subject or an object (see introduction). Most of the material traces of a mobile people are ephemeral and do not survive in the archaeological record. What survives is evidence of the activities people performed while stopped along their journeys—activities such as making or retouching tools, butchering, cooking and consuming animals, gathering seasonally available plants, and constructing temporary dwellings. Consequently, rather than even observing proxies of movement, archaeologists are able only to observe the proxies of impermanence or temporary stasis.

This distinction is important when we consider the two objectives of this book—namely, to reconceptualize settlement and to examine the bias toward sedentism that has underlay the anthropological study of indigenous peoples and state policies toward them. For the very epistemology of archaeology—one that relies on empirical observation and analogical reasoning—is limited to the observation of static remains that allow inferences of impermanence. It does not allow for the observation of movement—or if it does, only through several layers of inference; for example, from the excavated bones of an anadromous fish and contemporary observations of the migration patterns of the same species, one can make the abduction (*sensu* Peirce 1997; see also Douven 2011) that when the population was not fishing for smelt in this harbor they were moving to other locations, where they were conducting other temporarily stationary practices.[6] Thus, movement is inferred archaeologically through the absence of evidence of permanent settlement. Here we see that Massumi's (2002) critique—that cultural theory since the mid-twentieth century gives priority to position and sidelines the dynamism that explains how subjects are created as they flow through these positions—goes much deeper than the poststructuralist turn. It is ingrained into the methodological and epistemological foundations of the disciplines that have traditionally been the most influential on our understandings of the lifeways of indigenous peoples.

Recognizing our methodological and epistemological limits is the first step toward revitalizing the anthropological study of mobility. If archaeologists are able only to observe the remains of temporary sedentism—in effect, impermanence—then how do we analyze the significance of that impermanence in the lives of past subjects and in the lives of present subjects who claim descent from them? The Maligomish midden provides one case study for examining such significance. The remains of artifacts, animals, and plants contained within the midden are evidence of temporary—but repeated—human use of Maligomish stretching back at least fifteen hundred years before the present (BP). Like those found in comparable middens along the Atlantic coast of Nova Scotia and northern New England, the recovered remains of anadromous fish such as striped bass (*Morone saxatilis*) and smelt (*Osmerus mordax*) suggest that the ancestors of the contemporary Mi'kmaq may have been using Maligomish for only part of the year, likely the winter and late spring to summer. Other species recovered from the midden—including moose (*Alces americana*), porcupine (*Erethizon dorsatum*), and beaver (*Castor canadensis*)—would have been available year-round.[7]

These remains were recovered in the stratigraphic layers of the midden that I excavated with my assistants over two field seasons. Disentangling shell midden stratigraphy is notoriously difficult because of the variable activities that contribute to their formation processes (see Claassen 1986, 1991; Sanger 1981; Stein 1992). Middens are primarily formed through individual dumping episodes during which collections of discarded shells are deposited. These accumulating deposits of fragmenting shells appear to have been attractive places for constructing temporary camps, evidenced by the presence of what archaeologists describe as "living floors"—in other words, the compression that comes with walking, sitting, and sleeping in a confined area of the midden (Black 1991, 1993). The twenty-five centimeters of the Maligomish midden that our field crew was able to excavate include evidence of other activities such as the processing, preparation, and consumption of nonshellfish food (e.g., smelt, sea bass, and deer) and the manufacture of tools made from various lithic materials and animal bones. While stratigraphically shallow, the midden's depositional history appears to be temporally deep. As indicated in the bottom section of figure 5, the radiocarbon dates obtained from the profiles of two of the excavated units demonstrate that the oldest deposits date to around 1500 BP. The remaining radiocarbon dates cluster around 500 BP. The upper section of figure 5 illustrates what may be a shift over time in the dominant shellfish species represented in the midden (see Lelièvre 2017). In the deepest layers, oyster (*Crassostrea virginica*) dominates. In Nova Scotia, the appearance of oyster appears to be unique to the shell middens found along the

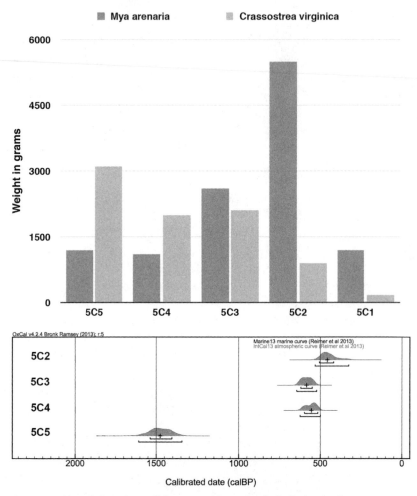

FIGURE 5. Top: Comparison of the proportions of soft-shell clam and eastern oyster for each level of test unit 5C at site BjCo-02 (by weight). Bottom—Calibrated radiocarbon dates for levels 2–5 of test unit 5C. All dates were calculated from soft-shell clam samples. All dates were calibrated using OxCal's (v. 4.2.4) IntCal 13 curve. The Marine13 calibration curve was applied to dates obtained from marine shells (see Reimer et al. 2013). The Δ R value for the Pugwash Basin (-60 +/-40) was applied for the Marine13 calibration (see McNeeley et al. 2006). Figure created by the author.

Northumberland Strait. The proportion of oyster shell in the midden appears to decline gradually over time as higher proportions of clam appear.[8] There are also shifts in the presence of some vertebrate species over time; for example, the remains of large mammals, such as moose and bear, were recovered from level two of unit 5C in higher quantities than from the other four levels. However, changes in vertebrate species are not as dramatic as the changes in shellfish, which may suggest an environmental change—such as increased water salinity and decreased water temperature—that made the waters of Merigomish Harbour less hospitable for oyster and more welcoming to clam. The possible change in species over time may also be due to cultural changes in the harvesting of certain species or in the use of the shell midden.

The materials recovered during our excavations were too few and too degraded to be able to draw strong conclusions about the specific activities undertaken at the midden.[9] However, the perdurance of impermanent human activity suggests that the ancestors of the Mi'kmaq had emplaced themselves on Maligomish over a thousand-year period. While there appears to be a significant gap in this long history between approximately 1500 and 500 BP, the archaeological evidence of repeated use indicates that knowledge of the midden—and the rich resources of the surrounding harbor and estuaries—may have been passed down through generations of Mi'kmaq for at least a millennium.[10] This knowledge became sedimented in the layers of the midden as its creators procured, processed, consumed, and discarded the resources found within it. With each successive movement to the midden—each accumulation of discarded materials—its creators were emplacing themselves on Maligomish and the surrounding harbor.[11]

Intersecting Narratives

1914

Historical evidence for the Mi'kmaq's emplacement on Maligomish stretches back to at least 1759 when Abbé Maillard dated his will from Maligomish after having fled the French town of Louisbourg before it fell to the British (see Burns 1936–37). Local histories describe Mi'kmaw and settler knowledge of Mi'kmaw activity during the mid-eighteenth to late nineteenth centuries (see G. Patterson 1877). In the course of my research, I was unable to learn any Mi'kmaw oral histories or stories about the pre-contact activities that occurred on Maligomish; I learned about such activities from archaeological materials and documentation alone. While the human and environmental processes that have contributed to the shell midden's formation have been at work since at least 1500 BP, this accumulation of shellfish remains did not become an archaeological feature until 1914. In the summer of that year, Harlan Smith was the first archaeologist to identify the midden as an archaeological site, which, as will be discussed below, established the first moment of intersection between the archaeological and local Mi'kmaw narratives of the midden's history.

Long before Harlan Smith's first visit to Maligomish, the documented archaeological exploration of Merigomish Harbour had begun with the Reverend George Patterson, a local Presbyterian minister, journalist, and antiquar-
ian who excavated grave and camp sites (see Patterson 1877, 1889). Over his
lifetime, Patterson had traveled widely, including to Scotland to attend university. Most of his travels, however, were contained within the Maritime
provinces, including his explorations of locales around Pictou County, which
formed the basis of his 1877 *History of the County of Pictou*. Patterson's excavations on the Big Island of Merigomish and at Kerr's Point on the south side
of Merigomish Harbour yielded lithic, ceramic, and faunal artifacts, which
formed the basis for the collection he donated to Dalhousie College (now
Dalhousie University) in Halifax in 1889.

A generation later, in 1913, William Wintemberg traveled from the Victoria Memorial Museum in Ottawa to Nova Scotia on a reconnaissance field
trip to build the museum's collection of artifacts from the Maritimes. The
Victoria Memorial Museum (now the Canadian Museum of History) was a
national museum, funded and operated by the Canadian federal government
as a division of Geological Survey of Canada.[12] While in Nova Scotia, Wintemberg studied the archaeological collections at the provincial museum in
Halifax and Patterson's collection at Dalhousie College before making his way
north to Pictou County. Wintemberg spent a very productive two weeks in
Pictou County, identifying several shell middens located along the Northumberland Strait, including six in Merigomish Harbour. His notes indicate that
he spent four days exploring the middens of Merigomish Harbour, collecting
surface finds and meeting with local farmers who had found artifacts in their
fields (see CMH-A 1913). Several of these farmers presented their artifacts
to Wintemberg, who took them back to Ottawa for the Victoria Memorial
Museum. Unlike Patterson—who made no reference to the contemporary
Mi'kmaq who dwelled in the area of Merigomish Harbour—Wintemberg
mentions Maligomish in his field notes and refers to a local Mi'kmaw man
named Joseph Phillip, who was living on the island and had found artifacts
on the neighboring Big Island of Merigomish (CMH-A 1912).[13]

Thus, when Harlan Smith arrived on Maligomish in the summer of 1914,
the surrounding harbor had already been identified as an important area for
archaeological research. Smith revisited the sites around Merigomish Harbour
that Wintemberg had investigated the previous year, identifying twelve additional shell middens (H. Smith 1929, 3). Among these new sites was the Maligomish midden, which Smith later identified as "shell-heap B" (H. Smith
1929, 7–8). Smith conducted extensive excavations of several middens, which
resulted in a collection of several hundred artifacts, which he took with him
for the Victoria Memorial Museum.

Harlan Smith returned to Ottawa in August 1914, soon after Canada had joined several other nations in declaring war on Germany. Although he wrote brief updates on his fieldwork in annual government reports, he did not publish a full report on his Merigomish Harbour research until 1929 (see H. Smith 1914, 1915, 1929). In this report, Smith briefly mentions the Mi'kmaq who frequent Maligomish: "Micmac Indians still live on Indian Island [Maligomish], fish and make baskets on and about the harbor, and even collect from the shell-heaps archaeological objects which they sell to tourists" (H. Smith 1929, 2). His description of the Maligomish midden makes no mention of excavations. He notes that he purchased five worked bone artifacts, which most likely originated in shell-heap B, from Joseph Philip (see H. Smith 1929, 8)—the Mi'kmaw whom William Wintemberg first mentioned in his field notes as living on Maligomish.

Following the publication of Smith's report, the archaeological narrative of the Maligomish midden was suspended until 1962, when John Erskine published the results of his investigations in Merigomish Harbour. In addition to describing the artifacts and features that he unearthed on Maligomish, Erskine related another archaeological ghost story of sorts in the 1962 edition of his "Micmac Notes." This time, it was the ghost of Harlan Smith who was haunting Erskine as he prepared to excavate on the island.

> In 1960 Kenneth Hopps and I searched a number of the Merigomish Islands and shores in the hope of finding sites which Wintemberg and Smith had overlooked in 1913–14. We found two on Point Betty [Olding] Island and one on Indian Island [Maligomish], but these were all marked on Smith's map as having been dug. Later, however, we met one of Smith's companions . . . and he told us that they had dug on Indian Island for only half a day and had found it very rich. The Indian caretaker, however, had warned them off as they were trespassing on the reserve. I tried to get permission both from the Indians and from the Department of Indian Affairs, but I heard from the latter only when the season was past. This year, fortified with departmental permission, I obtained permission from Chief Francis of Pictou Landing, and we prepared to dig. (Erskine 1962, 21)

In his unpublished notes, Erskine offered a few additional details to the story: "There was also the partially excavated site on Indian Island which we had considered excavating. Smith's crew had begun excavation there but before they finished, the Indian caretaker asked them to leave because the site was on land belonging to the Pictou Landing reserve. Smith had said that it would take too long to get permission from Ottawa, so they left" (Erskine 1986, 72).

Although these reports are based on Erskine's retelling of an eyewitness account that was almost fifty years old, the summary of his conversation with Smith's field assistant seems to indicate strongly that Smith did, in fact, excavate the midden on Maligomish in 1914—contrary to his annual updates and final report. More significant, however, is the role played by the Mi'kmaw "caretaker" who did not accept that Smith had a right to be there. Although told by non-Mi'kmaw archaeologists, the story of Smith's dismissal introduces a Mi'kmaw narrative of the Maligomish midden. The identity of the caretaker and the nature of his duties are currently unknown. In my conversations with members of the Pictou Landing First Nation and reviews of archival documents related to the island, I have not encountered the category of "caretaker." One of the few references to any kind of representative for the people of the island appeared in James Dawson's letter to Joseph Howe in June 1842, when he spoke with John Sapier, the elder who was on the island with the community's women and children while the younger men were engaged in the cod and herring fisheries elsewhere (see LAC 1842c). Was the caretaker in 1914 fulfilling a comparable role? Or did he have a mandate from the federal government to care for this piece of Crown land? Was this person Joseph Phillip, whom both Smith and Wintemberg encountered on their research trips to Merigomish Harbour?

Regardless of his identity, the caretaker's dismissal of Smith marks a moment of intersection between the archaeological and Mi'kmaw narratives of the shell midden on Maligomish. In this moment, the caretaker reinforced the Mi'kmaq's continued emplacement on Maligomish several centuries after the last remains had been deposited in the midden. Whether the caretaker was acting as a representative of the Crown, as a Mi'kmaw who had personal and social ties to the island, or as some combination of the two, he was asserting Mi'kmaw authority over the island and, consequently, over Harlan Smith as a representative of the Crown. It matters that this incident occurred on federal land reserved for the Mi'kmaq. Indeed, Smith was not deterred from his excavations on islands a mere stone's throw from Maligomish. The caretaker's authority was vested both in the status of the land being owned by the Crown and in his own status as a Mi'kmaw. He acted as a political subject the moment he asserted that authority and had it legitimated when Harlan Smith left Maligomish. The nature of that subjectivity is more difficult to articulate. If we follow Ortner's (2005, 31) conception of subjectivity as "the ensemble of modes of perception, affect, thought, desire, fear, and so forth that animate acting subjects . . . as well the cultural and social formations that shape, organize, and provoke those modes of affect," then we can understand the caretaker's subjectivity as constituted in the moment of his assertion of authority, as an entanglement of his experiences as a Mi'kmaw and as a ward of the settler state. In thwarting Smith's excavations, the caretaker reinforced the Mi'kmaq's claim to that land. As such, his assertion of authority was an act of emplacement. He positioned himself as acting within the authority of the local Mi'kmaw community and the Crown to protect the integrity of the reserved land.

The caretaker's assertion of authority defined a new role for Mi'kmaq in Nova Scotia's archaeographic narrative. Until Erskine recorded this story, the archaeological literature had cast Mi'kmaq as living fossils, as the race that had driven the Eskimos northward, or as the direct descendants of the people who created features such as shell middens.[14] In other words, Mi'kmaq were associated with the past. The caretaker of Maligomish disrupted this narrative because he intervened in the contemporary process of constructing the midden as an object for archaeological study.

1933

After their removal from sites such as the Maligomish shell midden, archaeological artifacts may circulate along many different paths. If they are the result of looting, the artifacts may get traded on the illegal antiquities market. If they are excavated by weekend treasure-seekers working without a permit, they may end up in a personal collection adorning a mantel or decorating a lawn. If they are excavated by a qualified archaeologist holding a permit to excavate, those artifacts most likely move to a university, museum, or government-sponsored facility where they are (ideally) curated and stored in perpetuity. Increasingly in North America, if materials are excavated on lands either owned by or reserved for indigenous peoples, the responsibility for curation and interpretation is being undertaken by qualified individuals and organizations within those communities (see Atalay 2008; Ferguson 1996; Isaac 2007; Phillips and Allen 2005).[15] In the early twentieth century, the artifacts excavated in the Maligomish midden by Harlan Smith and John Erskine followed a path out of the community and into federal and provincial museums where they remain to this day.[16]

But archaeologists are not the only vehicles for transferring artifacts to museum collections. Indeed, after Smith and Wintemberg's (1929) excavations in the early twentieth century, there was very little archaeological research conducted in Nova Scotia until John Erskine's work in the 1950s and 1960s; yet, hundreds of archaeological artifacts made their way into the provincial museum's collection. Some were opportunistic finds collected by farmers from their

FIGURE 6. Peter Wilmot at the Millbrook reserve in 1932. Photograph taken by Clara Dennis. P113/76.180.588/N-14,811. Reproduced with permission from the Nova Scotia Museum.

ploughed fields. Others were sold or donated to the museum after having been in a personal collection for several years. And a small but significant portion of archaeological artifacts acquired by the provincial museum in the first half of the twentieth century were purchased from Mi'kmaw collectors, including Jerry Lonecloud, Abraham Paul, and Charlie Wilmot.[17] Using details recorded in the Nova Scotia Museum's accession ledgers, and archival data from archaeological investigations, it is possible to trace the movements of these Mi'kmaq as they collected and sold artifacts—and, hence, to explore another moment of intersection between the archaeological and Mi'kmaw narratives of places like Maligomish.[18]

I am particularly interested in Charlie Wilmot because of his close ties to the Pictou Landing First Nation. I had first heard Charlie Wilmot's name in my many conversations with Katalin Thomas, the Mi'kmaw elder who was my coresearcher on our road trip to Pugwash. Katalin counted Charlie and his father, Peter Wilmot, among her relations. Peter had been the chief of the Pictou Landing First Nation in the late nineteenth and early twentieth centuries. He later moved to what would become the Millbrook First Nation near Truro, Nova Scotia, located approximately eighty kilometers southwest of Pictou Landing (see fig. 6).

I next encountered Charlie as I examined the Nova Scotia Museum's artifacts and archival records associated with John Erskine's excavations on Maligomish. While I was examining Erskine's collection, the curator who was assisting me, Steve Powell, mentioned that there were other artifacts from Maligomish at the Nova Scotia Museum, most of which had been purchased from Charlie Wilmot. Recalling Wilmot's name from my conversations with Katalin, my curiosity was piqued. I asked if Mr. Wilmot had sold artifacts from other middens. Steve consulted the museum's database and very graciously generated a list that included the types of artifacts, the locations from where Charlie collected them, and their accession numbers. With the accession numbers, it was possible to consult the original accession ledgers, which, at the time of Wilmot's collecting, were kept by the Nova Scotia Museum's first full-time curator, Harry Piers. The accession ledgers are a wealth of ethnographic detail about the artifacts that Piers acquired, including detailed drawings and—in the case of items collected from Mi'kmaq—biographical and genealogical information about the collector. In his annual report for 1933 to 1934, Piers copied his entry for this lot of artifacts from the accession ledger: "76 stone implements obtained by Charles Wilmot in Sept. 1934, in another ancient Indian shell-heap on a bank 500 ft. from the shore, and 100 yds. or so south of the R.C. Chapel, on the southeast side, near the northeast end, of Indian Island, Merigomish Harbour, Pict. Co." (Province of Nova Scotia [Piers, H.] 1935, 32).

By focusing on these details, it was possible to trace some of Charlie Wilmot's movements. Like his father, Peter, Charlie Wilmot was born at Pictou Landing, but by the time he was selling artifacts to Piers in the 1930s, he was living at the Millbrook First Nation. Piers recorded that Charlie married Charlotte Paul, who was the daughter of Matthew Paul, also from Pictou Landing (see fig. 7). Mrs. Wilmot had sold several artifacts to Harry Piers for the Nova Scotia Museum's ethnology collection (see Province of Nova Scotia [Piers, H.] 1933, 1934). The first time that Charlie Wilmot's name appears as the source of archaeological artifacts sold to the museum is in December 1933. Between August 1934 and January 1937, Wilmot sold fourteen lots of archaeological artifacts to the museum. When Harry Piers recorded these transactions in the accession ledgers, he noted details that provide insight into Wilmot's travels and the frequency of his collecting (see table 1). The locations were concentrated in northeastern Nova Scotia, closer to the Pictou Landing First Nation than Wilmot's home of Millbrook.[19] He sold two lots of artifacts that he collected from sites at the mouth of North River, near Millbrook. However, Wilmot collected the majority of his artifacts from sites located comparatively far from the home that Piers recorded in his ledgers. Some artifacts were from places as far away as Bayfield Road and Pomquet Harbour in Antigonish County, approximately 135 kilometers northeast of Millbrook. Most, however, were from locations around Pictou County (see fig. 8). Of the

Acc. No. **8690.**

FIGURE 7. Charlie Wilmot and his wife, Charlotte, on the Millbrook Reserve, circa 1936. P113/37.41/10,641. Reproduced with permission from the Nova Scotia Museum.

Pictou County sites, only the shell midden on Maligomish and the collection sites at Pictou Landing were on land reserved for the Mi'kmaq. The other sites—on Barney's Point at the east end of Merigomish Harbour, and several points along Pictou Harbour—were located outside of Mi'kmaw reserves.[20] All of the sites that Wilmot visited have in common their proximity to Mi'kmaw communities and to rail lines, which Charlie Wilmot may have used to travel throughout northeastern Nova Scotia.[21]

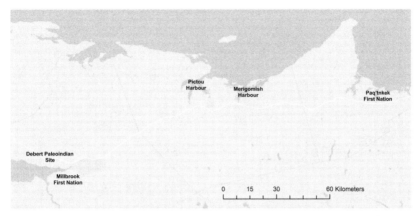

FIGURE 8. Map of northeastern Nova Scotia indicating Charlie Wilmot's artifact collecting areas. Map created by the author.

There are archaeological sites closer to Wilmot's home of Millbrook, including one of the most famous in North America, the Debert Paleoindian site, located a mere fifteen kilometers from Millbrook. Yet Wilmot collected few artifacts in this archaeologically rich area of the province. It is possible that his kin relationships in Pictou Landing—or a childhood familiarity with the locations of archaeological sites—were strong draws to the area. Katalin, the Pictou Landing elder who counted Charlie among her relations, recalled seeing him on Maligomish during the annual mission celebrating St. Anne's Day.

The information contained in the accession ledgers allows us not only to trace spatial locations but also to observe some temporal patterns in Wilmot's collecting. For example, Piers distinguishes in the accession ledgers the difference between the date of collection (in other words, the date when Charlie Wilmot visited the archaeological sites) and the date of accession (meaning the date that Piers received the item) (see table 1). The ten lithic tools belonging to lot 7931, for example, were collected during the first week of September 1934 and sold to the museum on September 17. Most of the other accessions appear to have had a comparable time lag of two to three weeks and came to Halifax via Henry Cruikshank, a Truro taxidermist and frequent vendor to the Nova Scotia Museum. Most of Wilmot's sales, then, did not require him to travel the ninety kilometers from Millbrook to Halifax. Between June and August 1935, Charlie collected four lots of artifacts from sites in Merigomish Harbour. What is unclear from the accession ledgers is whether Charlie traveled from Millbrook to Pictou County for each of these collecting episodes, or whether Charlie was staying in the area, perhaps at Pictou Landing or on Maligomish, during the summer of 1935. What is clear is that Charlie

Table 1. Summary of the artifacts collected by Charlie Wilmot and sold to the Nova Scotia Museum between 1934 and 1937. The information presented in this table was recorded from the Nova Scotia Museum accession ledgers kept by former curator Harry Piers. The figures appearing in the last column have been corrected for inflation to the year 2016 using the Bank of Canada's inflation calculator (http://www.bankofcanada.ca/rates/related/inflation-calculator/; last accessed July 18, 2016).

Accession Number	County	Site	Collection Date	Accession Date	Amount Paid	Corrected for Inflation
34.112–34.155	Pictou	Pig Island	Aug. 10, 1934	Aug. 24, 1934	$16.00	$286.22
34.156–34.162	Colchester	Savage Island (near Truro)				
34.1	Pictou	Maligomish	First week of Sept. 1934	Sept. 17, 1934	$23.00	$411.44
34.177–34.187	Pictou	Rustico Beach				
34.218–34.222	Pictou	Brown's Point	Oct. 1934	Oct. 16, 1934	$19.00	$339.89
34.223	Pictou	King's Head				
34.224	Pictou	Maligomish				
35.94	Pictou	Barney's Point	early June 1935	June 22, 1935	$28.00	$500.89
35.95–35.104	Pictou	Maligomish	July 1935	July 24, 1935	$15.00	$268.33
35.131–35.136	Pictou	Pig Island	July 1935	Aug. 3, 1935	$35.00	$626.11
35.145–35.153	Pictou	Quarry Island	Aug. 1935	Sept. 3, 1935	$20.00	$357.78
35.154	Pictou	Olding Island				
35.181	Antigonish	Close to chapel at Pomquet Harbour	Sept. 1935	Oct. 12, 1935	None recorded	N/A
35.256–35.261	Antigonish	Bayfield Road				
35.262	Pictou	Brown's Point	April 1936	May 8, 1936	None recorded	N/A
36.93–36.94; 36.102	Pictou	Big Island	Aug. 2, 1936	Aug. 21, 1936	$0.75	$13.23
36.186–36.187	Pictou	Big Island	Aug. 1936	Aug. 28, 1936	None recorded	N/A
36.194	Pictou	Abercrombie Point	Summer 1936	July 10, 1936	$15.00	$264.66
36.244–36.250	Pictou	Lighthouse Beach	Oct. 1936	Jan. 11, 1937	None recorded	N/A
37.6–37.12	Pictou	Smash'em Head	May 1937	June 10, 1937	None recorded	N/A
37.136–37.137	Pictou	Christie's Point				
37.138						
TOTAL					$171.75	$3,068.55

collected most of his artifacts between the months of May and October, when these mostly coastal sites were free of ice and snow.

Charlie Wilmot's collecting patterns throughout northeastern Nova Scotia represent one of the impermanent but recurring practices that have emplaced Mi'kmaq on Maligomish and at several other locations in the region. Wilmot emplaced himself at Maligomish, and at sites outside of Mi'kmaw reserves, when he moved great distances to places that he knew well through his kin relationships. As the Nova Scotia Museum's accession ledgers indicate, Wilmot returned to some of these collecting sites, including Maligomish, over the three years that he sold artifacts to the museum. He was, in effect, staking a claim to these sites—not through the permanent settlement or use of them, but by using such places persistently and innovatively.

Wilmot's collecting may have been motivated by the amount of money he was able to earn. Between 1934 and 1937, he was paid at least $171.75 for the archaeological artifacts he collected and more for the ethnological artifacts that he and his wife, Charlotte, manufactured and sold to the museum. When this amount is adjusted for inflation, Wilmot was paid at least $3,068.55 in 2016 Canadian dollars, a small proportion of the overall cost of living, but significant when compared to monies that could be earned from the manufacture of ax handles, baskets, and other crafts sought by non-Mi'kmaq. Indeed, the annual reports from the Department of Indian Affairs and census data from the Canadian federal government indicate that the per capita annual Mi'kmaw income for this period was $19.26 (Gonzalez 1981, 142). Yet, although Wilmot was supplying a demand for a non-Mi'kmaw market, he was not bound by that market's mode of production. Artifact collecting was an economy whose relations of production very much favored Mi'kmaq, whose movements across the land and knowledge of ancestral Mi'kmaw places made them familiar with the likely areas for archaeological sites. As Tanner (1979) and others who work on indigenous-settler economies have demonstrated, the indigenous participants exercised a great deal of flexibility in how and when they supplied demand.[22] The artifact trade was part of a broader suite of mobile activities that contributed toward Mi'kmaw subsistence in the twentieth century (see Gonzalez 1981).[23] Hunting, fishing, gathering, craft manufacture and sale, door-to-door sales, and wage labor were all activities that emplaced Mi'kmaq as they moved across their ancestral lands and waters.

2008

While Charlie Wilmot and other Mi'kmaw collectors were certainly contributing to the growth of the Nova Scotia Museum's archaeological collections, we would not classify their participation in the artifact trade as archaeological fieldwork. Indeed, any disturbance of an archaeological site without a government-issued permit is now illegal in Nova Scotia.[24] The 2008 field seasons on Maligomish marked a unique moment of intersection between the archaeological and local Mi'kmaw narratives of the Maligomish midden for two reasons. First, members of the Pictou Landing First Nation were involved in planning the project. Through a series of community meetings—and through speaking to community members individually—we were able to negotiate a research plan that would minimize disturbance of the island. The plan allowed my field crew and me to conduct subsurface testing only in the shell midden. Other possible archaeological features on the island would be measured, mapped, described, and photographed, but they would not be excavated. Thus, like the caretaker who appears to have banished Smith from Maligomish in 1914, the Mi'kmaq of Pictou Landing were asserting their right to determine whether an archaeological research project would happen at all, and, perhaps more significantly, how that research would be conducted.[25]

The 2008 field seasons were also unique because they involved local Mi'kmaq in conducting the actual surveys and excavations. And more than just serving as "shovel bums," my field assistants, Mary Irene Nicholas and Edie Nicholas, helped to shape the archaeological fieldwork as it evolved. For example, as we began our work, new concerns were raised over its potentially negative impacts. Mary Irene Nicholas was uneasy that our measuring, digging, and recording might have been disturbing the spirits that dwell at the island. She suggested that we conduct the *pekitdne'man* or sweet grass ceremony each morning before we began our work (see Murdena Marshall n.d.). The sweet grass ceremony is commonly performed at the commencement of many Mi'kmaw events in order to purify those gathered. On Maligomish, we burned braids of sweet grass, some of which I had gathered with the help of other community members the previous summer. Mary Irene instructed our field crew to wave the burning braids toward our heads, hearts, and bodies while asking the spirits on Maligomish to keep our minds and hearts open and thanking them for allowing us to work on the island and keeping us safe. Mary Irene also suggested offering tobacco to the spirits on the island. Tobacco is used by many indigenous peoples in North America as an offering of respect. It may be offered to elders in appreciation of their knowledge, to animals for having offered themselves in a hunt, or, in our case, to the spirits on Maligomish (see Johnson 2007; Sunshine 2007). We offered tobacco by sprinkling it on the ground surrounding us.

In conducting these rituals, we were not only acknowledging the presence of the nonhuman (and noncorporeal) subjects on Maligomish, but also respecting their efficacy to do work in the corporeal world. This respect manifested in choices we made about how and where to excavate the shell midden. For example, we planned our test pits and excavation units to avoid the several trees that were growing in the midden. Although this decision might have obscured the profiles of the test unit, the potential threat to the trees seemed to outweigh any possible loss of archaeological information.

Long after the excavations were completed, I attempted to balance the observation and interpretation of sufficient archaeological information from the Maligomish midden with the imperative to respect the sacredness that most community members attributed to the island. Some residents of the Pictou Landing First Nation were concerned about what would happen to the materials that were removed from the shell midden. While most community members had eventually accepted the excavations, many were concerned that the artifacts would be separated from the community. My field assistants and I held periodic community meetings to update members of the Pictou Landing First Nation about our work on Maligomish. I explained that some materials would have to be removed in order to conduct postfield analyses at laboratories that had the necessary facilities. I planned to process soil samples at the paleoethnobotany laboratory at the Memorial University of Newfoundland in St. John's, and at the Bedford Institute of Oceanography in Dartmouth, Nova Scotia. I also planned to submit charcoal and shell samples for radiocarbon dating to the Accelerated Mass Spectrometry Laboratory Group at the University of Arizona. For some community members, the distance from Maligomish that these materials would be traveling made a difference in their level of concern. Dartmouth and St. John's were more tolerable than removing the materials to the United States.

To alleviate some of these concerns, something of a compromise was reached on the ultimate destination of the excavated materials. Although the requirements of the permits under which I conducted my fieldwork on Maligomish required me to deposit the recovered artifacts with the Nova Scotia Museum, members of the museum staff, the Pictou Landing Chief and Council, the Confederacy of Mainland Mi'kmaq, and I worked together to devise an alternative solution that would allow the artifacts to be stored properly and securely while still keeping them within the Mi'kmaw community. The Pictou Landing Chief and Council signed a band resolution in which they requested that the Nova Scotia Museum accept the collection as a transfer and store it until an appropriate Mi'kmaw facility became available.[26] This resolution stipulated the conditions of the transfer, including those for accessing the collection while in storage at the Nova Scotia Museum and the mechanism for transferring the collection back to the Mi'kmaw community. The Nova Scotia

Museum agreed to accept the collection as a temporary transfer and to store it in trust for the Pictou Landing First Nation. Negotiating this arrangement was important not only for maintaining my working relationship with the Pictou Landing First Nation but also for establishing the first steps toward breaking the mold of how Mi'kmaw communities—and the predominately non-Mi'kmaw heritage sector in Nova Scotia—interact.

Indeed, one of my objectives for the research was to compensate for the loss of artifacts and knowledge that the Mi'kmaq of northeastern Nova Scotia experienced as a result of previous archaeological fieldwork—a loss amplified by the federal government's decision in 2012 to close several regional storage facilities operated by Parks Canada and to consolidate its archaeological collections in Ottawa.[27] Archaeological research conducted in First Nations communities has often resulted in artifacts being removed from these communities, often without their knowledge. The postfield research involved not only preliminary analyses of the excavated materials but also the inventorying of artifacts, notes, and publications associated with past projects so that Pictou Landing First Nation members would know where the remains of their past have been disseminated. While much information about materials from the Merigomish area exists, it is scattered in annual reports and museum publications and archives, which can be difficult for individuals who are unaffiliated with a university or research institution to access. This "gray literature" often contains details that remain unknown to local communities. For example, the archaeological collections from Merigomish Harbour collected by Harlan Smith, which are now housed at the Canadian Museum of History, include eleven fragmented or complete human bone and tooth remains.

The year 2008 marked not only an intersection between Mi'kmaw and non-Mi'kmaw archaeological perspectives of the Maligomish midden but also a moment in which several branches in the archaeological genealogy of Maligomish converged. Just as Erskine was haunted by Smith, whose digging had "so thoroughly ruined" the camp sites he claimed to have uncovered, our field crew was haunted by Erskine, whose backfilled units encroached upon our carefully mapped and stratigraphically excavated site. The year 2008 was also a moment that continued the legacy of Mi'kmaw intervention on the archaeology of Maligomish. When members of the Pictou Landing First Nation expressed their concerns about the consequences of the excavation and postexcavation analyses—and when Mary Irene suggested performing a daily *pekitdne'man*—they were joining Charlie Wilmot and the Mi'kmaw caretaker of Smith's era in asserting their authority on Maligomish.

In doing so, these Mi'kmaq have blurred the categories "Mi'kmaq" and "archaeologist." While there are many thriving indigenous-led archaeological programs across North America and in other settler colonies, there remains an underlying assumption that archaeologists are nonindigenous outsiders who come to study the "Other's" past. Mary Irene and Edie defied this dichotomization by training and working as archaeologists and, furthermore, helping to set the agenda for how that archaeology would be performed—at times in ways that defied the ideal prescriptions for systematic archaeological fieldwork. Thus, a century after Harlan Smith had made the Mi'kmaq of northeastern Nova Scotia and their ancestors objects of archaeological study, the descendants of those Mi'kmaq were becoming the producers of new archaeological knowledge.[28]

These moments also became connected as subsequent research at the Canadian Museum of History, Library and Archives Canada, and the Nova Scotia Museum began to circulate some of the previously constructed archaeological knowledge back to the community. This knowledge included the names and images of Mi'kmaq whom Smith had photographed on Maligomish while conducting his fieldwork in 1914. It also included the presence of human remains now housed in the Canadian Museum of History's storage facilities in Gatineau, Québec. This information flowed back to the community through public meetings and a short report written specifically for the Pictou Landing First Nation that provided a sample of images, catalog entries, and archival documents (see Lelièvre 2014). This redirection of knowledge is simply that. Members of the Pictou Landing First Nation may now know where the remains of their ancestors are located, but those remains continue to be—in the words of Maori scholar Linda Tuhiwai Smith (1999, 11)—"imprisoned" in the display and storage cases of museums far from their original resting places in Merigomish Harbour.

Emplacing Impermanence

By tracing the movements of people, objects, and knowledge to and from the shell midden, we add to our understanding of Maligomish as a place that embodies mobility. The pre-contact contents of the midden evidence the availability of seasonal resources that attracted Mi'kmaq to Merigomish Harbour. They also suggest a possible environmental shift that may have made the harbor no longer hospitable for oyster and, perhaps, might explain the thousand-year gap that currently exists in the archaeological record of the Maligomish midden. And yet the gap in the archaeological record may not necessarily mean a gap in human occupation of Maligomish, as radiocarbon dates from sites along the Northumberland Strait indicate activity during this period.[29] Nevertheless, the evidence for a resumption of activity on Maligomish circa 500 BP suggests that knowledge of the island and its resources survived or was revived even in the absence of archaeological evidence of continued occupation. Indeed, Erskine reported from Bear River that in the nineteenth-century Mi'kmaq had been observed camping on the pre-contact site he was investigating (Erskine 1958, 14). Such persistent practices are further evidence of the Mi'kmaq's faith in their rights to access and use their traditional lands—especially those lands outside of their reserves— and not only for traditional purposes. These repeat visits demonstrate the impermanent but recurring nature of many Mi'kmaw practices.

In the post-contact period, the archaeographic and oral-historical record of Maligomish provides another perspective on the impermanent but recurring practices that contribute to the emplacement of Mi'kmaq on Maligomish. Archaeological fieldwork is one such practice—and one engaged not only by non-Mi'kmaw, academically trained archaeologists. George Patterson, William Wintemberg, Harlan Smith, John Erskine, and I were all non-Mi'kmaq engaged in archaeological fieldwork who traveled from places of varying distances to work temporarily on the island. In each of the three moments discussed in this chapter, Mi'kmaq have influenced the production of archaeological knowledge. And while Charlie Wilmot's collecting cannot be considered as "archaeology" per se, his work has contributed to our current understanding of the location and distribution of pre-contact Mi'kmaw places. Moreover, his travels to such places not only demonstrate his right to access the land but also suggest the longevity of the knowledge that some Mi'kmaq had regarding the indigenous association with these places—knowledge that did not disappear with the arrival of European settlers.

3

Settled but Not Sedentary

MI'KMAW DWELLING ON MALIGOMISH AND BEYOND

Assimilating Maligomish

FOR MOST OF ITS POST-CONTACT HISTORY, Maligomish has been a site where both the Church and the Crown have attempted various strategies to assimilate the Mi'kmaq by "civilizing" them. In the mid-nineteenth century, Maligomish was briefly caught up in the efforts to transform the Mi'kmaq into sedentary farmers. It was considered as a possible site for permanent settlement until James Dawson finally visited the island in June 1842 and discovered it was too small for this purpose (see LAC 1842c). The island later became a site where Catholic priests—who often also served as Indian agents—preached the benefits of "progress" (see chapter 4, this volume). In the twenty-first century, Maligomish has been the site of a new manifestation of the sedentarist ideology, this time in the form of a state effort to fix in time and space the island's relatively impermanent cabins. In April 2008, Mary Irene Nicholas and I assisted two geographical information systems (GIS) specialists from the Confederacy of Mainland Mi'kmaq, who came to Maligomish to record the geospatial locations of all the island's buildings. They were collecting these data for the province of Nova Scotia, which was planning to use the geospatial information to assign a civic number to each building on Maligomish.[1] Unlike the nineteenth-century efforts to settle Mi'kmaq on reserved lands that they would farm, or the mid-twentieth-century centralization policy to move all Nova Scotia Mi'kmaq into two large reserves, the civic numbering project on Maligomish did not aim to sedentize subjects. The attempt to assign civic numbers to the cabins—and the addition of this spatial information to provincial databases—effectively fixed these buildings in time and space, thus making them legible.[2]

The attempt to make the camps on Maligomish legible throws into sharp relief the quotidian ways in which that place is actually created and used by the people who dwell there. The underlying assumption of the civic number-ing project was that the buildings on Maligomish could be commensurated with those on other Mi'kmaw reserves and in non-Mi'kmaw communities—that they are permanent structures, built on subterranean foundations, and associated with a discrete parcel of land that had been surveyed and demar-cated by boundary lines. Yet the Maligomish camps are very different from their mainland counterparts. For example, the styles of houses on the main reserve at Pictou Landing—and other Mi'kmaw communities in Nova Sco-tia—tend to be not unlike those outside reserves. Many are prefabricated, split-story or bungalow designs with vinyl siding. These types of houses are especially common in the recently expanded sections of the main reserve at Pictou Landing. In contrast, the styles of camps on Maligomish are more di-verse. Although it is federal Crown land, the Maligomish reserve does not appear to be subject to the same federal guidelines for construction that dic-tate architectural design on more permanently occupied reserves such as Pic-tou Landing. Neither the federal government nor the local bands appear to regiment construction on reserved lands such as Maligomish and Potlotek (Chapel Island) in Cape Breton, which are occupied impermanently.[3] Conse-quently, there are no property divisions, no zoning regulations, and—at least in the case of Maligomish—no band-level guidelines on how, when, or where to build camps. The individuals and families who build on Maligomish make these decisions. However, while there are no planning ordinances for the is-land, the spatial patterning of cabins is not haphazard. Many families con-struct their camps in areas of the island long associated with their ancestors' settlement. The lack of regulation on Maligomish means that owners are very flexible in how, when, and where they construct, occupy, and abandon their camps, making futile the attempt to freeze these impermanent buildings in space by assigning them civic numbers.

Flexibility and impermanence are two of the qualities of movement that are embodied in the camps on Maligomish. My conception of embodiment is influenced by Weiss (1996), Keane (2003), and especially Munn (1986). These authors understand material objects—including constructed dwell-ings—to be not only reflective of the social values of a community but also productive of them. Munn uses Peircean semiotics to explain how certain objects in the Gawan world exhibit within themselves qualities of positive or negative values that do work in the social world (1986, 16–17). On Gawa and its neighboring islands, the positive values of objects such as canoes (e.g., speed and lightness) serve to increase what Munn describes as "intersubjective spacetime," which she defines as "a spacetime of self-other relationships formed in and through acts and practices" (1986, 9). In his study of the everyday practices of the Haya in northwestern Tanzania, Weiss describes Haya homes as "'representations' or 'embodiments' of sociocultural processes" (1996, 30). He draws on Marx ([1867] 1906) and Mauss ([1925] 2002), writing that these authors "conceptualized the problem of objects in terms of the capacity of certain objects to condense within themselves the qualities that are characteristic of their wider social worlds" (Weiss 1996, 9). Building on Munn, Keane writes that in a semiotic approach to material objects, "The goal is to open up social analysis to the historicity and social power of material things without reducing them either to being only vehicles of meaning, on the one hand, or ultimate determinants, on the other" (2003, 411). In other words, objects are neither simply symbols of social meaning, nor tools for directing social action; they operate in a complex semiotic system that changes with social and historical contexts. Like the shell midden discussed in chapter 2, these camps embody mobility because they are constitutive of the practices, perceptions, and conceptions of movement that work to emplace Mi'kmaq on the island. They are also productive of social relationships on Maligomish. While their construction and location may be impermanent, the camps' roles in the shaping of the Mi'kmaw social world—roles that can be traced through the post-contact period—make them important objects in the embedding of Mi'kmaq on Maligomish.

The current chapter analyzes the Maligomish camps at two spatial scales. The first is the scale of the building itself. I place the contemporary Maligomish camps in historical context by offering an overview of Mi'kmaw dwellings in the post-contact period and the settler state's attempted interventions on them. It considers the history of Mi'kmaw dwellings both on and off reserved lands. The impermanent and dynamic nature of Mi'kmaw dwellings has been evident not only in the camps but also in other Mi'kmaw dwelling types such as wigwams—whose materials and construction techniques evolved over time—and "tar-paper shacks," which were used in the late nineteenth through mid-twentieth centuries on Maligomish and elsewhere. The chapter then transitions from a discussion of the history of Mi'kmaw dwellings throughout Mi'kma'ki to a focused description of the camps on Maligomish. I discuss the surface survey conducted on Maligomish during the 2007 and 2008 field seasons and how the Maligomish camps became the primary object of observation. I then describe the various phases in the life history of a typical camp, including its construction, layout, use, abandonment, and eventual destruction. The second scale of analysis considers the distribution of camps across the island in these different phases. Considered together, the individual camps and their spatial distribution demonstrate the fluid nature of settlement on Maligomish.

Indeed, in demonstrating how the camps and their distribution embody impermanence and dynamism, the current chapter makes an argument for settlement without sedentism. In its recent history, few Mi'kmaq have lived permanently on Maligomish. Yet the historical and archaeological evidence, combined with oral history data, suggests that the island has been used year-round on an impermanent basis, at least within the living memory of the Mi'kmaq at Pictou Landing. Despite the impermanent nature of its occupation, settlement patterns related to intergenerational kin and intercommunity ties are visible on the island. As such, Maligomish has endured as a Mi'kmaw place for centuries through the Mi'kmaq's persistent but temporary settlement of the island.

Constructing Houses, Constructing Subjects

The construction and use of Mi'kmaw dwellings has been of interest to non-Mi'kmaw observers since the earliest European explorers visited eastern Canada.[4] Nicholas Denys described the Mi'kmaw *cabanne* in his 1672 description of Acadia. He reported the gendered division of labor in relation to camp construction and transportation as Mi'kmaw communities moved across the landscape. Mi'kmaw wives and daughters carried the coverings of the *cabanne* and everything else, while the husbands and sons carried nothing. Mi'kmaq constructed a *cabanne* when they arrived at a new location. Denys differentiated between smaller, round cabins, which were designed for about ten to twelve people, and larger, longer wigwams for about double that number (Denys 1672, 368–70). Nietfeld speculated that these larger structures might have been associated with chiefs (1981, 396). In his 1748 survey of Nova Scotia, Surveyor General Charles Morris provided a detailed description of the construction of a wigwam, which he noted could be completed in "three or four hours": "They are Poles stuck one end in the ground and encompass 8 feet square. They are fastened in the Centre being bent archwise, and the whole covered with bark. Their Fire place is in the middle and a Little whole [*sic*] made for a Door, or else in this manner a threshold of about 6 feet high, the back threshold is Less, are stuck in the ground and are joined by 4 Poles on the Top and this is covered on the Top and three of the sides the Front being left open before which they make a fire in the open air" (LAC 1748).

Morris suggested that the uniformity of the design and construction facilitated the Mi'kmaq's movements for hunting, fishing, and fowling: "[I]t is no difficulty with them to shift their Habitations when they please" (LAC 1748). Although he does not provide descriptions, Titus Smith notes that he encountered both "winter" and "summer" camps during his tour of the eastern interior of mainland Nova Scotia in June 1801 (see NSA 1801–1802a, 1801–1802b). Some of the Mi'kmaw words for the materials used in constructing dwellings—including *masgwi* (white birch bark), *nimnoqn* (birch), *pqaw* (spruce bark), and *stoqn* (fir branches)—are grammatically animate, conveying a sense that the buildings themselves are dynamic and alive.[5] The animacy of Mi'kmaw dwellings is also suggested in the Mi'kmaw story of an encounter in the forest with a stranger who carries a multiroom wigwam on his head.[6]

In the mid-nineteenth century, Mi'kmaw dwellings shifted from being objects of curiosity to being sites of state and settler intervention in the efforts to sedentize Mi'kmaq. Contemporary sources, such as the addresses to the Nova Scotian Institute of Science and photographs available through the Nova Scotia Museum's Mi'kmaq [*sic*] Portraits Collection,[7] provide some indication of Mi'kmaw dwellings during this period. As discussed in chapter 1, the nineteenth-century project to transform the Mi'kmaq from mobile "savagery" to sedentary "civilization" used material means to achieve ideological ends. One such material means was to move Mi'kmaq out of portable dwellings such as wigwams and into permanent houses built on the recently established reserves around the province. But this material objective would not be successful without also reshaping Mi'kmaw consciousness—in other words, not only making the Mi'kmaq aware of the differences between their ways and those of the European settlers, but also convincing them of the deficiencies of the former and the benefits of the latter.[8] As such, moving Mi'kmaq into permanent dwellings was insufficient for "civilizing" them; Mi'kmaq also had to develop—in the words of physician and gentleman scientist J. Bernard Gilpin—"a sense of the necessity of all these wants" (1877, 280).

The "civilizing" ideology manifested in the settlers' encouragement of permanent Mi'kmaw dwelling and their attempts to discipline the Mi'kmaw body (*sensu* Foucault 1977).[9] In his 1877 address to the Nova Scotian Institute of Science, Gilpin suggested that the Mi'kmaq living at the St. Francis Xavier reserve along the Bay of Fundy showed promise of soon emulating the dwelling practices of European, nuclear families. He described the reserve as consisting of twenty-five families, each residing "in its own house" (1877, 279). These houses "were small frame ones, with glazed windows, shingled, and each with a porch. Inside they had good floors, chimney, cook-stove, table, but few chairs, and walls not plaistered [*sic*], though some were papered with *Illustrated London News*. A porch and single room formed the lower floor, but there was an upper loft, approached by a ladder, which formed sleeping apartments" (Gilpin 1877, 279). Gilpin commented that although Mi'kmaq had permanent winter houses, not all of the occupants slept in beds, but "they at least sleep on floors of wood during the cold winter, instead of on the hard ground covered by spruce bushes" (Gilpin 1877, 272).[10] He later noted that the Mi'kmaq in this community had separate sleeping rooms (1877, 280), suggesting a transformation of the Mi'kmaw worldview based on collectivity to a European worldview focused on the individual. Encouraging the Mi'kmaq to identify themselves as individuals, rather than a collective nation, was a broader objective of the nineteenth-century "civilizing" project, as Gilpin declared: "It is evident that the time has long passed to consider them as a nation, in approaching them for their good. The sooner all national feeling, language and traditions are gone the better. They must be approached as individual men and women" (Gilpin 1877, 275).[11] From the perspective of the European settlers who encouraged permanent Mi'kmaw dwelling, communities such as the St. Francis Xavier reserve served two purposes: First, they eased the management of the Mi'kmaq by keeping them fixed in one location. Second, they facilitated the assimilation of the Mi'kmaq into settler society by transforming their bodily practices.

Yet, if living in these permanent dwellings affected Mi'kmaw comportment, it had little success in inspiring Mi'kmaw sedentism. In the same address to the Nova Scotian Institute of Science, Gilpin conceded that while Mi'kmaq used their permanent houses in the winter months, their summer camps were "still as of old" (1877, 272). A generation later, Mi'kmaq continued their seasonal movements, as Harry Piers reported in his 1912 address to the Nova Scotian Institute of Science. He reported that "some of them cultivate a little land, having small houses on reservations but going into conical birch-bark wigwams or 'camps' as they are called, in the summer" (Piers 1912, 103). During his 1914 fieldwork in eastern Canada, Speck observed Mi'kmaw dwelling construction. The photograph of the wigwam that appears in Speck's monograph is covered in birch bark; however, Speck noted that wigwams were occasionally covered in tar paper because of the scarcity of bark in Nova Scotia (Speck 1922, 114).[12]

The images in the Mi'kmaq [sic] Portraits Collection indicate a variety of styles and materials used in the construction of Mi'kmaw dwellings in the late nineteenth and early twentieth centuries. Well into the twentieth century, variations of the conical, pyramid, and A-frame wigwam could be seen in Nova Scotia and elsewhere in eastern Canada, sometimes next to more permanent constructions, as seen in figure 9 (top). Wigwams were covered in birch bark, tar paper, or canvas. Similarly, more permanent cabins were made

FIGURE 9. Top: Portrait of Mi'kmaw group in front of cabin circa 1894, possibly from Lennox Island. Public Archives and Records Office of Prince Edward Island, Heritage Foundation of PEI Collection, Mitchell Neg. 7. Accession no. 3466/HF72.66.1.13. Photo no. P0001004. Reproduced with permission from the Public Archives and Records Office of Prince Edward Island. Bottom: Harry Piers (in the middle) at the summer camp of Henry and Susan Sack in September 1935. P113/ 36.118/N-7693. Reproduced with permission from the Nova Scotia Museum.

of rough-hewn logs or sawn planks. Some had frames that were covered in tar paper or filled in with lumber. Mi'kmaw hunting guides built lean-tos and lodges or raised canvas tents for their non-Mi'kmaw clients. As this variety of construction types demonstrates, although more permanent house types were being built as early as the mid-nineteenth century, their appearance did not mean the end of temporary living in wigwams and other impermanent dwellings.[13]

Indeed, as late as 1935, Piers was photographed with Henry and Susan Sack in front of their summer wigwam at Fox Point near Hubbards, Nova Scotia (see fig. 9 bottom). This Mi'kmaw couple was from the reserve of Shubenacadie, located ninety-five kilometers northeast of Hubbards. From the photograph, we see that the campsite is located close to the water and, presumably, within an easy distance to ash or maple trees from which to make splints for the baskets that they likely would have sold as a means to support themselves through the summer. The notes accompanying the photograph indicate that Piers purchased for the museum's collection the wood-splint fishing creel featured in the foreground of the photo. On this visit Piers also purchased a pair of moccasins from the Sacks. In the accession ledgers of the Nova Scotia Museum, Piers recorded the dimensions of the Sacks' wigwam. It measured approximately ten feet high and fifteen feet wide (~3×4.5 meters) with a three-foot (~1 meter) fire pit in the middle. The photograph also indicates that the skeleton of the wigwam was filled in with what appears to be rough-hewn boards, rather than birch bark. A similar construction was illustrated in the photographs taken on Maligomish by Harlan Smith in 1914.

Temporary Mi'kmaw dwellings in the first half of the twentieth century were not, however, strictly summer camps. For example, as described in the introduction, the camp that Olive Wilson described at Avondale Station was built by the Sylliboys over the winter of either 1945 to 1946 or 1946 to 1947. Olive recalled the Sylliboys' camp consisting of two structures, each built with rough-hewn logs and tar paper. Each building had two rooms that were created by hanging blankets. A woodstove heated the camp. Mrs. Wilson remembered there were three women, three or four men, and one child among the party. Test excavations at this site did not yield definitive evidence of a camp, but fragments of lumber, asphalt roofing materials, and tar paper were recovered from the area that most closely matched Mrs. Wilson's description (see Lelièvre 2005).

As the above examples illustrate, Mi'kmaw settlement patterns were still very mobile well into the twentieth century. Some Mi'kmaq who had permanent houses on reserves—such as the Sacks of Shubenacadie—left them in the summer months to live in temporary structures. Others, such as the Sylliboys, who lived outside of the main reserves, left their home communities even in the winter months. Still others, such as Louis Thom, had relatively permanent homes on reserves, but they left them and used temporary dwellings at various times of the year. The materials used to construct these temporary dwellings were those that were readily available—if the preferred birch bark was scarce, the lightweight, waterproof, and inexpensive alternative of tar paper would suffice. The resulting palimpsest of Mi'kmaw dwellings—temporary and permanent, wigwams and cabins, conical and linear, covered in birch bark or tar paper, and all copresent on the post-contact Mi'kmaw landscape—defies the nineteenth-century social-evolutionary logic underlying the sedentarist ideology. The Mi'kmaq did not step tidily from living in impermanent and portable dwellings to being fixed in one location in a permanent house. Movement and emplacement continued to define their settlement patterns into the mid-twentieth century, albeit in new and innovative ways.

The palimpsest of both temporary and more permanent housing has also been visible on Maligomish. A census taken by the Diocese of Antigonish in 1906 lists eight families living on Maligomish, with a total of twenty-seven people, suggesting a small but steady population (Diocese of Antigonish, 1906). On the one hand, accurate enumeration of Mi'kmaq in the nineteenth and early twentieth centuries was notoriously difficult given their movements and the practice of some Mi'kmaq of changing their names in different localities. Thus, it is impossible to conclude that these families considered themselves permanent residents of Maligomish. On the other hand, photographic and archaeological evidence of dwellings on Maligomish suggest that some of these buildings were constructed for more permanent occupation. For example, a photograph of the east end of Maligomish taken by Harlan Smith during his archaeological investigations around Merigomish Harbour in the summer of 1914 indicates several buildings, including the church, community hall, and three houses, which are visible at the northeast corner of the island (see fig. 10 top). The house closest to the shore has a north-facing gable window. This upper-story window is not a feature of most of the current cabins on Maligomish. It indicates an upper floor—perhaps a sleeping loft—for which the window provided light and ventilation. Such a feature may indicate that the building was one of the more permanent houses, similar to the style described by Gilpin at the St. Francis Xavier reserve.

Another example of more permanently constructed housing on Maligomish is the cement foundation of a structure located in this same northeastern corner of the island, which was recorded during our surface survey in the spring of 2008 (see fig. 10 bottom). Edie Nicholas and Dorie Sapier identified this foundation as belonging to the grandfather of Dorie's husband,

FIGURE 10. Top: Shell-heap on Donald MacDonald's farm, Olding Island, Pictou County, Nova Scotia, by Harlan I. Smith, 1914. Canadian Museum of History, 27728 (detail approved). The author has cropped the original image to highlight the eastern end of Maligomish. The arrow indicates an upper-story window. Reproduced with permission from the Canadian Museum of History. Bottom: Remains of foundation possibly belonging to the grandfather of Fred Sapier. Photograph taken by the author.

FIGURE 11. Tar-paper shack on Maligomish circa 1965. Still image captured from DVD transfer of Super 8 film. Original film shot by Noel Martin, Pictou Landing First Nation. Reproduced with permission from Noel Martin.

Fred, who was born in 1923. The 1906 census includes two Sapier households—those of Frank and Louis. Louis is listed as having one son. Frank is listed as having no children. Although the accuracy of the census is questionable, it is possible that one of these gentlemen was Fred's grandfather.

Figure 10 (top) shows houses whose structure and exterior walls appear to be constructed entirely of wood, but many Mi'kmaq and non-Mi'kmaq were at this time covering their homes in tar paper. When recalling their past experiences on Maligomish, many of the Mi'kmaq with whom I spoke focused on a period from the mid-twentieth century when Mi'kmaq from Pictou Landing and other reserves in Nova Scotia would travel to the island in late July and stay for a week or more during the St. Anne's mission. Some recalled constructing and living in a temporary "tar-paper shack." Tar-paper shacks were a popular form of early twentieth-century North American vernacular architecture among populations as diverse as homesteaders on the American prairie, workers in seasonal logging camps, and residents of the various Hoovervilles of the Great Depression. The tar-paper shacks on Maligomish were small dwellings, generally less than fifteen square meters.[14] Their structure included a wood frame over which tar paper is stretched. In figure 11, there appears to be an asphalt roof covering the shack. While conducting our surface survey of Maligomish, Mary Irene recalled her childhood visits to the island for the St. Anne's mission. She described the construction process consisting of building the frame of the shack, which stayed in place throughout the year, and covering the frame with fresh tar paper each year a family returned to the island (Lelièvre field notebook, vol. 15:70).[15]

An eight-millimeter film shot by Noel Martin in the mid-1960s captures some of the different dwelling types on Maligomish at that time, including tar-paper shacks and canvas tents. In the second half of the twentieth century, as accessing the island became easier, families began constructing more durable cabins that are now the dominant type of dwelling on Maligomish. But even as these more robust buildings became the most ubiquitous material object on the island, they have continued to embody qualities of impermanence and dynamism.

Surveying Maligomish

The analysis of the impermanence inherent in Maligomish's camps was possible because of the data that our research team gathered during a systematic surface survey to inventory any previously unidentified archaeological sites on the island.[16] This survey relied not only on the systematic and objective techniques of archaeology but also on the subjective local knowledge shared by my field assistants, Edie Nicholas and Mary Irene Nicholas. An archaeological survey is systematic if it is designed to cover a defined area of land in a rational, objective, and statistically significant way. As the island was only sixteen hectares, it was possible to conduct a survey of Maligomish with 100 percent coverage, meaning the entire island was studied. Archaeologists usually conduct surface surveys (also known as pedestrian surveys) by establishing a baseline and walking transects spaced at regular intervals across a defined study region. On Maligomish, Edie Nicholas and I established our first baseline along a north-south axis across the widest portion of the island near its west end. We spaced the transects at twenty-meter intervals and walked them following an east-west compass bearing. By the time we completed the survey, we had traced an imaginary Cartesian grid over Maligomish, rendering it neutral for scientific observation and recording (see fig. 12).[17]

We conducted the systematic survey in the autumn and spring to allow for better lines of sight through the dense hardwood stands on Maligomish. We examined the island's surface for remnants of campfires, foundations, building materials, mounds, and changes in the topography, vegetation, or soil that might indicate an archaeological site. During the first few days of survey, it

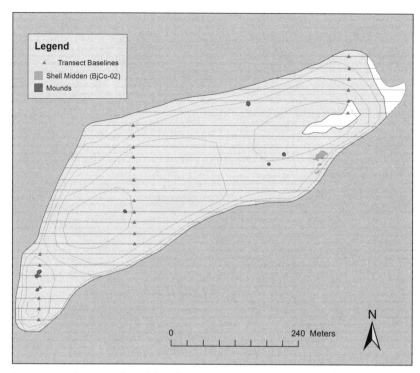

FIGURE 12. Map of Maligomish indicating the 2007 survey transect baselines and the major features identified. Geospatial data courtesy of Technical Services, Confederacy of Mainland Mi'kmaq. Map created by the author.

became clear that there were likely going to be few archaeological features to record beyond the earth mounds that many Mi'kmaq of the Pictou Landing First Nation believe to be burials. However, we decided to use the systematic survey as an opportunity to record the most ubiquitous cultural feature of the island—the cabins. Generally, the cabin is the principal structure of a camp, which also includes features such as a fire pit, the occasional storage building, and an outhouse. We used the GPS units to record the Universal Transverse Mercator (UTM) coordinates of the cabins. We also noted some of the features and objects associated with the camps, including picnic tables, chairs, the occasional canoe, and children's toys left behind from the previous summer.

We completed this systematic inventory of the Maligomish camps in May 2008. The data we recorded allowed for the creation of a map, which indicated the locations of these camps across the island (see fig. 13).[18] In a typical archaeological survey of a landscape occupied centuries or millennia ago, it may be impossible to connect the artifacts and features recorded to the people

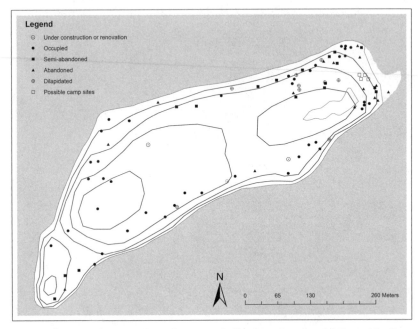

FIGURE 13. Map showing the palimpsest of all camp phases on Maligomish. Geo-spatial data courtesy of Technical Services, Confederacy of Mainland Mi'kmaq. Map created by the author.

who may have used them in the past or are continuing to use them in the present. However, because our crew included two Mi'kmaq from the local community, the information we recorded included much more than locations and empirical observations. Mary Irene and Edie were able to identify the owners—and, in some cases, the previous owners—of each camp. Recognizing the value of this information, I asked Mary Irene and Edie to revisit each camp on the island—this time, not following the east-west transects of our systematic survey, but walking along the paths that Mi'kmaq themselves use to access the camps. The three of us circled the island together, and over the two days that we conducted this survey, we switched from an objective rendering of Maligomish as a *space* to a subjective understanding of Maligomish as a *place* (*sensu* Casey 1997; Cresswell 2006).[19] Indeed, the knowledge produced during our supplementary survey was solely based on Mary Irene and Edie's personal experiences and memories. In addition to identifying the family or families associated with each camp, Mary Irene and Edie often referred to an area of the island by the name of a particular family whose camps are or had been located there. For example, the northeast corner of the island is commonly known among the Mi'kmaw inhabitants as "Waycobah Corner" or the "Waycobah Side" because most of the camps there belong to Mi'kmaq from the Waycobah First Nation on Cape Breton Island.[20] Sometimes Mary Irene and Edie were aware of the current owner and whether he or she had built the cabin or had purchased it from a previous owner. Their knowledge was invaluable for drawing my attention to camps that I would not have recognized as such. For example, they were able to trace the former owners of some abandoned camps to other areas of the island where these owners had built new camps. Edie had spent more time on the island than Mary Irene, and she was more familiar with its changing occupation patterns—so much so that she was able to identify where some camps were once located, even if no standing structure remained.

Recording the camps and their associated outbuildings and features in Cartesian space allowed for the observation of spatial patterning on Maligomish—for example, the density of camps at the eastern end of the island, as illustrated in figure 13. Recording the details provided by Edie, Mary Irene, and other interlocutors from the Pictou Landing First Nation—combined with my own participant observation on Maligomish—allowed for an interpretation of the life histories of the camps on Maligomish and the roles they play in the social lives of Mi'kmaq. Combining both the "objective" spatial data and the "subjective" knowledge of local residents allowed for the observation of the fluid nature of the camps.[21] The result is a palimpsest of seemingly static camps, which are, in fact, in dynamic flux—some are under construction, some occupied, some abandoned, some dilapidated, and some have no material trace and exist only in the memories of residents (see Lelièvre 2010). All, however, are copresent on Maligomish and contribute to how Mi'kmaq have emplaced themselves on the island. Understanding the Maligomish camps as dynamically in flux challenges the sedentarist ideology that assumes stasis and permanence to be normative and impermanence and movement as deviating from that norm.

Building(s) in Flux

Anthropology has a long tradition of studying house forms and how these forms both reflect and constitute social lives. Unlike studies such as Morgan's ([1881] 1965), which offers a broad overview of architecture, communal living, and practices of hospitality from peoples across North America, and Elsie Clews Parsons's (1926), which provides a detailed description of the construction of one Mi'kmaw wigwam, I offer here a composite life history of a typical camp on Maligomish.[22] I draw from several camps on the island to illustrate the dynamic phases of a Maligomish camp—from the first scouting of a particular location to its eventual abandonment.

* * *

Before a camp can be built, a location must be selected and cleared. On Maligomish there are neither property boundaries nor building guidelines. In principle, therefore, Mi'kmaq are free to build where they like. In practice, the choice of camp location is often based on proximity to extended family members. As discussed above, Mary Irene, Edie, and other Mi'kmaq from the Pictou Landing First Nation often refer to particular areas of the island by the name of the family whose camps predominate or—in some cases—by the name of the owners' home community if they are not from Pictou Landing. For example, "the Francis Side" and "Waycobah Corner" are commonly heard on Maligomish.[23]

There are several ways that these clusters of extended family camps develop. For example, Ralph and Lorraine Francis built their camp on the south end of Maligomish soon after they were married in the mid-1970s. They chose this area because that was where Ralph's family had camped. By 2008, ten other buildings belonging to extended family members were built in close proximity to Ralph and Lorraine. These included camps belonging to Ralph's second daughter, his sister, and two of his sororal nieces. The camp owned by his sister, however, was in disrepair, and she had not occupied it for several years. In some cases, camps are inherited by, or given to, children or grandchildren. A family or couple may build a new camp in the vicinity of their old one and pass on the old camp to their adolescent or adult children. For example, when Pictou Landing's former *Keptin*, Raymond Francis, passed away in the winter of 2008, his large cabin passed to one of his grandsons.

Clusters of family camps may also shift locations within Maligomish. During our surface survey, Edie Nicholas identified now-abandoned camps just west of Waycobah Corner that had belonged to Martin (Junior) Sapier and the family of his wife, Louise. This extended family now has camps located on the south side of Maligomish. Their cluster includes four camps, which belong to Junior and Louise and Louise's children from a previous marriage. An individual or family may also choose to purchase a camp from another resident. In such cases, there may be no other family members with camps nearby.

The location of a camp may also be determined by cultural norms shared by occupants of the island. For example, some community members claim that, until recently, no one built camps at the west end because it was considered to be a burial ground. The existence of burials in this area has not been

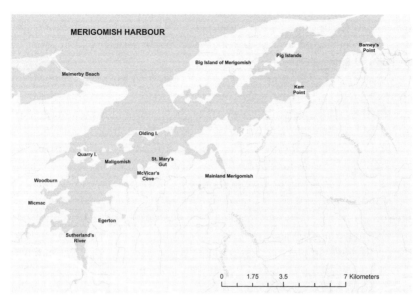

FIGURE 14. Map of Merigomish Harbour and the mainland of Merigomish. Map created by the author.

confirmed, but many community members believe the three mounds we recorded during our surface survey are burials.

Shifts in water access may have some bearing on the choice of camp location. Although there are a few camps located in the "interior" of the island, most stretch along the perimeter and are oriented toward the water. Changes in the physical environment of the island and surrounding waters may have influenced the expansion of settlement beyond its eastern end. At one time, Mi'kmaq accessed Maligomish either by taking a boat directly from Pictou Landing or by driving or taking the train to the closest point on mainland Merigomish and launching a boat from there.[24] A photograph taken by the anthropologist Frederick Johnson during his visit to Maligomish in 1930 indicates that a route southeast from Maligomish was likely taken, as the entrance of the church—which faces east—is visible in the background of the photograph (see cover photo). More recently, the water separating the east end of Maligomish from the west end of Olding Island (see fig. 14) is only navigable at high tide. The northern side of the island is less easily accessible by boat in the summer, given the dense beach grasses that grow along the shore. There are fewer camps along the northwestern shoreline in particular. We recorded several abandoned camps in this area, some of which succumbed to the winter storms that pound Maligomish's north shore. The deeper waters along the west and southwest of the island make it easier to anchor and launch a boat.

Contemporary camps are usually small, one-story structures, measuring approximately five meters by five meters. If the site of a camp has not been cleared, then the owner will have to remove the trees and brush from the area. The sound of chain saws is not uncommon on Maligomish. Some builders have brought all-terrain vehicles to the island to assist in the construction process. The materials for these buildings may be bought new, brought from homes on the mainland, or salvaged from previously abandoned structures on the island. The length of time to complete construction depends not only on preparing the site, obtaining materials, and recruiting some helping hands but also on finding adequate transportation and favorable weather to travel to the island. For example, the most common type of vessel among the Mi'kmaq who frequent Maligomish is a fifteen-foot, aluminum fishing boat with a fifteen- to thirty-horsepower outboard motor. Such vehicles are able to handle small shipments of materials. Larger, heavier materials require constructing or borrowing a flat-bottomed float that can be towed by more powerful vessels. Depending on the availability of transportation and materials, the time to complete a camp can vary from several days to several months or longer.

The camps do not have subterranean foundations but are raised off the ground using wood blocks and/or ready-made concrete footings. A frame for the building is constructed from two-inch by four-inch pine studs. Sheets of plywood are nailed to the frame to form walls and a roof, and the roof is covered in asphalt shingles. There is generally one entrance, which may have an interior wooden door and an exterior screen door. Depending on the size of the camp, it may have two, three, or more windows. Many have exterior porches, which serve as convenient areas for food preparation.

* * *

How Mi'kmaq use their camps on Maligomish very much depends on the time of year. When Edie and I started the surface survey in November 2007, we shared the island with only a few rabbits, deer, and the hunters who were after them. In the spring of 2008, when our crew resumed the surface survey, we were generally the only people on the island because no hunting was underway. By October 2008, when we were in the midst of our test excavations of the shell midden, there were more people on Maligomish because of the annual salmon run at the mouth of Sutherland's River (see fig. 14).

But the busiest season on Maligomish is summer. Some families move to the island for the entire summer but travel frequently to the mainland to restock supplies and enjoy a hot shower. With Maligomish offering few conveniences, the Mi'kmaq who stay for the summer need to bring almost everything with them. It has been many years since the few wells on Maligomish yielded potable water, so residents must bring enough water for drinking, making *pitewey* (tea), cooking, cleaning, and bathing. Supplies of gasoline, propane, and batteries are needed for powering generators, camp stoves, barbeques, and lanterns. Beyond these basic necessities, some occupants equip their camps with many of the conveniences of home. Generators power TVs, refrigerators, and even satellite dishes. Woodstoves provide much-needed warmth on chilly nights and help prevent dampness from creeping into a camp's walls. Many camps have built-in platforms that can accommodate single- and double-sized mattresses.

Other families may visit their camps on day trips to Maligomish but not stay overnight. Most families from Pictou Landing will only stay overnight one or two weekends in a summer, and one of these weekends is almost always coincident with the St. Anne's mission in late July. The population of Maligomish explodes during this weekend. The sounds of children's screams as they dive off the main wharf are mixed with the drones of outboard motors powering boats that carry pilgrims traveling to and from Maligomish. On the island itself, the increasingly common gas generators are heard day and night as they power electric lights and stereos and recharge mobile devices. During the mission weekend, some camps are transformed into compounds as small cities of tents pop up around the main building (see fig. 15).

As seen in figure 15, most socializing and food preparation happens outside of the main cabin. Some camps have exterior porches that accommodate tables and chairs. Others have picnic tables set up in the yard, often close to the fire pit. The camp where I stayed while conducting the subsurface testing of the shell midden belongs to Gladys Wilson.* Many Maligomish residents and visitors consider Gladys's camp to be one of the best on the island because of its clever use of interior and exterior space. A deck stretches the length of cabin and looks out over Merigomish Harbour to the shoreline of mainland Merigomish and the Pictou Highlands beyond. Trees growing in the bank below provide shelter from the sun and unwanted prying eyes and a home for the area's many squirrels. This deck is a favorite space for residents of—and visitors to—Maligomish to gather to enjoy a cup of *pitewey* with Gladys and the friends with whom she shares this small part of the island. A propane-fueled camp stove rests on a make-shift kitchen counter on the deck. The stove cooks food and heats water for *pitewey* and cleaning. Inside the cabin is a single bed, which I made more comfortable during my stay by salvaging some plywood from a nearby camp that was under construction. The camp also has a counter and cupboard unit that stores dishes, utensils, linens, and first-aid supplies.

FIGURE 15. Photographs of Lawrence Christmas and Elaine Knockwood's* camp in the spring of 2008 (*top*) and in July 2008 (*bottom*). Photographs taken by the author.

FIGURE 16. Fred and Dorie Sapier's home in 2008. Photograph taken by author.

Gladys stores as many of these items as possible in plastic containers to keep them safe from animals and mildew. Despite its compact size, Gladys's cabin can accommodate guests. She has a chair that converts to a narrow mattress. She also keeps an old cushion from a camper strapped to the wall with a bungee cord. When I was staying in the camp in October and November, I used Gladys's small woodstove to heat the building at night.

The conveniences of Gladys's camp reflect the temporary nature of its occupation. Its layout and features work so well because stays generally do not last longer than three or four nights. In contrast to the typical camp on Maligomish is the former home of Fred and Dorie Sapier, which is more typical of a single-story house found on the main reserve at Pictou Landing. Between the mid-1970s and 2000, Dorie and Fred lived year-round on the island. Their house reflects the permanent nature of their occupation on Maligomish (see fig. 16). The walls are insulated, and the exterior is covered in vinyl siding. It also has a cement foundation. The interior of the house is divided into rooms, unlike the open plan of most of the island's camps. Fred and Dorie also had outbuildings for storage.

* * *

Unfortunately, when Fred grew ill in 2000, he and Dorie were forced to leave their home on Maligomish, and they were never able to resume living on the island. In the time since they unexpectedly left Maligomish, their house has fallen into disrepair. When Mary Irene and I took Dorie to the island in 2008, we glimpsed the extent of the damage. The ceiling in the main room had collapsed. Animals and human intruders had ransacked most of the Sapiers' furniture and belongings. Although some Mi'kmaq from Pictou Landing had expressed an interest in purchasing Fred and Dorie's home and refurbishing it for their own use, as of the summer of 2015 Dorie had not yet given up hope of one day being able to use her home again. In the meantime, it continues to succumb slowly to the island's destructive forces.

Unlike Fred and Dorie's home, most camps on Maligomish do not have foundations or insulation. Consequently, the most common challenge on Maligomish is preventing dampness from seeping into the plywood walls and floor. Some people who use their camps for three or four seasons of the year may use insulation and vapor barrier to protect the building from moisture. When the damp and mildew become overwhelming, owners must contemplate abandoning their camp. Ralph Francis boasted that his first camp lasted thirty years, a life span that far exceeds most on Maligomish. In 2009, he described having to confront losing his camp to mildew. The camp lasted his family two more summers, but they spent less time in their camp because of the dampness. In 2012, Ralph razed the old camp and had a new one built in the same location. In an effort to extend the life of the new camp, Ralph had it built approximately fifty centimeters off the ground and added vapor barrier to the roof. Although Ralph opted to demolish his rotted camp, some owners find it easier to burn a mildewed camp where it stands (see fig. 17, left and right).

Mildew is not the only reason for abandoning a camp. Some Mi'kmaq with whom I spoke seemed to indicate that they gradually spent less time on Maligomish as their children grew up. If an abandoned camp is left stand-

FIGURE 17. Photographs of burned camps in 2008. Photographs taken by author.

FIGURE 18. Photographs of collapsed camps in 2008 (right and left). Photographs taken by author.

ing, it is susceptible to the winter storm surges and coastal erosion that are perennial problems on Maligomish (see fig. 18, left and right). For example, the camp on the right of figure 18 was originally located on the southern side of the northeastern tip of the island. Over the winter of 2008, it had been picked up and moved approximately one hundred meters to the southeastern corner. Depending on the state of decay, the materials surviving from these abandoned camps can become sources for new camps under construction. Windows, roofing material, and studs that have been undamaged can all be reused.[25] Indeed, some Mi'kmaq have opted to renovate abandoned camps that still have sound frames rather than construct a new camp from the ground up. For example, between the spring of 2008 and the summer of 2010, one of the abandoned camps we recorded in our surface survey was transformed into a new inhabited camp (see fig. 19, top and middle). Robert and Sherrie Christmas* purchased (or inherited) a camp once belonging to Robert's grandfather. Over twenty-six months, the couple stripped the rotted plywood from the exterior and used what remained to repair the frame, rebuild the windows, and repanel the exterior. The camp from July 2010 bore only a faint resemblance to the skeleton of May 2008. By July 2014 some wear could be seen on the camp's roof (see fig. 19, bottom).

* * *

Seen from the perspective of an individual camp, its typical life history on Maligomish occurs over multiple temporal scales and shifting spatial dimensions. A camp's initial construction may take only days or several months. The materials for its construction may be hauled from off-island or salvaged from an abandoned camp. It may remain habitable for a few years or a few decades. Its life may be extended by a renovation. It may end where it stood, or it may drift in a storm surge or slide down an eroded bank. Its death may happen quickly by the torch or slowly through rot and decay. Or a camp may

FIGURE 19. Before and after photographs of a renovated camp on Maligomish. Top: 2008. Middle: 2010. Bottom: 2014. Photos taken by the author.

Table 2. Phases of a typical camp on Maligomish.

Phase	Description
Under construction / under renovation	Camps with incomplete floors and house frames and, in some cases, scattered building materials such as sheets of plywood.
Occupied	Camps in use by their owners. These camps may only be used for one weekend a year, but their owners maintain them so that they are fit for occupation.
Semi-abandoned	Camps for which it is unclear whether they are abandoned or in use. Camps that appear too neglected to be occupied may still be reclaimed.
Abandoned	Camps that are no longer fit for occupation, but are still standing.
Dilapidated	Abandoned camps that have succumbed to erosion, winter storms, and/or have been burned by their owners. They have been reduced to rubble, yet are still recognizable as having once been camps.
Possible camp sites	The locations of former camps whose only traces are scattered building materials and remains of household items.

be reincarnated with its materials being salvaged for new and renovated buildings. Thus, few camps on Maligomish remain static for long; they are continuously progressing through construction, occupation, semi-abandonment, full abandonment, reclamation, and, finally, dilapidation (see table 2). For some camps, their progress through these phases means they are quite literally moving—either by the island's forces of erosion and storm surge or by the circulation of salvaged materials in the construction and renovation of other camps.

Nor is the distribution of the camps across the island static through time. Indeed, the distribution depicted in figure 13, which was based on data collected in April 2008, was already out of date three months later. At least one new camp was being built during the 2008 St. Anne's mission, and another had been burned. A longer timescale of shifts in camp locations is apparent when we compare the distribution of camps in these different phases. For example, considered as a palimpsest (that is, with all camps from all phases considered together), the highest density of occupation is at the east end of the island, which is how many Mi'kmaq remember Maligomish's settlement pattern in the mid- to late twentieth century. This density is due, in part, to the topography in the area; the eroding shorelines and steep banks mean that camps must crowd into limited space.

However, the palimpsest view obscures some of the social logics at work in the spatial patterning. For example, the density of camps in the northeast and southeast corners of the island also reflects the social ties of the camp owners, particularly those from the Mi'kmaw community of Waycobah on

Cape Breton Island and the extended Francis families. To the northeast is "Waycobah Corner" where several families from the Waycobah First Nation have camps and extended family members pitch tents during the St. Anne's mission. To the southeast is the Francis area, where Ralph and Lorraine Francis and their extended family members have their camps. A third concentration of camps is located near the wharf on the south side of the island. This cluster includes the camp of Gladys Wilson and those of some of her extended family and fictive kin.

In contrast to the palimpsest, when we separate out camps in the first stages of their life histories—in other words, those that were either under construction, under renovation, or occupied in the spring of 2008—we see a more evenly distributed settlement pattern, with just over half of the camps being located in the middle or west end of the island (see fig. 20). The general distribution of occupied camps and camps under construction or renovation suggests that the eastern end of Maligomish is no longer the most heavily populated—a hypothesis bolstered by the map showing the distribution of semi-abandoned, abandoned, and dilapidated camps, which are concentrated at the east end of the island (see fig. 21). During a community meeting in the summer of 2013, some Pictou Landing Mi'kmaq suggested that this shift

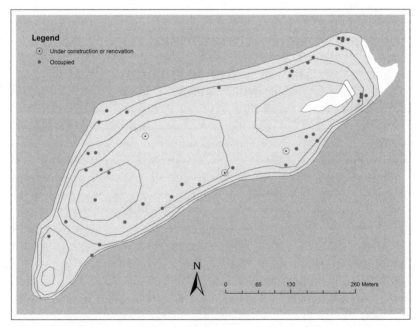

FIGURE 20. Map indicating camps under construction, under renovation, and/or occupied on Maligomish in 2008. Map created by the author.

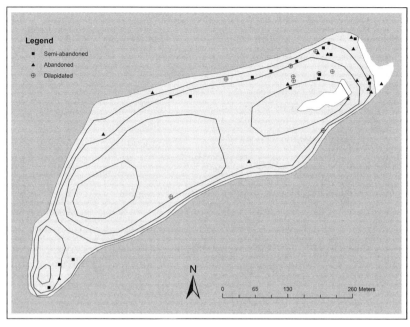

FIGURE 21. Map indicating semi-abandoned, abandoned, and dilapidated camps on Maligomish in 2008.

might be related to accessibility. Maneuvering and anchoring a boat have become increasingly difficult off the eastern end of Maligomish.[26]

The distribution maps represented in figures 20 and 21 are useful for indicating some of the spatial patterns of dwelling on Maligomish that are lost in the palimpsest. Yet these phases should be understood neither as discrete categories nor as inevitable in the life history of a camp. Ralph and Lorraine Francis, for example, were unable to sleep in their camp in 2011 because of the mildew that had seeped into its walls. However, they never abandoned the camp or allowed it to become dilapidated. They simply demolished it when they were ready to construct their new camp in 2012. They were able to salvage some materials from the demolished remains and use them to build the new camp. The Francis camp thus exemplifies the dynamic flux of dwellings on Maligomish.

From Systematic Survey to Dynamic Flux

The dynamism of the camps on Maligomish has implications for our understanding of mobility and settlement. In the fluidity of their life cycles and the shifting patterns of their locations, the camps simultaneously embody qualities of impermanence, flexibility, and rootedness, which emplace Mi'kmaq on Maligomish. These qualities serve to reinforce family and community relationships on Maligomish by ensuring that buildings can be constructed according to the resources of their owners, in a time frame that accommodates those resources, and in areas that maintain social ties. Moreover, these ties extend beyond the current spacetime of Maligomish. The Mi'kmaq who build and maintain camps on the island travel not only from Pictou Landing but also Millbrook and Waycobah, thus connecting Maligomish to the broader social world of Mi'kma'ki. And the abandoned camps that currently exist on Maligomish work to extend the island's social landscape into the past. When Edie Nicholas named the owners of the camps we encountered in our "subjective" surface survey, she included the abandoned and collapsed camps along with the camps that were still in use. She sometimes narrated the genealogy of the camps by including the names of previous owners. Edie even noted the locations of former camps for which there is now little or no trace. She connected a few scattered remnants of building materials, pieces of an iron stove, and scraps of garbage to her memories of the presence of a Mi'kmaw family. In documenting these ephemeral places, this family's presence continues on Maligomish. The map of the camps in all phases of life (see fig. 13) illustrates the palimpsest effect of Mi'kmaw settlement on the island. However temporary the camps may be, their material remnants remain on the land, reminding residents of who "used to live here." Combined, the abandoned and occupied camps on Maligomish contribute to a social landscape where the past is very much a part of the present.

The continued use of Maligomish from at least the late nineteenth century to the present has implications, too, for understanding indigenous responses to settler colonialism in North America. In the late nineteenth and early twentieth centuries, even as more Mi'kmaq moved to reserves and lived in permanent houses, many maintained some kind of residential impermanence. Indeed, as late as the 1970s Mi'kmaw families from Pictou Landing traveled to Maine each summer to harvest blueberries and potatoes, staying in lodgings provided by their employers. As demonstrated by Louis Thom's cabin outside Pugwash Junction and the Sylliboys' temporary residence near Avondale Station, some Mi'kmaq have maintained their right to access off-reserve lands that have long been encroached upon by settlers. Even though both Louis Thom and the Sylliboys were obliged to ask permission from the non-Mi'kmaw landowners to build camps, their decisions to live temporarily on private lands outside their home reserves worked to emplace them in areas from which their ancestors had been distanciated and disembedded (*sensu* Jacka 2005, 645).[27] Thus, for Mi'kmaq in the post-contact period, settlement has not meant sedentism.

If, as Patrick Wolfe (1999) has argued, settler colonialism is based on dispossession, then Mi'kmaw practices of (re-)embedding themselves—at various temporal intervals and spatial scales—challenge ongoing debates regarding indigenous sovereignty and political authority. Settlement on Maligomish, with few exceptions, has been temporary and fluid in nature. This fluidity has implications not only for anthropological conceptions of mobility and settlement but also for legal definitions of "exclusive occupation" as referenced in the Supreme Court of Canada's decision in the case of *R. v. Marshall, R. v. Bernard* (2005). If, as Justice LeBel argued, indigenous relationships to land and water should be used to reconceptualize common law definitions of *property* and *ownership*, then the impermanent settlement practices of Mi'kmaq in places such as Maligomish, Avondale Station, and Pugwash Junction become important evidence for precipitating this change.

Coda

At the end of that April day in 2008 when Mary Irene and I returned to Quarry Island with the GIS specialists from the Confederacy of Mainland Mi'kmaq, we ran into Lawrence Christmas,* who was en route to his camp on Maligomish. We explained that we had been recording information so that civic numbers could be added to the island's camps to ensure swift responses from Emergency Health Services (EHS). Lawrence chuckled. In all his many years visiting Maligomish, he had never seen EHS responders actually on the island. He said the closest they came was Quarry Island, three hundred meters to the west across a deep and sometimes treacherous channel. One of the GIS specialists expressed concern, saying that because all 911 calls are received by police, fire, ambulance, and the coast guard, there was no reason a boat couldn't be dispatched to Maligomish. Lawrence seemed doubtful that he would ever see EHS on the island, and he implied that the lack of door-to-door service had everything to do with Maligomish being a Mi'kmaw place. And Lawrence's skepticism seems well founded. Despite the effort that the GIS specialists from the Confederacy of Mainland Mi'kmaq made to record the locations of each occupied camp, the province of Nova Scotia has not added all of these data to the provincial database of civic numbers, which is available online through the government of Nova Scotia's website.[28] As of the summer of 2016, no civic numbers had been affixed to any of the camps on Maligomish. With no numbers affixed to buildings—and inaccurate information listed in the database—it is difficult to imagine a timely and effective EHS response to an emergency on Maligomish.

The attempt to include Maligomish in the civic numbering system is the latest example in the evolution of the Crown's efforts to use state technologies to assimilate Mi'kmaq and their places. In the nineteenth and twentieth centuries, the Crown attempted to make Mi'kmaq legible as political subjects by enumerating them and incentivizing them to settle into nuclear family units. In the twenty-first century, it has attempted to fold Maligomish and other Mi'kmaw places into its broader digital infrastructure. The fifteen points on Maligomish in the provincial civic-number database assume that this Mi'kmaw place can be made commensurate with nonindigenous and mainland indigenous communities in Nova Scotia, even if this means imposing an artificial impermanence to buildings in flux.[29] In most communities a building can be relied upon to remain in one location in the long term. But for Maligomish, the provincial database inaccurately fixes in space and time the fifteen camps it displays. Moreover, the poorly executed attempt to make Maligomish conform to the provincial system imperils the people who visit and use the island.

The inefficacy of the civic-number database for Maligomish may have less to do with the latent racism implied by Lawrence and more with the different levels of government—and the camp owners themselves—which would have to align in order to bring the civic numbers into reality. And yet Lawrence's skepticism reveals the inherently self-defeating nature of the Crown's assimilationist policies. By attempting to assimilate places like Maligomish, these initiatives further mark such places as *indigenous*. Lawrence seemed to believe that Maligomish does not receive EHS responders because it is marked as an exclusively Mi'kmaw place. At the same time, what makes Maligomish an exclusively indigenous place is that its occupants cannot rely on receiving the basic services—such as timely emergency response—that most nonindigenous Canadians take for granted. Despite upholding their obligations, many Mi'kmaq and other indigenous Canadians do not benefit from being subject to their social contract with the Crown. Moreover, the Crown's attempt to make Maligomish more visible to the nonindigenous gaze by rendering its occupation in terms of fixed addresses has further obscured the mobility inherent in the Mi'kmaq's settlement of this place.

4

Pilgrimage and Propagation

THE MISSION OF MI'KMAW CATHOLICISM

Processing St. Anne

THE 2010 ST. ANNE'S MISSION on Maligomish was notable for many reasons. The mission priest that year was young, affable, and recently ordained. He drew larger than normal crowds, who at first just seemed curious to meet a rare Catholic priest under the age of forty. But his easy manner and frank admission of the Church's past failings brought many people to the Masses and recitations of the Rosary that he officiated over the weekend. Also unusual in 2010 was the presence of the bishop of the Diocese of Antigonish, who concelebrated the Sunday ceremonies along with the mission and parish priests.

Immediately following Sunday's Mass, the procession of St. Anne began much as it had during the previous four missions that I had attended (see fig. 22). Four men picked up a small statue of St. Anne (approximately sixty centimeters), which was attached to a litter, and carried her out of the church. They were led by the crossbearer, who was a *Keptin* from the Grand Council. Following St. Anne were other *Keptins*, the priests, the bishop, and the general congregation—some of whom carried banners that represent different Mi'kmaw communities.

The order in which the participants appear in the procession appears to have varied over time. For example, *The Casket* reported the following processional order from the 1935 mission on Maligomish:

As it proceeded, the choir, chanting canticles all along the line of march, it was headed by the cross-bearer and also the chief of the Micmac tribe, Mattie Francis. Then followed the pastor and visiting clergymen. . . . Three altar boys carried banners of St. Ann, "Our Lady of Perpetual Help" and

FIGURE 22. Photographs of the procession of St. Anne on Maligomish in 2008 (left, right). Photographs taken by the author.

the "Canadian Martyrs." The statue of St. Ann was carried by four of their number, and little Micmac maidens, gaily dressed, with bouquets of flowers, added beauty to the scene. (Diocese of Antigonish Archives 1935)

Super 8 film footage shot by Noel Martin on Maligomish in the 1960s shows a slight variation with the crossbearer leading the procession, followed by the priest, altar boys, the shrine of St. Anne, *Keptins*, girls carrying banners, and, finally, the congregation. What all procession orders appear to have in common, both on Maligomish and on Potlotek (Chapel Island), is that the congregation must stay behind St. Anne.[1]

Generally, on Maligomish, the participants process counterclockwise around the churchyard and along the north side of the church to reach the procession path. If the weather is fine and the path is dry, the procession will follow this path west about 350 meters. Each pilgrim walks the procession at his or her own pace. Exposed tree roots and scattered leaves can make the footing precarious, especially if the ground is wet. The Pictou Landing First Nation sends a maintenance team to the island before each mission to mow the grass in the churchyard and clear any debris from the paths.[2] Wires and speakers that are part of the church's audio system are strung between the trees that line the procession path. The audio system has not been used in several years, but when it was operational, an organist and choir members performed hymns in Mi'kmaw that were broadcast during the procession. During some processions a member of the congregation will lead the group in song or prayer. While some walk in solemnity, others are engaged in conversations with friends and family while keeping one eye on children who are dashing in and out of the procession.

The western end of the procession path opens onto a clearing approximately thirty-five meters in diameter that some Mi'kmaq refer to as "the place of the cross." A common English description for this area is "the grotto," evoking the "caves" where shrines to Christian saints are often constructed.[3] Indeed, at the western edge of this clearing is a trellised archway symbolizing a grotto, which volunteers have decorated with ribbons and artificial flowers. St. Anne is set down beneath this archway. Next to the archway is a crucifix with a slightly hollowed stone at its base. Here, the priests, bishop, *Keptins*, and community members who are participating as readers flank St. Anne and face the rest of the congregation. Members of the congregation are assembled in the middle of the clearing and along its edges. The parish priest leads prayers to St. Anne, and the *Keptins* and lay community members recite petitions and invocations.[4]

FIGURE 23. Photograph of pilgrims queuing in the "grotto" on Maligomish to venerate before St. Anne. 2010. Photograph taken by the author.

In 2010, the procession started as usual, the weather being dry enough to walk from the church to the clearing or "grotto." When the procession reached the grotto, St. Anne was placed in the archway, and the parish priest poured holy water into the stone at the base of the crucifix. The priests, *Keptins*, and community members recited prayers to St. Anne. Following the prayers, the priest invited community members to bless themselves and to venerate before St. Anne (see fig. 23). The congregants queued to bless themselves with the holy water and then proceeded to venerate. Some congregants knelt or bowed before the statue. Others kissed or touched it. Many left monetary offerings.

While the pilgrims were venerating, the parish priest instructed an organizing committee member to tell one of the *Keptins* from Pictou Landing to lead the bishop, the mission priest, and the congregation back to the church. There were grumblings from some of the community members about the priests leaving the grotto before St. Anne. Had the *Keptin* left the grotto at the moment the parish priest requested, the members of the congregation who had completed their venerations would have likely followed, leaving St. Anne to trail sometime after them. Some of the community members exchanged a few words, debating whether to mention to the priest this affront to St. Anne. A few were uncertain if he would listen to their concerns. Finally, as the *Keptin* started to leave with the priests and bishop following, a mission organizer called out to him from the other side of the grotto saying, "Isn't St. Anne supposed to go first, Father?" Conceding his mistake in protocol, the parish priest waited with his concelebrants at the eastern edge of the grotto. When all of the pilgrims had paid their respects to St. Anne, the *Keptin* bearing the cross led her back to the church with the priests and congregation following.

This incident was notable for me because in the previous four missions that I had attended, no such disruption had occurred. Even in 2008, when the community was recovering from the recent death of *Keptin* Raymond Francis—who had for many years been the primary organizer of the mission—the procession appeared to unfold seamlessly. The disruption in 2010 was the exception that illuminated the St. Anne's mission as a dense site for examining the relationships between the Church, the Crown, and the Mi'kmaq and the role that mobility plays in mediating those relationships.[5] Many factors contributed to the interruption of the 2010 procession. On the one hand, the authority of the Catholic Church in Mi'kmaw and non-Mi'kmaw communities has been deteriorating for several decades due in no small part to the abusive treatment of Mi'kmaw and other indigenous children in Canada's residential schools. The compromised relationship, combined with greater Mi'kmaw autonomy and political power beyond the realm of the Church, provided the conditions of possibility for the community member to challenge the parish priest's decision to leave before St. Anne. On the other hand, the priest's misstep may have been due more to him being distracted than to a calculated assertion of authority. But many Mi'kmaq admire the virtue of patience, and the parish priest's haste to leave—in addition to his affront to St. Anne—appears to have been a step too far. The community member's determination to have the proper order of the procession respected meant asserting an authority based on her status not only as a Mi'kmaw on Mi'kmaw land but also as a Catholic. In calling out to stop the priest, she was, quite literally, a voice aware of her own vocality (Trouillot 1995, 23) and, hence, a political subject.

* * *

The current chapter continues to explore how mobility has mediated sociopolitical relationships in post-contact Nova Scotia by examining how movement and emplacement are inherent to Mi'kmaw Catholicism. It does so, first, by discussing some of the key concepts for this chapter—namely, mission, pilgrimage, and agency. The chapter then examines primary and secondary historical sources to describe the movements and emplacement of missionaries and priests from the seventeenth to early twentieth centuries.[6] Mobility was key for the Jesuit, Recollect, Capuchin, and Spiritan missionaries who were sent forth from their European seminaries to propagate the Catholic faith in the New World.[7] Mobility later mediated the Church's collusion with the Crown in attempting to sedentize the Mi'kmaq in the nineteenth and early twentieth centuries. These attempts included efforts not only to settle Mi'kmaq permanently at mission sites and centralized reserves but also to consolidate them periodically at events such as the St. Anne's mission and to discipline their movements by attempting to dictate how and when they could visit priests.

This discussion traces the gradual shift in the roles played by these subjects—a shift away from serving as spiritual advisors and advocates for the Mi'kmaq (and occasionally as recruiters for the French military) toward serving as bureaucrats for the management of the Mi'kmaq under the British colonial and Canadian federal governments. This shift is key to understanding the transformation of Mi'kmaq in the eyes of colonial authorities from that of a nation with and against whom wars were fought and treaties were negotiated, to that of wards of the state. The seeds of the Mi'kmaq's political status as children of a paternalistic state—which was made official with the introduction of the Indian Act in 1876 and reached its full flowering during the dark period of centralization and residential schools—were planted in the early nineteenth century when both the ecclesiastical and colonial authorities recognized the Church's influence and sought to use it to "civilize" the Mi'kmaq.

Mi'kmaw Catholicism has not only been a site for the Church and Crown's missionizing; it has also been a site where Mi'kmaq have celebrated their faith independently and, occasionally, in defiance of these institutions. Here I focus specifically on how Mi'kmaq have celebrated their Catholic faith through practices of pilgrimage. I define *pilgrimage* broadly to include not only the annual movement of Mi'kmaq to sacred sites such as Maligomish and Potlotek to celebrate the feast of St. Anne on July 26 but also the more quotidian movements for religious purposes that were of such concern to Crown and Church administrators in the nineteenth century.[8] This discussion draws on primary and secondary historical documents as well as my observations of the ten St. Anne's missions on Maligomish that I attended between 2006 and 2016. This four-day celebration in late July draws Mi'kmaq from several communities in Nova Scotia with both sacred and secular activities. Even for those Mi'kmaq who no longer participate (or have never participated) in the religious rituals, "mission time" is part of their memories and imaginaries of Maligomish.

A Four-Hundred-Year Mission

Despite its four-hundred-year presence, the modus operandi of the Catholic Church in Mi'kma'ki continues to be that of a "mission," a sending forth of the Church's agents to meet and live with Mi'kmaq in order to convert, preach, serve, and manage their spiritual—and occasionally temporal—needs. In making this argument, the current chapter considers how mobility at once structured while at the same time undermined the mission as a colonial project in Nova Scotia. Underlying this argument is an understanding of authority as constituted in agency—the capacity to act (Comaroff and Comaroff 1986, 2). Throughout their quadricentennial relationship, the Mi'kmaq and the Catholic Church have not had equal capacities to act. Indeed, the Catholic Church seems to have acted upon Mi'kmaw culture and language to an extent that not even the British Empire could rival. Missionaries such as Abbé Pierre Maillard, who adapted the early ideographic Mi'kmaw writing form developed by LeClerq to compile a complete prayer book and liturgy for the Mi'kmaq, seem to have inspired a fervent devotion to the Church and some of its most prominent figures—Jesus Christ; his mother, the Virgin Mary; and especially his maternal grandmother, St. Anne. A French observer, de la Varenne, opined from Louisbourg in 1756 that the Mi'kmaq's commitment to the true faith was all for show: "[E]very one knows that the savages are at best but slightly tinctured with it [Catholicism], and have little or no attachment to it, but as they find their advantage in the benefits of presents and protection, it procures to them from the French government" (cited in Maillard 1758, 86–87). However, almost a century later, the steadfastness of the Mi'kmaq's faith was noted by more than one source. The Mi'kmaq demonstrated their commitment to the Catholic Church in very material ways, such as volunteering their labor to construct churches in their own communities and lending money for the construction of St. Mary's cathedral in Halifax (Diocese of Antigonish Archives 1837).[9] With such accounts of the Mi'kmaq's spiritual and temporal devotion to the Church, it would appear as though their consciousness had been well and truly colonized (*sensu* Comaroff and Comaroff 1992). However, the Catholicism that the Mi'kmaq had been practicing since the late eighteenth century was very much their own, being based on the rituals included in Maillard's prayer book and the Mi'kmaq's own innovations developed in the scarcity—and sometimes complete absence—of missionaries and priests.

Lycett (2004, 358) has discussed the multiple meanings of *mission* in colonial settings, arguing that the term can be conceptualized "simultaneously as a place, an emergent community, and as an institutional logic or colonial project." He notes that, while relationships within a mission context are often asymmetrical, they are "also reciprocal and mutually constitutive" (2004, 359). In the Nova Scotia context, the relationships between Catholic missionaries and Mi'kmaq have changed significantly over the four centuries of the mission, and their effects have been experienced differently by the Church, the Mi'kmaq, and the Crown. Although never as materially or administratively structured as the Spanish mission system in the New World (see Graham 1998; Lycett 2004), by the early eighteenth century a structure was beginning to emerge in Nova Scotia, due in part to the increasing French and Acadian populations. Resident missionaries were based in more densely populated areas such as Louisbourg, Port Toulouse (now St. Peter's), and Port Dauphin (now Englishtown/St. Ann's) on Cape Breton Island (see fig. 1). In addition to serving these settlements, the resident priests were also responsible for "dependent missions," which were smaller communities with populations of only fifty to 150 people (A. A. Johnston 1960, 35). The priests traveled from their resident community to minister to their "missions." The relationship between a priest's resident community and that community's missions was similar to that between the *cabecera* and the *visitas* in colonial New Mexico (Lycett 2004, 363), although neither the resident community nor the mission would have had the infrastructure and economic activity typical of so many Spanish missions. What both the Spanish and French mission structures share, however, is a direct relationship between the density and relative sedentism of a congregation and the relative itinerancy of its missionary priest. This "core and periphery" model is important for understanding the development of the relationship between the Catholic Church and the Mi'kmaq. For even as Mi'kmaw communities became more densely and regularly populated throughout the late nineteenth and early twentieth centuries, they almost invariably remained "missions" of larger, non-Mi'kmaw Catholic parishes.

Understanding the continuing role of the Catholic mission to the Mi'kmaq is key for conceptualizing Mi'kmaw political subjectivity in the post-contact period. The 1610 baptism of Chief Membertou and his family was not simply a spiritual act. The conversion of the Mi'kmaq was also a political act to secure the concordat between the Holy See and the Mi'kmaw nation. This compact with the Vatican has been critical to the Mi'kmaq's assertion of their sovereignty to secular political authorities, including the French and British Crowns (see Lawrence 2002). And the Mi'kmaq's political connection to the Catholic Church has outlived both of these empires.

Even though the concordat formally ended with the Treaty of Westphalia in 1648, the Church remained an important presence in what is now Nova Scotia through the seventeenth and eighteenth centuries. Its influence did not disappear after the fall of New France. Consequently, since the late eighteenth century, there have been two states with colonial authority in the province: the British Crown and the Vatican. The Vatican operated in Nova Scotia first through the Diocese of Québec and then through the Vicariate Apostolic of Nova Scotia, which was established in 1817. The northern areas of the Vicariate Apostolic became the Diocese of Arichat in 1844 and the Diocese of Antigonish in 1886.[10] These administrative units had their own quasi-governmental technologies for managing their populations, including conducting occasional parish surveys and censuses and mapping parish boundaries. One survey conducted in 1885 listed—among other information—the number of parishioners, the numbers and locations of mission churches, and a chronological list of parish missionaries and priests. Mi'kmaq are mentioned in some of these reports; for example, the Christmas Island parish report noted that 180 of the 1303 parishioners were Mi'kmaq from Eskasoni (Diocese of Antigonish Archives 1885). A 1906 census recorded 114 Mi'kmaw families living at Pictou Landing and twenty-seven families on Maligomish (Diocese of Antigonish Archives 1906). However, these parochial censuses were taken irregularly and—like those taken by the Crown—did not account for people who may have been living in the area only temporarily or people who may have been absent at the time the enumeration was made.

Like many nonindigenous Catholics, some Mi'kmaq have turned away from the Catholic Church and toward "traditional" and "Pan-Indian" spirituality (see Poliandri 2011; Robinson 2005). Despite this phenomenon, Catholicism remains an influential spiritual and cultural force in the lives of many Mi'kmaq. In 2010, several hundred Mi'kmaq participated in the quadricentennial celebrations of the Mi'kmaq's conversion, which included an official visit by Queen Elizabeth II.[11] And the St. Anne's mission at Potlotek (Chapel Island) in the southwestern area of the Bras d'Or Lakes continues to draw hundreds of pilgrims from Mi'kmaw communities in Cape Breton and around Mi'kma'ki. However, the objective of the current chapter is not to understand the complicated role that Catholicism plays in contemporary Mi'kmaw life.[12] Instead, it takes a long-term perspective to consider the practices associated with Mi'kmaw Catholicism as a further nexus of relations between the Crown, the Church, and the Mi'kmaq.

From Propagating Missionaries to Paternalistic Bureaucrats

At the broadest level, the mission as "institutional logic" (*sensu* Lycett 2004, 358) required a significant mobilization of people and resources to dispatch missionaries from their European-based religious orders to the New World and to sustain them while they fulfilled their duties to propagate the faith. In 1629, for example, the Jesuit missionaries Fathers Barthélemy Vimont and Alexander de Vieuxport received royal patronage from Anne of Austria, the

Queen Mother of France, for their voyage to Nova Scotia. They arrived sepa-
rately and both eventually made their way to Captain Charles Daniel's fort at
St. Ann's on Cape Breton Island. Father de Vieuxpont only reached St. Ann's
after being shipwrecked near Canso, chancing upon a Mi'kmaw who was willing to guide him to the fort, and traveling approximately one hundred kilometers by canoe through the Bras d'Or Lakes (A. A. Johnston 1960, 13).[13]

The scarcity of priests and the mobile nature of the indigenous populations meant that a missionary could not remain settled in any one community
for long. All of the seventeenth-century missionaries whom A. A. Johnston
profiles in his history of what is now the Diocese of Antigonish spent comparatively little time in one location.[14] For example, the Capuchin missionary
Balthazar de Paris, who was based in northern New Brunswick between 1648
and 1654, toured Acadia traveling distances as far as three hundred kilometers.[15] And those missionaries who sought to learn an indigenous language
could do so only by living, and therefore traveling, with a community.[16]

In the early eighteenth century, many mission communities were populated by French and Acadian settlers who were engaged in modest agricultural pursuits and the fisheries. Others were missions specifically devoted to
the Mi'kmaq. In *Memoire sur les missions des Sauvages Mikmaks et de l'Acadie* (ca.
1738–39) the unnamed author lists thirteen such communities in what is
now Nova Scotia, Prince Edward Island, and New Brunswick.[17] The *Memoire*
describes priests being stationed at specific residences, but moving annually
to visit the other places where Mi'kmaq gathered: "*Quoy {sic} que ces Mission-
naires fassent leur principale résidence à Miraguaoueche (Malagawatch), à Malpec
(Malpeque) et à Chebnakadie (Shubenacadie), ils vont tous les ans faire leur mission
dans les autres villages des Sauvages*" (Diocese of Antigonish 1738–1739). For
example, Abbé Maillard, the missionary at Malagawatch, was responsible for
the missions on Cape Breton Island and in Antigonish, approximately eighty
kilometers to the southwest.[18] The missionary at Malpèque on Ile St. Jean
(now Prince Edward Island) also served missions across the Northumberland
Strait, on the north shore of Nova Scotia, including Pictou (Diocese of Antigonish 1738–1739).

The missionary residences became sites of emplacement. Not only did the
missionaries embed themselves in the colonial landscape of Nova Scotia by
building churches and presbytery houses. They—along with French colonial
officials—also emplaced the Mi'kmaq by encouraging them to settle permanently in the vicinity of the missions. Malagawatch was proposed for this purpose as early as 1713 (A. A. Johnston 1960, 32). Balcom and A. J. B. Johnston
(2006) describe a period in 1724 when French officials joined the Church's
efforts to bring Mi'kmaq from British-controlled Acadia to Malagawatch on
Isle Royale. The mission site's long distance from the Mi'kmaw lands on main-

land Nova Scotia and New Brunswick—and the area's poor soil—made it un-
suitable for enticing Mi'kmaq to settle (Balcom and A. J. B. Johnston 2006,
124; Diocese of Antigonish 1738–1739). In Antigonish and Malpèque, however, the Mi'kmaq were able to keep gardens. The Mi'kmaq at Shubenacadie
built that mission's church themselves (Diocese of Antigonish 1738–1739).
While none of these locations became permanent settlements for the Mi'kmaq
in the eighteenth century (Chute 1992, 51), the Church did not give up its
attempts to sedentize the indigenous population and control their movements.

A more successful strategy for attracting Mi'kmaq to one place was the
annual distribution of presents from the King of France. The author of the
Memoire describes Mi'kmaw chiefs assembling in June or July at Port Toulouse in Cape Breton and on Prince Edward Island where they would receive
gifts of muskets, powder, shot, and axes and renew their fidelity to the French
Crown. The chiefs would then take these supplies back to distribute in their
home communities, thus extending the influence of the Crown across the
whole of l'Acadie (Diocese of Antigonish 1738–1739; see also Chute 1992,
51–52).

The missionaries and government officials who arranged these political
gatherings may have timed them to coincide with the intraregional meetings
of Mi'kmaq from across Mi'kma'ki, which Chute (1992) identifies as having
occurred anytime between April and September. In his *History of the County of
Pictou*, George Patterson ([1877] 1916) describes an annual celebration that
occurred in September on the south side of Pictou Harbour, which drew large
numbers of Mi'kmaq from Prince Edward Island, Antigonish, and other
places: "A person brought up at the latter place, has told me that he has
counted one hundred canoes at one time drawn up on the shore, and it was
said that they would sometimes number one hundred fifty. . . . These gatherings continued yearly till a vessel with smallpox was sent to quarantine at the
mouth of Middle River, about the year 1838" (G. Patterson ([1877]) 1916,
121). Several scholars argue that the St. Anne's mission can trace its roots to
these cultural and political assemblies (Balcom and A. J. B. Johnston 2006;
Chute 1992; Hornborg 2002; Upton 1979).[19] Churches were being devoted
to St. Anne as early as 1629, and St. Anne's status as the grandmother of Jesus
had salience with the Mi'kmaq whose Kluskap stories prominently feature
Nukumi, the culture hero's *kiju* or grandmother (Battiste 1997, 13). Despite
the reverence for St. Anne, the annual commemoration of her feast day on
July 26 was not a fixture of the missionary calendar until the mid-eighteenth
century (see Chute 1992).[20]

By the late eighteenth century, Catholic missionaries and priests were no
longer serving only Mi'kmaq and the few Acadians who had avoided the
Grand Dérangement, but also a growing Irish and Highland Scot population.[21]

With more non-Mi'kmaw Catholics to serve, focus on the Mi'kmaq's spiritual needs was diminished. Over the course of the nineteenth century, missionaries and priests became more closely involved in the temporal needs of the Mi'kmaq, often working with the British Crown to manage the indigenous population. During most of this period, priests continued to move vast distances to serve their congregations. In the autumn of 1858, for example, the bishop of the Diocese of Arichat traveled approximately seven hundred kilometers from Antigonish to Catholic communities in Nova Scotia and New Brunswick (Diocese of Antigonish Archives 1858). In addition to such diocesan and missionary tours, new modalities of mobility were being introduced in the nineteenth century as the Church attempted to discipline the Mi'kmaq's spiritual movements.

As discussed in chapter 1, sedentizing the Mi'kmaq was one of the primary means by which the British Crown had hoped to "civilize" the colony's indigenous population. The commissioner for Indian Affairs, George Henry Monk, recognized in the early nineteenth century the potential power of the Catholic missionaries to help the Crown achieve this goal: "It would be in the power of the Roman Catholick [*sic*] Priests . . . to assist in persuading the Indians to change their way of Life, their Habits, and their Dress; and to become orderly Subjects. . . . Were their Priests to recommend the Cultivating small Fields in Villages, and regularly to visit the Indians in those Settlements, and commend their steadings, and Industry, it would be a great inducement to a Change of Life and Habits" (NSA 1808). The representatives of the Catholic Church in the New World agreed with Monk's observations. During a visit to Nova Scotia in 1815, the bishop of the Diocese of Québec (of which Nova Scotia was then a part) made appeals to Nova Scotia's lieutenant governor that something be done to alleviate the suffering of the Mi'kmaq, whom he described as *"errans, pauvres, abandonnés à l'ivrognerie"* (NSA 1815). In this letter, the bishop expressed a rather low opinion of the Mi'kmaq's capacity for—and interest in—work. The tone of the letter suggests that he did not consider hunting, fishing, and food gathering to be valuable forms of work. He noted that the Catholic missionaries had always had more influence on the conduct of the Mi'kmaq than civil or military officials. He suggested founding communities organized by Trappist monks who would teach Mi'kmaq to read and cultivate the land, instill good morals, and inspire a work ethic (NSA 1815). Although a Trappist community was eventually established near Tracadie, Nova Scotia (see fig. 1), the work communities the bishop envisioned did not come to pass.

Yet the desire to instill Mi'kmaq with a work ethic predicated on sedentism persisted among the Catholic missionaries. In 1860, the bishop of the

Diocese of Antigonish wrote a report to the Vatican in which he praised the colonial government for its persistent encouragement of the Mi'kmaq to settle permanently. Unfortunately, the bishop reported, the Mi'kmaq had not complied. However, the encroachment that Europeans had made upon the Mi'kmaq's traditional hunting and fishing grounds had compelled Mi'kmaq "to assume more steady habits, and procure by manual labor of some craft his daily bread" (Diocese of Antigonish Archives 1860).[22] If the bishop was optimistic that the Mi'kmaq would adopt a Protestant work ethic, he had no fear of their spiritual conversion. He noted the "formness [*sic*] and stability" of their faith (Diocese of Antigonish Archives 1860).

Archival and secondary sources from the nineteenth century testify to the Mi'kmaq's steadfast faith by referencing their constant prayer, their careful study of the books left to them by Abbé Maillard, and their persistent movements for personal devotion and to receive sacraments and blessings from priests. The latter practice was a cause of concern for both the colonial officials and the Catholic Church. For example, in August 1812, the bishop of the Diocese of Québec wrote to a priest in Prince Edward Island regarding the Mi'kmaq of northeastern Nova Scotia: "Since the Indians dispersed along the shores of Pictou and Merigomish have no fixed residence, they may go to your mission to receive instruction and approach the Sacraments. . . . They are not to come seeking your services in every place where you happen to be, but only at Lennox Island; and you are to give them due notice of the time when they can find you at the latter place" (quoted in A. A. Johnston 1960, 253). The bishop was indirectly instructing the Mi'kmaq not only on what priest to visit but also on when and under what circumstances they could visit him. Here we see the ecclesiastical incarnation of the colonial government's attempts to make order out of the conceived chaos of Mi'kmaw movements. The bishop was not attempting to sedentize the Mi'kmaq—indeed, he was actually requiring the Mi'kmaq to travel farther to consult a priest, since Lennox Island is located across the Northumberland Strait, approximately 120 kilometers northwest of Pictou, off the north shore of Prince Edward Island (see fig. 1). Rather than trying to keep the Mi'kmaq in one location, the bishop was attempting to discipline the Mi'kmaq's movements. This disciplining is a further example of the Church's emplacement of Mi'kmaq by positioning them to adapt their spiritual needs to the Church's temporal ones. Whether the bishop's instructions were ever related to the Mi'kmaq of Nova Scotia's north shore matters little; Mi'kmaq continued to move for religious purposes, seemingly at their will, throughout the nineteenth century.

While a more autonomous episcopal structure developed for the non-Mi'kmaw faithful, the relationship between the Mi'kmaq and the Catholic

Church remained that of a "mission," with chapels and churches in Mi'kmaw communities being missions of a parent parish. Records from Stella Maris parish in Pictou indicate that, for the year between August 1854 and August 1855, seven Mi'kmaw families had their children baptized. While some of these entries indicate where the children were born, they do not specify if the baptisms took place at the home church in Pictou or at the mission church in Maligomish. In the case of the mission at Maligomish, the relationship with its parent parish appears to have depended on the pastor. Some, like Father Roderick McDonald, took a very active interest in the Mi'kmaw mission. Between the late 1880s and late 1890s, he was the pastor at two different parishes that had Maligomish as one of its missions.

Father McDonald also served as the Indian agent, reporting on the activities around Pictou County to the federal government in Ottawa, which inherited responsibility for indigenous peoples after the British Crown confederated four of its former colonies to form the Dominion of Canada in 1867. The records of the federal Department of Indian Affairs include a detailed correspondence between the department's bureaucrats and McDonald as he raised funds and planned the construction of two mission churches on the island between 1890 and 1897.[23] In July 1890, Father McDonald hired the steamboat "Egerton" to take non-Mi'kmaw Catholics on an excursion to Maligomish scheduled for the day following the St. Anne's Day celebrations. Each passenger was charged fifty cents (Diocese of Antigonish Archives 1890a). The newspaper, *The Casket*, reported the following week that the picnic had raised the not immodest sum of eight hundred dollars (Diocese of Antigonish Archives 1890b).

Many priests were appointed as Indian agents, and they received a salary for their work (see LAC 1893). Although they were still occupied with attending to the spiritual needs of the Mi'kmaq, the priests paid more attention to ways of inspiring independence through hard and provident work. In an 1891 letter to the Department of Indian Affairs, Father McDonald demonstrates the entanglement of these roles. He wrote asking for funds to construct a new church on the island. Speaking of the St. Anne's mission, he writes:

> The gathering of the tribe in this place and on this occasion has many advantages. It furnishes the pastor and agent the opportunity of instructing them in the way of progress—of industry, economy of providing for future want, of contentment and gratitude to the Government for what it does for them, of sobriety, and morality of conduct. . . . There is nothing that would foster the spirit of gratitude and attachment to the Department than an interest in their spiritual matters as well as their temporal. (LAC 1891)

McDonald may have been selectively emphasizing the benefits of the mission in order to convince the department officials that they would be making a good investment by providing funds to construct a new church. Even so, his remark that the Department of Indian Affairs would make more progress toward "civilizing" the Mi'kmaq if the department provided for their spiritual needs suggests McDonald was quite conscious of the role the Church was playing in their management. McDonald's exhortation of the virtues that could be instilled in the Mi'kmaq during the St. Anne's mission echoes the strategies employed by the French missionaries of the eighteenth century. If sedentizing the Mi'kmaq was a hopeless cause, then the solution was to gather them regularly in one place for their instruction in "civilization," thus making these missions sites of emplacement. By supporting the periodic events that drew large numbers of Mi'kmaq together, the Church was colluding with the federal government to proselytize the virtues of remaining in one place. Yet, well into the early twentieth century, many Mi'kmaq remained mobile for at least part of the year.

The collusion between the Crown and the Church over the management of the Mi'kmaq deepened in the early twentieth century when priests' roles as spiritual advisors and Indian agents became more entangled. The Church became complicit in the state's schemes to sedentize and assimilate the Mi'kmaq. For example, the centralization plan introduced in 1942 sought to persuade Mi'kmaq from across Nova Scotia to settle into two large reserves with promises of new houses and access to education and medical services. The plan involved centralizing not only the Mi'kmaq but also the bureaucracy that managed them. As a result, the administrative buildings and residential compounds for the non-Mi'kmaw staff, including priests and nuns, were constructed on the reserves (Paul 2000, 281). When Shelia Steen conducted her doctoral fieldwork with the Eskasoni Mi'kmaq in 1950, she noted that the community had its own church with a priest in "continual residence," meaning that the church was no longer a mission of a parent parish.[24] Steen wrote that this priest "exerts his influence upon the Micmac in order to ensure their cooperation with the centralization program" (Steen 1951, 75). One consequence of the priest's constant presence was that most of the Mi'kmaw contributions to religious ceremonies were discontinued. According to Steen's interlocutors, before Eskasoni had a resident priest, elders led prayers, and Mi'kmaw dances and songs were a part of the Christian rituals. After the establishment of the centralization program, Mi'kmaq no longer organized or directly participated in these celebrations (Steen 1951, 75). Wallis and Wallis (1955) echo this report in their comparative study of Mi'kmaw communities in Nova Scotia and New Brunswick. When Wilson Wallis returned to the Maritime provinces in 1953 to follow up on fieldwork he had conducted in

1911, he observed substantial differences in the St. Anne's mission celebrations—most notably, the lack of what he considered to be "Mi'kmaw" rituals. He commented that the St. Anne's ceremonies in Mi'kmaw communities could be little distinguished from those conducted in Acadian parishes. St. Anne's Day had become a lucrative way for priests to raise money for the Church by attracting non-Mi'kmaw Catholics with picnics and bingo (Wallis and Wallis 1955, 291).

However, in communities, such as Pictou Landing—where no priest was in residence—Mi'kmaq combined formal instruction from the Church with local practices led by their chiefs and elders. In response to a question I asked about traveling to attend Mass as a child, elder Sadie Francis responded that she had few memories of going to church. Instead, she recalled from her childhood occasionally being told by her parents that a community meeting was being held and that she was expected to attend. She said the meetings were led by the chief and included some teaching but also food, dancing, and socializing. Sadie also said that the teaching might have been themed according to events on the ecclesiastical calendar.

During Sadie's childhood, the parish priest in charge of the Pictou Landing mission was A. A. Johnston, the author of the two-volume *A History of the Catholic Church in Eastern Nova Scotia* (1960, 1971). Records kept by Johnston during his tenure as parish priest of Stella Maris appear to complement Sadie's memories. Johnston kept a booklet that listed all of the announcements made during the Sunday Mass at Stella Maris. These announcements included banns of marriage, charity picnics, and funerals, among other parish business. They also included the days when Father Johnston would visit the mission church at Pictou Landing. For example, Johnston would travel across the harbor to say a weekday Mass, to hear confessions (often alternating genders from one week to the next), and to conduct special rituals, such as the Forty Hours Adoration.[25] In a letter to his bishop, Johnston remarked that his Mi'kmaw parishioners claimed to be unable to pay the ten-cent ferry fare to cross the harbor to attend Sunday Mass in Pictou. Therefore, they only heard Mass once a month when he traveled to Pictou Landing (Diocese of Antigonish Archives 1933a). An examination of the announcements in Father Johnston's booklets confirms this report for the period between 1932 and 1938; however, these monthly visits were restricted to between April and November.[26] Father Johnston appears to have moved more frequently to the Mi'kmaw congregation than that congregation moved to him.

Priests were not the only non-Mi'kmaq to travel to Mi'kmaw churches. The dispensations that the Church made to the Mi'kmaw people, which made "their church" possible, seem to have made them objects of curiosity for some non-Mi'kmaw Catholics. Elsie Clews Parsons observed one such group attending the Sunday celebrations of the St. Anne's mission at Potlotek (Chapel Island) in 1923:

> An excursion steamer from Sydney anchors off the Island, bringing about one hundred White visitors, the majority Catholics. They are seated on the right side of the centre aisle [of the church], and each pays twenty-five cents for a seat, besides which there is a collection. These visitors are welcome as a source of revenue (there is a charge of twenty-five to fifty cents for bringing them off the steamer in row boats); likewise as a source of prestige for the celebration. After the religious service they crowd into the wigwam of the Grand Chief to shake hands, and without giving offense they look into or enter any other wigwam at pleasure. (E. Parsons 1926, 466)

Parsons' observation that not all of the visitors were Catholic suggests that at least a portion of the party attended for reasons other than saintly devotion. Indeed, in her reflection on this passage, Hornborg described the non-Mi'kmaw visitors to Chapel Island as tourists (Hornborg 2002, 242). The description of white visitors entering wigwams and tents following the Mass indicates that the Mi'kmaq were very much on display, further exoticizing them.

Parsons' description of white pilgrims/tourists visiting Chapel Island highlights the role that mobility has played in the history of the Catholic Church's mission to the Mi'kmaq. Mi'kmaq have not been the only subjects in post-contact Nova Scotia moving for religious purposes. The Catholic Church's mission was dependent upon itinerant missionaries who would seek out and even follow communities of Mi'kmaw converts. And even in the nineteenth and twentieth centuries, as the more sedentary European settler population narrowed priests' spheres to their parishes, most who served Mi'kmaw communities continued to travel to them. On some occasions—such as the St. Anne's mission—these priests brought non-Mi'kmaw parishioners and others to experience Mi'kmaw Catholicism. Such excursions to Mi'kmaw places may have served to objectify the Mi'kmaq and their religious practices, but these instances also demonstrate the need to reimagine the role that movement played in nineteenth-century Mi'kmaw society. While their persistent movements marked the Mi'kmaq as "Other," those of their non-Mi'kmaw fellow Catholics were not considered outside the norm. Yet the movements of all these subjects were working to reshape the social and political relationships between them. Indeed, one of the unintended consequences of the Church's continued mission to the Mi'kmaq was the development of a Mi'kmaw

Catholicism that has afforded opportunities for Mi'kmaq to assert themselves as political subjects.

Mi'kmaw Catholicism

As a mediator of sociopolitical relationships in post-contact Nova Scotia, mobility can also be examined to understand Mi'kmaw responses to the changing policies and practices of the Catholic Church and the British Crown.[27] In the two centuries following the assertion of British sovereignty over Nova Scotia, the Catholic missionaries and priests who ministered to the Mi'kmaq had been transformed from advocates to bureaucrats. This transformation affected how Mi'kmaq adopted and adapted the Catholicism in ways unimagined by the first propagators of the faith.

In spite of the Crown's hope that the Mi'kmaq would convert to Protestantism, Mi'kmaw devotion to Catholicism by the mid-nineteenth century appeared to be unshaken. Several nineteenth-century observers noted the Mi'kmaq's devoutness. In his 1832 report, the commissioner for Indian affairs, Abraham Gesner, observed that Mi'kmaq from around the province regularly traveled to Halifax for religious purposes: "At Christmas and other seasons of the year hundreds of the Indians collect about the confines of the City to attend to their religious observances" (NSA 1832). In 1843, Joseph Howe, the superintendent of Indian affairs, remarked on the reverence in which Mi'kmaq held the prayer books that were given to their ancestors in the previous century by Abbé Maillard: "Their books, which contain prayers and portions of their religious services, are more numerous than I at first supposed, and if not found in every wigwam, are carefully preserved and constantly referred to in every encampment" (NSA 1843).

But the Catholicism that the Mi'kmaq practiced in the mid-nineteenth century was not the same as that of their Acadian, Irish, and Highland Scot contemporaries. In the absence of resident missionaries and priests, Mi'kmaw chiefs often led prayers and conducted rituals for their communities. Maillard's ideographic prayer book, which included liturgies and catechisms sanctioned by the mid-eighteenth century Catholic Church, became the guiding text for such ceremonies. As the decades passed, the Mi'kmaq adapted and innovated some of these practices. As Steen (1951) has discussed, until the Church actively sought to ban rituals such as the war dance, Mi'kmaw practices were often included in Catholic ceremonies.[28] The syncretic nature of Mi'kmaw spiritual practice has been discussed by previous researchers (Chute 1992; Hornborg 2002; E. Parsons 1926; Robinson 2005; Wallis and Wallis

1955). Yet, seen through the lens of mobility, Mi'kmaw Catholicism appears to be less an attempt to reconcile old and new beliefs and more a new form of Catholic practice, which had evolved from the mid-eighteenth century.[29]

In addition to the observations of Protestant colonial agents such as Monk, Gesner, and Howe, a key source for examining the mobility of Mi'kmaw Catholicism in the nineteenth century is an 1867 article titled "The Catholic Church in the Wilderness," which appeared in the *Irish Ecclesiastical Record*. The author is not named, although the references to Pomquet and the date of publication suggest the article was written by Christian Kauder, a Redemptorist missionary from Luxembourg.[30] Throughout the article, the author emphasizes Mi'kmaw practices that are either unfamiliar to him or have become passé in the Roman Catholic Church, many of which required movement at various temporal and spatial scales. In emphasizing the foreignness of these practices, the author goes so far as to describe them as comprising "their Church"—in other words, the Mi'kmaw Church. One such practice was that of "churching," in which new mothers presented themselves at a chapel or a church for blessing by a priest. By the mid-nineteenth century, the Vatican no longer required women to present themselves for the "benediction *post-partum*." However, the author stated that convincing the Mi'kmaq of this change was difficult because "[t]he hieroglyphic book of rites which they possess tells the women that they have to receive the churching before confession" (Anonymous 1867, 244–45).[31] These Mi'kmaq did not, however, completely disregard the authority of the missionaries and priests. The author describes the rituals performed during the final hours of an illness—a dying person's family gathered as he was "exhorted to pronounce in his heart Jesus, Mary, Joseph, St. Anne, while they [the family] are singing the prescribed prayers and psalms." But if a priest was present, "they will perform none of their own ceremonies, but leave the whole over to him" (Anonymous 1867, 246–47).

A persistent theme in "The Catholic Church in the Wilderness" is the various types of pilgrimage that Mi'kmaq made to fulfill their spiritual duties. Their reverence for St. Anne motivated many of these movements. Mi'kmaq from all parts of Mi'kma'ki had been traveling to sites such as Maligomish for the annual St. Anne's mission since the mid-eighteenth century. However, the author noted that the Mi'kmaq's devotion to St. Anne was not limited to large communal gatherings celebrating her feast day:

> When they are in great danger on the sea in their canoe, or in the winter hunting in the woods, or to obtain the grace of baptism for a child not yet born, or to be restored to health, or to obtain some other favours from heaven through the intercession of St. Anne, they make a vow to visit one

of the places where she is honoured, and to offer some presents in that place. . . . In general they make the vow to go to the Indian Island, CB. [Cape Breton], and to other chapels, and also to places where crosses are erected. (Anonymous 1867, 239)

More symbolic pilgrimages were performed by reenacting the passion of Christ through the ritual of *via crucis* or the "Way of the Cross." The anonymous author commented that "[i]n all their chapels the stations of the Way of the Cross are erected. . . . If they are living in the neighbourhood of the chapel, they will make on every Friday the *via crucis*" (Anonymous 1867, 254). In the early twentieth century, Elsie Clews Parsons observed another ritualized pilgrimage at the St. Anne's Day celebration on Chapel Island. To honor St. Anne, many pilgrims would crawl to her shrine on their knees. In 1923, the pilgrims began at the steps to the mission church: "The men headed the procession of kneelers, who moved three or four knee-lengths or strides between prayers, i.e. all moved together and prayed together, movement and prayer alternating" (E. Parsons 1926, 468).[32]

Unlike the Crown's bureaucrats, who were lamenting the continuous movements of the Mi'kmaq for religious purposes, the author of "The Catholic Church in the Wilderness" praised the distances that the Mi'kmaq's devotion would inspire. In this article he conveyed a conception of movement that was positively valued. On the Fridays of Lent, Mi'kmaq prayed before the large crucifixes erected in every chapel's cemetery: "I know Indians who go there every Lent, though they are living several miles from it. No inclemency of weather can prevent them" (Anonymous 1867, 254). Mi'kmaq also made long pilgrimages to attend the sick: "If any one is sick, every one visits him continually; they will travel twenty to forty miles to visit him . . . if his sickness increases, every one considers it as an honour to go for the priest, even if the priest's house be very far off" (Anonymous 1867, 240). The author also noted that Mi'kmaq traveled great distances to be able to make the sacrament of confession to a priest who spoke and understood Mi'kmaw: "I saw women walking through the snow, a distance of eighty miles, in order to have the happiness to confess in their own language. Many of them come every year from the remotest parts of the country to confess in their own language" (Anonymous 1867, 250–51).[33]

The author also provides some insight into the sensual perceptions Mi'kmaq would experience along these journeys, describing how they would sing in the woods "beautiful hymns and canticles in honour of the Blessed Virgin Mary, St. Anne, St. Joseph, or hymns for Christmas and Easter" (Anonymous 1867, 252). And such practices appear to have had spiritual benefit to the Mi'kmaq who performed them. The 1857 Ordo of Halifax noted that "[w]hen three or more families pray or sing hymns together in the woods," they would receive a partial indulgence of three years. The same indulgence would be offered to those who prayed or sang canticles on Sundays and holy days "either in some Church, or in their wigwams" (cited in Ste. Anne de Ristigouche [sic] Frères 1910, 82).

Fundamental to Mi'kmaw pilgrimage were the places to which Mi'kmaq traveled to express their devotion. The anonymous author wrote in 1867 that the Mi'kmaq had "great respect for their chapels, graveyards, and all things connected to them. . . . They behave also in it and towards it as if it was the house of God" (Anonymous 1867, 254). Mi'kmaq appear to have expected from their non-Mi'kmaw neighbors the same respect toward their sacred sites. The anonymous author describes an incident at a St. Anne's Day cele-bration during which two white Catholics were dancing near the chapel: "As soon as the Indians heard of it, all the men ran to that place, and the white fellows had a narrow escape. They were highly scandalized at the conduct of such Catholics" (Anonymous 1867, 254).[34] In July 1933, *The Casket* an-nounced that at the recent mission on Maligomish "[s]plendid order pre-vailed; and it is reported that a couple of bootleggers from the mainland who brought a quantity of their wares to the island during the week were set on by the Indians and given a rough handling" (Diocese of Antigonish Archives 1933b). The Mi'kmaq's care for Potlotek and Maligomish in particular may be related to the increased significance of islands in the late nineteenth and early twentieth centuries. As the federal government sought to curtail Mi'kmaw movements through programs like centralization, islands such as Maligomish became important places of refuge (Confederacy of Mainland Mi'kmaq the Robert S. Peabody Museum of Archaeology 2001, 69).

The predictability of pilgrimages to mission sites such as Maligomish for the feast of St. Anne was perhaps less threatening to Crown and Church offi-cials than the frequent journeys Mi'kmaq made "along the Coast, on the Riv-ers, and Lakes, and through the Forests" (NSA 1808) in search of a priest to offer prayers for the dying or to hear confessions. Maligomish has been a mis-sion site since at least 1758. It appears as though the earliest reference to a chapel devoted to Mi'kmaq in the area dates to 1835. A petition to the pro-vincial government dated June 11 mentions that "with some assistance and much labour" the Mi'kmaq had erected a house of worship in Merigomish (NSA 1835). Whether this chapel was on the island of Maligomish or on mainland Merigomish is unclear. Seven years later, however, James Dawson described a chapel and burying ground during his visit to Maligomish in June 1842 (LAC 1842c).

By the mid-nineteenth century, the St. Anne's mission was well established as an annual tradition on Maligomish. In his 1860 report on the diocese to the Vatican's *Congregation de Propaganda Fide*, the bishop of the Diocese
of Arichat described the St. Anne's Day celebrations at Maligomish, Potlotek,
and Paqtnkek (Afton): "On this day all the Indians, young and old, in each
Mission, assemble at their respective churches, where they remain very often
a fortnight, attended by the neighboring Catholic pastors. As it is reasonable
to suppose, during these Missions a great deal of good is performed, contributing very materially to the spiritual and temporal welfare of the tribe" (Diocese of Antigonish Archives 1860).

Today, Mi'kmaq from the Pictou Landing First Nation refer to the four-
day weekend closest to the July 26 feast day of St. Anne as "mission time."
For many Mi'kmaw Catholics, the feast of St. Anne not only invites them to
reflect on the life of their patron saint but also inspires a pilgrimage from
Pictou Landing and other Mi'kmaw communities around Mi'kma'ki to spiri-
tually significant places such as Maligomish and Potlotek. As a religious event,
mission time combines several Catholic traditions. The Catholic Church cate-
gorizes this four-day event as a "parochial mission," as distinguished from apostolic missions targeted toward nonbelievers. The objective of a parochial
mission is to renew and deepen the faith of believers. Such missions take place
over several days, are led by mission priests, and are organized around a systematic course of prayer and teaching.[35]

Catholics make a pilgrimage to Maligomish because it is a shrine to
St. Anne. The church on Maligomish is devoted to St. Anne, and it houses a
shrine in the form of a statue depicting the saint and her daughter, the Virgin
Mary. Pilgrims pray for St. Anne's intercession with God the Son (Jesus Christ)
and God the Father. As a shrine, Maligomish has been the scene of healing
miracles attributed to St. Anne. However, the St. Anne's mission has always
been more than a religious event. Anthropologists have long recognized the
mission as a social construction that combines both sacred and secular expressions of Mi'kmaw identity (see Chute 1992; Hornborg 2002; Larsen 1983; E.
Parsons 1926; Poliandri 2011; Reid 2013; Robinson 2005; Wallis and Wallis
1955).[36] What follows is a composite description of both the sacred and mundane practices, perceptions, and conceptions of movement that pilgrims to
Maligomish experience during the mission weekend. This description tacks
between the memories shared by members of the Pictou Landing First Nation
(which date to as early as the 1930s) and my observations of the ten missions
that I have attended. In weaving both perspectives through this description, I
aim to capture something of the "mission time" experience; it is an event for

which the past always informs the present. These observations of the daily life of mission time demonstrate how pilgrimage works to emplace Mi'kmaq on Maligomish.

Mission Time on Maligomish

Although the contemporary mission starts on Thursday, most people arrive on Friday in late afternoon or early evening.[37] Families with small children, groups of teenagers and twenty-somethings, and young to middle-aged couples represent the typical demographic of the "mission time" population. Those who arrive early park close to the wharf on Quarry Island, along the ever-dwindling shoreline. Latecomers park along the narrow, gravel Quarry Island Road and have to lug their gear to the wharf. The Pictou Landing First Nation generally lends one or two of its boats to transport people from Quarry Island to Maligomish. Mi'kmaq who have their own boats are usually happy to take another passenger (or several) and their supplies. As people wait for a boat, sleeping bags, pillows, coolers, backpacks, suitcases, and other supplies pile up along the narrow wharf.

In the late nineteenth and early twentieth centuries, Mi'kmaq traveling from Cape Breton, Millbrook, or Paqtntkek would take the train to the village of Egerton and wait there for a boat to the island (M. Martin 1989, 2). In the 1930s, when few people at Pictou Landing owned a vehicle, families either shared a car or hitchhiked to Maligomish. In her conversations with me, Madeline Martin recalled some Mi'kmaq walking the roughly fifteen kilometers from Pictou Landing to Quarry Island. She knew a non-Mi'kmaw family from Little Harbour (about halfway between Pictou Landing and Quarry Island) who provided water to the passing Mi'kmaw pilgrims. Others piled into a lobster boat piloted directly to Maligomish from Pictou Landing (Lelièvre field notebook, vol. 14:95; see also M. Martin 1989, 1). Madeline reported that the lobster boats could "take two or three families with their food, clothing and bedding" (M. Martin 1989, 1). Mary Irene Nicholas recalled from the mid-twentieth century that she and her family would wait several hours or even camp overnight on Quarry Island before catching a ride to Maligomish. Because transportation to Maligomish was limited, many families planned to stay on the island for a week or longer (M. Martin 1989, 1). Noel Martin's film footage of missions during the 1960s captures the perceptions of movement that many families experienced en route to Maligomish. In one sequence a man is seen speeding along the island's shore in a small boat with an outboard motor. Moments later the film resumes, the same boat puttering through the water laden with the weight of passengers, luggage, and mattresses. Today, the greater number of boats—and the construction of better wharves—have helped to cut the wait for a ride to seldom more than half an hour. The ride itself is usually less than ten minutes.

If the camp is the center of family life on Maligomish, then the churchyard is the focus of community activity. It serves as a kind of public square and hub during the mission. All of the main footpaths on the island lead to the churchyard. There are picnic tables and lawn chairs that invite people to stop and socialize. This area is especially popular with teenagers after dark.[38] There is also a canteen located to the north of the church that has a constant stream of customers. Pop and hip-hop music occasionally plays from a stereo powered by the canteen's generator. The churchyard is also the site of activities organized for children and adults. Some activities, such as making rosary beads, are provided by the mission's organizing committee. Others are organized through ad hoc committees that also arrange sporting events, card tournaments, bingo, and evening socials. In recent years, youth volunteers from the Red Road Project have organized activities such as scavenger hunts for younger children.[39] In 2014 and 2015 the missions included a sacred fire located at the eastern end of the island between the church and the north shore just south of Waycobah Corner. An elder attends the fire to ensure it burns throughout the mission. The sacred fire has become a new gathering place where mission attendees share stories about the island and Mi'kmaw traditions. These activities appear to be more popular than the religious rituals observed during the mission. Although Maligomish's population swells during mission time, proportionally few Mi'kmaq participate in either the gathering circles or the Stations of the Cross, Rosary services, and Masses. However, the variety of—and participation in—all of these activities may vary from year to year.

Until the mid- to late twentieth century, the officiating priest or priests generally stayed on Maligomish for the duration of the event. Father Roderick McDonald wrote to the Department of Indian Affairs that he had a residence built for himself in 1891 because he spent "every year over a fortnight continuously among them and had up to the last summer to rent a camp from one of the Indian families for use" (LAC 1891; see also M. Martin 1989, 1). Today the priests do not stay on the island. The glebe house where they once stayed has fallen into disrepair. Instead, they travel back and forth each day. Some missions will have a "mission priest," who is generally not the parish priest but a visiting pastor or deacon. The mission priest will generally travel to the island each day of the mission and lead the planned events, which include public recitations of the Rosary, praying the Stations of the Cross, and candlelight processions around the cemetery. A mission priest may also select a theme that will inform his homilies for the weekend. Recent themes have included "The Community as Family" and "Progress, Not Perfection."

If a mission priest is not present, then an elder, a *Keptin* of the Grand Council, and/or a member of the mission's organizing committee will lead the spiritual activities, often inviting members of the congregation to participate by, for example, saying a decade of the Rosary. When laypeople lead these rituals, there may be more Mi'kmaw practices included than if the mission priest had been present. For example, in 2009, Sadie Francis opened the mission by explaining its significance to those gathered. She then burned sweetgrass and sage and prayed to the spirits of the four cardinal directions to bless the mission and to keep its participants safe during their stay on Maligomish.

On the Saturday of the mission, the women of the organizing committee—and other interested female community members—gather at the church to dress the statue of St. Anne. The statue is approximately 1.5 meters tall and stands in a litter that is enclosed on three sides (see fig. 24 left and right). St. Anne is wearing simple clothing. Her daughter, the Virgin Mary, is depicted as a young child standing in prayer at St. Anne's feet. The supplies to dress the statue are taken to Maligomish by one of the organizing committee members. These include bolts of pastel-colored fabrics, ribbons, lace, cloth flowers, and rosettes. Most of the dressing happens on the litter, rather than on St. Anne herself. The exterior and interior surfaces of the litter are covered in cloth, leaving St. Anne visible. Ribbons are attached to either side of the litter, framing St. Anne. Rosettes conceal any staples used to attach the cloth and ribbons. Mary is sometimes given a pair of rosary beads that are draped over her hands. St. Anne herself is crowned with a wreath of braided sweetgrass gathered from the shores of one of the neighboring islands. Cloth is gingerly gathered around St. Anne's feet. Atop the cloth is placed a plastic bowl into which pilgrims can place money as they offer prayers to St. Anne. Like other images of saints and holy figures in the Catholic tradition, the statue of St. Anne is a focal point for the veneration of the saint herself, and the care with which these women prepare the statue suggests that they consider it to be more than an object. They often refer to the statue using the pronouns "her" and "she" rather than "it."

The dressed shrine of St. Anne remains in the church during the mission. A smaller statue is carried during the procession that follows Mass on the Sunday of the mission.[40] This Mass and the procession are the religious highlights of the mission weekend. The Mass usually begins around 2:00 p.m. The population on Maligomish grows even larger on Sunday because many

FIGURE 24. Photographs of women in the process of dressing the shrine of St. Anne (left) and of St. Anne dressed and prepared for the Sunday Mass (right), 2010. Photographs taken by the author.

people only attend the Sunday events. This group of day-trippers might include Mi'kmaq who live in other communities but have ties to the Pictou Landing First Nation, community members who do not keep camps on the island, elders whose health makes the climb into and out of boats and up the hill to the church quite difficult, and non-Mi'kmaq who have friends in the community and/or are curious to visit Maligomish. At least until the 1930s, the St. Anne's Day celebrations on Maligomish—especially the Sunday Mass and procession of St. Anne—were attended by local non-Mi'kmaq in addition to Mi'kmaq from around the region. Today, comparatively few non-Mi'kmaq attend.[41]

For many of the Mi'kmaq who stay on Maligomish during the mission, the Sunday ceremonies will be the only religious event they attend. During the first few missions I attended, the sacrament of Eucharist or First Communion was held during the Sunday Mass. In these years, the congregation was quite large as proud parents and their extended families watched their children receive the Holy Eucharist for the first time. Before Mass, children around age eight and nine, dressed in suits and white dresses, queued in the churchyard and then proceeded into the church, following their religious-studies teacher. The *Keptins* and flag bearers led the way.

During the mission's Sunday Mass, the *Keptins*, each wearing a light blue and white sash, sit in the front rows of the church. The procession of the statue of St. Anne to the "grotto" immediately follows the Mass. With the exception of the slight disruption in 2010, generally when all of the pilgrims have venerated, the priest ends the ceremony and St. Anne is picked up, processed down the path, and returned to the church. By the time the procession has ended, the organizing committee and volunteers have rearranged the picnic tables in the churchyard so that the St. Anne's feast can be served. In the first years that I attended the mission, the feast included snow crab that had been donated by the community's fishermen. Recently the menu has included stew or soup, *lu'sknikn* (a Mi'kmaw bannock), strawberry shortcake with strawberries donated from a community member, hotdogs for the children, and lots of *pitewey*. Often the meal has been prepared by volunteers, but in recent years a caterer from the Pictou Landing First Nation has been hired. The feast is open to anyone on the island. It draws the largest crowd of all the mission events. The feast attracts a broad cross-section of the Pictou Landing First Nation and visitors from other communities. People of all ages sit on lawn chairs, at picnic tables, on the church steps, and on the grass to enjoy their food while catching up with friends and family.

Following the feast, there is generally a rush to pack up and leave the island while the band boats are still running regularly. Most of the island's weekend residents amble down the path from the churchyard to the wharf, carrying as many of their belongings as they can. Others linger in the churchyard, helping to clean up after the feast. For those who stay on the island after the feast, the quiet of Sunday evening and Monday is particularly pleasant after a busy weekend. This peacefulness sets the tone for the mission's concluding ceremony—a cemetery Mass that honors the community members who are buried on Maligomish. This Mass has special significance for some Mi'kmaq, in part because it is held in the cemetery itself, which is located just west of the church on one of the highest points on Maligomish. Several large hardwood trees provide much-needed shade from the July sun. The quiet solemnity of the cemetery Mass marks the end of the St. Anne's mission and the departure from the island of most of the remaining pilgrims.

The journeys to and from Maligomish for the St. Anne's mission are part of the genealogy of pilgrimage that has been a hallmark of Mi'kmaw Catholicism. As early as 1808, Crown officials had observed the literal lengths Mi'kmaq would go to visit a priest for blessings and to receive sacraments. Despite the efforts of Bishop Plessis in 1812 to curtail the Mi'kmaq's religious journeys, the anonymous author of "The Catholic Church in the Wilderness" claims that few Mi'kmaq followed this prescription. Pilgrimage, whether prescribed by their ideographic prayer books or necessitated by the distance between priests and their missions, became a new way for Mi'kmaq to emplace themselves on Nova Scotia's colonial landscape by moving across it. These were innovative practices based on traditions introduced by a colonial power.

Mobility and Mi'kmaw Catholicism

Examining the Catholic mission through the lens of mobility allows us to understand the "reciprocal and mutually constitutive" (Lycett 2004) nature of the relationships between the Church's agents and Mi'kmaw subjects. Catholicism has become a significant aspect of some Mi'kmaq's identity; yet Mi'kmaq have never been wholly assimilated even into an institution as powerful and universal as the Catholic Church. Early missionaries adapted their proselytizing and ministrations to the mobile lifestyles of their prospective converts by traveling with and between Mi'kmaw communities. The constant movements of the missionaries made the Catholic Church— like the Mi'kmaq themselves—a persistent, if not permanent, fixture on the colonial landscape. After the establishment of a diocesan structure in eastern Canada that was dominated by non-Mi'kmaq, the Church not only tolerated some of the uniquely Mi'kmaw Catholic practices—such as "churching"—but also encouraged them by granting partial and plenary indulgences. In 1910, the Church granted special indulgences to mark the tercentenary of the Mi'kmaq's conversion (see Ste. Anne de Ristigouche [*sic*] Frères 1910, appendix B). And in 1914 Father Pacifique wrote to the Diocese of Antigonish from his parish of Ste. Anne de Restigouche in Québec requesting funds toward the cost of printing a "Micmac Church Singing Book." The bishop of Antigonish responded with a donation of twenty dollars and the wish that "the liturgical parts of the work will not involve a departure from the authorised rules regarding these matters" (Diocese of Antigonish 1914). By the mid-twentieth century, this favored status seems to have diminished, as indicated by Sadie Francis's recollection of her grandmother's dismissal by a priest on Maligomish and Steen's report that Mi'kmaw participation in Catholic rituals at Eskasoni discontinued after centralization.

Disciplining Mi'kmaw spiritual behaviour was difficult, however, because of the Church's continued approach to ministration through missionizing. Their status as missions of a parent parish means that most Mi'kmaw communities in the Diocese of Antigonish have not had a resident priest. The lack of a resident priest has opened opportunities for Mi'kmaq to practice their own faith—at times, in ways that deviate from the orthodoxy of the Church. Chiefs and elders—some of whom were women—have taken leading roles in the spiritual lives of the Mi'kmaq.

But there is no denying the adverse effects that the Church has had on the lives of many Mi'kmaq who suffered abuse, neglect, and the loss of language and culture while attending residential schools. Church leaders—as much as their counterparts in the Crown government—paternalized Mi'kmaq, as evidenced in some of the correspondence between priests and the bishop of Antigonish. Responding to Father Johnston's request for reimbursement to the parish fund for an insurance policy for Our Lady of Perpetual Help, the bishop suggested that Johnston keep the source of funding hidden from the Mi'kmaw congregation: "lest they try to take advantage of it in the future. Hold the obligation over them, and so spur them up to industry and thrift" (Diocese of Antigonish Archives 1934). Yet such infantilization did not serve the bishop's intended objective of assimilating Mi'kmaq as independent, liberal subjects. Rather, it worked to further mark the Mi'kmaq as indigenous and, therefore, "Other" than non-Mi'kmaw Catholics.

Indeed, the mission structure of the Catholic Church's ministration to the Mi'kmaq has had the effect of marking this congregation as exceptional. Mi'kmaq have not been the only Catholics in the Diocese of Antigonish to be ministered through the mission system, but unlike their non-Mi'kmaw

Catholic neighbors, the mission structure is the norm in Mi'kmaw communities. Holy Family Church in Eskasoni is the only Mi'kmaw parish in the Diocese of Antigonish. During Father Johnston's tenure at Stella Marish parish in Pictou, Masses were held at Our Lady of Perpetual Help mission only once a month, unlike the multiple daily Masses that would have been said at the parish church. Adherence to long passé rituals, liturgies, prayers, and hymns in the Mi'kmaw language and devotion to St. Anne have further marked Mi'kmaq as different from nonindigenous Catholics in the Diocese of Antigonish and elsewhere.

These differences have made Mi'kmaw Catholicism an object of curiosity for some nonindigenous Catholics. The non-Mi'kmaq who attended the 1923 St. Anne's mission on Potlotek (see E. Parsons 1926) and the picnickers who came to Maligomish in 1890 may have been more curious onlookers than devout pilgrims. Yet, Parsons seems to imply that receiving curious strangers to the St. Anne's mission was not without benefit to the gathered Mi'kmaq who were able to collect funds for transporting them to the island and receive donations to the mission church.

Entangled in this complex, reciprocal, and mutually constitutive four-hundred-year Catholic mission to the Mi'kmaq was the disruption during the 2010 procession of St. Anne. Placed in its historical and comparative contexts, the calling out of the priest does not appear to be a significant conflict or deviation from the traditions of the mission procession. The observations reported from different periods of the twentieth century indicate that, with the exception of keeping the congregation behind St. Anne, the order of procession participants was very flexible (see Hornborg 2002, 251; Howard 1965, 9; Larsen 1983, 114; E. Parsons 1926, 467; Vernon 1903, 99). Priests and chiefs alternated between walking one in front of the other to processing side-by-side. These variations likely have as much to do with the contemporary relationships between the institution of the Catholic Church and the Mi'kmaw nation as they do with the very localized relationships between parish priests and their mission congregations.

The community member's capacity to act in protest to the affront to St. Anne was possible, in part, because it occurred on Maligomish. It is a site not only with a long history of Mi'kmaw occupation but also with overlapping, competing, and sometimes contradicting authorities. In addition to the priests and the local Mi'kmaw organizing committee, other authorities at work on Maligomish include the appointed or inherited offices of *Keptin*, Grand Chief, and Grand *Keptin* of the *Sante' Mawi'omi*; the elected band chief and council in each Mi'kmaw community; the federal department now known as Indigenous and Northern Affairs Canada;[42] and, occasionally, the Nova Scotia provincial government. All of these institutions have authority on Maligomish that varies depending on the historical moment.

Seen through the lens of mobility, however, the 2010 procession and the interruption illustrate the entangled processes of movement and emplacement at work during the mission, and further demonstrate the construction of Mi'kmaq as political subjects—here, specifically, through a subtle contestation between the authority of the local Mi'kmaq and that of the Catholic Church, represented by the parish priest. The priest's desire to change the order was not simply a violation of the accepted tradition but also an affront to St. Anne. For the women who carefully clean and dress the statue—and the pilgrims who pray before it—the statue is a visual reminder of St. Anne herself. The respect with which St. Anne is given by dressing her, conveying her from the church to the "grotto," and venerating before her was violated when she was at risk of being left behind by the officiating priests. The community member's insistence that St. Anne be shown her due respect by leading the recession back to the church demonstrates a conception of movement rooted in the positive values associated with maintaining the spatial order of the procession that has become the tradition of the mission on Maligomish. Not adhering to that order violated the accepted practice. Moreover, by insisting on this spatial order, the community member was emplacing the participants of the procession.

The multiscale pilgrimages of the St. Anne's mission have worked to emplace Mi'kmaq on Maligomish. At a very broad scale, Mi'kmaq from around Mi'kma'ki make their way by car and boat to the sacred site. Although accessing the island is easier now than it has ever been, the pilgrimage may still require sacrifice from those who lack the resources to prepare to camp away from home for several days. At a smaller scale, the procession of the statue of St. Anne is a ritualized pilgrimage to honor the saint and ask for her intercession. During the procession, the pilgrims' perceptions of walking are affected not only by their immediate interaction with the path, its roots, hills, and length, but also by their cumulative experiences of walking the same path over their lifetimes and the collective moment of sharing that journey with their fellow community members and outsiders such as myself who may be experiencing it for the first time.[43] The sensual experience of walking the procession path is heightened by the occasional signing of hymns, the recitations of the "Our Father" and "Hail Mary," and the gestures of veneration as participants kneel, bow, and kiss the statue of St. Anne.

Pilgrimage is a particularly powerful site of inquiry for the colonial and postcolonial periods in Nova Scotia. Many different subjects have been moving in order to practice and propagate the Catholic faith. The current chapter has drawn on historical sources and ethnographic observations to examine movements for religious purposes as practiced by the clergy, the Mi'kmaw faithful, and non-Mi'kmaw Catholics. These different instantiations of pilgrimage demonstrate how movement works to emplace—whether through the Church's assertion of authority over the religious landscape of colonial Nova Scotia, its attempt to discipline the Mi'kmaq's movements by restricting where and when they could visit priests, the Mi'kmaq's movements to offer devotions to St. Anne and honor the Cross, or one woman's assertion of Mi'kmaw authority over the St. Anne's procession on Maligomish. These pilgrimages provide further evidence for the need to reconceptualize settlement and its relationship to mobility.

Conclusion

The People's Journey

IN JANUARY 2013 seven young men set out from their Cree community of Whamagoostui in northern Québec to *walk* sixteen hundred kilometers to the Canadian capital of Ottawa.[1] Members of Cree and other Algonquian communities joined the men as they trekked south on what came to be known as the "Journey of Nishyuu"—or, "The People's Journey." By the time the walkers reached Ottawa in late March, their numbers had grown to almost four hundred. They were walking in solidarity with Theresa Spence, chief of the Attawapiskat First Nation, a James Bay Cree community in northern Ontario. Chief Spence underwent a six-week hunger strike in protest against the federal government's continued renegation of its social contract with Canada's First Peoples, manifesting in 2011 in an inadequate response to the housing crisis in her community, which left many families living in mold-filled houses or tents.

Perhaps no event better illustrates the incongruity of life on many reserves compared to the rest of Canada than the 2011 housing crisis in Attawapiskat. Canadian and international media brought to their audiences detailed descriptions and photographs of living conditions more commonly associated with the large urban slums of the global south than with the stereotypical image of Canada's Great White North. And yet Attawapiskat is not unique, as several other northern communities are suffering housing crises; nor are these crises new phenomena. The Crown has been failing to provide adequately for its indigenous subjects since the nineteenth century—a charge confirmed in a June 2016 report released by Human Rights Watch in which the organization noted that the provincial laws and regulations that protect the safety of drinking water for most Canadians do not extend to those who live on First Nations reserves (see Human Rights Watch 2016).

In different times and places over the colonial and postcolonial periods, the response of some indigenous peoples to this failure of the Crown has been to move. In the mid-nineteenth century, when the Nova Scotia government attempted to sedentize them, many Mi'kmaq were forced to move in order to supplement what little food they could coax from the often sterile lands that had been reserved for them. In the early twentieth century, when the federal government attempted to centralize all Nova Scotia Mi'kmaq into two large reserves, some families—such as the Sylliboys of Christmas Island—chose to travel several hundred kilometers and seek permission to camp near a train station rather than obey a government-mandated relocation.

Since 2012, and the rise of the Idle No More movement, many indigenous peoples are again choosing to move in response to the failure of the Crown. These movements, however, are less about the daily survival of a family or community and more about the survival of indigenous peoples within the settler state. Such was the purpose of the Journey of Nishyuu. When the walkers arrived on Parliament Hill in Ottawa on March 25, 2013, they were greeted by thousands of supporters and by representatives of the Canadian government, including the federal minister in charge of indigenous affairs. Yet what many people remember from that day is that then–Prime Minister Stephen Harper was not present, having chosen, instead, to greet two panda bears at the Toronto Zoo that had recently arrived from China.

The Journey of Nishyuu was one of many responses to the grassroots calls for political action made by Idle No More—a multisited political protest, which began among First Nations people in Canada in late 2012. Idle No More was precipitated by the increased frustration and anger felt by Canada's First Nations toward a federal government that has long undermined indigenous rights protected in Canada's constitution and has neglected to uphold its own environmental regulations in pursuit of oil, gas, and mineral development—often in the ancestral lands and waters of indigenous communities. Like its better-known political cousins Occupy and Black Lives Matter, Idle No More is characterized by its youthful leadership, social-media savvy, and use of spontaneous acts of protest, including flash round dances held in the food courts of shopping malls, rallies at busy intersections in urban centers, and blockades of highways and railroads.

Since March 2013 indigenous walkers have made many long-distance treks similar to the Journey of Nishyuu. In the winter of 2014 the Omushkegowuk walkers traveled seventeen hundred kilometers from the Attawapiskat First Nation in northern Ontario to Ottawa. In December 2014 a group of Cree youth marched from Mistissini, Québec, to Montréal to protest the development of a uranium mine in their traditional territory. The year 2015 saw a proliferation of long-distance walks, including Water Walks, often led by indigenous women hoping to draw attention to the need to protect fresh water supplies.[2] Mi'kmaw elder Dorene Bernard organized the 2016 Mi'kma'ki Water Walk to protest against the development of a natural-gas storage facility near Fort Ellis, Nova Scotia, which will see brine released into the Shubenacadie River.[3] Other walks have been precipitated by protest against the development of oil, gas, and mineral exploitation.[4]

Broadly speaking, the objectives of each of these journeys have been to raise awareness of the social and environmental crises that face many indigenous communities in Canada and the United States; to draw attention to the ways in which various levels of government have undermined their own regulatory mechanisms to push through oil, gas, and mining development; to deepen the spirituality of the walkers; and—in the case of the journeys to Ottawa—to meet with representatives of the settler state.

The political aspirations of the two journeys to Ottawa appear to be paradoxical: On the one hand, the discourse of the journeys is one that turns against or even ignores the Crown. In statements made to the media and on personal and group Facebook pages, the Nishyuu and Omushkegowuk walkers and their supporters are disparaging of the Canadian settler state, epitomized by the paternalistic and omnipresent federal Indian Act and the politicians who uphold it, including both the predominately nonindigenous members of the Canadian Parliament and also the elected indigenous chiefs who serve in the Assembly of First Nations. The members of both of these political organizations represent what elder Edmond Etherington of the Moose Cree First Nation has described as the "suits and ties."[5] In their frustration and anger with the settler state, the protagonists of Idle No More are appealing to what Danny Metatawabin, leader of the Omushkegowuk walkers, has described as "the grassroots peoples." In his speech on Parliament Hill at the end of his journey on February 25, 2014, Metatawabin emphasized that the walkers represent grassroots peoples who had been sent by the community's elders.[6] Similarly, the Journey of Nishyuu's official website declares that "[t]his Quest-Journey will establish and unite our historical allies and restore our traditional trade routes with the Algonquian, Mohawk and other First Nations."[7] During an interview with the Canadian Broadcasting Corporation, Jordan Masty, one of the Cree youth on the Journey of Nishyuu, stated: "This journey is to send a message across—to all First Nations to come together under one universe, one voice, one nation" (Masty 2013). Here the intended audience is other indigenous peoples in a transnational, pan-indigenous context—the walkers' political interlocutors are neither the Canadian federal government, nor the provincial government of Québec, nor the Assembly of First Nations. Thus, Idle No More and the long-distance journeys inspired by it appear to be attempting to reconfigure political alliances in settler colonies in ways that ignore those established by the sovereign.

On the other hand, the destination of these more than one-thousand-kilometer treks is not just the city of Ottawa but, more precisely, the front lawn of the Parliament buildings close to the Centennial Flame that commemorates Canada's one hundred years of confederation—the very heart of the state from which the Idle No More participants seem ready to turn. Unlike other indigenous long-distance treks, such as the Maori pilgrimages to Waitangi described by Sinclair (1992)—the Journeys of Nishyuu and the Omushkegowuk were not to places sacred only to the Cree as a First Nation. They were journeys to a place whose significance is shared by Canada's indigenous and nonindigenous peoples. This choice to walk to (and emplace themselves in) the nation's capital suggests that some faith in the settler state still exists—that there is some devotion to its potential (if not actual) power to uphold treaty promises; to recognize the sovereignty of First Nations; and to negotiate for access to, and the protection of, land and resources in a nation-to-nation context.

Examined through the lens of mobility, these acts of walking—and the conceptions and perceptions that are entangled with this movement—are working to remake sociopolitical relationships in Canada between different First Nations communities, between First Nations and nonindigenous communities, and between First Nations and the "suits and ties" who embody the settler state for many Idle No More supporters. When these journeys are placed in historical and ethnographic context, we see that they are working to construct an indigenous politics that draws on traditions of the secular and the sacred from both the past and the present. Indeed, by walking across the ancestral lands of several different Algonquian peoples to the capital of Ottawa, these walkers have been asserting themselves as political subjects of the sovereign Cree First Nation and of a pan-indigenous political sphere, rather than subjects of the Canadian settler state.

Conceptualizing mobility as the practices, perceptions, and conceptions of movement that work to emplace subjects is a useful tool for examining how the quotidian experiences of the Journeys of Nishyuu and Omushkegowuk have contributed to the construction of indigenous politics. Some details about the practices, perceptions, and conceptions of the walkers while they were on their journeys can be gleaned from their postings on social media and information shared on the journeys' websites. These updates provide details such as the average distance that the walkers aimed to complete each day and the number of hours spent each day, not only walking, but also arranging for food and lodging and planning the next stages of the journey. Danny Meta-tawabin described how the tempo and qualities of the walking changed from day to day—with the start of some days' walks being delayed because of logistical difficulties; some walkers moving slowly because of sore feet, an-kles, and knees; and others struggling to continue through cold and hunger.[8] The Journey's occurrence in the dead of a subarctic winter required a particu-lar assemblage of material culture.[9] The walkers were required to bring both snowshoes and hiking boots, indicating that the areas traversed would in-clude both paved roads and the open land. Even with the provisions of warm, woolen socks, mittens, and hats, several of the walkers on the Journey of Nishyuu perceived the topography and weather in quite visceral ways as they suffered frostbite and foot injuries over the two-month trek.

Entwined with the lived practices and sensuous perceptions of movement on these journeys are their represented and imagined conceptions. Many of the walkers described the journey in terms of their relationships to the land and its resources, both of which are imperiled by the energy and mineral exploitation occurring on their ancestral territories with perfunctory consultation. With faith in the settler state undermined, the walkers turned to the "grassroots people" in communities along the sixteen-hundred-kilometer route. The Cree and other Algonquian communities along the way provided the walkers with shelter, meals, hot drinks, and encouragement, thus rekindling social, eco-nomic, and political relationships along the "ancient trade routes" that the organizers of the Journey of Nishyuu reference in their mission statement.[10]

By trekking through the traditional territories of Cree and other Al-gonquian First Nations, these walks worked to emplace the participants and their supporters by reestablishing connections between First Nations, some of which had been established long before the arrival of Europeans. These jour-neys echo the seasonal movements that the indigenous peoples of this region made within and between their territories until the early twentieth century. L'Innu activist Mélissa Mollen-Dupuis told the Canadian Broadcasting Corpo-ration in late 2014 that the journeys were positive acts that demonstrate that indigenous peoples are still in their traditional territories and that they con-tinue to use the land for subsistence (Mollen-Dupuis 2014). Walking hun-dreds of kilometers demonstrates this persistence by marking the breadth of these territories in footprints—it stakes a claim to the rights promised to Cree and other First Nations peoples in treaties signed with the British Crown and later the government of Canada.

The Cree walkers were asserting these rights by moving from the periphery to the center of the settler state. But the symbolism of Ottawa as the heart of the state seems to be of secondary importance. Of primary importance in Ottawa—and why the walkers' choice to make it the focal point of their journeys is not a paradox—is the presence of the Queen's representative. In keeping with the broader discourse of Idle No More, the participants in the Journeys of Nishyuu and Omushkegowuk were no longer interested in the mechanisms the government has set up to devolve powers to First Nations communities. Instead, they sought to reclaim the sovereignty their ancestors had when they negotiated treaties with the British Crown. As sovereign nations, the Cree and other First Nations in Canada expect to deal with Canada's head of state—the Governor General—and the Governor General lives in Ottawa.

As demonstrations of their continued use of, connection to, and partnerships with the traditional lands of several Algonquian nations, the Journeys of Nishiyuu and Omushkegowuk evoked an indigenous politics that defies the liberal model of a subject population submitting to the will of a sovereign. In calling for nation-to-nation relationships, the participants of these walks and other Idle No More events are not simply imagining a political sphere in which multiple sovereign, indigenous nations coexist with a colonizing nation. Indeed, the vision statement of the Journey of Nishyuu and the broader discourse of Idle No More conceive of a pan-indigenous politics that bypasses the last two hundred years of nation-building in Canada in favor of the nation-to-nation relationship that was the foundation of the eighteenth-century treaties signed with the British Crown. Thus, seen in ethnographic and historical context, the tagline of the Omushkegowuk walkers' Facebook page: "Reclaiming Our Steps Past, Present and Future," suggests the construction of an indigenous politics that draws on pre-contact, post-contact, and possibly post-state experiences.

The Right to Move

Anthropologists have been predicting the death of the state for at least two decades. Appadurai (1996) inventoried the kinds of human movement that were threatening the nation-state, including economic opportunity, oppression, iterant labor, and environmental crises. His assertion that "human motion is often more definitive of social life than it is exceptional" (Appadurai 1996, 43) accurately describes the social lives of the 65.3 million people whom the UNHRC (the UN Refugee Agency) estimates were displaced in

2015.[11] These people include the 1.6 million who have crossed the Mediterranean since 2011 seeking refuge in Europe from civil war, religious persecution, and economic collapse in Syria, Afghanistan, Eritrea, Libya, and other regions within North Africa and the Middle East. They also include the almost thirteen thousand people who have died or gone missing attempting to cross the Mediterranean since 2011.[12] In fact, 880 of those died just in the last week of May 2016.[13]

Yet far from dissolving, European nation-states appear to be resurging in response to migration on this massive scale. As Kallius et al. (2016, 27) report from Hungary, the framing of the recent increase in migration as a crisis works to "fabricate 'the state' as a cohesive institution with authority and responsibility to remedy threats."[14] Hungary and other European countries have asserted their nation-state-ness by shutting borders, disciplining the movements of migrants within their borders, arbitrating how and when the migrants can move on to a state that will welcome them, and—in the case of the United Kingdom—voting "yes" to a June 2016 referendum that would take that country out of the European Union.

The migration "crisis" requires anthropological analysis, and the reports of Kallius et al. (2016) from Hungary, and Holmes and Castañeda (2016) from Germany, represent the forefront of this work (see also Albahari 2015 and Andersson 2014). Their descriptions of the movements of refugees and asylum seekers—and the efforts of humanitarian workers, government agencies, and private citizens to both facilitate and also discipline these movements—demonstrate the necessity of an anthropological concept of mobility built on the practices, conceptions, and perceptions of movement entangled with practices of emplacement. Holmes and Castañeda (2016) discuss the conceptions of the recent surge in migration, including the anxiety that some Germans share over allowing the "right" kind of migrant into the country. Here we see a variation on the theme of the mobile subject as "Other." Evoking rhetoric not unlike that expressed by the colonial government and its agents in nineteenth-century Nova Scotia, Holmes and Castañeda's interlocutors imagine the right kind of migrant to be a "deserving" one (2016, 15). A deserving migrant is, for example, a Syrian refugee who had no choice but to flee his or her home. A nondeserving migrant is one who left his or her home country by choice.[15] Both types of migrants are engaged in the kind of human movement that is a problem needing to be solved (Holmes and Castañeda 2016, 19).

And while the migrants wait to move from one state to the next, they are emplaced. They are emplaced by the states that keep them in detention centers and processing zones. They also emplace themselves as they make homes and communities in the parks, train stations, and abandoned warehouses where they wait. Kallius et al. (2016, 28) describe these locations as places of potential mobility; the migrant may be able to move once more when a train station becomes operational again or through a chance encounter with a human smuggler. Perhaps nowhere better embodied the concept of emplacement than "The Jungle"—the series of camps outside Calais, France, that was inhabited by thousands of migrants either seeking asylum in France or attempting to cross the English Channel to enter the United Kingdom. Before it was razed in October 2016, "The Jungle" exemplified the capacity for mobile subjects to build an impermanent community dense with overlapping social relationships and cultural meanings. In the months and years that The Jungle's migrants waited, economies developed, infrastructure was built, a mosque and church were constructed, a nightclub was opened, and neighborhoods—often based on the migrants' countries of origin—were founded.[16]

The academic and public discourse on the migrant "emergency" has criticized some European governments for denying refugees and asylum seekers the *right* of mobility (see Appadurai 1996, 46; Dalakoglou 2016, 180; Kallius et al. 2016, 27; Womack 2016). Indeed, Article 26 of the 1951 UN Refugee Convention states: "Each Contracting State shall accord to refugees lawfully in its territory the right to choose their place of residence and to move freely within its territory subject to any regulations applicable to aliens generally in the same circumstances."[17] The scholars, journalists, and activists commenting on the migrant surge appear to accept the right to move as universal, even though such a right is rooted in a liberal ideology that conflates mobility with freedom and—as such—is historically and socially contingent (see Langan 2001, 463). Indeed, the migrants currently seeking refuge in Europe and the nineteenth-century Mi'kmaq in Nova Scotia share the experience of realizing that the *right* to move doesn't always mean an *ability* to move. Being granted the right to move comes with both explicit and implied expectations of how, when, and for what purpose those movements are made.

Rethinking Settlement, Rethinking the Settler State

Although radically different in their subjectivities and historical circumstances, the millions of migrants and internally displaced peoples and the Mi'kmaq profiled in the previous chapters share an experience of mobility that demands a reexamination of some of the fundamental concepts of the postcolonial moment—foremost among them being *settlement*. The primary objective of this book has been to reimagine settlement by reconsidering the role that mobility has played in mediating social, political, and economic relationships among (post)colonial subjects and institutions. Casting mobility as a mediator between the Mi'kmaq, the Catholic Church, and the British Crown allows researchers to examine how the daily practices, personal perceptions, and imagined conceptions of movement worked to create and challenge sociopolitical relationships in a settler colony. By combining data from archival documents, ethnographic observations, and archaeological remains, this mediating framework contributes to a broader discourse in the social sciences and humanities that seeks to understand the genealogy of policies of assimilation and dispossession in settler societies (see Harris 2004; Li 2010; Parnaby 2008; Raibmon 2005, 2007; Roy 2010).

The Mi'kmaw practices described here have demonstrated that settlement can be at once intermittent, impermanent, and ephemeral, while also being persistent and enduring. In other words, it is possible to be settled but not sedentary. This statement is as true for the missionaries, priests, and Crown agents who first traveled to the New World and then moved throughout colonies such as Nova Scotia as it is for the Mi'kmaw hunters, fishers, pilgrims, and artifact collectors of the nineteenth and twentieth centuries.

At stake in recognizing the movement inherent in Mi'kmaw and other forms of settlement (e.g., the settlement needed to build a Catholic mission) is an acceptance of the consequences of the Church and Crown's efforts to reshape the Mi'kmaq as sedentary subjects. The Church and Crown's biases toward settlement as *sedentism* contributed to their increasingly paternalistic relationships with indigenous peoples, in part because it blinded the agents of these institutions to the power that persistent movements had to emplace a people in a region. Their attempts to "civilize" by assimilation have often been predicated on a sedentary population—one that can be enumerated and, as demonstrated by the civic-numbering project on Maligomish, can be tied to specific cartographic coordinates.

If we are to conceive a different indigenous politics, the bias toward sedentism must be acknowledged. The multidisciplinary scholarship on indigenous politics has for the past twenty years turned on the question of sovereignty (Barker 2005; Biolsi 2005; Bruyneel 2007; Cattelino 2008; Deloria and Lytle 1998; Harring 1994; Moreton-Robinson 2007; Shaw 2004; Simpson 2014; Smith and Kēhaulani Kauanui 2008; Thompson 2009). Increasingly, researchers are questioning whether sovereignty should be the organizing concept for an indigenous politics (see Rifkin 2009; Young 2002). Yet so much of the discourse surrounding indigenous sovereignty—scholarly and otherwise—is predicated on Western conceptions of "the state" that are bound up with notions of territory, borders, property, individual ownership, and commoditization (see Mitchell 1991; Scott 1998; Sparke 2005; Trouillot 2001). Although the individualizing power of the state has long been recognized as incongruent with many indigenous political traditions such as communal property, consensus decision-making, and the agency of nonhuman actors (see Byrd 2012; de la Cadena 2010, 2015), this book has aimed to draw attention to the ways in which focusing on the "space" of the state (borders, territories, etc.) has obscured the dynamism at work in the creation of these spaces. The movements of people such as Charlie Wilmot, Louis Thom, the Sylliboys, Mi'kmaw pilgrims, and the Cree walkers have created social relationships that at once transcend the various spatial boundaries imposed by settlers, while also demonstrating the historical contingency—and frailty—of those boundaries.

And the moral premise upon which liberal states are founded—that its subjects forego some individual will in return for the protection of a sovereign—appears null in former colonies such as Canada where the sovereign has been at best indifferent and at worst negligent in meeting its obligations to the indigenous subjects of its realm (see Ferris 2003; Human Rights Watch 2016; Lee Nichols 2005, 2013). Can such an entity call itself a state when the projects of statecraft, such as supplying basic infrastructure and ensuring the health, safety, and education of its subjects, are systematically denied to indigenous communities or granted in substandard form? Reimagining indigenous politics, therefore, requires questioning the very idea of a *settler state*. And this appears to be the conceit in the discourse of Idle No More. Believing the political apparatuses of band councils, the Indian Act, the Assembly of First Nations, and Parliament to be corrupt, the leaders of Idle No More call for First Nation–to–First Nation collaborations.

What emerges from this attention to dynamism is a conception of politics in settler colonies that is always in the process of becoming. The case study of post-contact Nova Scotia demonstrates that the institutions of the Catholic Church and the British Crown were constituted, in part, through their relationships to Mi'kmaw institutions and subjects. Institutions as powerful as the Vatican and the British Crown were not unaffected by their interactions with the Mi'kmaq. The Mi'kmaq's mobility influenced how the Church and Crown adapted their approaches to managing the indigenous population. Recognizing the unlikeliness of either converting the Mi'kmaq to Protestantism and/or making them completely sedentary, the Crown sought to discipline Mi'kmaw movements and to enlist the Church to aid their efforts of assimilation. And Mi'kmaq themselves have been affected by these interactions—from the historical adoption of Catholicism, which continues to be a powerful identity marker for some Mi'kmaq, to the suffering and resistance of residential school survivors (see Knockwood 2001). The complexity of all of these interactions has only been addressed superficially here. Indigenous politics in Nova Scotia is an entanglement of three levels of formal government; nongovernmental organizations such as the Confederacy of Mainland Mi'kmaq and the Kwilmu'kw Maw-klusuaqn Negotiation Office; organizations considered by many Mi'kmaq to be "traditional," such as the *Sante' Mawi'omi*; and social and kinship ties that stretch across Mi'kma'ki and beyond. Such entanglements complicate but also create the conditions of possibility for the assertion of Mi'kmaw authority. As demonstrated by the construction of camps on Maligomish—and the attempt of the provincial government to fix them in space—the multiple authorities at work in a place such as Maligomish at once create opportunities for Mi'kmaw agency while also structuring that agency.

This capacity for a subject to act even as the subject's actions are influenced by social structures remains one of the enduring questions of anthropology. This book imagines this tension in terms of mediation and process—that both subjects and institutions are constituted through their interactions with one another. Mobility is particularly important to analyze as a mediator because of the work it does to highlight the agency of indigenous individuals in post-contact Nova Scotia. The ethnographic examination of how practices, perceptions, and conceptions of movement have worked to emplace Mi'kmaq has illuminated moments in which Mi'kmaq have asserted themselves as political subjects. These brief moments—when a caretaker dismisses a perceived trespasser, when a husband and father supports his family by collecting artifacts from ancient places, when a community member challenges a priest's affront to St. Anne—represent the quotidian construction of political subjectivity. These intimate moments complement the more momentous events that have punctuated the political lives of the Mi'kmaq, such as the Royal Commission on the prosecution of Donald Marshall Jr. (see Hickman et al. 1989) and the 1999 Supreme Court of Canada's "Marshall Decision" granting treaty rights to Mi'kmaq to fish in order to earn what the court later clarified as "a moderate living." These events have become part of Canadian—not just Mi'kmaw—history, and they mark turning points in the relationships between the Mi'kmaq and the Crown. Rather than document the important work that a very public figure such as Donald Marshall Jr. has done for the political efficacy of Mi'kmaq, *Unsettling Mobility* has followed the more mundane practices of subject making and politics—the policies, legislation, enumerations, and ministrations—and how these were met with challenges, acceptances, and/or silences.

Of course, the subjectivity described here remains vague and fixed within the dynamics of the even broader categories of *indigenous* and *settler*. While highlighting a few individuals described in the historic and archaeographic records, the book has not considered the ways in which these categories break down through the intersection of identities constructed through categories based on race, gender, sexuality, ability, age, and class. However, the book has offered insight into how mobility has mediated the construction of a category like "Mi'kmaq." The Crown's support for the St. Anne's mission on Maligomish in the late-nineteenth century, the Church's entrenched missionization of its ministry to the Mi'kmaq, and the provincial government's civic-numbering project all represent the contradiction at the core of the settler project: the settler's failure to understand the structures and subjectivities at work in indigenous communities means that its efforts to assimilate indigenous populations further mark these peoples as "indigenous."

Rethinking the settler state may also require researchers to rethink settler colonialism—or at least to break down the assumptions inherent in the idea of *settler*, which has become shorthand for everything not indigenous. Are settlers simply the descendants of the people who first colonized the New World? Are they any newcomer? If the latter, then how do we parse the structures of inequality facing not only indigenous peoples but also the descendants of people brought to the New World against their will—including enslaved Africans, refugees, economic migrants, or the victims of human trafficking—from those that uniquely challenge the world's First Peoples? Analyzing the movements and emplacements of global shifts in human settlement can help to break colonial and postcolonial discourse out of a settler/indigenous dichotomy.

Abbreviations

CMH-A	Canadian Museum of History—Archives
JLCNS	Journal of the Legislative Council of Nova Scotia
LAC	Library and Archives Canada
NSA	Nova Scotia Archives

Notes

Introduction

1. The section title is quoted from Battiste (1997, 17).

2. *Mi'kmaq* is a plural noun and is used to describe the Mi'kmaq as a people. *Mi'kmaw* is a singular noun and is used as an adjective to modify both singular and plural nouns (see Pacifique 1990).

3. Raibmon (2007, 117) describes similar efforts of the Crown in British Columbia: "Civilized Indians were to be sedentary ones."

4. The early ethnohistorical sources for the Mi'kmaq include Cartier ([1598] 1993); Champlain (1603); Denys (1672); Gaulin (1750); LeClerq (1691) 1910; Lescarbot (1611); Maillard (1758).

5. At its most basic, settler colonialism is the colonization by nonindigenous peoples of lands where they eventually become the majority, outstripping the indigenous population. As Patrick Wolfe (1991, 1) describes them, "settler colonies were not primarily established to extract surplus value from indigenous labour. Rather, they are premised on displacing indigenes from (or *re*placing them on) the land." Most countries in North and South America, Australia, and New Zealand are examples of settler colonies. See also Krautwurst (2003).

6. See later in this Introduction for definitions of "movement" and "mobility."

7. My use of *mediating* has developed from conversations with my colleague Maureen Marshall. See Marshall and Lelièvre (2010) and Lelièvre and Marshall (2015) for a discussion of mobility as a mediator between political subjects and political institutions.

8. The *pays d'en haut* include what is today northwest Québec, most of Ontario, the area west of the Mississippi and south of the Great Lakes, and the region west to the prairies. See http://www.thecanadianencyclopedia.ca/en/article/pays-den-haut/; accessed June 17, 2016.

9. James Scott (1998) considers legibility to be the central problem of the modern state. He understands legibility as the state's attempt to "arrange the population in ways that simplified the classic state functions of taxation, conscription, and the prevention of rebellion" (J. Scott 1998, 2). States make populations legible by developing and deploying technologies such as censuses.

10. Raibmon (2007) makes this argument for late nineteenth-century British Columbia.

Ferris (2009, 38) cautions against interpreting the dispersed mobility of Ojibwa peoples in nineteenth-century southwestern Ontario as "wandering or nomadic." On sedentarist biases in the social sciences, see Cresswell (2002), Malkki (1992), and Sheller and Urry (2006). Sheller and Urry (2006, 208) define sedentarism as that which "treats as normal stability, meaning, and place, and treats as abnormal distance, change, and placelessness." I use the term *sedentism* to refer to a way of being that is largely associated with living in a fixed place of residence. Following Malkki, *sedentarist* refers specifically to the constellation of (often unconscious) beliefs that understand sedentism to be the norm and morally good (see Marshall 2003; Marshall and Lelièvre 2010; Lelièvre and Marshall 2015).

11. The earliest descriptions of the Mi'kmaq include those by Cartier ([1598] 1993); Champlain (1603); Lescarbot (1611); Denys (1672); LeClerq ([1691] 1910); and the documents contained in the Jesuit Relations (see Biard 1616). These accounts also describe other Algonquian and Haudenosaunee (Iroquois) peoples. For references to other early accounts of indigenous peoples in what is now Canada, see Biggar (1911) and Hoffman (1961). The documents referenced by Biggar, for example, include a translation of a 1501 Portuguese description of Labrador Naskapi (Biggar 1911, 64).

12. The work presented here is inspired by Wolfe's 1999 monograph on the co-constitution of assimilationist policies in the settler colony of Australia and anthropology. His approach is to analyze anthropology "in a manner adapted from Marcel Mauss, as a total discursive practice: in this case one that encodes and reproduces the hegemonic process of colonial settlement" (Wolfe 1999, 3).

13. Barnard (2014, 44) argues that the origins of the social category "hunter-gatherer" lie in the Scottish Enlightenment. Scholars such as Adam Smith and Daniel Wilson had turned from political to economic principles as the defining features of societies— hence, the emergence of a social category defined by the subsistence strategy of hunting and gathering.

14. In this way, the book is inspired by ethnographic archaeology and the archaeology of the contemporary past (see Buchli 2007; Castañeda and Matthews 2008; Hamilakis 2011; Mortensen and Hollowell 2009).

15. For the results of these projects, see the permit reports, which are on file with the Heritage Section of the Nova Scotia Department of Communities, Culture and Heritage in Halifax, Nova Scotia. Permit numbers A2007NS74, A2008NS02, A2008NS73.

16. For an excellent discussion of previous archaeological work conducted in Nova Scotia, see Rosenmeier (2010), especially chapter 4.

17. D. Marshall et al. (1989, 76) translate *Mi'kma'ki* as "land of friendship," which represents the seven traditional districts of the Mi'kmaq. A chief led each of these districts. These chiefs formed the Mi'kmaw Grand Council or *Sante' Mawi'omi*, which governed the Mi'kmaw people (Confederacy of Mainland Mi'kmaq 2007, 11).

18. The Pictou Landing First Nation's website describes a place called *A'Se'K* (or "the other room") near an estuary that was an important source of sustenance and materials for the pre-contact Mi'kmaq. This place may be what Pacifique describes as *Oisasôg* or Boat Harbour. He also lists *Esasok* for Boat Harbour (Pacifique 1934, 240).

19. The Pictou Landing First Nation consists of five parcels of reserved lands. Three of these are in the immediate vicinity of Pictou Landing. Two are known by their original name of "Fisher's Grant." The third is named for the inland harbor adjacent to the community known as "Boat Harbour." The majority of the community lives on the larger of the two Fisher Grant reserves. This area of Pictou Landing was also called "Indian Cove" in the late nineteenth and early twentieth centuries. The Franklin Manor reserve is located in Cumberland County and is shared with the Paqnetek (or Afton) First Nation. *Piwktuk* has also been known as *Piktuk*, and the Pictou Landing First Nation has been known as *Piktukewaq*.

20. "Registered" members are Mi'kmaq who have registered "Indian status" under the federal Indian Act.

21. Peter Wilmot was born in 1826 and died in 1932. He was the chief at Pictou Landing when William Wallis conducted his initial ethnographic research in the area in 1911 and 1912. Wilmot was also an informant for the folklorist Clara Dennis (see NSA, n.d., MG1 vol. 2867, no. 6).

22. An online search of the Library and Archives Canada database returned one entry for Louis Thom. The title of the entry is "Individual case files—Estates—Louis Thom—Micmac Band—Shubenacadie Agency." It dates from 1955 to 1956 and likely refers to the settlement of Thom's estate following his death. The LAC entry also states that this case file is "restricted by law."

23. Names marked with an asterisk are pseudonyms.

24. On legibility, see note 9 in this introduction. Describing Louis Thom's camp and recording its location made it visible to the provincial bureaucracy. It was visible only in the memories of local residents before it was recorded. *Landscape* is a term that social scientists often use unreflectively, and I am guilty of such laziness in parts of this monograph. Following the work of sociocultural anthropologists, archaeologists, and geographers who have thought critically about the genealogy of the concept (see Alcock 1993; Anschuetz et al. 2001; Basso 1996; Bender 1993; Cosgrove 1984; Ingold 1993; Adam T. Smith 2003), I invoke *landscape* metaphorically to refer to large-scale spaces (generally on the scale of a region) that hold meaning for individuals and collectivities because of their associations with particular places within those landscapes, often stretching over multiple temporal scales.

25. In her discussion of the importance of movement in Musqueam assertions of authority over place, Roy (2010, 14) argues similarly that there is a "need to understand Aboriginal territoriality as something much more than points fixed in time and space." Discussing the fluidity of the diverse Ojibwa territorial communities throughout nineteenth-century southwestern Ontario, Ferris (2009, 36) argues that these communities had defined but open boundaries.

26. Cf. Sayres (1956), who conducted several life history interviews in 1950 with "Sammy Louis," which was the pseudonym for a Mi'kmaw man from southwestern Nova Scotia who served in the army during the Second World War and traveled to the United Kingdom, Europe, and Africa.

27. Blueberry raking and potato picking in Maine were common wage-earning activities for Mi'kmaq from the Maritime provinces in the twentieth century. Several Mi'kmaq at Pictou Landing recalled traveling to Maine as children and young adults. The Maine Folklife Center at the University of Maine (Orono) has at least two interviews with farmers who hired Mi'kmaq to rake blueberries. See Maine Folklife Center (1989a, 1989b).

28. These definitions have been developed over several years. Foundational ideas, such as the "Othering" of mobile subjects, appear in Marshall 2003. Early definitions of the practices, perceptions, and conceptions of movement appear in Marshall and Lelièvre 2010. These definitions were revised and published in Lelièvre and Marshall 2015.

29. Roth (2015) notes that *mobility* has only become a keyword of interest to social and cultural thinkers within the last decade. He encourages scholars to "attend to the differences in mobility-related keywords in different languages" (Roth 2015, 403). Indeed, in some of the recent archaeological literature on mobility and movement, there are no definitions of the basic terms. See, for example, Beaudry and Parno (2013) and Sellet et al. (2006).

30. Trouillot (2001) discusses the difference between an object of observation and an object of study in his article on anthropological approaches to "the state." He argues that "the state" was never an object of observation—in other words, an observable, concrete fact. It was always "a construction—at worst an ideological construction, at best a theoretical construction, that is, an object of study" (Trouillot 2001, 136).

31. Referring to cultural theory that privileges structures that *position* predetermined subjects, Massumi (2002, 3) writes, "The very notion of movement as qualitative transformation is lacking. There is 'displacement,' but no transformation. It is as if the body simply leaps from one definition to the next." For a different critique of the primacy of displacement see Clifford (1997). See also Malkki (1992), who argues that the prioritization of displacement is deeply rooted in conceptions of the nation-state and ethnic identities and establishes the sedentarist bias that contributes to mobility's "Othered" status. See also Friedman's (2002) discussion of Clifford. Sheller and Urry (2006, 208) discuss the normative status of stasis. Cobb (2005) complicates the dichotomy between movement and stasis with his discussion of emplacement. See also Rockefeller (2011) on Bergson.

32. This triadic framework was first introduced by Lefebvre ([1974] 1991) in his analysis of the production of space; it has since been adapted by Harvey (1990) to understand spatial practice and by Adam T. Smith (2003) for his study of political landscapes (Lelièvre and Marshall 2015, 441). See Lefebvre ([1974] 1991, 37–45)—representational spaces (lived), representations of space (conceived), and spatial practice (perceived); Harvey (1990, 218–23)—material spatial practices (lived), representations of space (perceived), and spaces of representation (conceived); Adam T. Smith (2003, 72–75)—spatial experience (lived), spatial perception (perceived), and spatial imagination (conceived).

33. At the same time, heuristically separating practices, conceptions, and perceptions helps us to understand how they inform each other.

34. See Binford (1976) for a detailed discussion of the goods that accompanied the Nunamiut hunters with whom he conducted ethnoarchaeological research. Among other observations, Binford noted that the hunters distinguished between "Young Man's Gear," which tended to be store-bought, and "Old Man's Gear," which tended to be made in local communities (Binford 1976, 332).

35. For example, see Father A. A. Johnston's announcement booklet (Diocese of Antigonish 1932–38).

36. The Magdalene Islands are located approximately 180 kilometers from Pictou (see fig. 1).

37. See also William Nixon's description to Lieutenant Governor John Wentworth in November 1801 of the movements of Mi'kmaq fleeing illness (NSA 1801c).

38. Cf. Munn's (1986, 104) observations of Gawan gardening practices, which led her to describe the relationship between mobility and immobility as dialectical.

39. Pacifique appears to have used the orthography of the Baptist missionary Silas Rand (1867; 1894; 1902).

40. Battiste (1997) uses a variation on the Smith-Francis orthography.

41. Cf. Reiser's (2010) study of "Native communities" in the Housatonic River Valley of western Connecticut, and Pawling's (2010) consideration of *homeland* among the Penobscot, Passamaquoddy, and Wolastoqiyik (Maliseet) of northern Maine and New Brunswick. Studies of the post-contact period especially have begun to unravel the spatial, temporal, and social dimensions of movement.

42. One exception is Sable and Francis's 2012 volume, which includes discussions of the importance of movement in the Mi'kmaw worldview and in cultural expressions including dance.

43. Cf. Roy (2010), who makes a similar argument in relation to the Musqueam of British Columbia, as does Raibmon (2007) for several indigenous peoples in British Columbia in the late nineteenth and early twentieth centuries. Raibmon argues that, "rather than nullifying ownership, mobility was the idiom through which Aboriginal people exercised their ownership" (2007, 188). Wicken (2012) discusses the off-reserve practices of Cape Breton Mi'kmaq in the late nineteenth and early twentieth centuries. Referring to the 1752 treaty that "made peace and promised hunting, fishing, and trading rights" (Bernard et al. 2015), Wicken (2012, 132) argues that "the movement on and off reserve became part of how the men came to remember the treaty."

44. Ferris (2009, 1) describes the "changed continuities" of indigenous communities in southwestern Ontario who negotiated colonial encounters in the eighteenth and nineteenth centuries, arguing, "They maintained identity and historically understood notions of self and community, while also incorporating substantial material changes and revision to those identities."

45. The centralization plan introduced in 1942 sought to persuade Mi'kmaq from across Nova Scotia to settle into two large reserves with promises of new houses and access to education and medical services. The plan involved centralizing not only the Mi'kmaq but also the bureaucracy that managed them. This meant that administrative

buildings and residential compounds for the non-Mi'kmaw staff, including priests and nuns, were constructed on the reserves (Paul 2000, 281).

46. For a more complete list of promising anthropological research on mobility, see Lelièvre and Marshall 2015.

47. LeBel references Hepburn (2005) in his decision. Writing about the Australian context, Hepburn (2005, 49) suggests that "a pluralist property culture, where indigenous and non-indigenous title exist as equalised entities, can only be properly nurtured with the full and absolute abolition of the feudal doctrine of tenure," which is the foundation of Australian land law.

48. On the other hand, some skepticism of the intentions and practicalities of a "pluralist property culture" (Hepburn 2005, 29) is warranted. Marisol de la Cadena (2010) expresses such skepticism in her examination of the multiple cosmologies extant in contemporary Ecuador. She encourages scholars to recognize their coexistence in settler societies, but she cautions against trying to make different cosmologies commensurable (de la Cadena 2010, 361; see also M. Johnson 2008). To make Western conceptions of property law commensurate with Mi'kmaw ideas of how land should be accessed and used would require altering each, thus undermining the very purpose of considering Mi'kmaw perspectives in legal cases. De la Cadena discusses this problem in relation to the presence of "earth-beings" (nonhuman, animate entities) in Ecuadorian politics. She argues that bringing such beings into the political sphere requires analysts to reimagine them as political not just natural or cultural (de la Cadena 2010, 336). De la Cadena attributes the exclusion of "earth-beings" and other nonhuman actors (e.g., animals) from the political sphere to the deeply engrained modern, Western epistemology that separates "Humanity" from "Nature" (2010, 345).

49. Cf. Cipolla (2013, 24), who accepts the Foucauldian conceptualization of power as diffuse and adds to it "a pragmatic twist to explore the different restraints and limitations of subaltern agency, particularly that of Native peoples negotiating and enduring colonial encroachment."

50. The Mi'kmaw Covenant Chain should not be confused with the Covenant Chain associated with the Iroquois Confederacy. The Mi'kmaw Covenant Chain of treaties includes those that were made not only with Mi'kmaq but also with other Northeastern indigenous nations such as the Wolastoqiyik (Maliseet) and Passamaquoddy. The 1725 treaty was originally signed in Boston and later ratified by representatives from different regions of Mi'kma'ki in 1726 and 1728. The treaty signed in 1749 renewed the promises made in 1725. Other treaties were signed by some Mi'kmaw representatives in 1752, 1753, 1776, and 1779. Often included in the Covenant Chain are two proclamations— Belcher's Proclamation of 1762 and the Royal Proclamation of 1763. See Bernard et al. (2015, 106). See also J. B. Marshall (2006); Wicken (2002, 2012); and resources available from the Atlantic Policy Congress of First Nations Chiefs—www.apcfnc.ca.

51. In the post-contact period, the *Sante' Mawi'omi* has played an important role in maintaining Mi'kmaw political and spiritual traditions. The offices of the *Sante' Mawi'omi* include a Grand Chief (*Kji-Saqmaw*), a Grand Captain (*Kji-Keptin*), a Wampum-bearer (*Putu's*), and at least one Captain (*Keptin*) from each community. Traditionally

these roles were inherited through male lines. To date, no woman has served as a member of the *Sante' Mawi'omi*, and opinions differ on whether women should be allowed to hold these offices. See McMillan (1996) for a discussion of the changing roles of the *Sante' Mawi'omi*; see also Strouthes (2010).

52. Wicken (2002) discusses how this faith in the treaties operated in the late twentieth century. He describes how, in 1993, the Nova Scotia Mi'kmaw communities of Paqtnkek (Afton) and Membertou refused to sign licensing agreements that were negotiated with Fisheries and Oceans Canada (also known as DFO) under the Aboriginal Fisheries Strategy in wake of the Supreme Court of Canada's so-called Sparrow decision protecting indigenous fishing rights: "People in Afton and Membertou feared that by signing a licensing agreement and accepting federal jurisdiction, they would be undermining their treaty and aboriginal rights. They believed that any agreement they reached with the government would later be used by the DFO in future negotiations regarding the fishery" (Wicken 2002, 5–6).

53. Wicken (2002) provides a succinct discussion of the differences between an *aboriginal right* and a *treaty right* as understood in Canada. A *treaty right* "stems from the words used in an agreement between an aboriginal community and a European government" (Wicken 2002, 6). An *aboriginal right* "stems from the fact that aboriginal people were the first inhabitants of North America" (Wicken 2002, 6). The First Nations and Indigenous Studies Department of the University of British Columbia provides a more detailed discussion of the differences between aboriginal rights and treaty rights on its website: http://indigenousfoundations.arts.ubc.ca/home/land-rights.html; accessed June 3, 2016. This site also defines *aboriginal title* as the "inherent Aboriginal right to land or a territory."

54. Ivison et al. (2000) address this question of the appropriateness of a liberal politics in settler states in their introductory essay to the interdisciplinary volume *Political Theory and the Rights of Indigenous Peoples*. For a seminal anthropological analysis of historical negotiations of competing social structures, see Sahlins (1976). Jennings (2011), who is quite critical of anthropology's turn to sovereignty in the last decade, argues that, like "The State," sovereignty has become almost synonymous with "the political"—and this politics is a liberal one rooted in Hobbes. In describing the cosmopolitics at work in the Andes, where nonhuman animals and geological formations are political subjects, Marisol de la Cadena notes that "indigenous politics may exceed politics as we know them" (2010, 335). The Mohawk scholar Gerald Taiaiake Alfred (1999, 2005) also questions whether sovereignty is a productive concept for indigenous politics. See also Lee Nichols 2005, 2013.

55. Sparke (2005) cautions scholars about the risk of fetishizing particular spatial arrangements (for example, the nation-state) while ignoring the ongoing processes of spatial production, negotiation, and contestation. Appadurai (1996, 48) makes a similar point as he questions territoriality as "the critical diacritic of sovereignty." On the spatiality of Hannah Arendt's conception of citizenship and the political sphere, see Stanford Encyclopedia of Philosophy: http://plato.stanford.edu/entries/arendt/#CitPubSph. On the political landscape see Adam T. Smith (2003).

56. I use this relational conception of the political as a framework for understanding how Mi'kmaq have been constituted as political subjects within settler society (see Walls 2010). I do not examine Mi'kmaw conceptions of political subjectivity outside the colonial and postcolonial experience.

57. On the feelings of many indigenous people toward the research being conducted on (and in rarer cases, with) them, see Linda Tuhiwai Smith (1999). See Paul (2000, 220–29) for a discussion of the legal implications of what is commonly known in Nova Scotia as the "Boat Harbour Agreement." In September 2010, the Pictou Landing First Nation (PLFN) filed a lawsuit against the Province of Nova Scotia demanding the relocation of the effluent-treatment facility, although a lack of funding delayed the progress of the suit (see http://www.ngnews.ca/News/Local/2014-03-05/article-3638539/No-funding-for-Pictou-Landing%26rsquo%3Bs-Boat-Harbour-lawsuit/1; accessed October 23, 2016). In June 2014 members of the PLFN blocked access to the treatment facility after effluent spilled and flooded the surrounding area. The blockade ended when an agreement to close the provincially owned waste-treatment facility was reached between the PLFN and the provincial government (see Withers 2015).

58. Maps that indicate this island label it as Indian Island, but the local Mi'kmaq refer to it as *Maligomish*. It has several spellings including *Malegomich* and *Marogomish*. Rand translates the Mi'kmaw place-name as "the merry-making place" (Rand 1902). Throughout its history it has also been referred to as Chapel Island. This Chapel Island should not be confused with the Mi'kmaw community of Potlotek in Cape Breton, which is also known as the Chapel Island or Potlotek First Nation. This is the site of the largest St. Anne's Day celebrations in Mi'kma'ki.

59. Hallowell (1960, 21; cited in Hornborg 2006, 332) argues that personhood among the Northern Ojibwa is not "synonymous with human beings, but transcends it." Colin Scott (1989, 195) demonstrates that, for the James Bay Cree, "Human persons are not set over and against a material context of inert nature, but rather are one species of person in a network of reciprocating persons. These reciprocative interactions constitute the events of experience." Whitehead (1988, 4–5) suggests that, for the Mi'kmaq, "much more than trees or animals is regarded as animate. Stars are Persons, for example . . . Winds themselves are Persons, as are Seasons and Directions. The very geography is animate in the six worlds (that comprise the Mi'kmaw universe). Mountains are alive, and lakes, and the icebergs floating on the sea." Whitehead (1988, 13) identifies the Six Worlds from Mi'kmaw stories as World Beneath the Earth, World Beneath the Water, Earth World, Ghost World, World Above the Earth, World Above the Sky.

60. Leone (2005, chap. 3) applied this methodology in his investigation of eighteenth-century formal gardens in Annapolis. He states explicitly that his use of "archaeology, period literature, aerial photography, other photographs and living opinion . . . emphasized the differences among all these and did not dismiss any source as unworthy. The point was not to use one to corroborate the other; differences and

variation were hidden that way. The point was to highlight discrepancies and then to explain them" (Leone 2005, 78).

61. For exceptions, see Rosenmeier (2010), who recorded such sites as part of her dissertation research. See also Mi'kma'ki All Points Services' (formerly the Treaty and Aboriginal Rights Research [TARR] Centre) geographic information system that records hunting, fishing, gathering, and other sites from the oral testimony of Mi'kmaq.

62. Between 2003 and 2009, Adam T. Smith offered a graduate seminar at the University of Chicago entitled "Theory and Method in Archaeology: Archaeology and Archaeography." He referred to the archaeographic theme of the seminar as focusing "on an exploration of archaeological representation and overlapping issues raised in the sister field of historiography" (see http://blogs.cornell.edu/adamtsmith /files/2011/09/Arch-Sys-Syllabus-2009.pdf; accessed June 19, 2016). Several other definitions of the term exist. The Oxford English Dictionary defines *archaeography* as the "systematic description of antiquities." Michael Shanks, professor of classical archaeology at Stanford University, defines *archaeography* as the "convergence of archaeology and photography" (http://www.mshanks.com/about-the-blog/; accessed August 14, 2011). What all these definitions share is a focus on the representation of archaeology, whether in written or visual form.

63. These institutions included the Nova Scotia Archives, the Nova Scotia Museum, the Acadia University Archives, the Diocese of Antigonish Archives, the University of New Brunswick Archives, the Maine Folklife Center at the University of Maine (Orono), the Fortress of Louisbourg National Historic Site Archives, the Town of New Glasgow records office, Library and Archives Canada, and the Canadian Museum of History Archives.

64. Citing Vansina (1985), Klein distinguishes oral traditions from oral data. The former are "formally preserved, not always as narratives, but in some fixed form. They are part of the collective memory of the group and get passed on from generation to generation" (Klein 1989, 209). The latter is a body of data, which "individuals hold in memory, data about individual experience, data that consist essentially of things that people have seen and experienced. . . . [Oral data] are valid primarily during the lifetime of those being interrogated" (Klein 1989, 209).

65. Quoting Lescarbot (1611), Nietfeld writes that Mi'kmaw chiefs may have had more elaborate burials than the others in their bands. Chief Panoniac, for example, was buried on a "desolate island" off the south shore of Nova Scotia (Nietfeld 1981, 479).

66. Stephen Powell, Archaeology Assistant Curator, Nova Scotia Museum, 2006, pers. comm.

67. Today this association is known as the Mi'kmaq [*sic*] Association for Cultural Studies. Christmas also draws on the early texts of LeClerq ([1691] 1910) and Lescarbot (1611), although these sources do not include detailed descriptions of Pictou County.

68. See Meskell and Pels (2005).

69. The section title is quoted from NSA (1842c).

Chapter 1

1. The section title is quoted from LAC (1835).

2. Cf. Raibmon (2007, 178), who notes that some of the "civilizing" policies introduced by the colonial and provincial governments in British Columbia—including residential schools—actually "engendered the Aboriginal movement that colonial rhetoric condemned."

3. *L'Acadie* was the name of the French colony first settled in 1604, which included the territories that now comprise the Canadian provinces of Nova Scotia, New Brunswick, and Prince Edward Island. In 1713, all of these territories, with the exception of Isle Royale (now Cape Breton Island in Nova Scotia), were given to Britain under the Treaty of Utrecht. Acadia is the anglicized name of this region. Today many descendants of the original Acadian inhabitants of the region continue to refer to the area as *l'Acadie*.

4. Jennifer Reid (1995) reports that around thirty thousand Loyalists alone came to Acadia following the American Revolutionary War.

5. These agreements were signed by different Mi'kmaw communities—and different indigenous nations—at different times. The other signatories included leaders from the Passamaquoddy and Wolastoqiyik (Maliseet). Together with the Abenaki, these four nations are occasionally referred to collectively as the "Wabanaki" (see Wicken 2002). On the history of these treaties, see Bernard et al. (2015); D. Marshall et al. (1989); Prins (1999); Reid (2013); Speck (1915); Wicken (2002).

6. This chart is housed at the Beaton Institute at Cape Breton University in Sydney, Nova Scotia. The Beaton Institute's description notes that the chart is "unsigned but presumed to be DesBarres, modelled after Samuel Holland." Holland began a survey of the northern British colonies in 1764 for the Board of Trade (see http://www.biographi.ca/en/bio/desbarres_joseph_frederick_wallet_6E.html; accessed October 24, 2016).

7. See Cronon (1983, chap. 6–7) for a detailed discussion of how British land clearing, cultivation, and bounding practices undermined indigenous land use in New England.

8. Ferris (2009, 35) notes a similar complaint made by the Missionary Society of the Methodist Church in its annual report on the Ojibwa nations of Ontario.

9. Other researchers have identified underlying themes in the archives of other North American colonies. For example, Dawdy (2008, 28) describes a discourse of "disorder" that appears in the archival record of colonial New Orleans.

10. Barker (2005), citing Harring (1998), argues that such policies governing Mi'kmaw land distribution and management in Nova Scotia were influenced by the so-called Marshall trilogy of US Supreme Court decisions on the question of American Indian sovereignty. Barker attributes Chief Justice Marshall's opinion to influences such as John Locke who argued that hunter-gatherer societies had only usufruct rights to land, not ownership of it (Barker 2005, 7). See also Arneil 1996; Harris 2004.

11. Upton (1979, 160–61) discusses the parallel efforts of Protestant denominations to instill their ethic in the Mi'kmaq in Nova Scotia and New Brunswick.

12. The section title is a reference to Weber's 1905 *The Protestant Ethic and the Spirit of Capitalism*. I evoke Weber here consciously for two reasons. First, I wish to draw attention to the contrast in worldviews between the nineteenth-century Mi'kmaq, who had converted to Catholicism two centuries previously, and the colonial officials and settlers, who were predominantly Protestant. Second, this book is inspired by Weber's analysis of the factors contributing to the unique form of capitalism that developed in modern Europe. Where Weber connected the Protestant ethic of accumulating wealth through disciplined work and self-denial to European capitalism, which required a never-ending investment of labor and capital, the current study attempts to connect this same ethic with the Crown's efforts to "civilize" the Mi'kmaq. As will be argued in chapter 4, even the Catholic Church came to promote an ethic of provident, disciplined, private self-sufficiency as it colluded with the Crown to "civilize" the Mi'kmaq.

13. See Andrew Parnaby's (2008) discussion of these strategies in relation to the nineteenth-century Cape Breton Mi'kmaq. For an analysis of pre-contact Mi'kmaw cultivation, see Deal et al. (1987). See also G. Patterson ([1877] 1916, 120) and J. Hall (2015).

14. See, for example, Comaroff and Comaroff 1987. Raibmon (2005, 2007) discusses the importance of migrant indigenous labor for British Columbia's resource-dependent economy in the nineteenth and early twentieth centuries. See also Knight (1996) and Roy (2010). For discussions of Mi'kmaw involvement in resource harvesting, see Martijn (1989, 221) and Rand (1867, 3–5), who discuss what appear to be commercial fisheries operated by the Mi'kmaq. On Mi'kmaw wage labor, see Gonzalez (1981) and Prins (1996b).

15. See J. Bernard Gilpin's (1877) description of the St. Francis Xavier reserve at Beaver River in Digby County along the Bay of Fundy.

16. Jean and John Comaroff (1992) describe the "colonization of consciousness" as a critical moment in the British colonization of the Tswana of southern Africa. In simplified terms, the colonization of consciousness required two steps. First, the Tswana's recognition of *setswana* (Tswana ways) as "a coherent body of knowledge and practice in relation to *skegoa* (European ways)." Second, an induction "into the *forms* of European discourse; into the ideological terms of rational argument and empirical reason" (Comaroff and Comaroff 1992, 245) even as Tswana attempted to appropriate European cultural and technological power while maintaining their autonomy. Niezen (2009) and Povinelli (2005) discuss similar processes in colonial Canada and Australia, respectively. Understanding the process of colonizing the Mi'kmaw consciousness in late nineteenth-century Nova Scotia is complicated by the 250-year history of Mi'kmaw Catholicism by that time and centuries of interactions with Europeans and other indigenous peoples.

17. The author is thought to have been Christian Kauder, a Trappist missionary from Luxembourg who ministered to Mi'kmaq in northeastern Nova Scotia in the mid-nineteenth century. Robinson (2005) attributes the article to Kauder.

18. Sorrenson (1975) discusses the British attempt to "civilize" the Maori through commerce. Biolsi (1995) distinguishes between the "civilizing" efforts of the US government

toward the Lakota and other western Native American nations and the processes of subjection (*sensu* Foucault 1977) that created Lakota individuals in the second half of the nineteenth century. See also Raibmon (2005, 2007).

19. This definition elides two concepts that the Comaroffs (following Gramsci 1971) articulate: hegemony and ideology. Where hegemony "consists of constructs and conventions that have come to be shared and naturalized throughout a political community, [ideology] is the expression and ultimately the possession of a particular social group, although it may be widely peddled beyond" (Comaroff and Comaroff 1991, 24). I argue that the sedentarist ideology was "shared and naturalized" in colonial Nova Scotia—and in that way it was "hegemonic." And the shared and naturalized construct of sedentism as morally right had expression in the discourse surrounding indigenous assimilation in colonial Nova Scotia. The power of the Comaroffs' definitions is that they recognize hegemony and ideology as historically contingent and mutually constitutive: "Hegemony, we suggest, exists in reciprocal interdependence with ideology: it is that part of a dominant worldview which has been naturalized and, having hidden itself in orthodoxy, no more appears as ideology at all" (Comaroff and Comaroff 1991, 25).

20. Donovan (1980, 114) suggests that de la Varenne was a French official at Louisbourg, but states, "Unfortunately, Monsieur Varenne cannot be identified in the Louisbourg documentation."

21. My thanks to Kathleen Morrison (pers. comm. 2011) and Shannon Dawdy (pers. comm. 2011), who each cited the irony of European immigrants disapproving of Mi'kmaw movements.

22. Referring to seventeenth-century ethnohistorical sources, Nietfeld (1981, 403) writes that the Mi'kmaq's mobility was seasonally variable, with more movements happening in the winter months.

23. The section title is quoted from LAC (1835).

24. However, Speck did acknowledge that European encroachment on these hunting territories likely meant that similar territories in the past looked very differently from the ones he recorded in 1914.

25. A 1955 transcription of an 1857 edition of Titus Smith's report on his 1801–1802 survey of Nova Scotia includes descriptions of Mi'kmaw hunting territories in a section titled "General Observations of the Northern Tour." The transcription of the report, along with many pages from Smith's field notebook are available on microfilm (reel #15,411) at the Nova Scotia Archives (see NSA 1801–1802a; see also 1801–1802b). Unfortunately, Smith's original notes from the northern tour are not included on this reel. The original survey notes will have to be consulted to determine whether or not they were added by the transcriber. Elsie Clews Parsons (1926) noted the inheritance of land in Cape Breton in the 1920s, but not as hunting territories.

26. In contextualizing this debate within the political and academic climates of the early twentieth century, Feit (1991) argues that family hunting territories cannot be understood as private property. Regardless of their origins, Chute (see Chute and Speck 1999) has argued that Speck's research provided insight into Mi'kmaw perceptions of land and land use.

27. The question of the origins of the family hunting territory and other manifestations of land use and management remains relevant today as demonstrated in recent cases heard before the Supreme Court of Canada on the issue of aboriginal title and the limits of treaty rights (see Supreme Court of Canada 1999, 2005, 2011, 2014).

28. Here Hendry notes that he is quoting a letter dated August 18, 1862, from J. Courteau, the parish priest at l'Ardoise on Cape Breton Island.

29. Indeed, Arneil (1996) argues that Locke was explicitly defending a colonial philosophy based on Protestant ideals of labor and industry, which he contrasted to a Catholic colonialism dependent on violence against indigenous peoples.

30. See Upton (1979, chap. 6) for a more in-depth historical discussion of the development of the colonial government's management of the Mi'kmaq in Nova Scotia.

31. However, see Howe's 1843 report in which he mentions: "Besides the public lands, a few tracts are held by individuals, either under grant or by possession" (NSA 1843).

32. See also NSA 1820: "That your Excellencys [sic] humble Petitioner is an Indian of this Province who as well as his Father and Grand Father have from their Birth resided at or near River John in the District of Pictou which said River derives its name from that of your Petitioners Grand Father."

33. Cf. Raibmon (2005, 2007), who discusses a similar dilemma faced by indigenous peoples in the nineteenth and early twentieth-century Pacific Northwest. She argues, "Colonial authorities often equated seasonal movements away from homesteads as abandonment, justifying the encroachment of non-indigenous settlers" (Raibmon 2007, 181).

34. See Cronon (1983, chap. 4) for a detailed discussion of the problem of encroachment and property rights in colonial New England.

35. My thanks to Adam T. Smith (2010) for pointing out that the Mi'kmaw movements were not simply acts of resistance and for directing me to Geertz's 1983 article in which he makes the argument that movement across a territory works to assert a sovereign's authority over it.

36. Simpson (2011, 209) acknowledges this negotiation in her definition of indigenous sovereignty as "simultaneously tied to governmental forms, charters, and philosophical systems that are both prior to and embedded within settler systems, states, and imaginaries."

37. The section title is quoted from Morgan (1877, 19).

38. Williamson (2004, 178) notes that in nineteenth-century Australia the application of social evolutionism to the study of native Aborigines resulted in a shifting of blame for the decline in aboriginal welfare from European influence to the natural march of progress.

39. Note, however, that Morgan did not believe private property to be the endpoint of humanity's societal telos: "A mere property career is not the final destiny of mankind, if progress is to be the law of the future as it has been of the past" (Morgan 1877, 561).

40. John Lubbock, a contemporary of Morgan and Wilson, equated nineteenth-century indigenous peoples with prehistoric ones. One of his measures of "civilization" was population size. He contended that population size increases with the introduction of civilization (Lubbock 1865, 592–93).

41. See also the extensive twentieth-century literature on hunter-gatherer studies (e.g., Ingold et al. 1991a; Lee and Devore 1968; Myers 1988; Price and Brown 1985; Schrire 1984).

42. On the typologizing legacy of anthropological thought, see McNiven and Russell (2005, 39–40), Adam T. Smith (2003), and Trigger (1980, 682–86). Ferris (2009) is also critical of the "unreflexive" approach that anthropologists and archaeologists have taken to understanding the relationships created between indigenous peoples and settler populations.

43. This discussion on the renewed interest in social evolutionism appeared originally in Marshall and Lelièvre 2010 and was revised in Lelièvre and Marshall 2015 (p. 437). See also Asch (1979).

44. In discussing anthropology's linking of hunter-gatherers to mobility, Robert Kelly (1992, 43) has argued that "early concepts of mobility blinded us to the fact that mobility is universal, variable, and multi-dimensional."

45. However, see Eder (1984), McCabe (1994), and Townsend (1978) for examples of studies that describe motivations for moving beyond food procurement.

46. Post-contact archaeologists can use diaries, maps, and travel logs to make more direct inferences about the practices of human movement. See, for example, the authors in Beaudry and Parno 2013.

47. See, for example, Ingold (2007); Tilly (1994).

48. On the co-constitution of anthropology and colonialism, see Asad (1973); Dirks (2001); Stocking (1991); Thomas (1994); Trigger (1984, 1989); Trouillot (1991); and Wolfe (1999). On the relationship between anthropology and the assimilationist policies of colonial governments, see Nurse (2006). On the legal consequences of the sedentarist ideology on indigenous peoples, see Arneil (1996); Barker (2005); Harring (1998).

49. By *cultural* I refer to the learned behaviors and beliefs that shape and are shaped by an individual's membership and development within a society. This definition is broad in scope and is meant to include behaviors that fall within the categories of "political," "spiritual," and "familial."

50. Much of the recent archaeological research on abandonment is based in the American Southwest. Nelson (1999, 3) describes a shift in conceptual approaches away from equating abandonment to cultural collapse and toward understanding abandonment as "a strategy of land use that is suited to arid landscapes, as an aspect of the mobility of human groups."

51. Radiocarbon dates obtained from the midden cluster around 1500 BP and 500 BP. There appears to be a thousand-year gap in the cultural deposits recovered from the midden (see Lelièvre 2017; Mudie and Lelièvre 2013).

52. See Stewart's (1986) discussion of these species at the Delorey Island site, located approximately sixty-five kilometers east of Maligomish along the Northumberland Strait.

53. Note that one elder with whom I spoke stated that the foundations could not have belonged to Fred Sapier's grandfather. She stated that all of the Sapier family had their camps along the southern shore of Maligomish.

Chapter 2

1. See Borden and Wilson (1952) for an explanation of the Borden system for assigning site numbers in Canada.

2. Indeed, see Black's comments: "Settlement-subsistence change should not be conceived as Native groups selecting alternate patterns from an abstract array of ideal settlement-subsistence types. Rather, the temporal mosaic of settlement-subsistence systems is an *archaeological construct*, created by an averaging of the subsistence and settlement choices made by Native peoples living in specific environments, during periods that we, as archaeologists, designate for our purposes according to criteria that we select" (Black 2002, 307; emphasis added).

3. Specifically, Stoler argues that the Dutch colonial documents she uses serve "less as stories for a colonial history than as active, generative substances with histories, as documents with itineraries of their own" (Stoler 2009, 1).

4. See Power (2006) for an analysis of Alain Badiou's conceptions of active and passive political subjects.

5. This chapter focuses on the very local and personal experiences of Mi'kmaq in northeastern Nova Scotia who have been involved with archaeological collection and excavation. Previous scholars have discussed how indigenous communities—particularly those located in British Columbia—have used archaeological research and cultural resource management to support their claims of sovereignty (see Hammond 2009; Nicholas et al. 2007, 276–77; Roy 2010).

6. In the mid-twentieth century, Charles Sanders Peirce coined the term *abduction* to refer to a method of nondeductive inference that was different than induction (Douven 2011). Scholars of Peirce note that there is not a coherent theory of abduction in his works. Peircean abduction, which Douven suggests resides in the realm of discovery of scientific hypotheses, differs from the more common usage today, which resides in the realm of justification of hypotheses. See also Peirce 1997. Abduction appears to be required for both discovery and justification of the hypotheses generated by archaeological investigation.

7. The vertebrate animal remains recovered from BjCo-02 during the 2008 excavations were few and in very poor quality. My thanks to Mikael Haller, assistant professor in the Anthropology Department at St. Francis Xavier University, for sorting and identifying these remains. Most remains were identifiable only to class and differentiated by size. A report of the vertebrate fauna identification is on file with the Nova Scotia Department of Communities, Culture and Heritage (see Lelièvre 2009).

8. Other shellfish species were recovered from the midden in much smaller proportions. These species include *Mytilus edulis* (blue mussel), *Spisula solidissima* (Atlantic surf clam), *Mercenaria mercenaria* (hard clam or quahog), *Littorina sp.* (common periwinkle), *Crepidula sp.* (slipper limpet), and possibly *Buccinum undatum* (common whelk). See Lelièvre (2017) for a discussion of the sampling strategy and quantification methods, including possible biases that make the claim of species change over time only tentative.

9. However, see the notes published by John Erskine in which he reports that his excavations located the outlines of two camps (Erskine 1962, 22). Unfortunately, Erskine's excavation methods did not account for stratigraphy.

10. Although many archaeologists in the nineteenth and early twentieth centuries did not believe that the makers of this and other similar middens were the ancestors of the contemporary Mi'kmaq, Harlan Smith, who excavated a portion of this midden in 1914, rejected the idea that Eskimos may have occupied the region prior to the arrival of the Mi'kmaq. In his 1929 report, Smith stated, "The Micmacs are the only Indians known to have lived in this area, and the archaeology bears certain resemblances to the material culture of the modern Micmacs" (H. Smith 1929, 89).

11. Rosenmeier (2010) has made a comparable argument in her call for an "archaeology of descent." She draws on oral histories, historical documents, and archaeological evidence to argue for persistent Mi'kmaw presence in areas of present-day Guysborough County, Nova Scotia, such as Tracadie Harbour and Glenelg.

12. Many of Canada's national museums can trace their roots to the Geological Survey of Canada (GSC), which was established in 1841. Early in its institutional history, the GSC included a museum that served as a showcase for its findings. Ethnological and archaeological investigations were eventually incorporated into the mandate of the GSC. In 1910, an anthropology division was added. Edward Sapir was appointed the first head of this division. The museum branch was separated from the GSC in 1927 to become the National Museum of Canada. In 1968, the human history divisions of the museum became the National Museum of Man. In 1990, the Museums Act established the Canadian Museum of Civilization Corporation. In 2013, the museum was renamed the Canadian Museum of History. Archival records of the GSC's early archaeological investigations are now housed at the Canadian Museum of History Archives in Gatineau, Québec (see http://www.historymuseum.ca/about-us/about-the -museum/history-of-the-museum; accessed May 21, 2015).

13. There is some discrepancy between the dates of the published reports on archaeological fieldwork conducted in Nova Scotia and Wintemberg's field notes. The published reports indicate that Wintemberg was in Nova Scotia during the summers of 1913 and 1914. In 1912, he was reported as having conducted fieldwork in Ontario and Québec. However, the notebook containing the reference to Joseph Phillip is titled "Wintemberg, W.J. Field Notes. N.B., N.S. 1912" (see CMH-A 1912).

14. McNiven and Russell (2005) discuss several tropes in pre-contact archaeological research that have worked to dispossess indigenous peoples of their pasts. One of these tropes is "antiquation," which identifies indigenous peoples as "living fossils" (McNiven and Russell 2005, 8).

15. Under a 1992 amendment to the National Historic Preservation Act, federally recognized Native American tribes may create Tribal Historic Preservation Offices to oversee the management of archaeological resources on their lands. In British Columbia there has been a long-standing commitment to training indigenous peoples as archaeologists (see Nicholas 2006). In Nova Scotia, the Confederacy of Mainland Mi'kmaq has been planning the Mi'kmawey Debert Cultural Centre, which would

not only interpret the Debert Paleoindian site and surrounding landscape, but also preserve artifacts, oral histories, and traditional knowledge (see the Mi'kmawey Debert Cultural Centre website: http://www.mikmaweydebert.ca/home/; accessed June 3, 2016).

16. Harlan Smith's artifacts are housed at the Canadian Museum of History in Gatineau, Québec. Erskine's artifacts are at the Nova Scotia Museum in Halifax.

17. Analysis of these ledgers is ongoing. As of December 2015, I had reviewed four of the six accession ledgers, representing the years 1900–29 and 1933–37. Of the approximately 228 archaeological artifacts accessioned during these periods, 180 or 79 percent were collected and/or sold to the museum by Mi'kmaq. The most prolific collector—Mi'kmaw or otherwise—was Jerry Lonecloud. Between the years 1900 and 1911, all of the archaeological artifacts sold to the Nova Scotia Museum by Mi'kmaq were collected by Lonecloud. He developed a close relationship with Harry Piers, who was curator of the Nova Scotia Museum from 1899 to 1940 (see Whitehead 2002). While this chapter focuses on the collection of archaeological artifacts, the Mi'kmaq's participation in the manufacture and sale of ethnological artifacts (e.g., household objects, tools, games, and clothing associated with so-called traditional Mi'kmaw activities) also required accessing the land and resources to collect the materials necessary to create these items—sometimes as commissions for Harry Piers.

18. Artifact collecting was not limited to the Mi'kmaq whose names appear in the Nova Scotia Museum accession ledgers. For example, in his interviews with the anthropologist William Sayres, a Mi'kmaw man from southwestern Nova Scotia described his uncle "digging for arrowheads on the beach" (Sayres 1956, 5). In the second half of the twentieth century, the Nova Scotia Museum ceased purchasing archaeological artifacts taken from sites. Mi'kmaq could still find buyers for these artifacts, however, in private collectors and even a university professor. Noel Nicholas, for example, was an active collector at sites around Pictou Landing during the mid- to late twentieth century. In 1979, his collecting activities helped Ronald Nash, a professor at St. Francis Xavier University in Antigonish, to identify the Moodie Point site (BkCq-20), which is located at the mouth of the East River of Pictou. Nash purchased a collection of lithic artifacts from Nicholas, which he used as a comparison collection (Nash and Stewart 1986, 21).

19. Piers indicated Wilmot's home as Millbrook in the accession ledgers—except for one entry that listed Pictou Landing. Piers conformed to the curatorial standard by including an address for each accession Wilmot sold to the museum, which included the reserve name and place. Doing so may have inaccurately fixed Wilmot to one place.

20. The sites along Pictou Harbour include Brown's Point, Abercrombie Point, Christie Point, and Pictou Landing. These collection locations were provided by Stephen Powell, assistant curator of archaeology at the Nova Scotia Museum.

21. It is possible that Charlie Wilmot, like Louis Thom (see the introduction, this volume), used the rail lines to move about northeastern Nova Scotia. However, as Louis

Thom's story demonstrated, Mi'kmaq in the early twentieth century used many different means of transportation, including hitchhiking and walking.

22. Cf. Knight 1996.

23. Staley (1993) introduced the term "subsistence digger" to describe the indigenous peoples of St. Lawrence Island, Alaska, who primarily dig for ivory artifacts to sell to gallery owners and private collectors. He distinguishes these practices from looting or pothunting because the St. Lawrence islanders use the proceeds of their digging to support their "traditional subsistence lifestyle" (Staley 1993, 348). On subsistence digging, see also Hollowell (2006) and Hollowell-Zimmer (2002) and Matsuda (1998).

24. Since 1970 the Nova Scotia government has introduced various legislation aimed at preventing nonarchaeologists from collecting artifacts and destroying archaeological sites in pursuit of artifacts. The 1989 Special Places Protection Act requires anyone conducting explorations to hold a permit issued by the Heritage Division of the Department of Communities, Culture and Heritage. All artifacts recovered from excavations are the property of the province of Nova Scotia. Section 11 of the act enforces this point: "Where a heritage object has been recovered from any site in the Province by a person who is not a holder of a permit or by a permit holder in contravention of his permit, the Minister or a person authorized by him may seize the heritage object and deliver it to the Museum, which object becomes the property of the Province. R.S., c.438, s. 11; 1994–95, c. 17, s. 1." (Province of Nova Scotia 1989. See http://nslegislature .ca/legc/statutes/specplac.htm; accessed June 4, 2016). Despite the illegality of collecting without a permit, Mi'kmaq and non-Mi'kmaq continue to collect artifacts, and archaeologists occasionally work with amateur collectors. During a brief visit to Nova Scotia in the summer of 2011, many of the Mi'kmaq with whom I spoke reported finding artifacts and fossils along the shores of Merigomish Harbour. A particularly violent storm in December 2010 disturbed much of the coastline, churning up these materials.

25. All of my archaeological fieldwork was conducted under three Category "B" Heritage Research Permits (permit numbers A2007NS74, A2008NS02, and A2008NS73) issued by the province of Nova Scotia between October 2007 and September 2008 (see Lelièvre 2008a, 2008b, 2009). Under the Special Places Protection Act, all archaeological materials are the property of the province of Nova Scotia. However, the provisions of the act do not apply to federal Crown land, which includes most reserved lands in Mi'kmaw communities. Archaeological research conducted in Nova Scotia's national parks, for example, is not regulated by provincial legislation. Materials collected from federal Crown land managed by Parks Canada, which oversees national parks, are deposited and curated in the agency's own facilities. Therefore, I was not required to apply for a provincial permit to conduct archaeological research in these areas. However, given the history of poor or nonexistent documentation of archaeological activity on reserves, and on Maligomish in particular, I wanted to leave a record of the fieldwork that would be accessible to other researchers and members of the Mi'kmaw community. Field notes, photographs, drawings, artifacts, and other materials are on deposit with the Nova Scotia Museum in Halifax (part of the Nova Scotia Department of Communities, Culture and Heritage). A written summary of

all of the research conducted between 2007 and 2009 was presented during a community meeting with the Pictou Landing First Nation in 2013 (see Lelièvre 2014).

26. For example, the Mi'kmawey Debert Cultural Centre.

27. See the Canadian Archaeology Association's website for a list of these cuts and letters of protest from Canadian and international archaeological organizations: http://canadianarchaeology.com/caa/sites/default/files/page/draconian_cuts_to_parks_canada/pdf/details_on_cuts_o.pdf; accessed June 12, 2016.

28. A shift away from a Western scientific approach grounded in objectivity and systematicity—and a decentering of the production of knowledge away from academically trained, nonindigenous archaeologists—is part of the "decolonization" of archaeological practice at the heart of "indigenous archaeology" (see Atalay 2006, 2008, 2012; Colwell-Chanthaphonh et al. 2010; Conkey 2005; McNiven and Russell 2005; Nicholas and Andrews 1997; Silliman 2008; Watkins 2000).

29. Radiocarbon dates collected by Keenleyside at the Cox-Swanson site (BkCq-10, approximately forty kilometers west of Maligomish) and Nash at Delorey Island (BjCj-09, approximately eighty kilometers east of Maligomish) indicate occupation along the Northumberland Strait during the millennium gap that appears to exist in the BjCo-02 record. Nash's radiocarbon date from the Kerr site (BjCo-15) on the south side of Merigomish Harbour dates to several hundred years before the first dates recorded at Maligomish (see Lelièvre 2017).

Chapter 3

1. Civic numbers mark the physical address of a home or business. They are also known as "911 numbers." Depending on the jurisdiction, different levels of government may administer the assignment of civic numbers and manage the geospatial data associated with them. The main purpose of assigning civic numbers is to reduce the response time of Emergency Health Services (EHS) in emergency situations. In exchange for giving the GIS specialists a ride to Maligomish and guiding them around the island, they kindly offered to record the locations of our transect baselines, our datum points, and the archaeological features we had identified. They later shared the data and a preliminary map, which indicated not only the camps but also the baselines of our survey transects, the area of the shell midden, and the mounds that we recorded during our survey. Some of the data that were shared with us have been used to make maps that appear in this book.

2. See introduction, note 9, for a discussion of James Scott's concept of *legibility*.

3. However, unlike Maligomish, it appears as though all of the camps on Potlotek (Chapel Island) have individual civic numbers. The footpaths on Potlotek appear in Nova Scotia's online civic-number database as "Chapel Island #1 Trail," "Chapel Island #2 Trail," and so on. The difference between the two islands may be due, in part, to the fact that the Potlotek First Nation is not a member of the Confederacy of Mainland Mi'kmaq. The geospatial data may have been recorded by a different umbrella organization or directly by the province. Further research would be required to confirm.

4. Nietfeld (1981, 396–97) reviews these sources, which include Biard (1616). See also Denys (1672), LeClerq ([1691] 1910), and Thwaites (1896–1901). In this brief history I focus on post-contact dwellings. There is a long legacy of archaeological investigation in the Maritime provinces that has resulted in the identification of features associated with pre-contact dwellings. Matthew (1884) excavated pits at Bobec, New Brunswick, which he identifies as the floors of semi-subterranean houses. Davis (1974) used reports by Matthew (1884) and others (Byers and Johnson 1940; Hadlock 1939; Moorehead 1922; Preston 1971; Sanger 1971) to interpret what he identifies as house features at Teacher's Cove in the Passamaquoddy region of New Brunswick. Nash and Stewart (1990) identified postmolds at the Melanson Mi'kmaw site but do not attribute them to a pre-contact dwelling. Mike Sanders and Bruce Stewart identified a stone feature, which they describe as a tent ring, at the Sandy Lake Reservoir in Nova Scotia. They consider this feature to be associated with Nova Scotia's Archaic Period (7050 to 550 BC). My thanks to David Christianson, former Manager of Collections at the Nova Scotia Museum, for drawing my attention to the Davis (1974) and Sanders and Stewart (see Cultural Resource Management Group Ltd. 2001) studies.

5. All words except *masgwi* are taken from Pacifique 1990, which are recorded in the Smith-Francis orthography. *Masgwi* is taken from the Mi'gmaq-Mi'kmaq Online talking dictionary, which uses the Listuguj orthography. See http://www.mikmaqonline.org; accessed October 30, 2016. Note that Pacifique 1990 lists *maskwi* as inanimate, while the online dictionary lists *masqwi* as animate.

6. Tomah Josephs, a Passamaquoddy man from Dana's Point, Maine, told this story to Charles Leland (see Leland 1884, 290–93). In describing the power embodied in objects given during a potlatch, Mauss reported that several Northwest Coast peoples consider houses themselves as living beings, with their constituent parts being able to speak to each other, to spirits, to totem animals, and to the people occupying the house. Mauss also referred to Kwakiutl and Tsimshian stories collected by Franz Boas that described the magical qualities of some houses (Mauss [1925] 2002, 56, 160).

7. See http://novascotia.ca/museum/mikmaq/; accessed October 30, 2016.

8. See chapter 1, note 16, for a discussion of Jean and John Comaroff's (1986, 1992) concept of the "colonization of consciousness."

9. For Foucault the body is the site on which power relations are exercised as strategies for subjecting the individual. Power manifests diffusely; it is something that is exercised, not possessed. "It is not the 'privilege,' acquired or preserved, of the dominant class, but the overall effect of its strategic positions—an effect that is manifested and sometimes extended by the position of those who are dominated" (1977, 26–27). Foucault understands ways of disciplining the body, such as teaching soldiers to march in formation and creating spaces for the observation of workers, prisoners, and so on, as "political technologies of the body" (1977, 24) that work to create docility. These docile bodies can then be more easily dominated.

10. Gilpin does not seem to have appreciated the insulating and cushioning advantages of spruce boughs over wooden planks. He sketched some Mi'kmaw houses near Clementsport, Nova Scotia, in 1880, some of which are included in the Mi'kmaq Portraits

Collection (e.g., MP0251). See http://novascotia.ca/museum/mikmaq/?section=image&page=3&id=167&period=1850&region=; accessed October 30, 2016.

11. Despite being an advocate for the Mi'kmaq, the Baptist missionary Silas Rand also believed that year-round dwelling in permanent houses was preferable to the Mi'kmaq's mobile existence (see Abler 2006, 77).

12. Describing her visit to Potlotek for the 1923 St. Anne's mission, Elsie Clews Parsons notes that at that time birch trees could no longer be found on the island. Instead, sheets of birch bark or tar paper were imported to the island (1926, 462).

13. Parsons (1926, 462) notes some of the material changes to wigwams that were becoming more common: "In several wigwams or tents there was a stove, as there will be probably next year in the Morris wigwam or tent; that they were living in a stoveless wigwam rather than in a bestoved canvas tent was a hardship, much discussed."

14. Hornborg notes that Steen (1951) had witnessed tar-paper shacks and wigwams during the 1950 mission on Potlotek. Howard (1965) reported fifty wigwams during his visit to Potlotek in 1962, but only one was covered in birch bark—the rest were covered in tar paper (1965, 6). Hornborg states that the tradition had stopped by the time of her visit to Potlotek in 1996 (Hornborg 2002, 247).

15. Jarvenpa and Brumbach (1988) reported comparable construction strategies from their ethnoarchaeological investigations of Chipewyan winter staging communities in northern Saskatchewan. The camps that were built in these communities had log frames, which were kept in place. Each year families would return to these small villages, from which male hunters would set out to trap fur-bearing animals. Children, women, and the elderly would camp at the staging communities and dress the furs (Jarvenpa and Brumbach 1988, 602). This combination of permanent and temporary structural elements is less visible in the current camps on Maligomish.

16. The following description is a brief overview of the surface survey on Maligomish. For a more detailed description of the survey design and results, see Lelièvre 2008a and 2008b.

17. What Deleuze and Guattari would call (after Pierre Boulez) "striated space"—the space of royal science and the state—in contrast to the "smooth" space of the nomad (Deleuze and Guattari 1987, chap. 12).

18. In the spring of 2008, the information we recorded was updated by Theresa LeBlanc and Craig Marshall from the Confederacy of Mainland Mi'kmaq, who used a Trimble GPS device to record more precise locations for each camp.

19. Both Casey (1997) and Cresswell (2006) contrast space and place, with the former being abstract and objective and the latter being situated in particular social and historical contexts and, therefore, subjective.

20. From my preliminary inquiries among Mi'kmaq from Pictou Landing about the occupants of Waycobah Corner, it appears as though the matriarch of the group of families that comprises this cluster was originally from Pictou Landing but had moved to Waycobah when she married a man from that community.

21. Eldon Yellowhorn (2015) discusses his use of both the Western scientific methods of archaeology and local knowledge in his research with fellow members of the Piikani

Blackfoot Nation in southern Alberta. Michael Heckenberger (2009, 17, 25–26) describes field research as a "social relation" and argues that, when working collaboratively, archaeological and local narratives of the past "co-evolve and result in the creation of multi-vocal histories."

22. My thanks to Raymond Fogelson, professor emeritus of anthropology at the University of Chicago, for drawing my attention to Lewis Henry Morgan's ([1881] 1965) systematic study of dwellings and social organization in North America. Elsie Clews Parsons (1926, 462) provided a detailed description of the construction of the Mi'kmaw wigwam in which she stayed during the 1923 St. Anne's mission on Potlotek, including the number of poles used in the construction and the Mi'kmaw words that described the component parts of the structure. See also Binford (1990); Gamble and Boismier (1991); Kent (1990).

23. In order to protect the confidentiality of the relatively small number of people who have camps on Maligomish, I have also on occasion been purposely vague about the locations of their camps and their kin relationships.

24. Madeline Martin (1989) wrote that some Mi'kmaq from Cape Breton took the train to Egerton and waited for a boat at the mouth of Sutherland's River (see fig. 14). Using an aerial photograph of Merigomish Harbour, Dorie Sapier identified two launch areas: McVicar's Cove and St. Mary's Gut. A geological map from 1902 labels St. Mary's Gut as McDonald Gut. Current topographic maps list this area as Roy's Gut.

25. Salvaging materials from buildings on Maligomish is not a new activity. In an 1891 letter to the Department of Indian Affairs, Father Roderick McDonald reported: "Out of the material of the old church I had a glebe house built" (LAC 1891).

26. Comments made during a community meeting at Our Lady of Perpetual Help Church on July 30, 2013. The meeting was organized by the author to discuss the results of the research conducted between 2007 and 2011 with members of the Pictou Landing First Nation.

27. Referencing Giddens 1990 and Foster 2002, Jacka (2005, 645) describes emplacement as "a process in which people reembed social relations that have been 'distanciated' and 'disembedded' by the disruptions, dislocations, and deterritorializations of capitalist development, globalization, and Christianity." He distinguishes this definition of emplacement from Englund's phenomenological approach.

28. The provincial database of civic numbers includes only fifteen points on Maligomish. Four of these are numbered and have the address of "Indian Island Wa [sic], Merigomish Harbour 31, Municipality of the County of Pictou, Pictou County, B2H 5C4 (E911)." The remaining eleven points are listed as "o Indian Island Wa [sic]." Indian Island is the name for Maligomish that appears on all official maps. On the map included in the civic-number database, "Indian Island Wa" appears to be a road encircling the shoreline of the island; yet no such road exists. See http://nscaf1.nsgc.gov.ns.ca/civicviewer/civic.aspx?cmd=tabs&F=STR_KEY&value=map&V=400010401; accessed October 30, 2016.

29. Civic numbers have also been applied to the houses on the mainland Pictou Landing First Nation reserves of Boat Harbour and Fisher's Grant. On these reserves each

building has an individual civic number. The database also lists aliases for some of the street names on these reserves; for example, "Beach Road" is also known as "Shore Road," "Qasqe'k Awti Road," and "Situmkwe'l Awti Road." The inclusion of these aliases suggests that the province has a better understanding of how the mainland community operates on the ground compared to its understanding of how the island community on Maligomish operates. See http://nscaf1.nsgc.gov.ns.ca/civicviewer /civic.aspx?cmd=tabs&value=map&F=PNTID&V=85200005; accessed October 30, 2016.

Chapter 4

1. The procession order has also varied over time on Potlotek (Chapel Island) (see Hornborg 2002, 251; Howard 1965, 9; Larsen 1983, 114; E. Parsons 1926, 467; Vernon 1903, 99; cf. Reid 2013). The organizers of the Potlotek mission ensure the desired order by placing signs along the procession path reminding pilgrims not to walk in front of St. Anne. Cf. Poliandri (2011), who describes the procession of St. Anne at the Indian Brook First Nation in 2004.

2. Madeline Martin describes this work being conducted in the early to mid-twentieth century on the three or four weekends preceding the mission. Women scrubbed the church, canteen, and glebe house while men cut the grass with scythes (M. Martin 1989, 1).

3. Ralph Francis of the Pictou Landing First Nation described this area as "the place of the cross," which he spelled in Mi'kmaw as *klojowey*. The Mi'gmaq-Mi'kmaq Online dictionary (which uses the Listuguj orthography) translates "cross" as *guljie'wei* (see https://www.mikmaqonline.org/servlet/dictionaryFrameSet.html?argo=cross&method =searchFromEnglish; accessed October 31, 2016).

4. A booklet prepared by the Secretariat of the Basilica Saint Anne de Beaupré (Québec), titled "Prayer and Hymns to Saint Anne," was provided to pilgrims at a recent mission. The booklet includes prayers such as "Prayer Before the Statue and Relics of Saint Anne," "Prayer to Saint Anne for the Sick," and "Saint Anne Bless My Family."

5. Cf. Reid (2013), who discusses the St. Anne's mission on Potlotek as a site of Mi'kmaw politics.

6. I conducted much of the archival research for this chapter at the Diocese of Antigonish Archives in Antigonish, Nova Scotia. Most of the consulted sources are contained within the Father A. A. Johnston fonds, which include handwritten and typed notes, photocopies, photographic reproductions, maps, and index cards associated with the extensive research he conducted to write his two-volume *History of the Catholic Church in Eastern Nova Scotia* (1960, 1971). Johnston's archive contains valuable information for understanding the relationship between the Mi'kmaq and the Catholic Church, especially in the mid-nineteenth to mid-twentieth centuries. However, the consistency of Johnston's source referencing varies. I have tried to indicate throughout this chapter the references that will require verification from a primary source.

7. See Binasco (2004, chap. 1) for a detailed review of the historiographic resources available for missionaries in eastern Canada between the mid-seventeenth and mid-eighteenth centuries. His review includes references to primary and secondary sources, the latter of which include historical and anthropological studies of the political, economic, and cultural influences on the Mi'kmaq of missionaries from the Capuchin, Jesuit, and Recollect orders.

8. The current discussion departs from many other anthropological analyses of pilgrimage, which examine the construction of the sacred and the mundane and the collective transformation of individuals through what Victor Turner has described as *communitas* in both Christian and non-Christian religious traditions and also in the secular world (Turner 1974; Turner and Turner 2011; see also Coleman and Eade 2004; Coleman and Elsner 1995; Eade and Sallnow 1991; Eickelman and Piscatori 1990; Morinis 1984, 1992; Peña 2011; Sallnow 1987; Yamba 1995). The Turners examined the social phenomena of collective effervescence, *communitas*, and liminality, which they argued individuals experience while participating in the social practice of pilgrimage. Here, I use Deborah Ross's definition of pilgrimage, which is simply "journeys to sacred sites" (Ross 2011, xxix).

9. A. A. Johnston's research notes for his *History of the Catholic Church in Eastern Nova Scotia* (1960) include a typescript reference to the 1932 edition of the *Catholic Reference Book* in which he found this reference to the chiefs' contributions: "the parish recognized its indebtedness to the Indian Chiefs for the sums 'they had from time to time lent to the building of St. Mary's.'" Johnston believed the reference possibly dated to January 1, 1837.

10. Throughout this chapter I use the period-appropriate names for this territory, which are as follows (from A. A. Johnston 1960, 2): 1611–1657—religious orders in France; 1657–1659—the Archdiocese of Rouen, France; 1659–1817—the Vicariate Apostolic of New France, which became the Diocese of Québec in 1674; 1817–1844, the Vicariate Apostolic of Nova Scotia; 1844–1886—Diocese of Arichat; 1886–present—Diocese of Antigonish.

11. At least one Mi'kmaw publicly, though subtly, voiced criticism of the celebrations. Andrea Colfer, who, at the time, was an analyst for the Atlantic Policy Congress of First Nations Chiefs Secretariat, contributed an article to the August 2010 edition of *Mi'kmaq-Maliseet News* in which she described the traditional blessing and spirit-naming ceremonies that were performed for a male infant on the White Eagle Sundance grounds at the Elsipogtog First Nation on June 24, the date of the four-hundredth anniversary of Chief Membertou's conversion to Catholicism. She wrote, "I was compelled to contribute this piece as I saw it [the baby's blessing and naming ceremony] as a day of decolonization, this boy will learn his language, his culture and his spirituality" (Colfer 2010, 3).

12. For discussions of Catholicism in contemporary Mi'kmaw life, see D. Marshall et al. (1989), Poliandri (2011), Reid (2013), Robinson (2005).

13. Wallis and Wallis (1955, 183) report that these missionaries kept a promise to Queen Anne "by dedicating the first chapel they built in the New World to St. Anne

d'Apt." Chute, however, cautions scholars not to confuse "the first instances of Native reverence for St. Anne" with the "origins of the actual St. Anne's ceremony" (1992, 51). See also Krieger (1989, 2002).

14. A. A. Johnston reinforces this point by delineating the boundaries of the Diocese of Québec, which included Nova Scotia until 1817: "In 1800 the Diocese of Quebec was bounded on the east by Newfoundland and the Atlantic Ocean, on the south by the United States, on the west by the Pacific Ocean, and on the north by the Arctic Ocean" (A. A. Johnston 1960, 23–24). Johnston writes, "[T]he territory of the present Diocese of Antigonish has been successively under five ecclesiastical jurisdictions" (1960, 2).

15. A. A. Johnston reports that Balthazar de Paris made "missionary tours throughout Acadie as far as St. Peter's, in a radius of 100 leagues" (A. A. Johnston 1960, 20).

16. Indeed, language acquisition was the first step in what Dumont-Johnson has called *la technique missionnaire* (Dumont-Johnson 1970, 77).

17. Schmidt and Balcom (1993) attribute this report to Abbé Maillard, although the document's references to Maillard in the third person might suggest a different author. A transcript included in the A. A. Johnston papers at the Diocese of Antigonish Archives states that the report was unsigned with no date or location given. However, the information contained in the report suggests that it was written circa 1738 to 1739 (see Diocese of Antigonish Archives 1738–1739).

18. Following the fall of the Fortress of Louisbourg to British forces in 1758, Maillard fled the mission at Potlotek and wandered to other mission sites around Acadia. One of these sites was the island of Maligomish. Maillard also wrote his will at Maligomish in April 1759. In it he states that he, and his caretakers, M. and Mme. Louis Pettipas, had been living on the island since the fall of Louisbourg ("*Malegomich, où nous avons été obligez de nous réfugier après le prise de Louisbourg*"). Maillard states that his will was "*Fait à Malegomich, dans mon Oratoire*" (David 1926–1927, 153). This oratory may not have been much more than a small room or even wigwam. It may have been the first formal house of worship and prayer on Maligomish. Maillard soon after moved to Halifax, where he died in 1762. Along with notable British dignitaries, many Acadian Catholics and Mi'kmaq attended his funeral (David 1926–1927, 149; Lenhart [1921] 1995, vi).

19. Indeed, the tradition of alliance renewal survived in modified form in twentieth-century rituals of the mission, during which the *Sante' Mawi'omi's Putu's* would read the wampum that describes the Mi'kmaq's concordat with the Holy See (McMillan 1996, 95). McMillan notes that Isaac Alek was the last *Putu's* who was able to read the wampum and that this tradition died with him in 1965 (1996, 97).

20. Chute (1992, 52) argues that two conditions were necessary for the annual celebration to be instituted: first, the establishment of a regularity to the intraregional summer gatherings of Mi'kmaq and, second, the emergence of a charismatic leader with influence over the Mi'kmaq "to change their traditional beliefs and ceremonies." She further argues that Abbé Maillard was the person most likely to solidify St. Anne as the Mi'kmaq's patroness because of his command of the Mi'kmaw language, his

production of the ideographic prayer books, his personal expenditures toward the cost of building a chapel at the mission site on what is now Potlotek, Cape Breton, and his elevation to the post of grand vicar of the Acadian missions in 1751 (Chute 1992, 53). As grand vicar, Maillard had the power to organize processions for the Holy Year and therefore, Chute argues, was positioned to introduce an elaborate ceremony devoted to St. Anne, including the procession of her shrine (Chute 1992, 53–54).

21. In 1755, the British deported hundreds of Acadians who refused to swear an oath of allegiance to the British Crown. Some Acadians returned to France; others traveled to Louisiana and became the ancestors of the region's Cajun population. Still others eventually returned to eastern Canada.

22. Upton (1979, 160–61) discusses the parallel efforts of Protestant denominations to instill their ethic in the Mi'kmaq in Nova Scotia and New Brunswick.

23. These records are housed at Library and Archives Canada in Ottawa. See RG 10. Vol. 6608. File 4051–7RC.

24. Today, the Holy Family Parish in Eskasoni is the only church in a Mi'kmaw community in the Diocese of Antigonish that is its own parish. The other Mi'kmaw churches are either missions or members of pastoral units, which are amalgamations of former parishes whose congregations have diminished.

25. The Forty Hours Adoration or Forty Hours Devotion involves forty hours of continuous prayer before the Eucharist (see Diocese of Antigonish Archives 1932–1938).

26. The announcement books do not indicate why there were no visits to the Pictou Landing mission in the winter. Access to Pictou Landing was comparatively easier in the winter because the harbor would freeze, making it possible to travel on foot. It is possible that more Mi'kmaq were living at Pictou Landing during the summer months. In a letter to Father Roderick McDonald, dated October 1898, the local schoolteacher, Nelly Connolly, reported, "The number to attend during the winter months will be in the vicinity of forty, with a sure increase for the summer term" (LAC 1898).

27. Some of the discussion of Mi'kmaw pilgrimage in the nineteenth century has been presented in modified form in Lelièvre and Marshall 2015.

28. Elsie Clews Parsons (1926, 469) observed this dance in 1923 at Chapel Island. She referred to it as the "war medicine dance"—*nes'kawet*.

29. Cf. Reid (2013, 59), who questions the accuracy of describing Mi'kmaw Catholicism as syncretic, and Westerfelhaus and Singhal (2001), who discuss how the Aztecs transformed the Catholicism to which they were converted in the early sixteenth century.

30. See chapter 1, note 16, for a discussion of the author's identity.

31. This book also contained a directive that meat should not be consumed for the two days preceding the Sabbath. The anonymous author wrote: "It is very difficult to convince them that they can now eat it. They will say it is not good to change the commandments" (Anonymous 1867, 249).

32. Hornborg also noted this practice on Chapel Island when she visited in 1996: "To end the day everyone could, if they wished, crawl on their knees from the church stairs up to the statue of St. Anne and pray for the sick" (Hornborg 2002, 251). During her doctoral fieldwork in the late 2000s, Sherry Smith observed a group of Mi'kmaw pilgrims from Nova Scotia crawling to St. Anne's shrine at the pilgrimage site of Sainte Anne de Beaupré in Québec (S. Smith 2011, 107).

33. These descriptions should be approached with caution, considering that the author was likely a missionary himself and writing for an ecclesiastical audience. However, reports of the vast distances traveled by Mi'kmaq come from other sources. For example, Rankin writes that in 1814 the governor of the colony of Cape Breton established an overland postal-communication route between Sydney and Halifax (a distance of approximately three hundred kilometers) by "dispatching an Indian once a month during the winter, when Sydney Harbor was closed by ice" (Rankin 1940–1941, 54).

34. It is possible that the author was more scandalized than the Mi'kmaq. Dancing was a fundamental part of the St. Anne's mission until the Catholic Church discouraged it. The conversations that I had with elders from Pictou Landing suggest that in the early twentieth century, Mi'kmaq of that community were not scandalized by dancing near their chapel on Maligomish. Indeed, a building that some referred to as a "dance hall" was located north of the church. Madeline Martin (1989, 1) wrote that the square and step dances performed during her childhood "would last for hours." Some elders even recall the missionary priest occasionally joining the fun.

35. See "Catholic Encyclopedia" at "Catholic Online," http://www.catholic.org/encyclo pedia/view.php?id=9005; accessed November 1, 2016.

36. Hornborg says that the Mi'kmaq who visit Chapel Island refer to St. Anne's Day as going "to the mission." She also notes the religious and secular nature of the Potlotek mission, referring to one of her interlocutors who said that she goes to Potlotek "foremost as a Mi'kmaq, and not as a Catholic" (Hornborg 2002, 249; see also Hornborg's note 18).

37. This description is *contra* Poliandri (2011), who contrasts the St. Anne's missions on mainland Nova Scotia to the one held on Cape Breton Island at Potlotek. He writes, "Among the mainland Mi'kmaq, St. Anne's Day is mainly a religious experience with limited social significance" (Poliandri 2011, 208).

38. As Elsie Clews Parsons (1926), Howard (1965), and others have noted, the St. Anne's mission has long been a popular place for young Mi'kmaq to court.

39. The Red Road Project in Nova Scotia is a network of youth groups on reserves throughout the province. According to the Pictou Landing First Nation's Red Road Facebook page, "The Red Road Project is meant to ENCOURAGE and PROMOTE healthy choices, and to combat drug and alcohol abuse. We plan to do this through the development and delivery of cultural and non-cultural activities which will empower youth to take greater control of their lives as individuals." See https://www .facebook.com/groups/1467019200263418/; accessed November 1, 2016.

40. Noel Martin's film footage from the 1960s shows men carrying the larger statue of St. Anne during the procession.

41. Two weeks before the 1897 mission, *The Casket* reported on the events scheduled for the weekend, some of which were intended to include non-Mi'kmaq, such as "a picnic with field sports, boat and canoe races, etc. . . . Among the attractions will be a tug-of-war between Indians and white men. There will be excursion rates from Truro and Pictou and intermediate stations on the I.C.R. [Intercolonial Railway]" (Diocese of Antigonish Archives 1897a). After the mission, *The Casket* reported that non-Mi'kmaw Catholics from mainland Merigomish provided food for the Sunday meal, and the choir from Stella Maris sang during the ceremonies (Diocese of Antigonish Archives 1897b). In 2012, the Pictou Landing First Nation organized a St. Anne's Day event on the mainland for community members who were no longer able to travel to Maligomish for the annual mission.

42. This federal department has had numerous name changes and changes in mandate since the mid-twentieth century. It was most recently known as Aboriginal Affairs and Northern Development Canada (see http://www.thecanadianencyclopedia.ca/en/article/aboriginal-affairs-and-northern-development-canada/; accessed June 4, 2016).

43. Cf. Turner 1974; Turner and Turner 1978.

Conclusion

1. The chapter title is excerpted from a paper titled "In Restlessness There Is Power: Idle No More and Political Pilgrimage," delivered at the 2014 meeting of the American Anthropological Association. The title of this section is taken from an article by aboriginal writer and journalist Paul Seesequasis, which appeared on the website theTyee.ca in April 2013 (see http://thetyee.ca/Life/2013/04/06/Nishiyuu-Walkers/; accessed November 4, 2016.).

2. See http://www.motherearthwaterwalk.com/?page_id=2613; accessed November 4, 2016.

3. See https://www.facebook.com/Mikmakiwaterwalk2016/; accessed November 4, 2016.

4. On the Journey of Nishyuu, see http://www.huffingtonpost.ca/2013/03/25/nishiyuu-journey-ends-ottawa-harper-pandas_n_2950643.html; accessed November 4, 2016. On the Omushkegowuk Walkers, see http://www.cbc.ca/news/canada/ottawa/omushkegowuk-walkers-reach-ottawa-call-for-treaty-awareness-1.2548932; accessed November 4, 2016. See the Nibi Walk website for a list of some of the Water Walks in 2015: http://www.nibiwalk.org/posts/water-walks-in-2015/; accessed November 4, 2016. Other walks have included the multistage Nihigaal Bee Iiná (Our Journey of Existence) led by young Diné. The first two stages were a combined distance of 925 kilometers stretching from Dził Naa'oodiłii (Huerfano Mountain) in New Mexico to Dook'o'osliid (San Francsico Peaks) in Arizona. See http://indiancountrytodaymedianetwork.com/2015/05/06/young-dine-walk-another-350-miles-prayer-people-land-culture-160244; accessed November 4, 2016.

5. Edmond Etherington, Facebook post, November 29, 2013, https://www.facebook

.com/plugins/post.php?href=https%3A%2F%2Fwww.facebook.com%2Fperma
link.php%3Fstory_fbid%3D1381752645383046%26id%3D1381629508728693
or https://www.facebook.com/pages/Oskapewis-helpers/1381629508728693?fref=nf;
accessed November 4, 2016).

6. "Canada Must Recognize First Nations' Rights: Omushkegowuk Walkers' Historic
Journey Calls for New Arrangements," *The Marxist-Leninist Daily—Internet Edition*,
no. 22, March 4, 2014, http://cpcml.ca/Tmld2014/D44022.htm; accessed November 4, 2016.

7. See http://nishiyuujourney.ca/#!/?page_id=10; accessed November 4, 2016.

8. See https://www.facebook.com/pages/Reclaiming-Our-Steps-Past-Present-Future/7688
16863131863; accessed November 4, 2016.

9. See Journey Protocol (revised), February 6, 2013, p. 4, http://nishiyuujourney.ca
//wp-content/uploads/2013/02/JourneyProtocolRevised-1.pdf; accessed November 4, 2016.

10. See "Mission" at http://nishiyuujourney.ca/#!/?page_id=10; accessed November 5, 2016.

11. See http://www.unhcr.org/en-us/news/latest/2016/6/5763b65a4/global-forced-displace
ment-hits-record-high.html; accessed November 4, 2016.

12. See http://data.unhcr.org/mediterranean/regional.php; accessed November 4, 2016.

13. See http://www.unhcr.org/en-us/news/latest/2016/5/574db9d94/mediterranean-death
-toll-soars-first-5-months-2016.html; accessed November 4, 2016.

14. See also Andersson (2015); Dunn (2015).

15. Holmes and Castañeda (2016) also examine the public discourse of the migrant
emergency, noting that the conceptions of these human movements are often represented through aquatic metaphors—for example, waves, tides, floods, and so on.

16. See http://www.theguardian.com/media/ng-interactive/2015/aug/10/migrant-life-in
-calais-jungle-refugee-camp-a-photo-essay; accessed November 4, 2016. See also http://
www.theatlantic.com/photo/2016/10/france-dismantles-the-jungle-in-calais/505481/;
accessed November 4, 2016; and http://www.nytimes.com/2016/10/25/world/europe
/we-are-ready-to-leave-france-clears-out-the-jungle.html?_r=0; accessed November 4, 2016.

17. See http://www.ohchr.org/EN/ProfessionalInterest/Pages/StatusOfRefugees.aspx; accessed November 4, 2016.

References

Abler, Thomas S. 1990. "Micmacs and Gypsies: Occupation of a Peripatetic Niche." In *Papers of the Twenty-First Algonquian Conference*, edited by William Cowan, 1–11. Ottawa: Carleton University.

———. 2006. "A Mi'kmaq Missionary among the Mohawks: Silas T. Rand and His Attitudes toward Race and 'Progress.'" In *With Good Intentions: Euro-Canadian and Aboriginal Relations in Colonial Canada*, edited by Celia Haig-Brown and David A. Nock, 72–86. Vancouver: University of British Columbia Press.

Adams, Robert McCormick. 1966. *The Evolution of Urban Society: Early Mesopotamia and Prehispanic Mexico*. Chicago: Aldine Publishing Company.

Agbe-Davies, Anna. 2010. "An Engaged Archaeology for Our Mutual Benefit: The Case of New Philadelphia." *Historical Archaeology* 44 (1): 1–6.

Agamben, Giorgio. 1998. *Homo Sacer: Sovereign Power and Bare Life*, translated by Daniel Heller-Roazen. Stanford: Stanford University Press.

Albahari, Maurizio. 2015. "Riots, Rage and Populism: Voices from the Austere City." *Anthropology Now*, January 23, 2015, accessed November 3, 2016. http://anthro now.com/ online-articles/riots-rage-and-populism.

Alcock, Susan E. 1993. *Graecia Capta: The Landscapes of Roman Greece*. Cambridge: Cambridge University Press.

Alfred, Gerald Taiaiake. 1999. *Peace, Power, Righteousness: An Indigenous Manifesto*. New York: Oxford University Press.

———. 2005. *Wasáse: Indigenous Pathways of Action and Freedom*. Toronto: University of Toronto Press.

———. 2009. First Nation Perspectives on Political Identity. First Nations Citizenship Research and Policy Series: Building Towards Change. Ottawa: Assembly of First Nations. Accessed May 26, 2016. http://web.uvic.ca/igov/uploads/pdf/GTA .FN%20perspectives%20°n%20political%20identity%20(Alfred).pdf

Althusser, Louis. 1971. "On Ideology." From "Ideology and Ideological State Apparatuses (Notes towards an Investigation)." In *Lenin and Philosophy and Other Essays by Louis Althusser*, translated by Ben Brewster, 158–86. New York: Monthly Review Press.

Ames, Kenneth A. 1991. "Sedentism: A Temporal Shift or Transitional Change in Hunter-Gatherer Mobility Patterns?" In *Between Bands and States: Center for Archaeological*

Investigations, Occasional Paper No. 9, edited by S.A. Gregg, 108–34. Carbondale: Southern Illinois University Press.

Andersson, Ruben. 2014. *Illegality, Inc.: Clandestine Migration and the Business of Bordering Europe*. Oakland: University of California Press.

———. 2015. "Illegal Migration from Africa Is Now an Industry, Ethnographer Says." National Public Radio, Morning Edition, May 28, 2015, accessed November 3, 2016. http://www.npr.org/2015/05/28/410204957/illegal-migration-from-africa -is-now-an-industry-ethnographer-says.

Andrus, C. F. T., and D. E. Crowe. 2000. "Geochemical Analysis of *Crassostrea virginica* as a Method to Determine Season of Capture." *Journal of Archaeological Science* 27: 33–42.

Andrushko M., R. Buzon, A. Simonetti, and R. A. Creser. 2009. "Strontium Isotope Evidence for Prehistoric Migration at Chokepukio, Valley of Cuzco, Peru." *Latin American Antiquity* 20 (1): 57–75.

Anonymous. 1867. "The Catholic Church in the Wilderness." *The Irish Ecclesiastical Record* 4: 238–54.

Anschuetz, Kurt F., Richard H. Wilshusen, and Cherie L. Scheick. 2001. "An Archaeology of Landscapes: Perspectives and Directions." *Journal of Archaeological Research* 9 (2): 157–211.

Appadurai, Arjun. 1996. "Sovereignty without Territoriality." In *The Geography of Identity*, edited by Patricia Yaeger, 40–58. Ann Arbor: University of Michigan Press.

Arneil, Barbara. 1996. *John Locke and America: The Defence of English Colonialism*. Oxford: Clarendon Press.

Asad, Talal, ed. 1973. *Anthropology and the Colonial Encounter*. London: Ithaca Press.

Asad, Talal. 1979. "Equality in Nomadic Social Systems? Notes toward the Dissolution of an Anthropological Category." In *Pastoral Production and Society*, edited by L'Equipe ecologie et anthropologie des societies pastorals, 419–428. Cambridge: Cambridge University Press.

Asch, Michael. 1979. "The Ecological-Evolutionary Model and the Concept of Mode of Production." In *Challenging Anthropology*, edited by D. H. Turner and G. A. Smith, 81–99. Toronto: McGraw-Hill, Ryerson.

———. 1992. "Errors in the *Delgamuukw* Decision: An Anthropological Perspective." In *Aboriginal Title in British Columbia: Delgamuukw v. The Queen*, edited by Frank Cassidy, 221–244. Vancouver and Montréal: Oolichan Books and the Institute for Research on Public Policy.

Ashmore, Wendy, and A. Bernard Knapp, eds. 1999. *Archaeologies of Landscape: Contemporary Perspectives*. Malden, MA: Blackwell Publishers.

Atalay, Sonya L. 2006. "Indigenous Archaeology as Decolonizing Practice." *American Indian Quarterly* 30 (3): 280–310.

———. 2008. "Multivocality and Indigenous Archaeologies." In *Evaluating Multiple Narratives: Beyond Nationalist, Colonialist, Imperialist Archaeologies*, edited by Junko Habu, Clare Fawcett, and John M. Matsunaga, 29–44. New York: Springer.

———. 2012. *Community-Based Archaeology: Research with, by and for Indigenous and Local Communities*. Berkeley: University of California Press.

Augustine, Stephen J. 2008. "Silas T. Rand's Work among the Mi'kmaq." In *Aboriginal Oral Traditions: Theory, Practice, Ethics*, edited by Renée Hulan and Renate Eigenbrod, 45–51. Halifax, NS: Fernwood Publishing.

Bachand, B. 2006. "Preclassic Excavations at Punta de Chimino, Petin Guatemala: Investigating Social Emplacement on an Early Maya Landscape." PhD diss., Department of Anthropology, University of Arizona, Tucson.

Bakhtin, Mikhail M. 1981. "Discourse in the Novel." In *The Dialogic Imagination*, edited by Michael Holquist, translated by Caryl Emerson and Michael Holquist, 259–422. Austin: University of Texas Press.

Balbo, Andrea L., Marco Madella, Asumpció Vila, and Jordi Estévez. 2010. "Micromorphological Perspectives on the Stratigraphical Excavation of Shell Middens: A First Approximation from the Ethnohistorical Site Tunel VII, Tierra del Fuego (Argentina)." *Journal of Archaeological Science* 37: 1252–59.

Balcom, B. A., and A. J. B. Johnston. 2006. "Missions to the Mi'kmaq: Malagawatch and Chapel Island in the 18th Century." *Journal of the Royal Nova Scotia Historical Society* 9: 115–40.

Barker, Joanne. 2005. "For Whom Sovereignty Matters." In *Sovereignty Matters: Locations of Contestation and Possibility in Indigenous Strategies for Self-Determination*, edited by Joanne Barker, 1–31. Lincoln: University of Nebraska Press.

Barnard, Alan. 2014. "Defining Hunter-Gatherers: Enlightenment, Romantic, and Social Evolutionary Perspectives." In *The Oxford Handbook of the Archaeology and Anthropology of Hunter-Gatherers*, edited by Vicki Cummings, Peter Jordan, and Marek Zvelebil, 43–54. Oxford, Oxford University Press.

Barsh, Russell Lawrence. 2002. "*Netukulimk* Past and Present: Míkmaw Ethics and the Atlantic Fishery." *Journal of Canadian Studies* 37 (1): 15–42.

Barth, Frederic. 1961. *Nomads of South Persia: The Basseri Tribe of the Khamseh Confederacy*. Prospect Heights, IL: Waveland Press.

Basso, Keith H. 1996. *Wisdom Sits in Places: Landscape and Language among the Western Apache*. Albuquerque: University of New Mexico Press.

Battiste, Marie. 1997. Introduction. In *The Mi'kmaw Concordat*, edited by J. (Sákéj) Youngblood Henderson, 13–20. Halifax, NS: Fernwood.

Beaudry, Mary C., and Travis G. Parno, eds. 2013. *Archaeologies of Mobility and Movement*. New York: Springer.

Bemis, B. E., and D. H. Geary. 1996. "The Usefulness of Bivalve Stable Isotope Profiles as Environmental Indicators: Data from the Eastern Pacific Ocean and the Southern Caribbean Sea." *Palaios* 11: 328–39.

Bender, Barbara, ed. 1993. *Landscape: Politics and Perspectives*. Providence: Berg.

Bender, Barbara. 2002. "Time and Landscape." *Current Anthropology* 43: S103–12.

Bergson, Henri. (1889) 2001. *Time and Free Will: An Essay on the Immediate Data of Consciousness*. Translated by F. L. Pogson. Mineola, NY: Dover Publications.

Bernard, Tim, Leah Rosenmeier, and Sharon Farrell, eds. 2011. *Ta'n Wetapeksi'k: Understanding from Where We Come: Proceedings of the 2005 Debert Research Workshop, Debert, Nova Scotia, Canada*. Truro, NS: Eastern Woodland Publishing.

————. 2015. *Mi'kmawe'l Tan Teli-kina'muemk / Teaching about the Mi'kmaq*. Truro, NS: Eastern Woodland Publishing.

Bettinger, Robert L. 1991. *Hunter-Gatherers: Archaeological and Evolutionary Theory*. New
York: Plenum.

————. 2015. *Orderly Anarchy: Sociopolitical Evolution in Aboriginal California*. Oakland:
University of California Press.

Biard, Pierre. 1616. *Relation de la Nouvelle France*. Lyon: Chez Muguet.

Biggar, H. P., ed. 1911. *The Precursors of Jacques Cartier: 1497–1534. A Collection of Documents Relating to the Early History of the Dominion of Canada*. Ottawa: Government
Printing Bureau.

Binasco, Matteo. 2004. "The Role and Activities of the Capuchin, Jesuit and Recollet Missionaries in Acadia/Nova Scotia from 1654 to 1755." Master's thesis, Department
of History, Saint Mary's University, Halifax, NS.

Binford, Lewis R. 1976. "Forty-Seven Trips: A Case Study in the Character of Some Formation Processes of the Archaeological Record." In *Contributions to Anthropology: The
Interior Peoples of Northern Alaska*, edited by Edwin S. Hall Jr., 299–381. National Museum of Man Mercury Series. Archaeological Survey of Canada. Paper
No. 49. Ottawa: National Museums of Canada.

————. 1978. *Nunamiut Ethnoarchaeology*. New York: Academic Press.

————. 1980. "Willow Smoke and Dogs' Tails: Hunter-Gatherer Settlement Systems and
Archaeological Site Formation." *American Antiquity* 45: 4–20.

————. 1990. "Mobility, Housing, and Environment: A Comparative Study." *Journal of
Anthropological Research* 46: 119–52.

Binnie, Jon, Tim Edensor, Julian Holloway, Steve Millington, and Craig Young. 2007. "Edi-
torial: Mundane Mobilities, Banal Travels." *Social and Cultural Geography* 8 (2):
165–74.

Bird-David, Nurit. 2004. "No Past, No Present: A Critical-Nayaka Perspective on Cultural Remembering." *American Ethnologist* 31 (3): 406–21.

Biolsi, Thomas. 1995. "The Birth of the Reservation: Making the Modern Individual among
the Lakota." *American Ethnologist* 22 (1): 28–53.

————. 2005. "Imagined Geographies: Sovereignty, Indigenous Space and American Indian Struggle." *American Ethnologist* 32 (2): 239–59.

Black, David W., ed. 1988. *Bliss Revisited: Preliminary Accounts of the Bliss Islands Archaeology
Project Phase II*. Fredericton, NB: Archaeological Services, Provincial Parks and
Historic Sites, Tourism, Recreation and Heritage.

Black, David W. 1985. *Living in Bliss: An Introduction to the Archaeology of the Bliss Islands
Groups, Charlotte County, New Brunswick*. Fredericton, NB: Department of Historical and Cultural Resources.

————. 1991. "Stratigraphic Integrity in Northeastern Shell Middens: An Example from
the Insular Quoddy Region." In *Prehistoric Archaeology in the Maritime Provinces:
Past and Present Research*, edited by Michael Deal and Susan Blair, 201–15. Committee on Archaeological Cooperation, Reports in Archaeology 8. Fredericton,
NB: Council of Maritime Premiers.

————. 1993. *What Images Return: A Study of the Stratigraphy and Seasonality of a Shell Midden in Insular Quoddy Region, New Brunswick*. Manuscripts in Archaeology 27. Fredericton, NB: Archaeological Services, Department of Municipalities, Culture and Housing.

————. 2002. "Out of the Blue and into the Black: The Middle-Late Maritime Woodland Tradition in the Quoddy Region, New Brunswick, Canada." In *Northeast Subsistence-Settlement Change: A.D. 700–1300*, edited by John P. Hart and Christina B. Rieth, 301–320. Albany: University of the State of New York.

Black, David W., and Ruth Holmes Whitehead. 1988. "Prehistoric Shellfish Preservation and Storage on the Northeast Coast." *North American Arcahaeologist* 9 (1): 17–30.

Blair, Susan. 2004. "Ancient Wolastoq'kew Landscapes: Settlement and Technology in the Lower Saint John River Valley, Canada." PhD diss., Department of Anthropology, University of Toronto.

Bloch, Maurice. 1989. "From Cognition to Ideology." In *Ritual, History and Power: Selected Papers in Anthropology*, 106–36. London: Althone Press.

Bock, Philip K. 1966. *The Micmac Indians of Restigouche: History and Contemporary Description*. National Museum of Canada. Bulletin 213. Anthropological Series 77. Ottawa: Department of the Secretary of State.

Bonilla, Yarimar. 2011. "The Past Is Made by Walking: Labor Activism and Historical Production in Postcolonial Guadeloupe." *Cultural Anthropology* 26 (3): 313–39.

Bonzani, R. M. 1997. "Plant Diversity in the Archaeological Record: A Means Toward Defining Hunter-Gatherer Mobility Strategies." *Journal of Archaeological Science* 24: 1129–39.

Borden, Charles E., and Duff Wilson. 1952. "A Uniform Site Designation Scheme for Canada." *Anthropology in British Columbia* 3: 44–48.

Bourdieu, Pierre. 1977. *Outline of a Theory of Practice*. Cambridge: Cambridge University Press.

Bourque, B. J. 1973. "Aboriginal Settlement and Subsistence on the Maine Coast." *Man in the Northeast* 6: 3–20.

Bourque, B. J., K. Morris, and A. E. Spiess. 1978. "Determining the Season of Death of Mammal Teeth from Archaeological Sites: A New Sectioning Method." *Science* 199: 530–31.

Bradley, Richard. 2000. *An Archaeology of Natural Places*. London: Routledge.

Braidotti, Rosi. 1994. *Nomadic Subjects: Embodiment and Sexual Difference in Contemporary Feminist Theory*. New York: Columbia University Press.

Brightman, Robert. 1993. *Grateful Prey: Rock Cree Human-Animal Relationships*. Berkeley: University of California Press.

Brooks, Lisa. 2008. *The Common Pot: The Recovery of Native Space in the Northeast*. Minneapolis: University of Minnesota Press.

Bruchac, Margaret M., Siobhan M. Hart, and H. Martin Wobst. 2010. *Indigenous Archaeologies: A Reader on Decolonization*. Walnut Creek, CA: Left Coast Press.

Bruyneel, Kevin. 2007. The Third Space of Sovereignty: The Postcolonial Politics of U.S.-Indigenous Relations. Minneapolis: University of Minnesota Press.

Buchli, Victor. 2007. "Afterward: Towards an Archaeology of the Contemporary Past." In *Contemporary and Historical Archaeology in Theory: Papers from the 2003 and 2004 CHAT Conferences*, 115–18. BAR International Series 1677. Oxford: Archaeopress.

Burchell, Meghan, N. Hallman, B. R. Schöne, A. Cannon, and H. P. Schwarcz. 2014a. "Biogeochemical Signatures of Archaeological Shells: Implications for Interpreting Seasonality at Shell Midden Sites." In *The Cultural Dynamics of Shell Matrix Sites*, edited by M. Roksandic, S. Mendonça de Souza, S. Eggers, M. Burchell, and D. Klokler, 241–50. Albuquerque: University of New Mexico Press.

Burchell, Meghan, M. Betts, A. K. Patton. 2014b. "Preliminary Analysis of Stable Oxygen Isotopes and Shell Growth in the Soft-Shelled Clam *Mya Arenaria*: Implications Interpreting Seasonality and Shellfish Harvesting in Port Joli Nova Scotia." *North Atlantic Archaeology* 3: 91–106.

Burke, Adrian L. 2003. "Archetypal Landscapes and Seascapes: Coastal Versus Interior in the Archaeology of the Maritime Peninsula." *Northeast Anthropology* 66: 41–55.

Burns, John E. 1936–37. "The Abbé Maillard and Halifax." CCHA (Canadian Catholic Historical Association), *Report* 4: 13–22.

Byers, Douglas S., and Frederick Johnson. 1940. "Two Sites on Martha's Vineyard." *Papers of the Robert S. Peabody Foundation for Archaeology*, vol. 1, no. 1. Andover, MA: Phillips Academy.

Byrd, Jodi A. 2012. *The Transit of Empire: Indigenous Critiques of Colonialism*. Minneapolis, MN: University of Minnesota Press.

de la Cadena, Marisol. 2010. "Indigenous Cosmopolitics in the Andes: Conceptual Reflections Beyond 'Politics.'" *Cultural Anthropology* 25 (2): 334–70.

———. 2015. *Earth Beings: Ecologies of Practice Across Andean Worlds*. Durham, NC: Duke University Press.

Cameron, Alex M. 2009. *Power Without Law: The Supreme Court of Canada, the Marshall Decisions and the Failure of Judicial Activism*. Montréal: McGill-Queen's University Press.

Cameron, Catherine M., and Steve A. Tomka, ed. 1993. *Abandonment of Settlements and Regions: Ethnoarchaeological and Archaeological Approaches*. Cambridge: Cambridge University Press.

Cartier, Jacques. (1598) 1993. *The Voyages of Jacques Cartier*. Reprint, Toronto: University of Toronto Press.

Casey, Edward S. 1997. *The Fate of Place: A Philosophical History*. Berkeley: University of California Press.

Casgrain, Henri Raymond. 1895. *Memoire sur les missions de la Nouvelle-Ecosse du Cap Breton et de l'Ile du Prince-Edouard de 1760 à 1820*. Québec: Archdiocese of Québec.

Casimir, M. J., and A. Rao, eds. 1992. *Mobility and Territoriality: Social and Spatial Boundaries among Foragers, Fishers, Pastoralists and Peripatetics*. New York: Berg.

Castañeda, Quetzil E., and Christopher N. Matthews, eds. 2008. *Ethnographic Archaeologies: Reflections on Stakeholders and Archaeological Practices*. Lanham, MD: AltaMira Press.

Cattelino, Jessica. 2008. *High Stakes: Florida Seminole Gaming and Sovereignty*. Durham, NC: Duke University Press.

———. 2010a. "The Double Bind of American Indian Need-Based Sovereignty." *Cultural Anthropology* 25 (2): 235–62.

———. 2010b. "Anthropologies of the United States." *Annual Review of Anthropology* 39: 275–92.

Champlain, Samuel de. 1603. *Des Sauvages, ou, Voyage de Samuel Camplain, De Brovage, fait en la France nouvelle, l'an mil six cens trois*. Paris: Chez Claude de Monstr'oeil.

Chang, K. C. 1962. "A Typology of Settlement and Community Pattern in Some Circumpolar Societies." *Arctic Anthropology* 34: 286–94.

Charlevoix, Pierre. 1744. *Histoire et description générale de la Nouvelle-France*. Paris: Pierre-François Giffart.

Childe, V. Gordon. 1929. *The Danube in Prehistory*. Oxford: Oxford University Press.

———. 1950. "The Urban Revolution." *Town Planning Review* 21: 3–17.

Christmas, Peter. 1977. *Wejkwapniaq*. Sydney, NS: Micmac Association of Cultural Studies.

Chute, Janet E. 1992. "Ceremony, Social Revitalization and Change: Micmac Leadership and the Annual Festival of St. Anne." *Papers of the Twenty-Third Algonquian Conference*, edited by William Cowan, 45–61. Ottawa: Carleton University.

Chute, Janet E., and Frank G. Speck. 1999. "Frank G. Speck's Contributions to the Understanding of Mi'kmaq Land Use, Leadership, and Land Management." *Ethnohistory* 46 (3): 481–540.

Cipolla, Craig N. 2013. *Becoming Brothertown: Native American Ethnogenesis and Endurance in the Modern World*. Tucson: University of Arizona Press.

Clark, Andrew H. 1954. "Titus Smith, Junior, and the Geography of Nova Scotia in 1801 and 1802." *Annals of the Association of American Geographers* 44 (4): 291–314.

———.1968. *Acadia: The Geography of Early Nova Scotia to 1760*. Madison: University of Wisconsin Press.

Clarke, D. Bruce, and Lisa Patterson. 1987. *The Mi'kmaq Treaty Handbook*. Sydney, NS: Native Communications Society of Nova Scotia.

Claasen, Cheryl. 1986. "Temporal Patterns in Marine Shellfish-Species Use along the Atlantic Coast in the Southeastern United States." *Southeastern Archaeology* 5: 120–37.

———. 1991. "Normative Thinking and Shell-Bearing Sites." In *Advances in Archaeological Method and Theory*, vol. 3, edited by Michael B. Schiffer, 249–298. Tucson: University of Arizona Press.

———. 1998. *Shells*. Cambridge: Cambridge University Press.

Clifford, James. 1997. "Traveling Culture." In *Routes: Travel and Translation in the Late Twentieth Century*, 17–46. Cambridge, MA: Harvard University Press.

Coates, Kenneth. 2000. *The Marshall Decision and Native Rights*. Montréal: McGill-Queen's University Press.

Cobb, Charles R. 2005. "Archaeology and the 'Savage Slot': Displacement and Emplacement in the Premodern World." *American Anthropologist* 107 (4): 563–74.

Coleman, Simon and John Elsner, ed. 1995. *Pilgrimage Past and Present: Sacred Travel and Sacred Space in the World Religions*. Cambridge, MA: Harvard University Press.

Coleman, Simon, and John Eade, eds. 2004. *Reframing Pilgrimage: Cultures in Motion*. London: Routledge.

Colfer, Andrea. 2010. "The Wind Sings 400 Years after Chief Membertou." *Mi'kmaq-Maliseet News*, August.

Collignon, Béatrice. 2006. *Knowing Places: The Inuinnait, Landscapes and the Environment*, translated by Linna Weber Müller-Willie. Circumpolar Research Series 10. Edmonton, AB: Canadian Circumpolar Institute Press.

Colwell-Chanthaphonh, Chip. 2009. *Inheriting the Past: The Making of Arthur C. Parker and Indigenous Archaeology*. Tucson: University of Arizona Press.

Colwell-Chanthaphonh, Chip, and T. J. Ferguson. 2006. "Rethinking Abandonment in Archaeological Contexts." *The SAA Archaeological Record* 6 (1): 37–41.

Colwell-Chanthaphonh, Chip, and T. J. Ferguson, ed. 2007. "The Collaborative Continuum: Archaeological Engagements with Descendant Communities." Walnut Creek, CA: AltaMira Press.

———. 2008. *Collaboration in Archaeological Practice: Engaging Descendent Communities*. Walnut Creek, CA: AltaMira Press.

Colwell-Chanthaphonh, Chip, T. J. Ferguson, Dorothy Lippert, Randall McGuire, George P. Nicholas, Joe E. Watkins, and Larry J. Zimmerman. 2010. "The Premise and Promise of Indigenous Archaeology." *American Antiquity* 75 (2): 228–38.

Comaroff, John L., and Jean Comaroff. 1986. "Christianity and Colonialism in South Africa." *American Ethnologist* 13 (1): 1–22.

———. 1987. "The Madman and the Migrant: Work and Labor in the Historical Consciousness of a South African People." *American Ethnologist* 14 (2): 191–209.

———. 1991. *Of Revelation and Revolution: Christianity, Colonialism, and Consciousness in South Africa*, vol. 1. Chicago: University of Chicago Press.

———. 1992. "The Colonization of Consciousness." In *Ethnography and the Historical Imagination*, 235–63. Boulder, CO: Westview Press.

Confederacy of Mainland Mi'kmaq. 2007. *Kekina'muek: Learning about the Mi'kmaq of Nova Scotia*. Truro, NS: Eastern Woodland Publishing.

Confederacy of Mainland Mi'kmaq and the Robert S. Peabody Museum of Archaeology. 2001. *Mikwitelmanej Mikmaqik/Let Us Remember the Old Mikmaq*. Halifax, NS: Nimbus Publishing.

Conkey, Margaret. 2005. "Dwelling at the Margins, Action at the Intersection? Feminist and Indigenous Archaeologies." *Archaeologies* 1 (1): 9–59.

Cooper, John M. 1939. "Is the Algonquian Family Hunting Ground System Pre-Columbian?" *American Anthropologist* 41 (1): 66–90.

Cresswell, Tim. 2002. "Introduction: Theorizing Space." In *Mobilizing Place, Placing Mobility: The Politics of Representation in a Globalized World*, edited by Ginette Verstraete and Tim Cresswell, 11–29. Amsterdam: Rodopi.

———. 2006. *On the Move: Mobility in the Modern Western World*. New York: Routledge.

Cribb, R. 1991. *Nomads in Archaeology*. Cambridge: Cambridge University Press.

Cronon, William. 1983. *Changes in the Land: Indians, Colonists and the Ecology of New England*. Rev. ed. New York: Hill and Wang.

Culhane, Dara. 1998. *The Pleasure of the Crown: Anthropology, Law, and First Nations*. Burnaby, British Columbia: Talonbooks.

Cultural Resource Management Group Limited. 2001. "Archaeological Monitoring and Salvage Sandy Lake Reservoir, Halifax Municipality." Unpublished draft archaeological management and salvage report. Manuscript on file with Cultural Resource Management Group, Halifax.

Cunningham, Hilary, and Josiah McC. Heyman. 2004. "Introduction: Mobilities and Enclosures at Borders." *Identities: Global Studies in Culture and Power* 11: 289–302.

Custer, J. F., and K. R. Doms. 1990. "Analysis of Microgrowth Patterns of the American Oyster (*Crassostrea virginica*) in the Middle Atlantic Region of Eastern North America: Archaeological Application." *Journal of Archaeological Science* 17: 151–60.

Czeglédy, André P. 2004. "Getting Around Town: Transportation and the Built Environment in Post-apartheid South Africa." *City & Society* 16 (2): 63–92.

Dalakoglou, Dimitris. 2016. "Europe's Last Frontier: The Spatialities of the Refugee Crisis." *City* 20 (2): 180–85.

Dalakoglou, Dimitris, and Penny Harvey, eds. 2015. "Roads and Anthropology: Ethnography, Infrastructures, (Im)mobility." New York: Routledge.

Daly, Richard. 2005. *Our Box Was Full: An Ethnography for the Delgamuukw Plaintiffs*. Vancouver: University of British Columbia Press.

David, Albert. 1926–1927. "A Propos du Testament de l'Abbé Maillard." *Nova Francia* 2: 149–63.

Davis, Stephen. 1974. "The Teacher's Cove Site: An Archaeological Study of a Prehistoric Site on the New Brunswick Coast." Master's thesis, Department of Anthropology, Memorial University of Newfoundland, St. John's.

———. 1986. "Man, Molluscs and Mammals: A Study of Land Use and Resources in the Late Holocene of the Maritime Provinces of Canada." D.Phil. diss., Department of Archaeology, University of Oxford, Oxford.

Dawdy, Shannon Lee. 2008. *Building the Devil's Empire: French Colonial New Orleans*. Chicago: University of Chicago Press.

———. 2009. "Millennial Archaeology: Locating the Discipline in the Age of Insecurity." *Archaeological Dialogues* 16 (2): 131–42.

Dawson, John William. 1868. *Acadian Geology. The Geological Structure, Organic Remains, and Mineral Resources of Nova Scotia, New Brunswick and Prince Edward Island*. 2nd ed. London: MacMillan.

———. 1878. *Acadian Geology. The Geological Structure, Organic Remains, and Mineral Resources of Nova Scotia, New Brunswick and Prince Edward Island*. 3rd ed. London: MacMillan.

Deal, Michael, J. Corkum, D. Kemp, J. McClair, S. McIlquham, A. Murchison, and B. Wells. 1987. "Archaeological Investigations at the Low Terrace Site (BaDg2) Indian Gardens, Queen's County, Nova Scotia." In *Archaeology in Nova Scotia 1985 and 1986*, edited by S. Davis et al. Curatorial Report 63. Halifax, NS: Nova Scotia Museum.

Deal, Michael, ed. 1998. "Memoirs on the Prehistory of Nova Scotia, 1957–1967. By John Steuart Erskine." Nova Scotia Museum Special Report. Halifax, NS: Nova Scotia Museum.

De León, Jason. 2012. "'Better to Be Hot than Caught': Excavating the Conflicting Roles of Migrant Material Culture." *American Anthropologist* 114 (3): 477–95.

Deloria, Vine, Jr., and Clifford M. Lytle. 1998. *The Nations Within: The Past and Future of American Indian Sovereignty*. Austin: University of Texas Press.

Delugan, Robin M. 2010. "Indigeneity across Borders: Hemispheric Migrations and Cosmopolitan Encounters." *American Ethnologist* 37 (1): 83–97.

Deleuze, Gilles, and Felix Guattari. 1987. *A Thousand Plateaus: Capitalism and Schizophrenia*. Minneapolis: University of Minnesota Press.

Delucia, Christine M. 2015. "Locating Kickemuit: Springs, Stone Memorials, and Contested Placemaking in the Northeastern Borderlands." *Early American Studies: An Interdisciplinary Journal* 13 (2): 467–502.

Denny, Alex. 1992. "Beyond the Marshall Inquiry: An Alternative Mi'kmaq Worldview and Justice System." In *Elusive Justice: Beyond the Marshall Inquiry*, edited by Joy Mannette, 103–8. Halifax, NS: Fernwood Publishing.

Denys, Nicholas. 1672. *Description geographique et historique des costes de l'Amerique Septentrionale. Avec l'Histoire naturelle du Païs*, vols. I and II. Paris: Chez Louis Billaine.

Department of the Interior. 1874. *Annual Report. Year Ended 30th June, 1874*. Ottawa: MacLean, Roger.

Dirks, Nicholas B., ed. 2001. *Castes of Mind: Colonialism and the Making of Modern India*. Princeton, NJ: Princeton University Press.

Donovan, Ken. 1980. "A Letter from Louisbourg, 1756." *Acadiensis* 10 (1): 113–30.

Douven, Igor. 2011. Peirce on Abduction. *The Stanford Encyclopedia of Philosophy*. Spring 2011 ed., edited by Edward N. Zalta. http://plato.stanford.edu/archives/spr2011/entries/abduction/.

Duff, Andrew I. 2002. *Western Pueblo Identities: Regional Interaction, Migration, and Transformation*. Tucson: University of Arizona Press.

Dumont-Johnson, Micheline. 1970. *Apôtres ou agiteurs: La France missionnaire en Acadie*. Trois-Rivières: Le Boréal Express Ltée.

Dunn, Elizabeth Cullen. 2015. "The Failure of Refugee Camps." *Boston Review*, September 28, 2015, accessed November 3, 2016. http://www.bostonreview.net/world/elizabeth-dunn-failure-refugee-camps.

Eade, John, and Michael J. Sallnow. 1991. *Contesting the Sacred: The Anthropology of Christian Pilgrimage*. London: Routledge.

Eder, James F. 1984. "The Impact of Subsistence Change on Mobility and Settlement Pattern in a Tropical Forest Foraging Economy: Some Implications for Archeology." *American Anthropologist* 86: 837–53.

Eickelman, D., and J. Piscatori, ed. 1990. *Muslim Travellers: Pilgrimage, Migration, and the Religious Imagination*. Berkeley: University of California Press.

Engels, Friedrich. (1884) 1978. "The Origin of the Family, Private Property, and the State." In *The Marx-Engels Reader*, edited by Robert C. Tucker, 734–59. Reprint, 2nd ed., New York: W. W. Norton and Company.

Englund, Harri. 2002. "Ethnography after Globalism: Migration and Emplacement in Malawi." *American Ethnologist* 29 (2): 261–86.

Erskine, John S. 1958. "Micmac Notes, 1958." Wolfville, NS, for the Nova Scotia Museum of Science, Halifax, NS. On file at the Heritage Division of the Nova Scotia Department of Communities, Culture and Heritage, Halifax.

———. 1962. "Micmac Notes, 1961." Nova Scotia Museum. Occasional Papers 2, Archaeological Series 2. Halifax, NS.

———. 1986. Unpublished papers on the Archaeology of the Maritime Provinces. Compiled by Michael Deal, Department of Anthropology, St. Mary's University. Halifax, NS.

Evans, Susan, and Peter Gould. 1982. "Settlement Models in Archaeology." *Journal of Anthropological Archaeology* 1: 275–304.

Evans-Pritchard, E. E. 1940. *The Nuer: A Description of the Modes of Livelihood and Political Institutions of a Nilotic People*. Oxford: Oxford University Press.

Feit, Harvey A. 1991. "The Construction of Algonquian Hunting Territories: Private Property as Moral Lesson, Policy, Advocacy, Ethnographic Knowledge." In *Colonial Situations: Essays on the Contextualization of Ethnographic Knowledge*, edited by G. W. Stocking, 109–34. Madison: University of Wisconsin Press.

Ferguson, T. J. 1996. "Native Americans and the Practice of Archaeology." *Annual Review of Anthropology* 22: 63–79.

Ferguson, T. J., and Chip Colwell-Chanthaphonh. 2006. *History Is in the Land: Multivocal Tribal Traditions in Arizona's San Pedro Valley*. Tucson: University of Arizona Press.

Fergusson, Charles Bruce. 1966. *The Boundaries of Nova Scotia and Its Counties*. Public Archives of Nova Scotia. Bulletin 22. Halifax, NS.

Ferris, Neal. 2003. "Between Colonial and Indigenous Archaeologies: Legal and Extralegal Ownership of the Archaeological Past in North America." *Canadian Journal of Archaeology* 27: 154–90.

———. 2009. *The Archaeology of Native-Lived Colonialism: Challenging History in the Great Lakes*. Tucson: University of Arizona Press.

Fortes, Meyer, and E. E. Evans-Pritchard. 1940. "Introduction." In *African Political Systems*, edited by Meyer Fortes and E. E. Evans-Pritchard, 1–23. London: Oxford University Press.

Foucault, Michel. 1977. *Discipline and Punish: The Birth of the Prison*, translated by Alan Sheridan. New York: Pantheon Books.

Fowles, Severin. 2011. "Movement and the Unsettling of the Peublos." In *Rethinking Anthropological Perspectives on Migration*, edited by Graciela Cabana and Jeffrey Clark, 45–67. Gainesville: University Press of Florida.

Fratkin, Elliot, Kathleen A. Galvin, and Eric Abella Roth. 1994. *African Pastoralist Systems: An Integrated Approach*. Boulder, CO: Lynne Rienner.

Fried, M. H. 1960. "On the Evolution of Social Stratification and the State." In *Culture in History: Essays in Honor of Paul Radin*, edited by Stanley Diamond, 713–31. New York: Columbia University Press.

Friedman, Jonathan. 2002. "From Roots to Routes: Tropes for Trippers." *Anthropological Theory* 2: 21–36.

Gallivan, Martin. 2007. "Powhatan's Werowocomoco: Constructing Place, Polity, and

Personhood in the Chesapeake, C.E. 1200–C.E. 1609." *American Anthropologist* 109 (1): 85–100.

Gamble, Clive, and W. A. Boismier, eds. 1991. *Ethnoarchaeological Approaches to Mobile Campsites: Hunter-Gatherer and Pastoralist Case Studies*. Ethnoarchaeological Series 1. Ann Arbor, MI: International Monographs in Prehistory.

Gaulin, Antoine. 1750. Relation de la mission du P. Antoine Gaulin dans le pays de Mikmaks. Archives Nationales de France. K. 1232, no. 50.

Geertz, Clifford. 1973. "Ideology as a Cultural System." In *The Interpretation of Cultures*, 193–233. New York: Basic Books.

———. 1983. "Centers, Kings and Charisma: Reflections on the Symbolics of Power." In *Local Knowledge: Further Essays in Interpretive Anthropology*, 121–46. New York: Basic Books.

Giddens, Anthony. 1979. *Central Problems in Social Theory*. London: Macmillan Press.

Gilpin, J. Bernard. 1877. "Indians of Nova Scotia." *Proceedings and Transactions of the Nova Scotian Institute of Natural Science* 4: 260–81.

Glass, Aaron. 2006. "Conspicuous Consumption: An Intercultural History of the Kwakwaka'wakw Hamat'sa." PhD diss., Department of Anthropology, New York University, New York.

Glick Schiller, Nina G., L. Basch, and C. S. Blanc. 1995. "From Immigrant to Transmigrant: Theorizing Transnational Migration." *Anthropological Quarterly* 68: 48–63.

Gonzalez, Elice B. 1981. "Changing Economic Roles for Micmac Men and Women: An Ethnohistorical Analysis." *Canadian Ethnology Service Paper* 27. National Museum of Man Mercury Series. Ottawa: National Museums of Canada.

Gordon, Jolene. 1993. "Construction and Reconstruction of a Mi'kmaq Sixteenth-Century Cedar-Bark Bag." Curatorial Report 76. Halifax: Nova Scotia Museum.

———. 1995. "Mi'kmaq Textiles: Sewn-Cattail Matting BkCp-1 Site, Pictou Nova Scotia." Curatorial Report 80. Halifax: Nova Scotia Museum.

———. 1997. "Mi'kmaq Textiles Twining: Rush and Other Fibres BkCp-1 Site, Pictou, Nova Scotia." Curatorial Report 82. Halifax: Nova Scotia Museum.

Gramsci, Antonio. 1971. *Selections from the Prison Notebooks*, edited and translated by Quintin Hoare and Geoffrey Nowell Smith. New York: International Publishers.

Graham, Elizabeth. 1998. "Mission Archaeology." *Annual Review of Anthropology* 27: 25–62.

Graves-Brown, Paul M., ed. 2000. *Matter, Materiality, and Modern Culture*. London: Routledge.

Gupta, Anil. 1992. "The Song of the Nonaligned World: Transnational Identities and the Reinscription of Space in Late Capitalism." *Cultural Anthropology* 7: 63–79.

Gupta, Anil, and James Ferguson. 1997. *Anthropological Locations: Boundaries and Grounds of a Field Science*. Berkeley: University of California Press.

Hadlock, W. S. 1939. *The Taft's Point Shell Mound at West Gouldsboro*. Bar Harbour: ME: Robert Abbey Museum.

Hall, Jason. 2015. "Maliseet Cultivation and Climatic Resilience on the Wəlastəkw/ St. John River During the Little Ice Age." *Acadiensis* XLIV (2): 3–25.

Hall, Martin. 1988. "At the Frontier: Some Arguments against Hunter-Gathering and Farming Modes of Production in Southern Africa." In *Hunters and Gatherers 1: History, Evolution and Social Change*, edited by Tim Ingold, D. Riches, and James Woodburn, 137–147. New York: Berg.

Hallowell, A. Irving. 1960. "Ojibwa Ontology, Behaviour, and World View." In *Culture in History: Essays in Honor of Paul Radin*, edited by Stanley Diamond, 19–52. New York: Columbia University Press.

Hamilakis, Yannis. 2011. "Archaeological Ethnography: A Multi-temporal Meeting Ground for Archaeology and Anthropology." *Annual Review of Anthropology* 40: 399–414.

Hammond, Joanne. 2009. "Archaeology Without Reserve: Indigenous Heritage Steward-ship in British Columbia." Master's thesis, Department of Archaeology, Simon Fraser University, Burnaby.

Harring, Sidney L. 1994. *Crow Dog's Case: American Indian Sovereignty, Tribal Law, and United States Law in the Nineteenth Century*. Cambridge: Cambridge University Press.

———. 1998. *White Man's Law: Native People in Nineteenth-Century Canadian Jurispru-dence*. Toronto: Osgoode Society for Canadian Legal History, University of Toronto Press.

Harris, Cole. 2002. *Making Native Space: Colonialism, Resistance, and Reserves in British Co-lumbia*. Vancouver: University of British Columbia Press.

———. 2004. "How Did Colonialism Dispossess? Comments from an Edge of Empire." *Annuals of the Association of American Geographers* 94 (1): 165–82.

Harrison, Rodney, and John Schofield. 2010. *After Modernity: Archaeological Approaches to the Contemporary Past*. Oxford: Oxford University Press.

Hart, John P., and Christina B. Rieth, ed. 2002. *Northeast Subsistence-Settlement Change: A.D. 700–1300*. Albany: University of the State of New York.

Harvey, David. 1990. *The Condition of Postmodernity*. Oxford: Basil Blackwell.

Heckenberger, Michael J. 2009. "Mapping Indigenous Histories: Collaboration, Cultural Heritage, and Conservation in the Amazon." *Collaborative Anthropologies* 2: 9–32.

Henderson, Jason. 2013. "Street Fight: The Politics of Mobility in San Francisco." Boston: University of Massachusetts Press.

Hepburn, Samantha. 2005. "Feudal Tenure and Native Title: Revising an Enduring Fiction." *Sydney Law Review* 27: 49–86.

Hickman, T. Alexander, Lawrence A. Poitras, and Gregory T. Evans. 1989. *Royal Commis-sion on the Donald Marshall, Jr. Prosecution: Digest of Findings and Recommendations*. Halifax: Province of Nova Scotia.

Hirsch, Eric, and Michael O'Hanlon. 1995. *The Anthropology of Landscape: Perspectives on Space and Place*. Oxford: Clarendon Press.

Hobhouse, Leonard T., Morris Ginsberg, and Gerald CWC Wheeler. 1915. *The Material Culture and Social Institutions of the Simpler Societies: An Essay in Correlation*. London: Chapman and Hall.

Hoffman, Bernard. 1955. "The Historical Ethnography of the Micmac of the Sixteenth and Seventeenth Centuries." PhD diss., Department of Anthropology, University of California at Berkeley.

———. 1961. *Cabot to Cartier: Sources for a Historical Ethnography of Northeastern North America: 1497–1550*. Toronto: University of Toronto Press.

Hollowell, Julie. 2006. "Moral Arguments on Subsistence Digging." In *The Ethics of Archaeology: Philosophical Perspectives on Archaeological Practice*, edited by Chris Scarre and Geoffrey Scarre, 69–93. Cambridge: Cambridge University Press.

Hollowell-Zimmer, Julie. 2002. "The Legal Market in Archaeological Materials from Alaska's Bering Strait." *Revista de Arqueología Americana* 21: 7–32.

Holmes, Seth M., and Heide Castañeda. 2016. "Representing the 'European Refugee Crisis' in Germany and Beyond: Deservingness and Difference, Life and Death." *American Ethnologist* 43 (1): 12–24.

Hornborg, Anne-Christine. 2002. "St. Anne's Day—A Time to 'Turn Home' for the Canadian Mi'kmaq Indians." *International Review of Mission* 91: 237–55.

———. 2006. "Visiting the Six Worlds: Shamanistic Journeys in Canadian Mi'kmaq Cosmology." *Journal of American Folklore* 119 (473): 312–36.

Howard, James H. 1965. "The St. Anne's Day Celebration of the Micmac Indians, 1962." *Museum News* 26 (March–April): 5–13.

Human Rights Watch. 2016. "Make It Safe: Canada's Obligation to End the First Nations Water Crisis." HRW, June 7, 2016, accessed November 2016. https://www.hrw.org/report/2016/06/07/make-it-safe/canadas-obligation-end-first-nations-water-crisis.

Humphreys, A. J. B. 1987. "Prehistoric Seasonal Mobility: What Are We Really Achieving?" *The South African Archaeological Bulletin* 42: 34–38.

Hurtado, Albert L. and K. R. Hill. 1990. "Seasonality in a Foraging Society: Variation in Diet, Work Effort, Fertility and Sexual Division of Labor among the Hiwi of Venezuela." *Journal of Anthropological Research* 46: 293–346.

Ingold, Tim. 1993. "The Temporality of the Landscape." *World Archaeology* 25 (2): 152–74.

———. 2000. *The Perception of the Environment: Essays on Livelihood, Dwelling and Skill*. London: Routledge.

———. 2007. *Lines: A Brief History*. London: Routledge.

Ingold, T., D. Riches, and J. Woodburn, ed. 1991a. *History, Evolution and Social Change*. Vol. 1 of *Hunters and Gatherers*. New York: Berg.

———. 1991b. *Property, Power and Ideology*. Vol. 2 of *Hunters and Gatherers*. New York: Berg.

Isaac, Gwyneira. 2007. *Mediating Knowledges: Origins of a Zuni Tribal Museum*. Tucson: University of Arizona Press.

Ivison, Duncan, Paul Patton, and Will Sanders, ed. 2000. *Political Theory and the Rights of Indigenous Peoples*. Cambridge: Cambridge University Press.

Jacka, Jerry K. 2005. "Emplacement and Millennial Expectation in an Era of Development and Globalization: Heaven and the Appeal of Christianity for the Ipili." *American Anthropologist* 107 (4): 643–53.

Jarvenpa, Robert, and Hetty Jo Brumbach. 1988. "Socio-Spatial Organization and Decision-Making Processes: Observations from the Chipewyan." *American Anthropologist* 90: 598–618.

Jenness, Diamond. 1958. "The Indians of Canada." *National Museum of Canada*. Bulletin 65. Ottawa: Queen's Printer.

Jennings, Ronald C. 2011. "Sovereignty and Political Modernity: A Genealogy of Agamben's Critique of Sovereignty." *Anthropological Theory* 11 (1): 23–61.

Johnson, Lottie, ed. 2007. "Traditional Tobacco." Unpublished resource. Eskasoni, NS: Native Alcohol and Drug Abuse Couselling Association of Nova Scotia.

Johnson, Miranda. 2008. "Struggling Over the Past: Decolonization and the Problem of History in Settler Societies." PhD diss., Department of History, University of Chicago.

Johnston, Rev. Angus Anthony. 1960. *A History of the Catholic Church in Eastern Nova Scotia*. Vol. 1, *1611–1827*. Antigonish, NS: St. Francis Xavier University Press.

———. 1971. *A History of the Catholic Church in Eastern Nova Scotia*. Vol. 2, *1827–1880*. Antigonish, NS: St. Francis Xavier University Press.

Journal of the Legislative Council of Nova Scotia (JLCNS). 1863. Appendix 16:4.

Kallius, Annastiina, Daniel Monterescu, and Prem Kumar Rajaram. 2016. "Immobilizing Mobility: Border Ethnography, Illiberal Democracy, and the Politics of the 'Refugee Crisis' in Hungary." *American Ethnologist* 43 (1): 25–37.

Kaplan, Martha, and John Kelly. 1994. "Rethinking Resistance: Dialogics of 'Disaffection' in Colonial Fiji." *American Ethnologist* 21 (1): 123–51.

———. 1999. "On Discourse and Power: 'Cults' and 'Oriental' in Fiji." *American Ethnologist* 26 (4): 843–63.

Keane, Webb. 2003. "Semiotics and the Social Analysis of Material Things." *Language and Communication* 23: 409–25.

———. 2005. "Signs Are Not the Garb of Meaning: On the Social Analysis of Material Things." In *Materiality*, edited by Daniel Miller, 182–205. Durham, NC: Duke University Press.

Kelly, Robert. 1983. "Hunter-Gatherer Mobility Strategies." *Journal of Anthropological Research* 29: 277–309.

———. 1992. "Mobility/Sedentism: Concepts, Archaeological Measures and Effects." *Annual Review of Anthropology* 21: 43–66.

———. 1995. *The Foraging Spectrum: Diversity in Hunter-Gatherer Lifeways*. Washington, DC: Smithsonian Institution Press.

Kelly, Robert, and David Hurst Thomas. 2013. *Archaeology*. 6th ed. Belmont, CA: Wadsworth, Cengage Learning.

Kennedy, Gregory. 2013. "Marshland Colonization in Acadia and Poitou During the 17th Century." *Acadiensis* 42 (1): 37–66.

Kennett, Douglas J., and Barbara Voorhies. 1996. "Oxygen Isotopic Analysis of Archaeological Shells to Detect Seasonal Use of Wetlands on the Southern Pacific Coast of Mexico." *Journal of Archaeological Science* 23: 689–704.

Kent, Susan, ed. 1990. *Domestic Architecture and the Use of Space: An Interdisciplinary Cross-Cultural Study*. Cambridge: Cambridge University Press.

Kent, Susan. 1992. "Studying Variability in the Archaeological Record: An Ethnoarchaeological Model for Distinguishing Mobility Patterns." *American Antiquity* 57: 635–59.

————. 1993. "Models of Abandonment and Material Culture Frequencies." In *Abandonment of Settlements and Regions: Ethnoarchaeological and Archaeological Approaches*, edited by Catherine M. Cameron and Steve A. Tomka, 54–73. Cambridge: Cambridge University Press.

Kent, Susan, and Helga Vierich. 1989. "The Myth of Ecological Determinism: Anticipated Mobility and Site Spatial Organization." In *Farmers as Hunters: The Implications of Sedentism*, edited by Susan Kent, 96–130. Cambridge: Cambridge University Press.

King, Thomas F. 1978. "Don't That Beat the Band? Nonegalitarian Political Organization in Prehistoric Central California." In *Social Archeology: Beyond Subsistence and Dating*, edited by Charles R. Redman, Mary Jane Berman, Edward V. Curtin, William T. Langhorne Jr., Nina M. Versaggi and Jeffery C. Wanser, 225–48. New York: Academic Press.

Klein, Martin A. 1989. "Studying the History of Those Who Would Rather Forget: Oral History and the Experience of Slavery." *History in Africa* 16: 209–17.

Knight, Rolf. 1996. *Indians at Work: An Informal History of Native Labour in British Columbia, 1858–1930*. Vancouver, BC: New Star Books.

Knockwood, Isabelle. 2001. *Out of the Depths: The Experience of Mi'kmaw Children at the Indian Residential School at Shubenacadie, Nova Scotia*. Lockeport, NS: Roseway Publishing.

Kosiba, Steve, and Andrew M. Bauer. 2013. "Mapping the Political Landscape: Toward a GIS Analysis of Environmental and Social Difference." *Journal of Archaeological Method and Theory* 20 (1): 61–101.

Krautwurst, Udo. 2003. "What Is Settler Colonialism? An Anthropological Meditation on Frantz Fanon's 'Concerning Violence.'" *History and Anthropology* 14 (1): 55–72.

Krech, Shepard. 1981. *Indians, Animals, and the Fur Trade: A Critique of Keepers of the Game*. Athens: University of Georgia Press.

Krieger, Carlo J. 1989. "Ethnogenesis or Cultural Interference? Catholic Missionaries and the Micmac." In *Actes du vingtième congrès des Algonquinistes*, edited by William Cowan, 193–200. Ottawa: Carleton University.

————. 2002. "Culture Change in the Making: Some Examples of How a Catholic Missionary Influenced Micmac Religion." *American Studies International* 40 (2): 37–56.

Kroeber, Alfred L. 1939. "Cultural and Natural Areas of North America." *University of California Papers in American Archaeology and Ethnology*, vol. 38. Berkeley: University of California Press.

Langan, Celeste. 2001. "Mobility Disability." *Public Culture* 13 (3): 459–84.

Larsen, Tord. 1983. "Negotiating Identity: The Micmac of Nova Scotia." In *The Politics of Indianness: Case Studies of Native Ethnopolitics in Canada*, edited by Adrian Tanner, 37–136. St. John's: Institute of Social and Economic Research, Memorial University of Newfoundland.

Lawrence, Bonita. 2002. "Rewriting Histories of the Land: Colonization and Indigenous Resistance in Eastern Canada." In *Race, Space, and the Law*, edited by Sherene H. Razack, 21–46. Toronto: Sumach Press.

Layton, Robert H. 1995. "Relating to the Country in the Western Desert." In *The Anthropology of Landscape: Perspectives on Place and Space*, edited by Eric Hirsch and Michael O'Hanlon, 210–231. Oxford: Clarendon Press.

Leacock, Eleanor. 1954. "The Montagnais 'Hunting Territory' and the Fur Trade." *American Anthropologist* 56 (5): part 2, memoir no. 78.

LeClerq, Chrestien. (1691) 1910. *New Relation of Gasparia*. Paris. Reprint, Toronto: Publications of the Champlain Society.

Lee, Richard B., and Irven DeVore, eds. 1968. *Man the Hunter*. Chicago: Aldine Publishing Company.

Lee Nichols, Robert. 2005. "Realizing the Social Contract: The Case of Colonialism and Indigenous Peoples." *Contemporary Political Theory* 4 (1): 42–62.

———. 2013. "Indigeneity and the Settler Contract Today." *Philosophy and Social Criticism* 39 (2): 161–82.

Lefebvre, Henri. (1974) 1991. *The Production of Space*, translated by Donald Nicholson-Smith. Oxford: Basil Blackwell.

Lekson, Stephen, and Catherine M. Cameron. 1995. "The Abandonment of Chaco Canyon, the Mesa Verde Migrations, and the Reorganization of the Pueblo World." *Journal of Anthropological Archaeology* 14: 184–202.

Leland, Charles G. 1884. *The Algonquin Legends of New England*. Boston: Houghton Mifflin.

Lelièvre, Michelle A. 2005. "Heritage Research Permit A2004NS72: Final Report." Unpublished manuscript on file with Museum Operations, Nova Scotia Museum, Halifax.

———. 2007. *"Wijswin [sic]* ('You move from one place to another'): Understanding Mi'kmaw Mobility in Post-Contact Nova Scotia." PhD diss. proposal, Department of Anthropology, University of Chicago. Chicago.

———. 2008a. "Heritage Research Permit A2007NS74: Preliminary Report." Unpublished manuscript on file with Museum Operations, Nova Scotia Museum, Halifax, Nova Scotia.

———. 2008b. "Heritage Research Permit A2008NS02: Report on Surface Investigations and Sub-Surface Testing of Maligomish (Indian Island), Pictou County, Nova Scotia." Spring 2008. Unpublished manuscript on file with Museum Operations, Nova Scotia Museum, Halifax, Nova Scotia.

———. 2009. "Heritage Research Permit A2008NS73: Final Report." Unpublished manuscript on file with Museum Operations, Nova Scotia Museum, Halifax, Nova Scotia.

———. 2010. "The Maligomish Archaeology Project 2007–2008: Building(s) in Flux." Paper presented at the 75th annual meeting of the Society for American Archaeology, April 2010, St. Louis, MO.

———. 2012. *"Ajiwisin* (You move from one place to another): Mobility, Emplacement and Politics in (Post-)Colonial Nova Scotia." PhD diss., University of Chicago, Chicago.

———. 2014. "Report on the Maligomish Research Project 2007–2011." Unpublished report on dissertation research written for members of the Pictou Landing First Nation.

———. 2016. "Evidentiary Encounters: Reconstituting 'the Field' Through Collaborative Archaeologies." Paper presented to the 115th annual meeting of the American Anthropological Association, November, Minneapolis, MN.

———. 2017. "Temporal Changes in Marine Shellfish? A Preliminary Archaeological Perspective from the Northumberland Strait." *Journal of the North Atlantic*. Special Volume 10: 42–58.

Lelièvre, Michelle A., and Maureen E. Marshall. 2015. "'Because Life it selfe is but Motion': Toward an Anthropology of Mobility." *Anthropological Theory* 15(4): 434–71.

Lenhart, John M. (1921) 1995. Preface. In *Manual of Prayers, Instructions, Psalms, & Hymns in Micmac Ideograms*, by Christian Kauder. Ste-Anne-des-Monts, QB: Editions de la S.H.A.M.

Leone, Mark P. 2005. *The Archaeology of Liberty in an American Capital: Excavations in Annapolis*. Berkeley: University of California Press.

Lescarbot, Marc. 1611. *Histoire de la Novvelle-France*. Paris: Chez Jean Millot.

Lewis, Roger J. 2007. "Pre-Contact Fish Weirs: A Case Study from Southwestern Nova Scotia." Master's thesis, Department of Anthropology, Memorial University of Newfoundland, St. John's.

Li, Tania. 2010. "Indigeneity, Capitalism and the Management of Dispossession." *Current Anthropology* 51 (3): 385–414.

Lips, Julius E. 1947. "Naskapi Law. (Lake St. John and Lake Mistassini Bands.) Law and Order in a Hunting Society." *Transactions of the American Philosophical Society, New Series* 37 (4): 379–492.

Littlefield, Alice, and Martha C. Knack. 1996. *Native Americans and Wage Labor: Ethnohistorical Perspectives*. Norman: University of Oklahoma Press.

Little, Barbara J. 2009. "Public Archaeology in the United States in the Early Twenty-First Century." In *Heritage Studies: Methods and Approaches*, edited by Marie Louise Stig Sørensen and John Carman, 29–51. London: Routledge.

Locke, John. (1690) 1980. *Second Treatise of Government*, edited by C. B. Macpherson. Indianapolis, IN: Hackett Publishing.

Lowie, Robert H. 1920. *Primitive Society*. New York: Horace Liveright.

Lubbock, John. (1865) 1892. *Pre-Historic Times*. 5th ed., New York: D. Appelton and Company.

Lycett, Mark. 2004. "Archaeology Under the Bell." *Missionalia* 32 (3): 357–70.

Lyell, Charles. 1863. *The Geological Evidences of the Antiquity of Man*. 2nd ed. London: J. Murray.

Lyons, Natasha. 2013. *Where the Wind Blows Us: Practicing Critical Community Archaeology in the Canadian North*. Tucson: University of Arizona Press.

MacLeod, J. D. 1909. "Report to Government on Micmacs of Pictou County." New Glasgow, April 15, 1909. Published September 25, 1909. *Pictou Advocate*, p. 4.

Magaña, Rocio. 2011. "Dead Bodies: The Deadly Display of Mexican Border Politics. In *A Companion to the Anthropology of the Body and Embodiment*, edited by F. E. Mascia-Lees, 157–71. New York: Wiley-Blackwell.

Mailhot, José. 1986. "Territorial Mobility among the Montagnais-Naskapi of Labrador." *Anthropologica* 28 (1/2): 92–107.

———. 1993. *Au Pays des Innus: Les Gens de Sheshatshit*. Montréal: Société Recherches amérindiennes au Québec.

Maillard, Pierre Antoine Simon. 1758. *An Account of the Customs and Manners of the Micmakis and Maricheets Savage Nations, Now Dependent on the Government of Cape-Breton, from An Original French Manuscript-Letter, Never Published, Written by a French Abbot, Who resided many Years, in quality of Missionary, amongst them, To which are annexed, Several Pieces, relative to the Savages, to Nova Scotia, and to North-America in general*. Printed for S. Hooper and A. Morley, London.

———. 1759. *Liturgical Texts in Micmac*. Manuscript produced by the Séminarie du Québec Archives. Available on microfilm.

Malkki, Liisa. 1992. "National Geographic: The Rooting of Peoples and the Territorialization of National Identity among Scholars and Refugees." *Cultural Anthropology* 7:24–44.

Marshall, Donald Sr., Alexander Denny, Simon Marshall, and the Executive of the Grand Council of the Mi'kmaw Nation. 1989. "The Covenant Chain." In *Drumbeat: Anger and Renewal in Indian Country*, edited by Boyce Richardon, 73–103. Regina, SK: Summerhill Press.

Marshall, Joe B. 2006. "The Covenant Chain of Treaties." Published by the Atlantic Policy Congress of First Nations Chiefs. Available at the Virtual Museum of Canada, accessed November 4, 2016. http://www.virtualmuseum.ca/edu/View LoitDa.do;jsessionid=22F7FE5DB70243AC63032B651C9772C5?method =preview&lang=EN&id=711.

Marshall, Maureen E. 2003. "Barbarians at the Gate: A Proposal for the Archaeology of the Kaska Other and the Hittite State." Unpublished seminar paper, Department of Anthropology, University of Chicago, Chicago.

Marshall, Maureen E., and Michelle A. Lelièvre. 2010. "Mediating Subjects: Toward an Anthropological Theory of Mobility." Paper presented at the 109th annual meeting of the American Anthropological Association, November 18, 2010, New Orleans, LA.

Marshall, Murdena. n.d. "Values, Customs and Traditions of the Mi'kmaq [*sic*] Nation." Unpublished resource, University College of Cape Breton, Sydney, NS.

Marshall, Yvonne, ed. 2002. "Community Archaeology." *World Archaeology* 34 (2): special issue.

Martijn, Charles A. 1989. "An Eastern Micmac Domain of Islands." *Actes du Vingtieme Congres des Algonquinistes* 20: 208–31.

Martin, Calvin. 1978. *Keepers of the Game: Indian-Animal Relationships and the Fur Trade*. Berkeley: University of California Press.

Martin, Madeline. 1989. "Malegomish (the way I like to remember it)." Unpublished manuscript provided to Lelièvre by the author.

Marx, Karl. (1867) 1906. *Capital, A Critique of Political Economy*, translated by S. Moore. New York: Charles H. Kerr.

Massumi, Brian. 2002. *Parables for the Virtual: Movement, Affect, Sensation*. Durham, NC: Duke University Press.

Masty, Jordan. 2013. Interview by Carol Off. *As It Happens*, CBC, excerpted and rebroadcast on September 15, 2014.

Matson, R. G., William D. Lipe, and William R. Haase IV. 1988. "Adaptational Continuities and Occupational Discontinuities: The Cedar Mesa Anasazi." *Journal of Field Archaeology* 15(13): 245–64.

Matsuda, David. 1998. "The Ethics of Archaeology, Subsistence Digging, and Artifact Looting in Latin America: Point Muted Counterpoint." *International Journal of Cultural Property* 7 (1): 87–97.

Matthew, G. F. 1884. "Discoveries at a Village of the Stone Age at Bocabec, N.B."" *Bulletin of the Natural History Society of New Brunswick* 3: 6–29.

Mauss, Marcel. (1925) 2002. *The Gift: Forms and Functions of Exchange in Archaic Societies*, translated by D. Halls. London: Routledge.

McCabe, J. Terrence. 1994. "Mobility and Land Use Among African Pastorialists: Old Conceptual Problems and New Interpretations." In *African Pastoralist Systems*, edited by Elliot Fratkin, Kathleen A. Galvin, and Eric Abella Roth, 69–89. Boulder, CO: Lynne Rienner.

McDavid, Carol. 2002. "Archaeologies That Hurt; Descendants That Matter: A Pragmatic Approach to Collaboration in Public Interpretation of African-American Archaeology." *World Archaeology* 34 (2): 303–14.

———. 2009. "The Public Archaeology of African America: Reflections on Pragmatic Methods and Their Results." In *Heritage Studies: Methods and Approaches*, edited by Marie Louise Stig Sørensen and John Carman, 217–234. London: Routledge.

McGhee, Robert. 2008. "Aboriginalism and the Problems of Indigenous Archaeology. *American Antiquity* 73 (4): 579–97.

McMillan, Leslie Jane. 1996. "Mi'kmawey Mawio'mi Changing Roles of the Mi'kmaq Grand Council from the Early Seventeenth Century to the Present." Master's thesis, Department of Social Anthropology, Dalhousie University, Halifax.

McNeely, R., A. S. Dyke, J. R. Southon. 2006. Canadian Marine Reservoir Ages, Preliminary Data Assessment. Geological Survey Canada Open File 5049, Ottawa.

McNiven, Ian J. 1992. "Shell Middens and Mobility: The Use of Off-Site Faunal Remains, Queensland, Australia." *Journal of Field Archaeology* 19 (4): 495–508.

McNiven, Ian J., and Lynette Russell. 2005. *Appropriated Pasts: Indigenous Peoples and the Colonial Culture of Archaeology*. Lanham, MD: AltaMira Press.

McWeeney, Lucinda. 2002. "Cultural and Ecological Continuities and Discontinuities in Coastal New England: Landscape Manipulation." Thematic Issue: Native Coastal New England. *Northeast Anthropology* 64: 75–84.

Merleau-Ponty, Maurice. (1945). 1962. *Phenomenology of Perception*, translated by Colin Smith. New York: Humanities Press.

Meskell, Lynn, and Peter Pels, ed. 2005. *Embedding Ethics*. Oxford and New York: Berg.

Miller, Virginia. 1982. "The Decline of Nova Scotia Micmac Population AD 1600–1850." *Culture* 2: 107–20.

Mills, Antonia. 2005. *"Hang On to These Words": Johnny David's Delgamuukw Evidence*. Toronto: University of Toronto Press.

Milner, Nicky. 2001. "At the Cutting Edge: Using Thin Sectioning to Determine Season of Death of the European Oyster, *Ostrea edulis*." *Journal of Archaeological Science* 28: 861–73.

Mitchell, Timothy. 1991. "The Limits of the State: Beyond Statist Approaches and Their Critics." *American Political Science Review* 85 (1): 77–96.

Mollen-Dupuis, Mélissa. 2014. Interview by Susan Campbell. *Quebec AM*, CBC, November 25, 2014.

Monet, Don, and Skanu'u (Ardythe Wilson). 1992. *Colonialism on Trial: Indigenous Land Rights and the Gitksan and Wet'suwet'en Sovereignty Case*. Philadelphia, PA: New Society Publishers.

Monks, Gregory. 1981. "Seasonality Studies." In *Advances in Archaeological Method and Theory*, vol. 4, edited by M. B. Schiffer, 177–240. New York: Plenum Press.

Moorehead, Warren K. 1922. *A Report on the Archaeology of Maine*. Andover, Mass: The Andover Press.

Moreton-Robinson, Aileen, ed. 2007. *Sovereign Subjects: Indigenous Sovereignty Matters*. New South Wales: Allen and Unwin.

Morgan, Lewis Henry. 1877. *Ancient Society*. Chicago: Charles. H. Kerr and Company.

———. (1881) 1965. *Houses and House-Life of the American Aborigines*. Reprint, Chicago: University of Chicago Press.

Morinis, Alan. 1984. *Pilgrimage in the Hindu Tradition: A Case Study of West Bengal*. Delhi: Oxford University Press.

Morinis, Alan, ed. 1992. *Sacred Journeys: The Anthropology of Pilgrimage*. London: Greenwood Press.

Morphy, Howard. 1993. "Colonialism, History, and the Construction of Place: The Politics of Landscape in Northern Australia." In *Landscape: Politics and Perspectives*, edited by Barbara Bender, 205–43. Providence: Berg.

———. 1995. "Landscape and the Reproduction of the Ancestral Past." In *The Anthropology of Landscape: Perspectives on Place and Space*, edited by Eric Hirsch and Michael O'Hanlon, 184–209. Oxford: Clarendon Press.

Morrison, Kathleen D., and Laura L. Junker, eds. 2002. *Forager-Traders in South and Southeast Asia: Long Term Histories*. Cambridge: Cambridge University Press.

Mortensen, Lena, and Julie Hollowell, ed. 2009. *Ethnographies and Archaeologies: Iterations of the Past*. Gainesville: University Press of Florida.

Mudie, Peta, and Michelle Lelièvre. 2013. "Palynological Study of a Mi'kmaw Shell Midden, Northeast Nova Scotia, Canada." *Journal of Archaeological Science* 40: 2161–75.

Munn, Nancy D. 1986. *The Fame of Gawa: A Symbolic Study of Value Transformation in a Massim (Papua New Guinea) Society*. Cambridge: Cambridge University Press.

———. 1996. "Excluded Spaces: The Figure in Australian Aboriginal Landscape." *Critical Inquiry* 22: 446–65.

Murray, Tim. 2004. *The Archaeology of Contact in Settler Societies*. Cambridge: Cambridge University Press.

Myers, Fred. 1988. "Critical Trends in the Study of Hunter-Gatherers." *Annual Review of Anthropology* 17: 261–82.

Nash, Ronald J. 1978. "Prehistory and Cultural Ecology—Cape Breton Island, Nova Scotia." In *Papers from the Fourth Annual Congress, 1977*, edited by R. J. Preston, 131–56. National Museum of Man Mercury Series, Canadian Ethnology Service, Paper 40. Ottawa: National Museums of Canada.

Nash, Ronald J., and Virginia P. Miller. 1987. "Model Building and the Case of the Micmac Economy." *Man in the Northeast* 34: 41–56.

Nash, Ronald J., and Frances L. Stewart. 1986. *MI'KMAQ: Economics and Evolution: Faunal Remains from the Delorey Island Site (BjCj9) of Nova Scotia*. Curatorial Report 57. Halifax: Nova Scotia Museum.

———. 1990. *Melanson: A Large Micmac Village in Kings County, Nova Scotia*. Curatorial Report 67. Halifax: Nova Scotia Museum.

Nelson, Margaret C. 1999. *Mimbres During the Twelfth Century: Abandonment, Continuity, and Reorganization*. Tucson: University of Arizona Press.

Nelson, Margaret C., and G. Schachner. 2002. "Understanding Abandonments in the North American Southwest." *Journal of Archaeological Research* 10: 167–206.

Nelson, Margaret C., and C. Strawhacker, ed. 2011. *Movement, Connectivity, and Landscape Change in the Ancient Southwest*. Proceedings of the 20th Anniversary Southwest Symposium. Boulder: University Press of Colorado.

Nicholas, George P. 2006. "Decolonizing the Archaeological Landscape: The Practice and Politics of Archaeology in British Columbia." *American Indian Quarterly* 30 (nos. 3, 4): 350–80.

Nicholas, George P., and Thomas D. Andrews, eds. 1997. *At a Crossroads: Archaeology and First Peoples in Canada*. Burnaby, BC: Archaeology Press.

Nicholas, George P., J. Welch, and Eldon Yellowhorn. 2007. "Collaborative Encounters." In *The Collaborative Continuum: Archaeological Engagements with Descendant Communities*, edited by C. Colwell-Chathaphonh and T. J. Ferguson, 273–99. Walnut Creek, CA: AltaMira Press.

Nietfeld, Patricia K. L. 1981. "Determinants of Aboriginal Micmac Political Structure." PhD diss., University of New Mexico, Albuquerque.

Niezen, Ronald. 2009. *The Rediscovered Self: Indigenous Identity and Cultural Justice*. Montreal: McGill-Queen's University Press.

Nurse, Andrew. 2006. "Marius Barbeau and the Methodology of Salvage Ethnography in Canada, 1911–51." In *Historicizing Canadian Anthropology*, edited by Julia Harrison and Regna Darnell, 52–64. Vancouver: University of British Columbia Press.

Ong, A. 2005. "Splintering Cosmopolitanism: Asian Immigrants and Zones of Autonomy in the American West." In *Sovereign Bodies: Citizens, Migrants, and States in the Postcolonial World*, edited by T. B. Hansen and F. Stepputat, 257–75. Princeton, NJ: Princeton University Press.

Ortner, Sherry B. 2005. Subjectivity and Cultural Critique. *Anthropological Theory* 5: 31–52.

Pacifique, Père. 1934. *Le Pays des Micmacs*. Montréal: Chez Ducharme.

—. 1990. *The Micmac Grammar of Father Pacifique*, translated and retranscribed by John Hewson and Bernard Francis. Memoir 7. Winnipeg, MB: Algonquian and Iroquoian Linguistics.

Pandya, Vishvajit. 1990. "Movement and Space: Andamanese Cartography." *American Ethnologist* 17 (4): 775–97.

Panter-Brick, Catherine, Robert H. Layton, and Peter Rowley-Conwy, ed. 2001. *Hunter-Gatherers: An Interdisciplinary Perspective*. Cambridge: Cambridge University Press.

Parnaby, Andrew. 2008. "The Cultural Economy of Survival: The Mi'kmaq of Cape Breton in the Mid-19th Century." *Labour/Travail* 61: 69–98.

Parsons, Elsie Clews. 1926. "Micmac Notes. St. Ann's Mission on Chapel Island, Bras d'Or Lakes, Cape Breton Island." *Journal of American Folklore* 38: 460–85.

Parsons, Jeffrey R. 1972. "Archaeological Settlement Patterns." *Annual Review of Anthropology* 1:127–50.

Patterson, Rev. George. 1877. *A History of the County of Pictou, Nova Scotia*. Montreal: Dawson Brothers.

—. (1877) 1916. *A History of the County of Pictou, Nova Scotia*. Reprint, Pictou: Pictou Advocate.

—. 1889. "The Stone Age in Nova Scotia, as Illustrated by a Collection of Relics Presented to Dalhousie College." *Transactions of the Nova Scotian Institute of Natural Science* 7 (3): 231–52.

Pauketat, Timothy R., and Thomas E. Emerson. 1991. "The Ideology of Authority and the Power of the Pot." *American Anthropologist* 93 (4): 919–41.

Paul, Daniel. 2000. *We Were Not the Savages: A Micmac Perspective on the Collision of European and Aboriginal Civilization*. Halifax, NS: Nimbus Press.

Pawling, Micah. 2010. "Petitions and the Reconfiguration of Homeland: Persistence and Tradition Among Wabanki Peoples in the Nineteenth Century." PhD diss., Department of History, University of Maine, Orono.

Peirce, Charles. 1997. *Collected Papers of Charles Sanders Peirce*, edited by Charles Hartshorne, Paul Weiss, and Arthur W. Burks. Bristol: Thoemmes Continuum.

Pels, Peter. 2005. "'Where There Aren't No Ten Commandments': Redefining Ethics During the *Darkness in El Dorado* Scandal." In *Embedding Ethics*, edited by Lynn Meskell and Peter Pels, 69–99. Oxford: Berg.

Peña, E.A. 2011. *Performing Piety: Making Space Sacred with the Virgin of Guadalupe*. Berkeley: University of California Press.

Pentz, Benjamin C. 2008. "A River Runs Through It: An Archaeological Survey of the Upper Mersey River and Allains River in Southwest Nova Scotia." Master's thesis, Department of Anthropology, Memorial University of Newfoundland.

Petrie, W. M. Flinders. 1939. *The Making of Egypt*. London: Sheldon.

Phillips, Caroline, and Harry Allen, ed. 2005. *Bridging the Divide: Indigenous Communities and Archaeology into the 21st Century*. Walnut Creek, CA: Left Coast Press.

Pictou Advocate. 1913. "Of Local Interest." *Pictou Advocate*, July 26, 1913, p. 10.

Piers, Harry. 1912. "Brief Account of the Micmac Indians of Nova Scotia and Their Remains." *Proceedings and Transactions of the Nova Scotian Institute of Science* 13 (2): 99–125.

Pinkoski, Marc, and Michael Asch. 2004. "Anthropology and Indigenous Rights in Canada and the United States: Implications in Steward's Theoretical Project." In *Hunter-Gatherers in History, Archaeology and Anthropology*, edited Alan Barnard, 187–200. Oxford: Berg.

Poliandri, Simone. 2011. *First Nations, Identity, and Reserve Life: The Mi'kmaq of Nova Scotia*. Lincoln: University of Nebraska Press.

Potter, Parker B. 1994. *Public Archaeology in Annapolis: A Critical Approach to History in Maryland's Ancient City*. Washington, DC: Smithsonian Institution Press.

Povinelli, Elizabeth. 1995. "Do Rocks Listen? The Cultural Politics of Apprehending Australian Aboriginal Labor." *American Anthropologist* 97 (3): 505–18.

Power, Nina. 2006. "Toward an Anthropology of Infinitude: Badiou and the Political Subject." In *The Praxis of Alain Badiou*, edited by Paul Ashton, A. J. Bartlett, and Justin Clemens, 309–38. Victoria, Australia: Ashton and Rafferty.

Preston, B. 1971. "The Shubenacadie River Project." Unpublished manuscript submitted to the National Museum of Man, Ottawa (now Canadian Museum of Civilization, Hull, Québec).

Price, T. Douglas, and James A. Brown, eds. 1985. *Prehistoric Hunter-Gatherers: The Emergence of Cultural Complexity*. San Diego: Academic Press.

Prins, Harald E. L. 1996a. *The Mi'kmaq: Resistance, Accommodation, and Cultural Survival*. Fort Worth, TX: Harcourt Brace College Publishing.

———. 1996b. "Tribal Networks and Migrant Labor: Mi'kmaq Indians as Seasonal Workers in Aroostook's Potato Fields, 1870–1980." In *Native Americans and Wage Labor: Ethnohistorical Perspectives*, edited by Alice Littlefield and Martha C. Knack, 45–65. Norman: University of Oklahoma Press.

———. 1997. "Tribal Network and Migrant Labor: Mi'kmaq Indians as Seasonal Workers in Aroostook's Potato Fields, 1870–1980." In *After King Philip's War: Presence and Persistence in Indian New England*, edited by C. G. Calloway, 231–51. Hanover, NH: Dartmouth College/University Press of New England.

———. 1999. "Storm Clouds over Wabanakiak: Confederacy Diplomacy Until Drummer's Treaty (1727)." Passamaquoddy Tribe at Pleasant Point, accessed July 20, 2012. http://www.wabanaki.com/Harald_Prins.htm.

Province of Nova Scotia. 1842. "Act to Provide for the Instruction and Permanent Settlement of the Indians." Chapter 16 of the Revised Statutes.

———. 1844. "An Act to Regulate the Management and Disposal of the Indian Reserves in This Province." Chapter 42 of the Revised Statutes.

———. 1989. "Special Places Protection Act." Chapter 438 of the Revised Statutes. Amended 1990, c. 45; 1994–95, c. 17; 2004, c. 6, s. 31; 2005, c. 28.

Province of Nova Scotia (Piers, H.). 1933. Report on the Provincial Museum and Science Library for the fiscal year 1931–1932. Halifax, NS. Minister of Public Works and Mines, King's Printer.

———. 1934. Report on the Provincial Museum and Science Library for the fiscal year 1932–33. Halifax, NS. Minister of Public Works and Mines, King's Printer.

———. 1935. Report on the Provincial Museum and Science Library for the fiscal year 1933–34. Halifax, NS: Provincial Secretary, King's Printer.

Quitmyer, Irvy R., and Douglas S. Jones. 1997. "The Sclerochronology of Hard Clams, *Mercenarias*, from the South-Eastern U.S.A.: A Method of Elucidating the Zooarchaeological Records of Seasonal Resource Procurement and Seasonality in Prehistoric Shell Middens." *Journal of Archaeological Science* 24: 825–40.

Quitmyer, Irvy R., Douglas S. Jones, and C. F. T. Andrus. 2005. "Seasonal Collection of Coquina Clams (*Donax variavilis*) during the Archaic and St. Johns Periods in Coastal Northeast Florida." In *Archaeomalacology: Molluscs in Former Environments of Human Behavior*, edited by D. Bar-Yosef, 18–28. London: Oxbow Press.

Radcliffe-Brown, A. R. 1965. *Structure and Function in Primitive Society: Essays and Addresses*. New York: The Free Press.

Raibmon, Paige. 2005. "Authentic Indians: Episodes of Encounter from the Late-Nineteenth-Century Northwest Coast." Durham, NC: Duke University Press.

———. 2007. "Meanings of Mobility on the Northwest Coast." In *New Histories for Old: Changing Perspectives on Canada's Native Past*, edited by Ted Binnema and Susan Neylan, 175–95. Vancouver: University of British Columbia Press.

Rand, Silas T. 1867. *Report Micmac Mission for the Year Ending December 31, 1866*. Halifax, NS: T. Chamberlainx.

———. 1894. *Legends of the Micmacs*. New York: Longmans, Green

———. 1902. *A Dictionary of the Micmac Language*. Charlottetown, PEI: The Patriot Publishing Company.

Rankin, Rev. D. J. 1940–1941. "Laurence Kavanagh." CCHA (Canadian Catholic Historical Association). *Report* 8: 51–76.

Rast, Tim, M. A. P. Renouf, and Trevor Bell. 2004. "Patterns in Precontact Site Location on the Southwest Coast of Newfoundland. *Northeast Anthropology* 68: 41–55.

Reid, Jennifer. 1995. *Myth, Symbol and Colonial Encounter: British and Micmac in Acadia, 1700–1867*. Ottawa: University of Ottawa Press.

———. 2013. *Finding Kluskap: A Journey into Mi'kmaw Myth*. University Park: The Pennsylvania State University Press.

Reimer, Paula J., et al. 2013. "IntCal13 and Marine13 Radiocarbon Age Calibration Curves 0-50,000 Years cal BP." *Radiocarbon* 55: 1869–87.

Reiser, Christine N. 2010. "Rooted in Movement: Spatial Practice and Community Persistence in Native Southwestern New England." PhD diss., Department of Anthropology, Brown University, Providence.

Renfrew, Colin, and Paul G. Bahn. 1996. *Archaeology: Theories, Methods, and Practice*. 2nd ed. London: Thames and Hudson.

———. 2012. *Archaeology: Theories, Methods, and Practice*. 6th ed. London: Thames and Hudson.

Reno, Joshua. 2011. "Beyond Risk: Emplacement and the Production of Environmental Evidence." *American Ethnologist* 38 (3): 516–30.

Renouf, M. A. P., and Trevor Bell. 2000. "Integrating Sea Level History and Geomorphology in Targeted Archaeological Site Survey: The Gould Site (EeBi-42), Port au Choix, Newfoundland." *Northeast Anthropology* 59: 47–64.

Richardson, C. A. 2001. "Molluscs as Archives of Environmental Change." *Oceanography and Marine Biology: An Annual Review* 39: 103–64.

Rifkin, Mark. 2009. "Indigenizing Agamben: Rethinking Sovereignty in Light of the 'Peculiar' Status of Native Peoples." *Cultural Critique* 73 (Fall): 88–124.

Rivers, W. H. R. 1914. *The History of Melanesian Society*. Cambridge: Cambridge University Press.

Robinson, Angela. 2005. *Ta'n Teli-ktlamsitasit (Ways of Believing)—Mi'kmaw Religion in Eskasoni, Nova Scotia*. Canadian Ethnography Series 3. New York: Pearson-Prentice Hall.

Rockefeller, Stuart A. 2011. "Flow." *Current Anthropology* 52: 557–78.

Rosenmeier, Leah. 2010. "Towards an Archaeology of Descent: Spatial Practice and Communities of Shared Experience in Mi'kma'ki." PhD diss., Department of Anthropology, Brown University, Providence.

Rosenmeier, Leah, Scott Buchanan, Ralph Stea, and Gord Brewster. 2012. "New Sites and Lingering Questions at the Debert and Belmont Sites, Nova Scotia." In *Late Pleistocene Archaeology & Ecology in the Far Northeast*, edited by Claude Chapdelaine, 113–34. College Station: Texas A&M University Press.

Ross, Deborah. 2011 (1978). Introduction. In *Image and Pilgrimage in Christian Culture*, by Victor and Edith Turner, xxix–lvii. New York: Columbia University Press.

Roth, Joshua Hotaka. 2015. "*Hōkō onchi*: Wayfinding and the Emergence of 'Directional Tone-Deafness' in Japan." *Ethnos* 43 (4): 402–22.

Roy, Susan. 2010. *These Mysterious People: Shaping History and Archaeology in a Northwest Coast Community*. Montréal: McGill-Queen's University Press.

Rubertone, Patricia E. 2000. "The Historical Archaeology of Native Americans." *Annual Review of Anthropology* 29: 425–46.

———. 2001. *Grave Undertakings: An Archaeology of Roger Williams and the Narragansett Indians*. Washington, DC: Smithsonian Institution Press.

Rubertone, Patricia E., ed. 2009. *Archaeologies of Placemaking: Monuments, Memories, and Engagement in Native North America*. Walnut Creek, CA: Left Coast Press.

Sable, Trudy, and Bernie Francis. 2012. *The Language of this Land: Mi'kma'ki*. Sydney, NS: Cape Breton University Press.

Sahlins, Marshall. 1976. "Marxism and Two Structuralisms." In *Culture and Practical Reason*, 1–54. Chicago: University of Chicago Press.

Sahlins, Marshall, and Elman R. Service, ed. 1960. *Evolution and Culture*. Ann Arbor: University of Michigan Press.

Sallnow, M. 1987. *Pilgrims of the Andes: Regional Cults in Cusco*. Washington, DC: Smithsonian Institution Press.

Sanger, David. 1971. "Preliminary Report on Excavations at Cow Point, New Brunswick." *Man in the Northeast* 1: 34–47.

———. 1981. "Unscrambling the Messages in the Midden." *Archaeology of Eastern North America* 9: 37–41.

———. 1982. "Changing Views of Aboriginal Seasonality and Settlement in the Gulf of Maine." *Canadian Journal of Anthropology* 2 (2): 195–203.

————. 1996. "Testing the Models: Hunter-Gatherer Use of Space in the Gulf of Maine, USA." *World Archaeology* 27 (3): 512–26.

Sassen, Saskia. 1998. *Globalization and its Discontents: Essays on the New Mobility of People and Money*. New York: New Press.

Sayres, William C., ed. 1956. *Sammy Louis: The Life History of a Young Micmac*. New Haven, CT: The Compass Publishing Company.

Schmidt, David L. and B. A. Balcom. 1993. "The Règlements of 1739: A Note on Micmac Law and Literacy." *Acadiensis* 23 (1): 110–27.

Schrire, Carmel, ed. 1984. *Past and Present in Hunter-Gatherer Studies*. Orlando, FL: Academic Press.

Scott, Colin. 1989. "Knowledge Construction among the Cree Hunters: Metaphors and Literal Understanding." *Journal de la Société des Americanistes* 75: 193–208.

Scott, James C. 1998. *Seeing Like a State: How Certain Schemes to Improve the Human Condition Have Failed*. New Haven: Yale University Press.

Sellet, Frédéric, Russell Greaves, and Pei-Lin Yu, ed. 2006. *Archaeology and Ethnoarchaeology of Mobility*. Gainesville: University Press of Florida.

Service, Elman R. 1962. *Primitive Social Organization; An Evolutionary Perspective*. New York: Random House.

————. 1975. *Origins of the State and Civilization: The Process of Cultural Evolution*. New York: W. W. Norton and Company, Inc.

Shackel, Paul A., and Erve J. Chambers. 2004. *Places in Mind: Public Archaeology as Applied Anthropology*. New York: Routledge.

Shannon, Jennifer. 2007. "Informed Consent: Documenting the Intersection of Bureaucratic Regulation and Ethnographic Practice." *PoLAR: Political and Legal Anthropology Review* 30 (2): 229–48.

Sharma, Sarah, and Armond R. Towns. 2015. "Ceasing Fire and Seizing Time: LA Gang Tours and the White Control of Mobility." *Transfers* 6 (1): 26–44.

Sharer, Robert J., and Wendy Ashmore. 2003. *Archaeology: Discovering Our Past*. 3rd ed. Columbus, OH: McGraw Hill Education.

Shaw, Karen. 2004. "Creating/Negotiating Interstices: Indigenous Sovereignties." In *Sovereign Lives: Power in Global Politics*, edited by Jenny Edkins, Véronique Pin-Fat, and Michael J. Shapiro, 165–87. New York: Routledge.

Sheets-Johnstone, Maxine. 1999. *The Primacy of Movement*. Amsterdam: John Benjamins Publishing Company.

Sheldon, Helen. 1988. *The Prehistory of Nova Scotia as Viewed from the Brown Site*. NSM Curatorial Report. Halifax: Nova Scotia Museum.

Sheller, Mimi, and John Urry. 2006. "The New Mobilities Paradigm." *Environment and Planning A* 38: 207–26.

Silliman, Stephen W., ed. 2008. "Collaborative Indigenous Archaeology: Troweling at the Edges, Eyeing the Center." In *Collaborating at the Trowel's Edge: Teaching and Learning in Indigenous Archaeology*, edited by Stephen W. Silliman, 1–21. Amerind Studies in Archaeology. Tucson: University of Arizona Press.

Simpson, Audra. 2003. "To the Reserve and Back Again: Kahnawake Mohawk Narratives of Self, Home and Nation." PhD diss., Department of Anthropology, McGill University.

———. 2011. "Settlement's Secret." *Cultural Anthropology* 26 (2): 205–17.

———. 2014. *Mohawk Interruptus (Political Life Across the Borders of Settler States)*. Durham, NC: Duke University Press.

Sinclair, Karen. 1992. "Mission to Waitangi: A Maori Pilgrimage." In *Sacred Journeys: The Anthropology of Pilgrimage*, edited by Alan Morinis, 233–56. Westport, CT: Greenwood Press.

Smith, Adam T. 2001. "The Limitations of Doxa: Agency and Subjectivity from an Archaeological Point of View." *Journal of Social Archaeology* 1 (2): 155–71.

———. 2003. *The Political Landscape: Constellations of Authority in Early Complex Politics*. Berkeley: University of California Press.

———. 2010. Discussant Remarks on "Moving Bodies, Being Subjects: Ethnographic, Archaeological, and Historical Approaches to Mobility." Invited session for the 109th annual meeting of the American Anthropological Association, November 18, 2010, New Orleans, LA.

———. 2011. "Archaeologies of Sovereignty." *Annual Review of Anthropology* 40: 415–32.

Smith, Andrea, and J. Kēhaulani Kauanui. 2008. "Native Feminisms Engage American Studies." *American Quarterly* 60 (2): 241–49.

Smith, Eric Alden. 1983. "Anthropological Applications of Optimal Foraging Theory: A Critical Review (and Comments and Reply)." *Current Anthropology* 24(5): 625–51.

Smith, Harlan I. 1914. "Archaeology." In *Sessional Paper No. 26. Summary Report of the Geological Survey Branch of the Department of Mines for the Calendar Year 1913*, 380–388. Ottawa.

———. 1915. "Archaeology." In *Sessional Paper No. 26. Summary Report of the Geological Survey. Department of Mines. For the Calendar Year 1914*, 177–181. Ottawa.

———. 1929. "The Archaeology of Merigomish Harbour, Nova Scotia." In *Some Shell-Heaps in Nova Scotia*, edited by Harlan I. Smith and William J. Wintemberg, 1–104. Bulletin 47. Anthropological Series 9. Ottawa: National Museums of Canada.

Smith, Harlan I., and William J. Wintemberg. 1929. *Some Shell-Heaps in Nova Scotia*. Bulletin 47. Anthropological Series 9. Ottawa: National Museums of Canada.

Smith, Linda Tuhiwai. 1999. *Decolonizing Methodologies: Research and Indigenous Peoples*. London: Zed Books.

Smith, N. R. 1989. "The Economics of the Wabanaki Basket Industry." *Papers of the Algonquian Conference* 20: 306–16.

Smith, Sherry A. 2011. "Encountering Anne: Journeys to Sainte Anne de Beaupré." PhD diss., Department of Religious Studies, McMaster University, Hamilton. Open Access Dissertations and Theses, paper 6235.

Smithers, Gregory D. 2015. *The Cherokee Diaspora: An Indigenous History of Migration, Resettlement, and Identity*. New Haven, CT: Yale University Press.

Snead, James E., Clark L. Erickson, and J. Andrew Darling, ed. 2009. *Landscapes of Move-*

ment: Trails, Paths, and Roads in Anthropological Perspective. Philadelphia: University of Pennsylvania Museum of Archaeology and Anthropology.

Snow, Dean R. 1968. "Wabanaki 'Family Hunting Territories.'" *American Anthropologist* 70: 1143–151.

Sorrenson, M. P. K. 1975. "How to Civilize Savages: Some 'Answers' from Nineteenth-Century New Zealand." *New Zealand Journal of History* 9 (2): 97–110.

Sparke, Matthew. 2005. *In the Space of Theory: Postfoundational Geographies of the Nation-State*. Borderlines 26. Minneapolis: University of Minnesota Press.

Speck, Frank G. 1915. "The Family Hunting Band as the Basis of Algonkian Social Organization." *American Anthropologist* 17 (2): 289–305.

———. 1922. *Beothuk and Micmac*. New York: Museum of the American Indian Heye Foundation.

Speck, Frank G., and L. Eiseley. 1939. "The Significance of Hunting Territory Systems of the Algonkian in Social Theory." *American Anthropologist* 41 (2): 269–80.

Spiess, Arthur E. 1976. "Determining Season of Death of Archaeological Fauna by Analysis of Teeth." *Arctic* 29: 53–55.

Spiess, Arthur E., Kristin Sobolik, Diana Crader, John Mosher, and Deborah Wilson. 2006. "Cod, Clams and Deer: The Food Remains from Indiantown Island." *Archaeology of Eastern North America* 34: 141–87.

Staley, David P. 1993. "St. Lawrence Island's Subsistence Diggers: A New Perspective on Archaeological Sites." *Journal of Field Archaeology* 20 (3): 347–55.

Ste. Anne de Ristigouche Frères Mineurs Capuchins. 1910. *Sist gasgemtelnaganipongegeoei Migoitetemagani oigatigen*. Souvenir of the Micmac tercentenary celebration, 1610–1910, accessed June 13, 2016. https://archive.org/details/souvenirduniiiecoostea.

Steen, Shelia. 1951. "The Psychological Consequences of Acculturation among the Cape Breton Micmac." PhD diss., Department of Anthropology, University of Pennsylvania, Philadelphia.

Stein, Julie K., ed. 1992. *Deciphering a Shell Midden*. San Diego: Academic Press.

Stenning, Derrick. 1957. "Transhumance, Migratory Drift, Migration: Patterns of Pastoral Fulani Nomadism." *Royal Anthropological Institute of Great Britain and Ireland* 87 (1): 57–73.

Steward, Julian H. 1955. *Theory of Culture Change: The Methodology of Multilinear Evolution*. Urbana: University of Illinois Press.

Stewart, Frances L. 1986. "Faunal Remains from the Delorey Island Site (BjCj-9) of Nova Scotia." Curatorial Report 57, 105–51. Halifax: Nova Scotia Museum.

———. 1989. "Seasonal Movements of Indians in Acadia as Evidenced by Historical Documents and Vertebrate Faunal Remains from Archaeological Sites." *Man in the Northeast* 38: 55–77.

Stocking, George W. 1991. *Colonial Situations: Essays on the Contextualization of Ethnographic Knowledge*. Madison: University of Wisconsin Press.

Stokes, R. J., and B. J. Roth. 1999. "Mobility, Sedentism, and Settlement Patterns in Transition: The Late Pithouse Period in the Sapillo Valley, New Mexico." *Journal of Field Archaeology* 26: 423–34.

Stoler, Ann L. 2009. *Along the Archival Grain: Epistemic Anxieties and Colonial Common Sense*. Princeton, NJ: Princeton University Press.

Strouthes, Daniel P. 2010. *Settlement, Nesting Territories and Conflicting Legal Systems in a Micmac Community*. New Haven: Yale University Press.

Sullivan, M. E. 1984. "A Shell Midden Excavation at Pambula Lake on the Far South Coast of New South Wales." *Archaeology in Oceania* 19 (1): 1–15.

Sunshine, Ron. 2007. "Tradition [*sic*] Tobacco by Ron Sunshine." In "Traditional Tobacco," edited by Lottie Johnson, unpublished resource. Eskasoni, NS: Native Alcohol and Drug Abuse Counselling Association of Nova Scotia.

Supreme Court of Canada. 1999. *R. v. D. Marshall*. 1999. 3 S.C.R. 456 (September 17, 1999) and 3 S.C.R. 533 (November 17, 1999).

———. 2005. *R. v. Marshall, R. v. Bernard*. 2005. 2 S.C.R. 220. July 20, 2005.

———. 2011. *Lax Kw'alaams Indian Band v. Canada (Attorney General)*. 2011. 3 S.C.R 535. November 10, 2011.

———. 2014. *Tsilhqot'in Nation v. British Columbia*. 2014. 2 S.C.R. 256. June 26, 2014.

Swidler, Nina, Kurt Dongoske, Roger Anyon, Alan Downer, ed. 1997. *Native Americans and Archaeologists: Stepping Stones to Common Ground*. Lanham, MD: AltaMira Press.

Tanner, Adrian. 1979. *Bringing Home Animals: Religious Ideology and Mode of Production of the Mistassini Cree Hunters*. New York: St. Martin's Press.

———. 1986. "The New Hunting Territory Debate: An Introduction to Some Unresolved Issues." *Anthropologica* 28 (1–2): 19–36.

Thomas, Bryn H., and James W. Thomson. 1992. "Historic Treatment of a Prehistoric Landscape." In *Deciphering a Shell Midden*, edited by Julie K. Stein, 61–70. San Diego: Academic Press.

Thomas, Nicholas. 1994. *Colonialism's Culture: Anthropology, Travel, and Government*. Princeton, NJ: Princeton University Press.

Thompson, Kara. 2009. "A Romance with Many Reservations: American Indian Figurations and the Globalization of Indigeneity." PhD diss., Department of English, University of California, Davis.

Thwaites, Reuben Gold, ed. 1896–1901. *The Jesuit Relations and Allied Documents: travels and explorations of the Jesuit missionaries in New France, 1610–1791*. Cleveland, OH: Burrows Bros.

Tilly, Christopher. 1994. *A Phenomenology of Landscape: Places, Paths and Monuments*. Oxford: Berg.

Townsend, P. K. 1978. "The Politics of Mobility among the Sanio-Hiowe." *Anthropological Quarterly* 51 (1): 26–35.

Trigger, Bruce G. 1980. "Archaeology and the Image of the American Indian." *American Antiquity* 45 (4): 662–76.

———. 1984. "Alternative Archaeologies: Nationalist, Colonialist, Imperialist." *Man* 19 (3): 355–70.

———. 1989. *A History of Archaeological Thought*. Cambridge: Cambridge University Press.

Trouillot, Michel-Rolph. 1991. "Anthropology and the Savage Slot: The Poetics and Politics of Otherness." In *Recapturing Anthropology: Working in the Present*, edited by Richard G. Fox, 17–44. Santa Fe, NM: School of American Research Press.

———. 1995. *Silencing the Past: Power and the Production of History*. Boston: Beacon Press.

———. 2001. "The Anthropology of the State in the Age of Globalization: Close Encounters of the Deceptive Kind." *Current Anthropology* 42: 125–38.

Truitt, Allison. 2008. "On the Back of a Motorbike: Middle-Class Mobility in Ho Chi Minh City, Vietnam." *American Ethnologist* 35 (1): 3–19.

Turner, Victor. 1974. "Pilgrimage and Communitas." *Studia Missionalia* 23: 305–27.

Turner, Victor and Edith Turner. 1978. *Image and Pilgrimage in Christian Culture*. Reprinted in 2011. New York: Columbia University Press.

Upton, L. F. S. 1979. *Micmac and Colonists: Indian-White Relations in the Maritimes 1713–1867*. Vancouver: University of British Columbia Press.

Vansina, Jan. 1985. *Oral Tradition as History*. Madison: University of Wisconsin Press.

Vernon, C. W. 1903. *Cape Breton Canada at the Beginning of the Twentieth Century: A Treatise of Natural Resources and Development*. Toronto: Nation Publishing.

Villagran, Ximena S., Andrea L. Balbo, Macro Madella, Assumpció Vila, Jordi Estevez. 2011. "Experimental Micromorphology in Tierra del Fuego (Argentina): Building a Reference Collection for the Study of Shell Middens in Cold Climates." *Journal of Archaeological Science* 38 (3): 588–604.

Waguespack, Nicole M. 2005. "The Organization of Male and Female Labor in Foraging Societies: Implications for Early Paleoindian Archaeology." *American Anthropologist* 107 (4): 666–76.

Wallis, Wilson D., and Ruth S. Wallis. 1955. *The Micmac Indians of Eastern Canada*. Minneapolis: University of Minnesota Press.

Walls, Martha E. 2010. *No Need of a Chief for This Band: The Maritime Mi'kmaq and Federal Electoral Legislation, 1899–1951*. Vancouver: University of British Columbia Press.

Waselkov, Gregory A. 1987. "Shellfish Gathering and Shell Midden Archaeology." *Advances in Archaeological Method and Theory* 10: 93–210.

Watkins, Joe. 2000. *Indigenous Archaeology: American Indian Values and Scientific Practice*. Walnut Creek, CA: Alta Mira Press.

Weber, Max. (1905) 1976. *The Protestant Ethic and the Spirit of Capitalism*, translated by Talcott Parsons. Reprint, New York: Scribner.

Weiss, Brad. 1996. *The Making and Unmaking of the Haya Lived World: Consumption, Commoditization, and Everyday Practice*. Durham, NC: Duke University Press.

Wendrich, W., and H. Barnard. 2008. "The Archaeology of Mobility: Definitions and Research Approaches." In *The Archaeology of Mobility: Old and New World Nomadism*, edited by H. Barnard and W. Wendrich, 1–23. Los Angeles: Cotsen Institute of Archaeology, University of California.

Westerfelhaus, Robert, and Arvind Singhal. 2001. "Difficulties in Co-Opting a Complex Sign: Our Lady of Guadalupe as a Site of Semiotic Struggle and Entanglement." *Communication Quarterly* 49 (2): 95–114.

White, Leslie A. 1943. "Energy and the Evolution of Culture." *American Anthropologist* 45 (3): 335–56.

White, Richard. 1991. *The Middle Ground: Indians, Empires and Republics in the Great Lakes Region, 1650–1815*. Cambridge: Cambridge University Press.

———. 2006. "Creative Misunderstandings and New Understandings." *William and Mary Quaterly* 63 (1): 9–14.

Whitehead, Ruth Holmes. 1988. *Stories from the Six Worlds: Micmac Legends*. Halifax, NS: Nimbus Publishing.

———. 1989. *Six Micmac Stories*. Halifax: Nova Scotia Museum.

———. 2002. *Tracking Doctor Lonecloud: Showman to Legend Keeper*. Fredericton, NB: Goose Lane Editions.

Wicken, William C. 1994. "Encounters with Tall Sails and Tall Tales: Mi'kmaq Society 1500–1760." PhD diss., Department of History, McGill University, Montreal.

———. 2002. *Mi'kmaq Treaties on Trial: History, Land and Donald Marshall Junior*. Toronto: University of Toronto Press.

———. 2012. *The Colonization of Mi'kmaw Memory and History, 1794–1928: The King v. Gabriel Sylliboy*. Toronto: University of Toronto Press.

Wilcox, Michael V. 2009. *The Pueblo Revolt and the Mythology of Conquest: An Indigenous Archaeology of Contact*. Berkeley: University of California Press.

Williamson, Christine. 2004. "Contact Archaeology and the Writing of Aboriginal History." In *The Archaeology of Contact in Settler Societies*, edited by Tim Murray, 176–199. Cambridge: Cambridge University Press.

Wilson, Daniel. 1862. *Prehistoric Man: Research into the Origin of Civilisation in the Old and the New World*. London: MacMillan.

Winterhalder, B., and E. A. Smith, ed. 1981. *Hunter-Gatherer Foraging Strategies: Ethnographic and Archaeological Analyses*. Chicago: University of Chicago Press.

Withers, Paul. 2015. "Boat Harbour Compensation Being Negotiated with Nova Scotia." *Chronicle-Herald*, December 19, 2015, accessed November 4, 2016. http://www.cbc.ca/news/canada/nova-scotia/boat-harbour-compensation-pictou-landing-first-nation-1.3372761.

Wolf, Eric. 1981. *Europe and the People Without History*. Berkeley: University of California Press.

Wolfe, Patrick. 1991. "On Being Woken Up: The Dreamtime in Anthropology and in Australian Settler Culture." *Comparative Studies in Society and History* 33 (2): 197–224.

———. 1999. *Settler Colonialism and the Transformation of Anthropology: The Politics and Poetics of an Ethnographic Event*. London: Cassell.

Womack, Helen. 2016. "Fearing Rejection in Hungary's Cold Comfort Transit Zones." UNHCR, June 7, 2016, accessed November 4, 2016. http://www.unhcr.org/en-us/news/latest/2016/6/5756b4374/fearing-rejection-hungarys-cold-comfort-transit-zones.html.

Woodborne, Stephan, Ken Hart, and John Parkington. 1995. "Seal Bones as Indicators of the Timing and Duration of Hunter-Gatherer Coastal Visits." *Journal of Archaeological Science* 22: 727–40.

Woodburn, James. 1980. "Hunters and Gatherers Today and Reconstruction of the Past. In *Soviet and Western Anthropology*, edited by Ernest Gellner, 95–119. New York: Columbia University Press.

Wylie, Allison. 2015. "A Plurality of Pluralisms: Collaborative Practice in Archaeology." In *Objectivity in Science: New Perspectives from Science and Technology Studies*, edited by Flavia Padovani, Alan Richardson, and Jonathan Y. Tsou, 189–210. Dondrecht, Netherlands: Springer.

Yamba, C. B. 1995. *Permanent Pilgrims: The Idea of Pilgrimage in the Lives of West African Muslims*. London: Edinburgh University Press.

Yellowhorn, Eldon. 2015. "Just Methods, No Madness: Historical Archaeology on the Piikani First Nation." In *Ethics and Archaeological Praxis*, edited by Cristóbal Gnecco and Dorothy Lippert, 245–56. New York: Springer-Verlag.

Yesner, David R. 1980. "Maritime Hunter-Gatherers: Ecology and Prehistory." *Current Anthropology* 21: 727–50.

Young, Iris Marion. 2002. *Inclusion and Democracy*. Oxford: Oxford University Press.

Primary Sources

Canadian Museum of History—Archives (CMH-A). n.d. Archaeological Photographs—Nova Scotia. Manuscript No. BO/113. File 200?

———.1912. Wintemberg, William J. "Wintemberg, W.J. Field Notes. N.B., N.S. 1912." Manuscript No. 196. Vol. 5. p. 28.

———. 1913. Wintemberg, William J. "Nova Scotia. Bibliography Working Copy (Do not disarrange). Archaeology." Wintemberg, William J. Fonds. Box 43. File 8.

———. 1913. Wintemberg, William J. "Catalogue of Rev. Geo. Patterson Collection. Dalhousie College, 1913." Wintemberg, William J. Fonds. Box 44. File 3.

———. 1913. Wintemberg, William J. Geological topopgraphic maps. William J. Fonds. Box 44. File 5.

———. 1914. Smith, Harlan. Photographs: 27728; 27745; 27750; 27766; 27770.

———. 1914. Wintemberg, William J. "Pictou County, Nova Scotia. Vol. I. Archaeological Sites. Contents (to be inserted), Introduction, Bibliography, References to Comparative Material, Informants, Collections, Maps, Sites." William J. Fonds. Box 45. File 14.

———. 1914. Wintemberg, William J. "Nova Scotia, Pictou County. Vol. II. Archaeological Sites. Contents (To be inserted, Introduction, Bibliography, References to Comparative Material, Informants, Collections, Maps, Sites." William J. Fonds. Box 45. File 15.

———. 1972. Keenlyside, David. "Keenlyside 1972. N. Scotia." Keenlyside, David Fonds. Box 6. File 228.

———. 1978. Keenlyside, David. "PEI/NS. Field Research 1978. A Preliminary Report on Activities." Manuscript No. 1406.

———. 1980. Keenlyside, David. "Maritimes 1980. Field Catalogues. PEI & N.S." Manuscript No. 88-1721. Vol. 8.

Diocese of Antigonish Archives: 1738–1739. Fonds 8. Series 7. Sub-series 3. Box 296.

Folder 13—"Isle Royale correspondence etc." Transcript of *Memoire sur les missions des Sauvages Mikmaks et de l'Acadie*. C11B. Vol. 1. Folios 249–254. Archives des Colonies. Archives Nationales.

———. 1827. Fonds 8. Series 8. Sub-series 1. Boxes 198–199. Folder? Notes on priests, parishes and episcopal affairs.

———. 1837. Fonds 8. Series 8. Sub-series 2. Boxes 299–301. Folder 14. "Indexes 1840–1852."

———. 1854. Fonds 8. Series 5. Sub-series 1. Box 288. Folder 58. "Parishes: Pictou."

———. Fonds 8. Series 8. Sub-series 2. Boxes 299–301. Folder 15. "Indices from the Antigonish Casket." Excerpt from *The Casket*. Tuesday, September 28, 1858.

———. 1860. Fonds 8. Series 9. Sub-series 1. Box 302. Folder 1. "Roman Documents 1824–1860's." Transcript of Bishop Colin MacKinnon's report on the Diocese of Arichat to Cardinal Barnabo. January 12, 1860.

———. 1862. Fonds. 8. Series 8. Sub-series 2. Boxes 299–301. Folder 16. "Indexes 1861–1865". Transcript from *The Casket*. August 28, 1862, p. 2, col. 5.

———. 1885. Fonds 3. Series 4. Sub-series 1. Box 229. Folder 86.—"Diocese Census 1885."

———. 1890a. Fonds 8. Series 6. Sub-series 3. Box 294. Folder 25. Transcribed excerpt from *The Casket*. July 24, 1890. p. 3, c. 3. No headline transcribed.

———. 1890b. Fonds 8. Series 6. Sub-series 3. Box 294. Folder 25. Transcribed excerpt from *The Casket*. August 7, 1890. p. 3, c. 2. No headline transcribed.

———. 1897a. Fonds 8. Series 6. Sub-series 3. Box 294. Folder 25. Transcribed excerpt from *The Casket*. Thursday, July 8, 1897. p. 8, c. 1. No headline transcribed.

———. 1897b. Fonds 8. Series 6. Sub-series 3. Box 294. Folder 25. Transcribed excerpt from *The Casket*. Thursday, July 29, 1897. p. 8, c. 2. "Indian Church Blessed."

———. 1897c. Fonds 8. Series 6. Sub-series 3. Box 294. Folder 25. Transcribed excerpt from *The Casket*. Thursday, August 5, 1897. p. 2, c. 1. "Indian Island Mission, Pictou County."

———. 1906. Fonds 8. Series 1. Sub-series 2. Box 251. Folder 82. "New Glasgow—St. John the Baptist."

———. 1914. Parish census. Letter from Bishop James Morrison to Rev. Father Pacifique. October 6, 1914. Antigonish.

———. 1932–1938. Fonds 8. Series 5. Sub-series 1. Box 288. Folder 58. "Parishes: Pictou" Announcement booklets. Volumes I and II.

———. 1933a. Fonds 4. Series 1. Sub-series 1. Box 17. Folder 107. Letter from Father A. A. Johnston to Bishop James Morrison. December 16, 1933. Pictou.

———. 1933b. Fonds 8. Series 5. Sub-series 1. Box 288. Folder 58. "Parishes: Pictou." Excerpt of an article from *The Casket* pasted onto vol. 1, p. 64 of the 1932–1938 Announcement Booklets.

———. 1934. Letter from Bishop James Morrison to Father A. A. Johnston. January 3, 1934. Antigonish.

———. 1935. Fonds 8. Series 5. Sub-series 1. Box 288. Folder 58. "Parishes: Pictou." Clipping from *The Casket*. No page or column number. Reprinted from the *Eastern Chronicle*, New Glasgow, N.S.

———. 1937. Fonds 4. Series 1. Sub-series 1. Box 17. Folder 107. Letter from Bishop James Morrison to Father A. A. Johnston. October 28, 1937. Antigonish.

———. 1939a. Fonds 4. Series 1. Sub-series 1. Box 17. Folder 107. Letter from Father Ernest Chaisson to Bishop James Morrison. March 30, 1939. Thorburn.

———. 1939b. Fonds 4. Series 1. Sub-series 1. Box 17. Folder 107. Letter from Father A. A. Johnston to Bishop James Morrison. April 12, 1939. New Waterford. (The map to which Johnston refers in this letter appears to be missing.)

Library and Archives Canada (LAC). 1722. Série C11B. Correspondence générale; Isle Royale. M. Le Normant de Mézy au ministre. December 27, 1722. Louisbourg.

———. 1748. MG18. F10. Charles Morris Fonds. *A Brief Survey of Nova Scotia.* 1748.

———. 1835. RG 88. RG10, R216-683-X-E. v. 11210F. Files 1-8. Responses to 1835 circular requesting information on the number and condition of Mi'kmaq in counties in Nova Scotia.

———. 1842a. RG10. R216–683-X-E. Vol. 11210. File Folder 3. Letter from James Dawson to Joseph Howe. January 26, 1842. Pictou.

———. 1842b. RG10. R216–683-X-E. Vol. 11210. File Folder 3. Letter from James Dawson to Joseph Howe. May 19, 1842. Pictou.

———. 1842c. RG10. R216–683-X-E. Vol. 11210. File Folder 3. Letter from James Dawson to Joseph Howe. June 25, 1842. Pictou.

———. 1842d. RG10. R216–683-X-E. Vol. 11210. File Folder 3. Letter from James Dawson to Joseph Howe. September 29, 1842. Pictou.

———. 1842e. RG10. R216–683-X-E. Vol. 11210. File Folder 3. Letter from James Dawson to Joseph Howe. November 30, 1842. Pictou.

———. 1842f. RG10. R216–683-X-E. Vol. 11210. File Folder 3. Letter from James Dawson to Joseph Howe. December 8, 1842. Pictou.

———. 1843. RG10, R216–683-X-E. v. 11210F. Files 1–8. Originals in RG88, vol. 494. Letter from Joseph Howe to James Dawson. May 8, 1843. Halifax.

———. 1891. RG10. Vol. 6608. File 4051–7RC. Letter from Father Roderick McDonald to the Superintendent General of Indian Affairs. April 28, 1891. Pictou.

———. 1893. RG10. Vol. 6608. File 4051–7RC. Letter from the Deputy Superintendent General to the Superintendent General of Indian Affairs. March 1, 1893. Ottawa.

———. 1898. RG10. Vol. 6046. File 253–1, part 1. Letter from Nelly Connolly to Father Roderick McDonald. October 18? 1898. New Glasgow.

———. 1918. RG10. Vol. 6608. File 4051–7RC. Letter from J. D. MacLeod to A. MacGregor. March 22, 1918. New Glasgow.

———. 1920. RG10. Vol. 6810. File 470–2-3, vol. 7, 55 (L-3) and 63 (N-3).

———. 1926. RG10. Vol. 6608. File 4051–7RC. Letter from J. D. MacLeod to R. H. MacKay. March 11, 1926. New Glasgow.

———. 1941. RG10, Vol. 7918. File: 41048–2. Memorandum from W. S. Arneil, Inspector of Indian Agencies, Department of Indian Affairs to Dr. McGill. July 12, 1941.

Maine Folklife Center. 1989a. Native American Related Collections. Transcript of interview with Phil Cunningham. March 25, 1989. Accession no. 2096(003).

———. 1989b. Native American Related Collections. Transcript of interview with Osmon Merill. April 26,1989. Accession no. 2098(004).

Nova Scotia Archives (NSA). n.d. MG1. Vol. 2867. No. 6. Notebook included in the Clara Dennis Papers.

———. 1800. RG1. Vol. 430. Doc. 34. Copy of letter from the Committee of His Majesty's Council and House of Assembly to Edward Irish and Timothy W. Hurliky. 10 December 1800 with supplies for the relief of distressed Indians. December 10, 1800. Halifax.

———. 1801a. RG1. Vol. 430. Doc. 47. Response to Edward Mortimer's report on the population of Mi'kmaw in Pictou County. 1801. Halifax.

———. 1801b. RG1. Vol. 430. Doc. 48 1/2. Circular from Brenton, Morris, Wallace and Tonge to representatives in districts around Nova Scotia inquiring about the Mi'kmaq. January 23, 1801. Halifax.

———. 1801c. RG1. Vol. 430. No. 88. Letter from William Nixon to Sir John Wentworth stating the situation of Indians about Guysboro? in Sydney County. November 20, 1801. Guysborough.

———. 1801–1802a. MG1. Vol. 1773. No. 34. A Natural Resource Survey of Nova Scotia in 1801–1802. by Titus Smith Jr. Transcription by Lloyd S. Hawboldt. Nova Scotia Department of Lands and Forest. 1955.

———. 1801–1802b. RG1, 380b. Journal of Titus Smith 1801–1802.

———. 1802. RG1. Vol. 430. Doc. 117. Letter from Sir John Wentworth to Michael Wallace. September 28, 1802.

———. 1807. RG1. Vol. 430. Doc. 143. Circular sent by George Henry Monk to representatives in districts around Nova Scotia inquiring about the Mi'kmaq. Halifax.

———. 1808. RG1. Vol. 430. Doc. 145. Letter from George Henry Monk to Sir George Provost. April 23, 1808. Halifax.

———. 1812. RG1. Vol. 430. Doc. 21. Letter from Abbé Sigogne to Lieutenant Governor Sherbrooke. May 9, 1812. Clare.

———. 1815. RG1. Vol. 430. Doc. 153. Letter from Bishop Plessis to Lieutenant Governor Sherbrooke. July 27, 1815. Halifax.

———. 1820. RG5. Series GP. Vol. 7, No. 9. Letter from Peter Wilmot to Lieutenant General George Dalhousie. 1820.

———. 1829a. RG1. Vol. 430. Doc. 168. Petition of Pictou Indians. James Lulan to Peregrine Maitland. March 2, 1829. Pictou.

———. 1829b. RG1. Vol. 430. Doc. 169. Petition of Pictou Indians. Peter Wilmot to Peregrine Maitland. March 2, 1829. Pictou.

———. 1832. RG1. Vol. 431. Doc. 62 1/2. Abraham Gesner. Report on Indian Affairs. March 4, 1832. Halifax.

———. 1835. RG 1. Vol. 431. No. 14. Petition from W. B. McLeod and J. W. Bannerman to Lieutenant Governor Sir Colin Campbell. June 11, 1835.

———. 1836. RG 1. Vol. 431. No. 23. Petition of Maltiel Sapier and other Mi'kmaq of the Pictou area to the Lt. Gov. Campbell requesting assistance, especially blankets and great coats. 1836. Pictou.

————. 1837. RG1. Vol. 431. No. 56. Notice to Trespassers on Indian Reserves. Provincial Secretary's Office. May 1, 1837. Halifax.

————. 1843. RG1. Vol. 430. Doc. 191. Joseph Howe. Annual Report of the Nova Scotia Commissioner of Indian Affairs.

————. 1844. MG15. Vol. 3. No. 80. Letter from Angus McDobald [*sic*] to Rt. Rev. Dr. Fraser, Bishop of Halifax, reporting on the success of Indian farming at Merigomish, 1844. November 18, 1844. Merigomish.

————. 1846. MG 15. Vol. 3. No. 99. Correspondence between William Anderson, Pictou Health Officer, and government concerning epidemic among the Mi'kmaq of "fever." June to November. 1846.

————. 1847. RG5. Series P. Vol. 45. No. 8. Dr. Anderson to Bishop Fraser, Diocese of Antigonish. January 20, 1847.

————. 1852. RG1. Vol. 431. Doc. 66. Silas Rand to Lieutenant Governor LeMerchant.

————. 1860. RG5. Series P. Vol. 49. No. 86. Petition of William Powell of Pictou for remuneration for damage sustained from his lands being occupied by Mi'kmaq. March 19, 1860. Fisher's Grant.

————. 1862. RG 5 Series P. Vol. 49, No. 121. Petition of Donald McArthur of Boat Harbour, Pictou County, asking for compensation for damages to his land upon which Mi'kmaq reside. July 15, 1862. Pictou.

Nova Scotia Museum (NSM). 1933–1937. Provincial Museum Accession Book. September 1933–November 1937. On file at the Heritage Division of the Nova Scotia Department of Communities, Culture and Heritage, Halifax.

Interviews

Francis, Sadie. 2004. Roundtable Discussion, Pictou Landing First Nation, December 14, 2004. Copy of transcript on file at the Pictou Landing First Nation band office.

Brothers, B. 2007. Oral History Interview, Pictou Landing First Nation, December 13, 2007.

Index

Page numbers in *italics* refer to illustrations.

About the Author

Michelle A. Lelièvre is an assistant professor at the College of William and Mary, jointly appointed to the Department of Anthropology and the American Studies Program; she earned her doctorate in anthropology at the University of Chicago. She conducted the research for *Unsettling Mobility* in collaboration with Mi'kmaq from the Pictou Landing First Nation in northeastern Nova Scotia. In 2015, she began a collaborative research project with the Confederacy of Mainland Mi'kmaq to document Mi'kmaw activity in the pre- and post-contact periods along the northeastern shore of Nova Scotia's Minas Basin. She was lucky enough to grow up on Unama'ki/Isle Royale/Eilean Cheap Bhreatainn/Cape Breton, which—however you say it—is the most beautiful island in the world. She lives in Richmond, Virginia.